Not Born a Refugee Woman

STUDIES IN FORCED MIGRATION
General Editors: Stephen Castles and Dawn Chatty

Not Born a Refugee Woman

CONTESTING IDENTITIES, RETHINKING PRACTICES

Edited By

Maroussia Hajdukowski-Ahmed
Nazilla Khanlou and
Helene Moussa

Berghahn Books
New York • Oxford

Published in 2008 by

Berghahn Books
www.berghahnbooks.com

Library of Congress Cataloging-in-Publication Data

Not born a refugee woman : contesting identities, rethinking practices /
edited by Maroussia Hajdukowski-Ahmed, Nazilla Khanlou, and
Helene Moussa.
    p. cm. — (Studies in forced migration ; v. 24)
Includes bibliographical references.
ISBN 978-1-84545-497-5 (hbk) -- ISBN 978-1-84545-704-4 (pbk)
1. Women refugees. 2. Identity (Psychology)—Social aspects.
3. Forced migration. I. Hajdukowski-Ahmed, Maroussia. II. Khanlou,
Nazilla. III. Moussa, Helene, 1931–

JV6346.N68 2008
305.48'96914—dc22

2008008211

British Library Cataloguing in Publication Data

A catalogue record for this book is available from the British Library

Printed in the United States on acid-free paper

ISBN 978-1-84545-497-5 hardback, ISBN 978-1-84545-704-4 paperback

Contents

Tables, Maps, and Illustrations

Acknowledgements

Many people have been directly and indirectly involved in the creation of this volume, too many to name individually. Our gratitude is of a kind, which can hardly be expressed in the form of a simple acknowledgement.

This book evolved from the International Conference *Saying 'I' is Full of Consequences. Refugee Women Reclaim their Identity*. The thought provoking papers at this conference inspired us to pursue the exploration of the complex refugee women's identity question and its vital implications. The conference was organized by the Program of Women's Studies at McMaster University and the Settlement and Integration Services Organization (SISO) of Hamilton, Canada. We gratefully acknowledge the financial assistance of the Social Sciences and Humanities Research Council of Canada and of the Program of Women's Studies of McMaster. We express our gratitude to The Settlement and Integration Services Organization of Hamilton for facilitating our collaboration with refugee women.

We express our respectful appreciation to each of the authors in this volume for their willingness to contribute to the enrichment of the ongoing interdisciplinary discourse on refugee women. Many authors tirelessly combine their scholarly pursuits with activities such as field work, advocacy, therapy, settlement, lecturing, or legal representation. Each author has forged new directions which will address root causes, and as is our hope, will enhance the visibility and presence of refugee women and ensure their rights. We thank them for the diligence in which they met deadlines and for their patience with the publication process.

We thank Charmaine Crawford and Michelle Lee for their contribution to various stages of the production of this book. Special thanks are extended to Khursheed Ahmed for his invaluable expertise with the innumerable technical and editorial tasks that go onto preparing and finalizing the manuscript.

We are grateful to colleagues and friends for their generous encouragements, for their insightful comments and suggestions.

The cover of this volume is a mural and the collective creation of refugee women emanating from workshops conducted by the Workers Arts and Heritage Center (WAHC) in partnership with the Immigrant Culture and Art Association (ICAA) and the Settlement and Integration Services Organization to produce community art works. Financial assistance was obtained from Status of Women Canada and the Ontario Arts Council. The workshops were initiated and facilitated by Renee Wetselaar and Inessa Petersen, Executive Director and Program Coordinator of the Worker's Arts and Heritage Center. The Center is an organization committed to providing artistic and educational programming on the historical and contemporary experience of working people in Canada with a special focus on non-white, immigrant, and gender-based experiences. As part of the *Saying 'I'* conference, refugee women were invited to explore and express their identity in words, drawings, and paintings. We extend our deep appreciation to Renee Wetselaar and Inessa Petersen, to Nazia Zeb (lead artist) and Yar Taraky (mentor artist), and to each of the refugee women who painted the mural: Khatol Rajic, Farkhonda Nazary, Nadia Areef, Belgin Onurlap, Seema Sultani, Fatia Abdullah, Maria Clemencia Olaya, and Ashtar Abudul Qader.

This publication was funded, in part, by the Center of Excellence for Research on Immigration and Settlement (CERIS) in Toronto, through Health Domain Leader funding to Nazilla Khanlou. We are grateful for this support.

We sincerely thank Marion Berghahn from Berghahn Books, as well as the editors of the *Refugee and Forced Migration Studies* at Oxford University and the editors of Berghahn Books in New York, for their professional guidance throughout the publishing process.

We thank our personal support networks, families, and friends, whose patience, understanding, and help were essential to the completion of this project.

And last but not least, we are profoundly indebted to all the refugee women who have directly and indirectly shared their knowledge, their wisdom, their creativity, their experience, their achievements, and their hopes with all of us.

We dedicate this book to all refugee women, with the hope readers will learn from them and work with and for them toward the eradication of all causes that force women and men, youth and children to leave their homes and the safety to which all human beings are entitled.

List of Abbreviations

AWR   Association for the Study of the World Refugee Problem
AWARE   Association of Women for Action and Research
BCSC   British Columbia Security Commission
CARE   Leading international humanitarian organization fighting global poverty
CBC   Canadian Broadcasting Corporation
CCVT   Canadian Center for Victims of Torture
CEDAW   Convention on the Elimination of all Forms of Discrimination Against Women
CERIS   Center of Excellence for Research on Immigration and Settlement
CIC   Citizenship and Immigration Canada
CIDA   Canadian International Development Agency
CIRPA   Canadian Independent Record Production Association
CTV   Canadian Television Network
DSM IV   Diagnostic and Statistical Manual of Mental Disorders Fourth Edition
FGM   Female Genital Mutilation
GAFM   Gender and Forced Migration
ICMEC   International Center for Migration, Ethnicity, and Citizenship
ICTY   International Criminal Tribunals on Yugoslavia
ICTR   International Criminal Tribunals on Rwanda
IDP   Internally Displaced Persons
IES   Impact of Events Scale
ILO   International Labour Organization
IMF   International Monetary Fund
INGO   International Nongovernmental Organizations

INS   Immigration and Naturalization Service
IOM   International Organization for Migration
IPTF   UN International Police Task Force
IPV   Intimate Partner Violence
IRB   Immigration and Refugee Board of Canada
ISIM   Institute for the Study of International Migration
IWGRW   International Working Group on Refugee Women
KFOR   Kosovo Force
KLA   Kosovo Liberation Army
LTTE   Liberation Tigers of Tamil Eelam
NAJC   National Association of Japanese Canadians
NGO   Non-Governmental Organization
ORR   Office of Refugee Resettlement
PAR   Participatory Action Research
PRET   Project for Rehabilitation through Education and Training
PRRA   Preremoval Risk Assessment
PTSD   Post-Traumatic Stress Disorder
RCMP   Royal Canadian Mounted Police
RMHP   Refugee Mental Health Program
RPD   Refugee Protection Division
RSC   Refugee Studies Center
SAMHSA   Substance Abuse and Mental Health Services Administration
SISO   Settlement and Integration Services Organization
SSHRC   Social Sciences and Humanities Research Council
UNHCR   United Nations High Commissioner for Refugees
WCC   World Council of Churches
WGRW   Working Group on Refugee Women
WICZNET   Women in Conflict Zones Network
WUSC   World University Services of Canada

Introduction

Maroussia Hajdukowski-Ahmed,
Nazilla Khanlou, and Helene Moussa

Setting the Context: Reflection on Two Decades of an Evolving Discourse on Refugee Women

Over the past twenty-five years, the discourse on the construction of refugee women's identities and their agency has followed several paths, often challenging assumptions about women in general and specifically about women who have been uprooted from their communities because of war, civil upheaval, and/or human rights violations.

In this introduction to the book, our reflection on the discourse on refugee women attempts to identify the main themes in research, policy, and practice from selected international and Canadian moments since the 1980s. The changing discourse that defined refugee women's identities and their agency will be highlighted. This reflection does not purport to be a comprehensive historical study or literature review, rather by linking international and the Canadian experience, it seeks to provide a contextual framework for our understanding of this volume.

Three basic premises which underlie our understanding of refugee women's identities and agency, as well as the rationale of this volume's focus on women are as follows: The first one is that 'refugee' is a legal category for a particular situation in which people find themselves. The second premise is that refugee women, as is the case with refugee men or other uprooted categories of people, have had multilayered and multifaceted identities even before the conditions that created their present status. The third premise recognizes that while men's and women's identities are impacted by war and the human rights violations that lead to uprooting from their communities and countries, women and girls are, on the one hand, disproportionately more vulnerable to violence, including sexual abuse and other forms of sexual and gender-based violence. They are vulnerable in flight and refugee situations in asylum, and in resettlement and return. And, on the other hand, in refugee and disaster situations, women often take on additional roles in caring for family members and maintaining the family and the community.

The 1980s—"The Forgotten Majority" on the International Agenda

Women have remained for long "the forgotten majority" on the international agenda.[1] United Nations world conferences on women[2] were significant signposts and catalysts toward the mobilization of women, advocating for the human rights of women at the local, national, and international levels. These international gatherings also served to raise awareness and build empirical data on the social, economic, and political situation of refugee women *vis-à-vis* men. As a result, the special needs of refugee women reached the international agenda.

The sexual violence perpetrated against refugee women in flight and in asylum was revealed for the first time by the "First World Survey on the Role of Women in Development" at the First United Nations World Conference on Women: Action for Equality, Development, and Peace which was held in Mexico in 1975. Following these revelations, the United Nations High Commissioner for Refugees' (UNHCR) presented a paper entitled "The Situation of Refugee Women the World Over" at the 1980 World Conference for the Decade on Women in Copenhagen (UNHCR 1980). In 1984 Dutch non-governmental organizations (NGOs), mobilized by women's groups in particular, organized a conference which tabled issues related to sexual violence experiences of women refugees in flight and first asylum countries (Dutch Refugee Association 1985). This was followed in the same year by the European Parliament calling on member states to recognize refugee women who experience gender-based persecution as a "social group" within the UN Convention on the Protection of Refugees. It was years into the 1980's before this proposal came to fruition at the UNHCR Executive meetings.

During this period, refugee women were seen as "victims" and "vulnerable." Uprooting, it was explained, had left these women without the family and community structures that would protect them under normal circumstances from such abuses. Furthermore, as victims and vulnerable, refugee women were perceived as a greater "burden" than men in countries of asylum and resettlement, or at best, having "special needs" which had to be accommodated.

While we can assume that refugee women have always existed in the exodus of people fleeing wars and human rights violations, awareness of the strikingly high percentage of women in the refugee population was catalyzed by the 1980 report of the UNHCR at the World Conference for the Decade on Women in Copenhagen (UNHCR 1980). To the surprise of many, this report revealed that 80 percent of the refugees under the protection of the UNHCR were women and their dependents. While this figure will vary according to particular refugee flow situations, it is still quoted to this day. This figure in and of itself does not vary in relation to the non-refugee population—women and children do constitute the largest percentage of a population. The significance of this figure is that it is women *and* their dependents who are in need of special protection because of the circumstances of uprooting. It was after the Copenhagen conference that the momentum accelerated and the special needs of refugee women was firmly on the agendas of international and NGO lobby groups and networks as was evidenced at the Third UN Women's Decade Conference in Nairobi, Kenya, 1985.

To ensure that issues related to refugee women would be sustained after the end of the first UN Decade for Women, the International Working Group on Refugee Women (IWGRW) was initiated in 1986 by the World Council of Churches and the World YWCA in Geneva, Switzerland. IWGRW's location in Geneva enabled it closely to lobby and to monitor policy decisions of the UNHCR Executive Committee. IWGWR was a loosely organized network never having more than one paid (often part time) staff member in the Geneva office. NGOs in different parts of the world were encouraged to set up national groups. The IWGRW's newsletter was the main tool of information exchanges.

In 1989, the IWGRW organized the First International Conference on Refugee Women. By this time, over one hundred NGOs from around the world were on the mailing list of the network. The UNHCR was also able to facilitate the participation of refugee women at the conference. A significant outcome of this conference was that it set the groundwork for international (and national) research, policy, advocacy, and programs to empower refugee women. A practical guide on responses to the special needs of refugee women was developed from the discussions in the areas of protection, health, employment, and cultural adjustment (Kelly 1989). Refugee women at the conference challenged academics and policy and program staff saying that their actions should also address refugee issues in the broader context of the root causes of displacement, of peace and of justice issues.

In Canada in 1985, the Working Group on Refugee Women (WGRW) was established at the Winnipeg Regional Consultation of the Standing Conference of Canadian Organizations Concerned with/about/for Refugees (SSCCOR), renamed as the Canadian Council for Refugees (CCR).[3] A small nucleus group of women working in agencies and church rganizations, as well as academics from Ottawa and Toronto, met the following year to formulate the issues and focus of the work agenda of the WGRW. Briefly, the focus was as follows: advocacy on the rights of refugee women and claimants, monitoring the Women at Risk Program, public education, research and information dissemination, and networking.

In response to WGRW's assertion that there was a critical need to collect data and information on the situation of refugee women in the world, in 1988 the WGRW, together with the YWCA of Metropolitan Toronto and the York University Center for Refugee Studies, sponsored a weekend workshop. The main objective was to identify gaps and inadequacies of services available to refugee women in Canada. Recognizing that women refugees would be the best judges of the topics for discussion at the workshop, refugee women participated in the planning and determined the content and issues to be addressed. Fifty refugee women living in the province of Ontario and coming from Africa, South and East Asia, Latin America, and the Middle East participated. Major themes of the workshop were: orientation (to Canadian society), discrimination, recognition, violence, and isolation. The report was also written by the participants (*Sharing Our Experiences* 1988). What came out loud and clear was that refugee women will speak for themselves. "[A]n enormous energy and enthusiasm was unleashed . . . , the vulnerabilities, strengths and resilience of the women came pouring out as did their determination to seek ways and means of being the transformer and not the helpless victim" (3). Perhaps one of the most poignant messages related to identity was when one of the women stated, "Consider us not as what we are now but as we were. Consider us as we can become our potential as individuals enabling others" (7). This was their way of stating that the refugee identity was one of many identities, and also a source through which their agency would be channelled. In the language of service providers, empowerment was a key action demand. At the spring CCR consultation in Montreal, papers were presented by members of WGRW and three refugee women gave testimonies. WGRW also sent representatives, including refugee women, to the First International Conference and presented a paper on cultural adjustment (Moussa with Allman and Ptolemy, in Kelly 1985: 146–153).

Following the Nairobi conference and subsequent lobbying by NGOs, a series of international resolutions, policy statements, and guidelines were developed in the UNHCR calling on states to recognize the vulnerability and special protection needs of refugee women in flight and in asylum.[4]

Surveying the literature on refugee women in the 1980s, Moussa wrote, "Women refugees—Footnote or Text?" (Moussa 1993: 16). Research was not only exploratory and descriptive but most often distinctions between men and women, let alone gender relations, were not made. It was safe to assume that the experience of men was the focus of research. In fact, the exclusion of women in a major research study on refugees in the Sudan was explained by the fact that women were busy during the day time and appointments could not be made with them. One such explanation only merited a footnote (Clay and Holcomb 1985: 54–55, 79, 109). In contrast, another study of the same population indicated that women were much more informed than men about the social and economic issues that affected the refugee community (Kibread 1987: 288).

In the same period, a major research project on the exile experience of the Brazilian *diaspora* from 1964 onward, discovered after the first phase of the study that although both sexes were represented in the sample, women's experiences were under-represented. An independent volume on the experience of women refugees was eventually published (Da Rocha Lima 1984: 81–83).

Not surprisingly, a significant difference between the literature on women refugees and refugees in general has been the discourse on family and community life and relationships. This not only filled the gap in the literature, but also expanded the understanding of the refugee experience. In the early 1980s, the gendered social, cultural, and political forces that caused refugee women to flee their homes and countries, and the gendered realities in flight and asylum, was little discussed until the sexual violence women experienced in flight and asylum was revealed by the UNHCR and NGOs working in the field, particularly by the Dutch women's NGOs noted above. In 1987, when Doreen Indra reviewed the extensive literature on South Asian refugees in Canada, she concluded that "People are refugees first, women and men second and gender is never a variable" (Indra 1987: 12–13).

At least three levels of discourse on identity and the agency of refugee women evolved in the late 1980s and persist to this day, albeit in different ways.

First, women refugees were/are perceived as victims, particularly of sexual violence. Their vulnerability was/is generally based on the assumption that they were/are dependent and passive in decision-making roles. At the same time, the perception associated with them of "victimhood" and "vulnerability" has pointed out the immense discrimination in relief work in refugee camps (e.g., in the distribution of food). Women refugees also were at greater risk of rape and/or sex trade because they did not have the protection of family and community and because international protection laws, and policies and practice, were gender-blind. More recently, we have also become aware of the similar risks experienced by internally displaced women and trafficked women.

Depicting women as victims and vulnerable because they are women gives a reason to recognize their *special circumstances* as women refugees, and therefore, the need for international protection of women in flight, in camps, and even in countries of asylum. However, as the image of victim and vulnerability took over, re-exploitation and revictimization has often occurred, particularly when women were asked to "tell their stories" to strangers as a way of "educating" or raising the awareness of listeners. As well intentioned as these efforts may be, this approach poses several dilemmas:

—women refugees often have to *re-live* the horrors of their experience and, such retelling, at its worst, constitutes a form of a voyeurism. Listeners as well do not know how to respond;

—it tends to evoke pity and pathologizes the tellers' countries of origin as horrifically misogynist and patriarchal societies, and as a consequence it racializes identities and violence as culture-specific;

—there is also a tendency to portray women as unable to survive and cope in hostile environments and even to adapt to new situations. Therefore, other (benevolent) people and countries have to rescue them from their situation.

Attempts to create more "sensitive" ways of telling such stories have often been developed, but too often the same misconceptions reemerge because refugee women are not in control of the process. In this context of storytelling, which focuses primarily on sharing the problem of refugee women, the root causes for uprooting and questions about the agency and multiple identities of refugee women are not central to the objectives.

Second, at the same time, in the mid-1980s, feminist discourse on gender relations also led to the application of a gender analysis to the refugee experience, which in turn influenced the perception of refugee women as victim*ized* rather than as victims *per se*. This shift in perspective led one to ask very different questions related to power relations, both at the private and public levels of society. Professionals working with refugee women were challenged to address the complex gendered, social, economic, and political realities of refugee women's lives, including the relationships between professionals and refugees.

Third, just as suddenly as it was realized in 1980 that most of the world's refugees were women and their dependents (UNHCR 1980), in the late 1980s the role refugee women played in holding the family together was recognized by researching scholars and professional staff working with them. These professionals recognized, as well, how women refugees organized themselves in their own traditional ways and how they resisted oppression. Despite the breakdown of family supports, the strength of women refugees was evident to all those who worked closely with them. In addition, refugee women were learning and taking decision-making responsibilities beyond sex-defined roles. Respect replaced pity in the discourse.

Though it may have come as a surprise to staff in these organizations and sometimes to the women refugees themselves, Moussa's research on the life histories of refugee women clearly showed that the roots of resistance and survival skills did not just begin when they were uprooted. They originated before the political/war crisis that led them to flee. It was this reservoir of power and strength that, consciously or unconsciously, they were able to draw on for their ability to cope and survive as uprooted women (Moussa 1993). At this time, the language of empowerment emerged in the discourse of strategies to enable refugee women to overcome their vulnerability. Programs for skills development, literacy, income generation projects, and so on were set up with the objective of building on refugee women's strength.

The 1990s and after—From Empowerment to Claiming Power

While people advocating for refugee women in the 1980s tended to be predominantly women who were not refugees and of "Western" cultures, in the 1990s in Canada, women of color and refugee women gradually held staff leadership positions in local and national service agencies, government policy decision-making positions, the women's movement, and in academe.[5] A perfectly natural outcome of "empowerment" strategies is that women who are empowered will seek to claim power at some point not only in their personal lives but also in the public realm.

At the same time, feminist research and community workers also delved into an analysis which intertwined race, culture, and gender relations. Questions were raised about cultural relativism and essentialist approaches in research, policy, and practice and about the construction of refugee women's identities. Nevertheless the same themes and dilemmas of the 1980s continued into the 1990s. For example, in 1991, after an experience where an African woman felt revictimized when telling the story of her refugee flight experience at a conference, an *ad hoc* group of refugee women of African backgrounds working as academics and in NGOs in Toronto, Ottawa, and Montreal (Canada), organized a workshop titled "African Women in Community." They invited academics, administrators and front line staff working with refugees. Both the format and content of the workshop challenged myths about African women and refugee women, and they demonstrated how respect for the dignity of women can be embedded in research and how services can respond to their needs.

The Second International Conference on Refugee Women entitled "Gender Issues and Refugees: Development Implications" was held in Toronto at York University from 9 to 11 May 1993. The conference was organized by the Center for Refugee Studies and the Feminist Research Center at York University. The working definition of the conference was that the refugee experience is gendered and that the way in which refugees are defined by the state is critical to their experiences as refugees. In contrast, past work had focused attention on the *problems of* refugee women.[6] One significant dynamic of this conference was the bringing together of a wide range of academic disciplines and professionals with scholars and professionals who focus on the "typical" refugee experience. This trend of the 1990s broadened the base of interest in the situation of refugee women and also contributed to the evolving discourse on refugee women's experience from a gender-integrated perspective. The challenge of this knowledge base, as it attempts to influence policy and practice that address the fundamental causes of the uprooting of people, must continue.

At the international level, the WGRW's most notable achievement in the early 1990s was the success of its advocacy campaign for a senior position within the UNHCR on Refugee Women. Ms. Anne Brazeau, a Canadian working in the Canadian International Development Agency (CIDA), was appointed to the position in 1991. WGRW continued to lobby for the implementation of UNHCR policies and to ensure that refugee women's issues are an integral part of all aspects of UNHCR activities. One of the last significant activities of WGRW was to take the lead together with the International Islamic Relief Organization in organizing the International Conference on Uprooted Muslim Refugee Women in Sharjah, United Arab Emirates from 12 to 14 September 1994. The rationale for the conference was that during this period Muslims represented 80 percent of the 25 million displaced people and, of these totals, 70 percent were women and children. While these refugees originated from or were hosted in Muslim communities, they were often assisted by non-Muslim organizations, which were not familiar with Muslim beliefs and practices. The recommendations of the conference offered culture-specific ways in which refugee women could be assisted (The Sharjah Declaration 1994: 1).

Largely due to lack of funding, but more perhaps because some of the WGRW's networks, such as the Norwegian Refugee Council, had developed the capacity to take a strong lead in the UNHCR arenas, WGRW's role as a catalyst diminished after 1994, and it ceased to exist after 1995. The NGO that has sustained continuing influence since the early 1990s is the well-staffed and well-financed Women's Commission for Refugee Women and Children, an independent affiliate of the International Rescue Committee based in New York and established in 1989.[7]

Amnesty International's 1990 report titled "Women at the Frontline: Human Rights Violations Against Women" was a key forerunner in defining sexual violence against women refugees as a human rights violation. During the early 1990s a growing movement of feminists began to claim that women's rights are human rights. The main catalyst of this movement was initially the Center for Women's Global Leadership at Rutgers University in New Jersey. This movement crystallized during the international campaign that led to the Vienna Conference on Human Rights in 1993. A significant outcome of the Vienna Conference was the acknowledgment that violence against women affects both public and private life, and that governments and international organizations are accountable for the equal status and human rights of women.[8] While this movement was led mainly by Northern white feminists, the "Women's Rights are Human Rights" campaign is another example in which women of color, Third

World[9] women, and refugee women were able to use this platform to affirm their priorities and assert their identities.

Three human rights themes during this period influenced the refugee women's discourse. First, women's rights as human rights in refugee protection discourse led to the recognition that "protection," as stated in refugee law and as interpreted from The Universal Declaration on Human Rights (1948), is a human right. At the same time, clauses in international treaties, such as the Convention on the Elimination of all Forms of Discrimination against Women, could be applied to women refugees. Uprooting was perceived as a gendered experience and a human rights violation. In 1993, the chairperson of the Canadian Immigration and Refugee Board (IRB) issued the *Guidelines on Women Refugee Claimants Fearing Gender-Related Persecution*. These guidelines were recognized internationally as groundbreaking since they were the first guidelines on gender-based persecution issued by an adjudicating body. The WGRW was one of the key advocates behind their establishment. At the international level, UNHCR policies and guidelines to assist staff on the ground were also ready for implementation in the early 1990s.[10]

The second theme in the human rights discourse during the 1990s was the right to safety and security. The Balkan wars (1992) and the Rwandan genocide (1994) moved the discourse on violence against women to a totally different level. In these conflicts, rape and sexual abuse were used as a means of "ethnic cleansing" and as "a weapon of war." Sexual violation of women (and men) was no longer indiscriminate, but a methodical strategy of war. Such violence is now considered a crime against humanity. The International Tribunal for the Former Yugoslavia has handed down convictions for rape as a weapon of war, and the Statute of the International Criminal Court also recognizes rape as a crime of war.

Third, ten years after the Nairobi Conference, the importance of women refugees as agents of change and particularly in peace building efforts was clearly evidenced at the 1995 NGO Forum preceding the UN Conference on the Decade of Women in Beijing. While refugee women acknowledged that they may be victims of war, they demonstrated that they can also be powerful agents of change. Particularly striking at the Beijing NGO Forum was that, every day, refugee and IDP (Internally Displaced Persons) women from all continents facilitated workshops showing how they were working toward human rights and peace in first asylum countries and in IDP camps. The official conference declaration was forthright in uplifting the situation of women in conflict areas, as well as in stating the actions that have to be taken by governments, national and international agencies, and NGOs (Platform of Action and the Beijing Declaration 1996).

The earliest documented efforts of refugee women organizing themselves in camps for peace and return to their homeland were the Guatemalan women in the 120 UNHCR refugee camps in Mexico and in the spontaneous settlements along the Mexican-Guatemalan border. While in Guatemala they had never realized they had rights. In Mexico it suddenly occurred to these women that they had an important role to play in the camps, which led to the establishment of their own organization, *Mama Maquin*. This organization was instrumental in setting up awareness-raising workshops and in ensuring that women participated in relief and development projects. *Mama Maquin* also played a critical role in the peace process in the 1990s and in organizing the return of refugees from the camps in Mexico to their home communities in Guatemala.[11] Back at home, the task of these returnees included building new villages, often in politically hostile environments. One of the concessions the *Mama Maquin* women won in the repatriation negotiations was the recognition, for the first time, of the principle of equal ownership of private and communal property. Although it took them a decade of lobbying pressure, this principle is now enshrined in Guatemalan law and jurisprudence, thus benefiting the entire population.

Since the Guatemalan experience, women refugees and women in many post-conflict areas have regrouped to respond to their situation. Achieving peace is of particular significance to them because of the violence they experienced and witnessed in war, and when forcibly displaced. For people who are uprooted, achieving peace means ensuring the rule of law, physical security, and the economic viability of returning home. While they seek to be included in peace negotiations, women refugees fully recognize that peace accords only signal the end of war and that peace is a lived experience, which has to be worked on within day-to-day power relations. Beyond the Beijing conference, refugee women's involvement in peace-building activities has been observed by professionals who work closely with refugees and displaced persons, as well as by scholarly researchers. Refugee women speak of healing relationships between family members, with neighbors, with the community, and with the nation. They speak of wanting to provide food security for their families and of the need for adequate housing, schools, and employment opportunities. They express the need to ensure the safety and dignity of women and girls. Above all they speak of different forms of governance based on nonviolent forms of relationships and respect for the human rights of all persons, including addressing the fundamental causes of uprooting.[12]

The campaign beyond the Beijing Conference led to Security Council Resolution 1325 (2000) which reaffirmed:

> [t]he important role of women in the prevention and resolution of conflicts and in peace building, and *stressing* the importance of their equal participation and full involvement in all efforts for the maintenance and promotion of peace and security, and the need to increase their role in decision-making with regard to conflict prevention and resolution. (UN Security Council Resolution 1325: 1)

In 2001, to ensure that protection of refugee women was central to the debates and the overall process of the Global Consultation of International Protection, twenty-five local consultations in all continents met with refugee women to review the achievements in the past ten years and the challenges for the future. The regional consultations culminated in a "dialogue" meeting with forty-seven refugee women in Geneva, Switzerland from 20 to 21 June 2001 that was titled "Respect our Rights: Partnership in Equality." The meeting was cosponsored by the UNHCR Senior Coordinator for Refugee Women/Gender Equality and the Women's Commission for Women Refugees and Children. The main themes of this meeting were "Respect our Rights: Safety and Security" and "Respect our Rights: Choice, Change and Livelihoods." The recommendations informed the Global Consultation of International Protection and, for the first time, a refugee woman addressed the UNHCR Executive meeting.[13]

In May 2002, an independent assessment by the Women's Commission for Refugee Women and Children titled "UNHCR Policy on Refugee Women and Guidelines on their Protection: An Assessment of Ten Years of Implementation" was published. The report acknowledged the significance of the progress the UNCHR has made ". . . in creating policies, guidelines and other tools to protect women but has had difficulty in translating these into practical measures in the field . . . [and] often [policies were] implemented inconsistently" (Women's Commission for Refugee Women and Children 2002). While the report notes that protection of refugees is a daunting task because the UNHCR operates in very difficult environments, and that states also fail to fulfill their obligations under international law, organizational barriers continue to prevail. For example:

—organizational commitment was lacking, such as standards of operating procedures, lack of female staff in the field, no mandatory gender training for staff, and lack of resources to implement guidelines;
—insufficient participation of refugee women in decision making leading to their inability to improve their living conditions, including a deprivation of basic services, such as food, shelter, and heath care;
—while many women and girls were found to suffer from sexual and gender-based violence (SGBV) throughout the refugee experience, such experiences go unreported as "there is little awareness about the problem, and few coordinated efforts to prevent abuses and respond when abuses occur" (ibid.)

From 28 February to 11 March 2005, the *Beijing +10* meeting was held in New York City. The meeting was convened by the United Nations Commission on the Status of Women (CSW) for a ten-year review of the commitment made in the Beijing Platform for Action emanating from the Fourth World Conference on Women. While it was generally agreed that progress had been achieved since the first world conference in Mexico (1975), and there were no obvious chances of backsliding, still a long road remained to make governments accountable to their commitments [See the report on the forty-ninth session of the United Nations Commission on the Status of Women (www.un/womenwatch/daw/csw/csw49/documents .htm/)]. The words of Noeleen Heyzer, Executive Director of the United Nations Development Fund (UNIFEM), succinctly expressed the need of continued focus and accelerating change at an International Women's Day Celebration on 8 March 2005 during the CSW meeting:

> And yet, while we celebrate progress, we know that it has been too slow. Thirty years after the beginning of the Decade on Women, and ten years after Beijing, it is still a woman's face we see when we speak of poverty, of HIV/AIDS, of violent conflict and social upheaval, of trafficking in human beings. Violence against women, already horrific in times of peace, intensifies during armed conflict with sexual violence now routinely used as a weapon of war. And women are everywhere disproportionately concentrated among the poorly paid, unsafe and insecure jobs, struggling to lift themselves and their families out of poverty (2005).

This reflection on the discourse on refugee women in the past three decades has demonstrated that the changing language to name refugee women's identities and agency, in theory, research, policy, and program, has challenged us and elicited change in our perceptions of refugee women and of our relationship with them. At the same time, well meaning yet "disempowering" perceptions and practices continue even when we adopt currently acceptable language. Memory of early struggles, gaps, and achievements is critical to move the discourse forward and make a difference in the lives of uprooted women.

The authors in this volume not only consider lessons learned from the past, they also raise critical questions at the conceptual and practical level, and pose new challenges for the future.

Continuing the Discourse: Breaking Paths

Visual media has also contributed to the construction of an identity discourse on refugee women. Many of us remember the piercing, frightened, and defiant stare of the refugee girl from Afghanistan whose photograph appeared on the cover of the *National Geographic Magazine* in June 1985. It is often referred to as "[t]he most famous anonymous photograph of our times." The photographer, Steve McCurry gained instant celebrity, but the refugee girl's *identity* remained unknown and her voice silenced for over fifteen years. It is that photograph of Sharbat Gula that was chosen to embody the theme of a three-day conference held between 19 and 21 March

2003 at McMaster University, Hamilton, Canada, entitled: *Saying "I" Is Full of Consequences. Refugee Women Reclaim Their Identity. Identity, Research, Education and Policy.*

The eye of the camera had commodified her, estheticized her, decontextualized her, deprived her of her voice, of her story, her identity, her agency, and of the monetary rewards reaped by the *National Geographic Magazine* while she continued living in poverty.[14] Her case exemplifies the situation of refugees around the world. It conceals the fact that identity and agency and their representation are predicated on factors that are interrelated such as historical and political context, gender, economic status, and power relationships. As Foucault (1979) and feminist poststructuralists have argued (Mulvey 1989; De Laureitis 1984; 1987), visual representation is associated with power and implies a subject-object relationship, and it is through voice and voicing that agency and power are reclaimed by marginalized groups, particularly women.[15] Visual media operate as a technology of power that constructs a dehistoricized *refugeeness*. Women are made into helpless and voiceless victims to be rescued, as L. Malkki remarked, "Indeed, it is not far fetched to say that a vigorous, transnational, largely philanthropic traffic in images and visual signs of refugeeness has gradually emerged in the half century" (Malkki 1996: 386). From a gender perspective—which is missing in Malkki's compelling analysis—we can further remark that the Western media reproduce a Christian gaze constructed through the Renaissance representation of the Madonna. "Under Western eyes" —to borrow the expression from Ch. Mohanty— that image of the Virgin Mary with Jesus became the blueprint of the imaginary Third World refugee mother. As best expressed in one of countless such analogies found on the Internet, "Mary knew exactly what it was like to be a single mom, a homeless woman, a seeker of shelter, a political refugee and the mother of an imprisoned and executed son" (Bishop Tobin 2004). Finally, the constructed and racialized exoticism of refugee women, as displayed for example by the strikingly colorful *Niqabs* (cloaks that cover both the face and the body worn by Muslim women in certain countries) of the Afghani women refugees in the film *Kandahar,* creates an "othering" distance which absolves the Western viewer from his/her accountability. Authors of this volume will deconstruct this othering distanciation, that is, the veiling of the West's responsibility for what happens "elsewhere" among "other"—strange or barbaric —populations (Murdocca, chapter 16).

Thus it is Sharbat Gula's photograph and the implicit discourse it conveys that inspired the theme of the *Saying "I"* conference, which in turn has led to the publication of this volume. Many of the authors of these chapters were also speakers at the conference. Several other contributors were invited to address a range of issues such as trafficking, racism, mental health, and policy.

The conference was intended to be a celebration of the tenth anniversary of the acknowledgement by Canada that gender-based persecution is a legitimate claim to obtain refugee status—the first country to do so.[16] In a cruel turn of irony, the news of the invasion of Iraq by the United States broke during the conference, and participants felt the need to interrupt the conference in order to collectively reflect on the event. They unanimously drafted resolutions in which they appealed to the Canadian government to stand firm in its decision not to join this war, and to reject the Safe Third Country Agreement between Canada and the United States (when a refugee lands in Canada or the US, he/she cannot apply for asylum in the other country), which it was perceived would be particularly harmful to refugee women. The resolutions were faxed to several appropriate government bodies (Canada did not join the war, but also did not reject the Safe Third Country Agreement until November 2007).[17]

A popular play written by Latina women for the occasion titled *I Was, I Am, and I Will Be,* an art exhibition, and a poetry recital brought together groups of refugee women from various countries and cultures, under the auspices of the Worker's Arts and Heritage Center in Hamilton. The large painting that they collectively produced to convey their common struggle for safety, self-fulfilment, and agency has been chosen as the book's cover.

The Objectives of This Volume

The concept of identity, which is very much debated in contemporary criticism, legitimately occupies a pivotal place in any investigation related to refugees. This is true of refugee women in particular, because defining their identity is indeed full of consequences. The title of this volume posits identity (that of refugee women, in particular) as a construct, links theory with practice, and focuses our attention on the processual, innovative, and forward-looking aspect of the volume's content. If any self is shaped as a multifaceted and multilayered entity always under construction, the self of refugee women constitutes a particularly complex process because of the multiplicity of contexts and intensity of circumstances which it encounters during its journey (Hajdukowski-Ahmed, chapter 1).

Why a book on *women,* one might wonder, in what some call the postfeminist era, and since "refugeeness" affects men and women, young boys and young girls alike? Numbers, specificities, and their transformations, as well as an increased awareness of the importance of gender by organizations themselves, warrant that a special case be made of refugee women in research and in practice. First, writing about women contextually cannot be done in isolation and implies a relational mode to men: to fathers, husbands, brothers, to political or religious leaders. Interconnectedness indeed constitutes a pivotal notion common to the chapters of this volume. Secondly, "[g]ender is a core organizing principle of social relations and opportunities" (Goździak, chapter 11); "a key relational dimension of human activity" (Indra 1999a: 2); and gender relationships are shaped by and in turn shape gendered structures and institutions of various historic and social settings. Furthermore, the concept of "refugeeness" as a legal category which has first been defined by the UN and UNHCR from a political—thus essentially male—perspective has gradually become gender-specific and is finding legitimacy in governments' policies (i.e., gender guidelines, gender-specificity of trafficking, increased participation of refugee women in UNHCR activities). The shift in the nature of today's conflicts is such that the militarization of economies and the technologization of wars have made civilians into targets of war, and by civilians we mean mostly women and children. In Columbia, for example, indigenous communities "have been targeted by irregular armed groups, who favour action against the civilian population over direct military confrontation" (UNHCR 2006: 170).

In this context, the body of women has increasingly become a site of violence and a weapon of war, as the tragedy in the former Yugoslavia has demonstrated (Gagnon, chapter 8; Valji 2000). Sexual violence such as rape occurs during all phases of the refugee situation; however the reporting of it is estimated at less than 10 percent of the total number of cases (UNHCR 2006: 36). Sexual violence is also treated differently for men and women, as raped women sometimes are further ostracized by their family and community members in certain cultural contexts (Gorman and Mojab, chapter 7; Cole 1992: 69).

Technologies of surveillance affect women in specific ways and intensities, from the bedroom to the refugee camps, and track them even when they are dispersed or in resettlement spaces. Conflicts such as nationalist or colonial struggles, as well as certain reactions to the Westernization brought by globalization (Chatterjee 2001: 331), tend to cast women in the role of guardians and transmitters of ethnocultural purity that suits patriarchal ideologies and purposes. As N.Yuval Davis has noted, "Women's membership [in] their national and ethnic collectivities is of a double nature. On the one hand, women are always included, at least to some extent, in the construction of the general body of members of national and ethnic collectivity and/or citizens of the state,—on the other hand—there is always, at least to a certain extent, a separate body of regulations (legal, and/or customary) which relate to them specifically as women, wives, mothers" (1995: 1).

Current dynamics of displacement compel us to reconsider and broaden the concepts of refugee and "refugeeness" and their gender-specificity. In the process, more women have become exposed to multiple risks. While the number of asylum seekers has decreased (20 percent to 36 percent in Western countries since 2001; UNHCR 2006: 14), the number of refugees—

of women refugees in particular—contained within the borders of nations, neighboring nations, and within the walls of refugee camps has increased in an inversely proportional manner. Within the female population of IDPs, "displaced girls are more vulnerable to sexual exploitation and pregnancy than other teenagers" (UNHCR 2006: 170). The dramatic increase in the number of protracted refugee situations—the number of years spent in camps nearly doubled from an average of nine years in 1993 to an average of seventeen years in 2004 (UNHCR 2006: 109)—increases the vulnerability of women.

They are "warehoused" in "isolated and insecure designated refugee camps, typically in border regions" (UNHCR 2006:114), in which suboptimal living conditions, domestic violence, alcoholism, and trafficking of women have increased (UNHCR 2006:117). High fertility rates among refugee women who are part of the 7.5 million "persons of concern"—1 in 5 women of reproductive age is "likely to be pregnant"—require that special attention be paid to their health and sexual care (UNHCR 2006: 20). An increase in HIV/AIDS "has been linked to extensive sexual violence by paramilitary groups and foreign troupes" (UNHCR 2006: 22).

The organization and the division of labor in camps are conducted along gender lines. In camps or in flight, issues of physical security, documentation, access to food and services, access to education, representation and participation, are still very much gender-informed (Introduction, this volume; UNHCR 2006, chapter 4; Cole 1992: 65). Displacement is undoubtedly affected by class, ethnicity, and location, which in turn shape the identity of refugee women. In most refugee-receiving countries, especially in the developed world, the majority of asylum seekers and refugees are men (UNHCR 2001, as mentioned by Valji et al., 2003: 62). When they come with their families, "[t]he existing practice of giving derivative refugee status to the partner and children of an asylum applicant is problematic" (Valji et al., 2003: 62). The derivative status may conceal the specificity of persecution based on *gender*, such as persecution of women based on kinship to "punish" male relatives, persecution that occurs in the private sphere of their life, or persecution by the state when it fails to protect them, particularly when that state is not listed as refugee-producing (Valji et al., 2003: 64). In conflict zones or under dictatorial regimes, men tend to be considered as "principle agents of political resistance and therefore the legitimate beneficiaries of protection as enshrined in the 1951 Convention Relating to the Status of Refugees" (Crawley 1999: 309).

The number of victims of natural disasters has tripled over the past decade and those displaced by "developments projects" have also augmented exponentially, with 211 million people affected every year (UNHCR 2006: 27); that is, five times the number of people affected by conflict over the past decade. For example, the December 2004 tsunami in Indonesia and neighboring regions has affected women in specific ways (UNHCR 2006:

21). It has been reported that the resulting economic destabilization and impoverishment have made women more vulnerable to the global trafficking of organs. In India, the state of Tamil Nadu and the city of Chennai (Madras) have emerged as the "the great kidney bazaar," and "[i]t is generally only women who are selected as donors. In most cases, the husbands of these women are daily wage workers and cannot afford such long absence from work" (Arun 2007: 1). It is the interplay of gender with other factors such as age (younger/healthier women), location (a tsunami affected-region where transplants are performed in fifty-four hospitals), caste/socioeconomic status and the resulting power relationship (low caste/poor vulnerable women and wealthy recipients) which impact this form of trafficking.

With border closings, visa restrictions, and the tightening of borders, measures which followed the tragedy of 11 September 2001 in New York, patriarchal fundamentalism has resulted as a form of retreat from Western influence and as an affirmation of traditional cultural identities, particularly in communities that feel targeted by the backlash (Murdocca, chapter 16). Another result of the tightening of borders is the increase in the smuggling and trafficking of people into industrialized countries (UNHCR 2006: 25), which present specific risks for women. Finally, there is increased evidence that other forms of violence against women, such as forced marriage or forced abortion or sterilization, forced prostitution, as well as sustained or systemic denial of education, employment, or healthcare, are cause for refugee determination, and "the next—or current—stage in refugee law may increasingly implicate economic and social rights" (Anker 150).

However, "refugeeness" can also be experienced as an opportunity for emancipation and agency, particularly for women. For example, resettlement is experienced differently by some women, who often feel they are becoming more like individuals than reproducers of the traditional roles of mother/daughter/wife (Cole 1992: 25). Also, feminist NGOs reject the patriarchal division of labor and organize training programs for women that include "men's" skills learning, such as welding (Hyndman and de Alwis, chapter 4). The militarization of women and their presence in combat zones creates a new division of labor and elicits new questions and perspectives, particularly for feminist scholars and practitioners (Yuval Davis 2004: 173). In all, refugee situations have changed, affecting women in specific ways and numbers, requiring conceptualizations, methodology, and practices which are reflective of those changes, and which respond to them effectively and justly.

In this volume we seek to understand how refugee women perceive themselves based on their own experiences, how they challenge their mono-logic (or monolithic and essentialized) constructed identity as helpless victims, how they redefine and reshape it on the strength of their knowledge, initiatives, and creativity. More precisely, certain questions are raised. What are the current (mis)conceptions and assumptions concerning women refugees that pervade research? How may these (mis)conceptions be dispelled? How is their identity transformed through various aspects and stages of the refugee experience? How ought the self-identification of refugee women affect research, as well as political initiatives and policies intended to support them in such areas as heath care, refugee laws, or settlement organizations? What new directions can we propose in these areas? All of the above questions are explored in the present global and local contexts and in the light of recent developments in politics, research, and policies.

Refugee women find themselves in continuous situations of crisis, that is, etymologically at turning points that create challenges but that also elicit critical judgment and open up new possibilities ("crisis" and "critique" share the same etymology *krinein*: to separate, to decide, to judge). The authors of this volume endeavour to break down walls and build bridges, as "thresholds to other realities" (Anzaldúa and Keating 2002: 1), bridges that link borders and banks of different territories. They destabilize rooted beliefs by breaking the walls that artificially separate dichotomized concepts such as helper and helped, academia and community, researcher and participant, home and state, past and present, here and there, memory and reality, theoretical work and field work, truth and untruth. The multiplicity and diversity of the identities and expertise of contributors alone attest to the pluridimensionality of this book. Many contributors themselves are people of the borderlands, whose activities straddle definitions and professional categories, challenging their artificial division. They are (or have been): refugee women, scholars, advocates, settlement experts, counselors, policy makers, students, therapists, and artists. They have worked and continue to work with refugee women. They come from many countries and venues. In their chapters, they develop and validate an epistemology and discourse of the borderlands, the peripheries, the intermediary spaces. Those spaces are cracks in life and discourses in which women refugees have fallen and are forced to live, both spatially and metaphorically. From the voices and experiential knowledge of refugee women, the contributors develop a feminist epistemology of the borderlands, not as the world's margins, but as their own refugee women's center, to paraphrase bell hooks (who chose not to capitalize her name). Those voices at times even challenged the researchers themselves.

Recent events require renewed reflection and intervention. We must examine the connection between manmade and nature-triggered tragedies, and between humanitarian aid and asylum. For example, the fallout from the tragedy of 11 September 2001 and the subsequent war on terrorism, account for the dramatic drop in the number of refugees who seek or obtain asylum, while their numbers in camps swell, mostly in poor neighboring countries, with a majority of them being women. Because many borders of wealthier countries have closed, the humanitarian aid keeps many women in precarious limbo within the boundaries of refugee camps. The occupation of Iraq, the war in Sudan, or the 2004 tsunami are painful reminders that our work is an unending process, and examples abound of refugees, particularly women, who face new dangers and new challenges every day. Global trafficking of women and girls around the world has not abated. In Sudan, women and girls are still being subjected to sexual violence in the camps where they have sought refuge (*Women's Human Rights Net,* http://www.whrnet.org/index.php, 2006). The 2004 tsunami resulted in the death of a significantly larger number of women and children than men, leaving the survivors facing specific challenges. As Becky Buel, Oxfam's policy director stated, "This disproportionate impact will lead to problems for years to come unless everyone working on the aid effort addresses the issue now." (http://www.oxfam.org.uk/press/releases/tsunami_women260305.htm, 2005). While they acknowledge that a certain progress regarding the status of refugee women and girls has taken place—although elderly women and men are still very neglected—recent reports such as *Displaced Women and Girls at Risk* published by the Women's Commission for Refugee Women and Children (2006) identify many challenges that refugee women still face because of their gender.

This volume is intended to be at once a homage to, a dialogue with, and a continuation of the thought process generated by previous authors. New circumstances, new voices, new developments, and a new awareness call for new or refined approaches to identity concepts, research, and policies. We are all participants in what we hope will be an entropic, collective task, the need for which should eventually be eliminated.

The Organization of the Book

The contributions to this volume provide thought provoking scholarship on refugee women and identity. Collectively they provide new and radical thinking in deconstructing prevailing assumptions about the ascribed category of refugee women and raise implications for the discourse and praxis of identity politics. Through its organization around four sections, this collection of chapters invites readers to engage in transformative thinking in challenging current representations of refugee women. The organization of the book is not only structural but also one that promotes dialogue about ideas raised across the chapters and with the readers. To facilitate the dialogue, we have also provided introductions to each of the sections. It is for this reason that detailed information on the specific chapters is not provided here, and the reader is encouraged to refer to the section-specific introductions prior to reading the chapters.

Our beginning point is more theoretical (see Section I: Reconceptualizing Identities), with a selection of four chapters from authors who address the concept of identity in connection to refugee women's experiences. While the authors draw from different disciplinary perspectives, including feminist critical theory, they go beyond a theoretical stance and make links to the lived experiences of displaced women. The politics of identity, citizenship, trafficking of women, war, and trauma are among the concepts examined and challenged by the authors.

By discussing and reflecting on their research approaches, the authors of the chapters in Section II (Challenging Methodologies. Challenging the Researcher) provide us with both substantive and empirical knowledge gained through their studies with refugee women. Through reflexive self-analyses of their methodologies, the researchers explore the relationship between the research approaches applied and implications for constructions of refugee women's identities that recognize their agency. Concepts of shifting positions and power relations in women's narratives and the challenging of researchers' methodologies by the study participants are explored.

Self-identity is recognized to be a central part of who we are as humans and an important aspect of mental well being. Section III (Rethinking Practices. Creating Spaces for Agency) of the book brings together chapters that address the multiple dimensions of refugee women's mental health. The displacement experiences of refugee women can pose significant challenges to their sense of identity. While discussing the implications of multiple challenges to refugee women's mental health, the authors also point toward the multiple resiliences utilized by displaced women in maintaining their own mental well being as well as that of their families. Among the concepts explored in this section are the dominance of trauma discourse, application of a developmental psychological perspective on the identity of refugee youth, religion and spirituality as part of refugee women's personal and collective identity, and the identity and mental health of refugee women during their resettlement years.

Law and policy define the identity of individuals within a state, which is crucial in delineating their access to rights and services. Current national and international policies and practices are considered in connection with implications for refugee women's legal and human rights in Section IV (Reviewing Policies. Taking Responsibility for the Rights of Refugee Women). Among the policies examined is the inclusion of gender in UNHCR policies and programs as well as the Canadian Guidelines on Women Refugees Fearing Gender-Related Persecution. The opportunities, gaps, and contradictions in the interpretation and implementation of existing policies are considered in this section of the book.

In unison, each of the sections of the book can be viewed as a complementary dimension contributing to the title of our book, *Not Born a*

Refugee Woman: Contesting Identities, Rethinking Practices. While the book is organized around four sections for the sake of clarity and overall thematic congruence, it is important to note that all chapters contribute to an intersectional understanding of identity, and place gender at the center of their analysis in examining the experiences of refugee women. The authors contributing to this book view refugee women as active agents in the construction of their identities and in embodying resiliences within the context of their multiple personal and systemic challenges. Yet, as the reader will observe in reading the chapters, the authors to this collection also take different positions and theoretical stances. The result is a new and dynamic contribution to the field of refugee, identity, and feminist studies, which, we believe, will challenge prevailing concepts and practices and move us toward a new paradigm shift in scholarship, advocacy, and praxis.

On a final note, we hope that the ideas and analyses presented in this book will move women back into the center of gender discourse. Impressive gains have been made in feminist scholarship and grassroots activism regarding women's rights and resiliences over the last decades. However, power relations continue to underprivilege women in policy and maintain inequitable access to resources from local to global levels.

Notes

1. "The Forgotten Majority" is a term used by Geneviève Camus-Jacques in one of the first publications on refugee women in a chapter titled "Refugee Women: The Forgotten Majority." In *Refugees and International Relations,* ed. Gil Loescher and Laila Monaham (Oxford, 1989: 141–147).

2. Mexico 1975; Copenhagen 1980; Nairobi 1985.

3. In an effort to move the work of the WGRW from Toronto to the national level, in 1990 the CCR established a Gender Working Group. In 1993 the name and function of this group was changed again to "Gender Core Group" so that it could serve all the CCR Working Groups. Its main function is to monitor and advocate for the rights of refugee women in Canada and abroad. One of the recent activities of the Gender Core Group has been a campaign for the protection of trafficked women who are in Canada.

4. Some of these resolutions are: UNHCR Executive Committee, 1985, 36th Session, *Resolution No.39, Refugee Women and International Protection.* www .refugeelawreader.org/files/pdf/61.pdf. Accessed 10 April 2007. UNHCR Executive Committee, 39th session, 1988, "Refugee Women" in *Conclusions on the International Protection of Refugees, Adopted by the Executive Committee of the UNHCR Program.* Geneva, UNHCR 1980–1988. www.unhcr.org/doclist/excom/3ba7175a1a .html. Accessed 10 April 2007.

5. No study was carried out on this development, but it was and is increasingly observable in regional and national CCR consultations, the women's movements, and other advocacy gatherings.

6. While proceedings of the conference were not published, a selected number of papers were published in *Development and Diaspora: Gender and the Refugee Experience,* ed. W. Giles, H. Moussa, and P. Van Esterik (Dundas, Ontario, 1996).

7. For more information on the U.S. Women's Commission on Refugee Women and Children see: www.womenscommission.org

8. For an account of this movement and the Vienna Conference, see Charlotte Bunch and Nianh Reilly, *Demanding Accountability: The Global Campaign and Vienna Tribunal for Women's Human Rights.* (Rutgers University and New York [UNIFEM], 1994).

9. "Third World" here is used to connote the countries of Africa, Asia, the Caribbean, Latin America, the Middle East, and the Pacific Islands that have been colonized and are still under the domination of the global cultural/economic/military system.

10. UNHCR *Policy on Refugee Women,* 1990; *Guidelines on the Protection of Refugee Women* (1991); *People Oriented Planning: A Practical Tool for Refugee Workers* (1993). These documents are available on the UNHCR Web site: www.unhcr.org. United Nations High Commissioner for Refugees. Sexual Violence against Refugees: Guidelines on Prevention and Response. Geneva: UNHCR, March 1995. Preface by Sadako Ogata.

11. In 1999, the UNHCR reported on the Guatemalan return process as a role model of best practices. See P. Worby, "Refugee Return and Reintegration in Guatemala. Lessons Learned by UNHCR through its Presence and Intervention 1987–1999." (Geneva, 2000). Available on UNHCR Web site: www.unhcr.ch/evaluate/reports99gtm.htm. And P. Worby, "Security and Dignity: Land Access and Guatemala's Returned Refugees," *Refuge* 19, no. 3 (2001): 17–24.

12. The research and publications of the Women In Conflict Zones NETwork (WICZNET) established in 1991 and affiliated with the Feminist Research Center at York University in Toronto are particularly relevant to the discussion on addressing root causes of violence against women if peace is to prevail in post-conflict areas. The following are two of the publications of the network: W. Giles et al., *Feminists Under Fire: Exchanges Across War Zones* (Toronto, 2003); W. Giles and J. Hyndman, *Sites of Violence: Gender and Conflict Zones* (Berkeley, 2004). Another useful resource on practical actions taken by women in conflict areas is "Best Practices in Peace Building and Non-Violent Conflict Resolution—Some documented African Women's Peace Initiatives." Edited and produced by Angela Ernest. The UNHCR, UNESCO, UNDP, UNFPA, UNICEF and UNIFEM published this document out of a workshop with the same title, held in Addis Ababa in 1997.

13. For the full report of the dialogue with refugee women, see 2002b. *Respect our Rights: Partnership for Equality. Report on the Dialogue with Refugee Women.* Geneva, Switzerland, 20–22 June 2001. http://www.womenscommission.org/pdf/unhcr_w.ref.pdf. Accessed 10 April 2007.

14. Photographed by Steve McCurry for *The National Geographic Magazine* in 1984 in Nasir Bagh refugee camp at the age of twelve, Sharbat Gula was located again in a remote village of Afghanistan in 2002, that is eighteen years later. She was married, poor, and the mother of four daughters, one of whom died in infancy. Steve McCurry promised to help Sharbat Gula with the education of her daughters and assisted the National Geographic Society in creating the Afghan Girl Fund. Another famous photograph of a refugee is that of Kim Phuc, taken by

Nick Ut, who was awarded the Pulitzer Prize for it. The naked and screaming Vietnamese girl was fleeing her napalm-bombed village during the American war in Vietnam in 1972. Both photographs have become emblematic of the plight of refugee girls and women.

15. Michel Foucault discussed the relationship between the eye and power in his concept of surveillance or *panoptikon* (See *Discipline and Punish: The Birth of the Prison*, trans. A. Sheridan (New York, 1995: 195–228). So did feminist theoricians such as Luce Irigaray, Laura Mulvey, Helene Cixous, Madeleine Ouellette-Michalska, and Teresa De Lauretis, who associated the eye with *patriarchal power*, for example in the visual arts.

16. In the decade 1993–2003, 2,331 cases of gender-related admissions were finalized in Canada.

17. The Federal Court of Canada ruled that the Safe Third Country Agreement violated the Canadian Charter of Rights and Freedoms on November 29, 2007.

Section I

Reconceptualizing Identities

INTRODUCTION

The authors of the first four chapters establish a conceptual framework for this book that challenges dichotomies and categorizations which silence or misrepresent refugee women and their experience, conceal their accomplishments, and limit their potential. From the challenges emerge new approaches to the conceptualization of refugee women's identity that impact research, policies, and practices.

In the first chapter, *A Dialogical Perspective on the Identity of Refugee Women and its Implications,* Maroussia Hajdukowski-Ahmed examines identity theories from a dialogical feminist perspective in relationship to the works of scholars/practitioners in feminist and refugee studies. From a dialogical perspective, the self is constructed socially through a process of interlocution shaped by the different and sometimes conflicting voices or worldviews it encounters along its lifelong transformation. It is expressed through language as discourse, language being understood both as verbal and corporeal. Refugee women experience dialogism particularly intensely because of the abnormal circumstances they have to confront, the migratory path they are forced to follow, and the various sociocultural environments to which they are sent. The author gives a brief overview of the stages in the evolution of the concept of identity, discusses the politics of the naming of refugee women and the impact it can have on their lives. She examines the process of "de-selving" or erosion of agency that refugee women undergo in various situations and in power relationships. She demonstrates how a dialogic approach unravels what appears to be contradictions, identifies and acknowledges counterdiscursive and enabling practices. Finally she explores the contributions a dialogical approach can make to research and therapy, to a politics of recognition of the complex identity of refugee women and their agency, to reassigning responsibilities for their uprootedness in our transnational world.

In her chapter, *The Gender Relations of Home, Security and Transversal Feminism: Refugee Women Reclaiming Their Identity,* Wenona Giles pursues her exploration of the link between war, homelessness, and citizenship. She defines citizenship as a concept shaped in industrial countries, predicated on property ownership and a fixed address, and constructed to serve the interests of those countries. She deconstructs the gendering of space, in which women's identity has been traditionally dependent on their association with home as their "natural" space. Such static gendering of space turns refugee women into a homeless, invisible, or deviant population. The word "home" in effect connotes different meanings and values depending on time and context. The concept of citizenship also has the effect of concealing the root causes of their dis-location and the agents responsible for their situation. Giles shows how conventional citizenship postulates sameness and equality before the law while obfuscating group differences, particularly among those groups which are disadvantaged. In the end, citizenship reflects inequities without challenging them. Furthermore, when they choose to provide humanitarian aid rather than welcome refugees into their midst, rich countries only prolong the "citizenship limbo" to which refugee women are confined. In her essay, Giles places violence at home and violence in war on a continuum. She also describes the homelessness caused by poverty and the homelessness caused by the situation of the refugee as consequences of the same inequities. A more inclusive and adaptive notion of transnational citizenship emerges as a constructive alternative, based on a concept of transversal feminist politics. Because of their predicament, refugee women create a crisis "around normative definitions of citizenship, north–south inequality and human rights," thus pointing to the position from which it is possible to challenge those definitions and to effect necessary changes.

Through a gendered analysis of an economic approach to women's bodies, Sarah Wayland and Viktor Malarek proceed to deconstruct the stereotyping and the "othering" of trafficked women as prostitutes, particularly those from Eastern Europe and the former USSR. Their chapter, *Always "Natasha": The Transnational Sex Trafficking of Women,* is based on the recently published book by Viktor Malarek, *The Natashas.* In trafficking—a term normally used for illegal dealing of merchandise, particularly drugs—a woman's body is considered as a commodity in a contemporary form of slave trade that has become global. Using Michel Foucault's theory from *History of Sexuality* (1978), the authors demonstrate how the same technologies of power control the body of a woman for the purpose of economic and sexual exploitation. The patriarchal construction of foreign women as exotic or promiscuous, as well as patriarchal global complicities that pervade the judicial and political spheres, only exacerbate the "othering" and the commodification of trafficked women. This is exemplified by the collective name "The Natashas" affixed to those women by the traffickers. Trafficked women should be considered as refugees, that is, as people who have been forced to migrate by adverse circumstances. The authors' analysis blurs the boundaries between commonly accepted, rigid oppositions such as virgin/prostitute, legal/illegal, and foreigner/citizen. Identities are shifting and contextual, and paradoxically, even the collective name "The Natashas" can also be subverted and converted into a shield behind which trafficked women conceal their real identity and in which they find refuge and solace. This chapter considers the means by which the scourge of trafficking can be reduced, and economic justice is perceived as the most effective way to eradicate the root causes of this transnational crime.

Over a period of two years, Jennifer Hyndman and Malathi de Alwis interviewed internally displaced women depending on humanitarian aid, as well as a gamut of professionals in organizations providing humanitarian assistance to internally displaced persons (IDPs) in Sri Lanka. Their objective was to examine specific ways in which gender identities of displaced women are shaped by humanitarian assistance. In their chapter *Reconstituting the Subject: Feminist Politics of Humanitarian Assistance*, the authors examine how conflict and displacement both increase the economic hardships for women, resulting in vulnerabilities, but also increase the potential to create new spaces in which traditionally gender-oriented training programs and gender relations are transformed.

The research illustrates how, by and large, the delivery of such assistance has reinforced the conventional gender roles and the division of labor rather than changed relationships. They argue that a gender analysis alone will not incorporate the different levels of power relations that shape women's (or men's) identities. They further contend that the application of a feminist analysis framework in humanitarian intervention must incorporate gender relations with other factors such as national identities. A contextually defined feminist framework is essential if such intervention is to address the gendered inequalities, trauma, and insecurity that shape women's lives, and at the same time provide the space for women's agency both in conflict and postconflict situations.

1

A Dialogical Approach to Identity

IMPLICATIONS FOR REFUGEE WOMEN

Maroussia Hajdukowski-Ahmed

"The oppressed are victims of social injustice; their significance, however, does not reside in the fact of their victimisation, but in the possibility that their agency will transform their lived relations." (Hitchcock 1993: 1).

"I have nothing" does not mean "I am nothing." (Nora, a refugee woman in *I Was, I Am and I Will Be*, Collective De Mujer a Mujer, 2003).

The question of identity is part and parcel of our modern world and has elicited a number of important works, such as Charles Taylor's *Sources of the Self* (1989) or Judith Butler's *Gender Trouble* (1990). The so-called "crisis of identity" is seen as part of a wider process of transformation which is dislocating the central structures and processes of modern societies—marked by demographic pluralism and mobility—and is undermining the frameworks which gave individuals stable grounding in the social world (Hall 1994). Identity is also at the heart of contemporary postmodernist and feminist debates born from narratives of the borderline (Anzaldua and Keating 2002). Those narratives are produced through an inclusion-ary process by various groups of women, minorities, and migrants, who carve a space for their difference, engendering new "critical-theoretical perspectives"(Bhabha 1994: 239–241). The question of identity and all its ramifications is particularly pressing and relevant for forcibly displaced people who experience multidimensional and discontinuous realities, and for those who live and work with them. People flee from poverty, from persecution and torture, from floods and deforestation, from occu-pation and dictatorship. Entire civil populations are displaced, dis-located, and put at risk. For uprooted people, every new situation and location deeply (re)shapes their identities, their sense of self, their agency, and their well being. Uprooted women in particular face multiple, distinct challenges that impact their identities.

This chapter expands upon existing theoretical and conceptual approaches to identity to explore questions of identity for refugee women. In particular, it applies a dialogical approach to unite strands of feminist theories and refugee studies, in the process making contributions to each. In refugee studies, for example, a "broader theoretical framework has been lacking" that goes beyond the multiplicity of specific anthropological case studies (Malkki 1995: 507). Feminist theory, on the other hand, has been caught between a politics of identity and difference, and the universalizing theory of gender oppression and global democracy. We agree with Seyla Benhabib who stated that "Unless feminist theory is able to develop a concept of normative agency robust enough to say something significant vis-à-vis such clashes . . . it loses its theoretical bite and becomes a mindless empiricist celebration of all pluralities. The question of the subject is central for contemporary feminist theory and practice" (Benhabib 1994: 2). In this chapter, we contend that a dialogic approach can correct these lacunae.

Dialogism views identity as a continuous and relational process rather than a fixed construct and is thus well suited to the task of understanding those whose lives have been radically transformed by trauma, upheaval, and resettlement. Its focus on the relational nature of language and identity allows it to operate as a conceptual bridge, making an organic connection between the contingent and the universal, history and story, the self and its context, philosophy and anthropology, the "here" and the "there," the past and the present, men and women in the lived context of their relations, tensions and movement. Processes do not progress in a linear fashion toward desired outcomes, yet—in contrast to postmodern thought—there is a horizon toward which our understanding moves, not a specific teleology, but a horizon characterized by equality and the recognition of fundamental human rights.

Central to the understanding of identity as process is the recognition of agency. Circumstances force people to become refugees and to be forcibly removed from place, kinship, culture, and other identity markers. As part of these experiences, these people are "continually being created and recreated as refugees by political decision makers, development planners and those who control the international market economy" (Giles et al. 1996: 15). In this context of uprootedness, women more than men find themselves "unequally located in structures of interpretation, representation, decision-making, policy-generation and program delivery" (Indra 1999a: 18). But even in the most disempowering circumstances, women always retain some specific forms of agency: they generate resisting discourses, work to reclaim their identity, and take initiatives in their everyday lives. Every new location or new situation challenges their sense of self, which is constantly renegotiated as they rebuild their lives, and in this process, is opened up to new possibilities. Any comprehensive understanding of refugee women and their identity must both recognize the agency of the subject and integrate culture and history into that understanding (Taylor 1983: 44–45).

Using a gendered, dialogical approach to theorize about the identity of refugee women is not merely a scholarly exercise. It is instrumental in the creation of policies and practices that are fair and appropriate to millions of women around the world. Even though over 75 percent of the world's refugees are women and children, the needs of refugee and asylum-seeking women are often overlooked in the legislation, social policies, and services that affect them. Policies and practices—such as those associated with re-settlement, reception centers, return programs, and zones of protection—may affect men and women differently. Yet there has been little analysis of how this situation has come about. From our perspective, conceptualization and practice are interdependent and should inform each other (Taylor 1983), continually and critically evolving according to changing circumstances.

This chapter works within a dialogical framework to examine questions of identity for refugee women, beginning with a discussion of how dialogism can help us to better understand refugee women. We then show the dialogical approach at work by discussing two examples: the importance of naming (what do we call women who have been forced to leave their homes) and the introduction of Gender Guidelines in the refugee determination criteria. Next, we analyze the concept of a dialogical self and its relevance to the process of identity transformation for refugee women, looking first at the factors that "de-self" them and then how they reclaim agency in their lives. We shall examine how identity expresses itself through the body and through language, both in verbal and nonverbal forms of communication. Finally, we explore ways of conducting research and therapy that draw upon a dialogical approach to the identity construction of refugee women. Throughout, examples from the author's own participatory community research with refugee women as well as from other sources are included.

Dialogism and Its Application

Our understanding of identity is informed by the work of the Russian philosopher, linguist, and cultural theorist Mikhail Bakhtin. Bakhtin viewed identity construction as *dialogic*, that is, formed through language as a process of social interaction. Later, H. Hermans and H. Kempen (1993) adapted Bakhtin's work to theories of psychological therapy and analysis of the self. Gender was not addressed by Bakhtin, but Bakhtinian feminists later included gender as constructed by society through language in a dialogical process (Bauer 1989; Hitchcock 1993; Malcuzynski 1992; Pearce 1994; Thomson 1989; Yaguello 1979). Feminisms of the difference such as Black, postcolonial or Latina feminisms, as well as development feminisms (Anzaldua and Keating 2002; bell hooks 1984; Marchand and Parpart 1995; Mohanty 2003; Spivak 1987) have enriched the conceptual debate over refugee women led by scholars such as D. Indra, L.Malkki, S. Forbes-Martin, and by the authors of this volume. Bakhtinian feminism is fundamentally relational and proceeds from an interdisciplinary perspective (Hajdukowski-Ahmed 1998).

However, while we agree that feminist agendas have to take into consideration the "'multiplexity' and multidimentionality of the identities involved" (Yuval-Davis 1995: 2), we cannot ignore that from those "multiplexities" emerge commonalities that link them globally. Those commonalities allow for a conceptualization of refugee women's predicament, resistance, initiatives, and solidarity. Like postcolonial criticism (Bhabha 1994; Spivak 1987; 1995), feminist dialogism accounts for the discourses of power, for the discourses of resistance, and for the "multiplexity" of identities. Feminist dialogism—like postmodernism—rejects the teleology of grand narratives and acknowledges contingency and difference. "It welcomes diversity, acknowledges previously subjugated voices and knowledge(s) and encourages dialogue between development practitioners and their clients" (Marchand and Parpart 1995: 17).

Dialogism is a philosophy of communication that maps the discursive territory of difference. It is a process of interlocution between distinct and competing voices. Dialogism is the space where differences between self and the other do not collapse when they meet but remain separate and embodied. In this space, all voices are heard in an historical context, shaped by factors such as gender, socioeconomic status, location, culture, sexuality, ability, race, and ethnicity that are at play within power relationships. It is also imbued with an ethics of recognition of the other, and an ethics of answerability because each subject is viewed as unique, invested with historical agency and responsibility, and as such, transforms and is transformed. A dialogic encounter with another voice/discourse does not result in fusion. Rather, each protagonist retains his or her own open, multifaceted, and moving identity. Conflicting worldviews within the same discourse are not considered as a defect of logic, but as forces at work in a normal life (De Santis 2001: 1). A refugee woman may experience a dialogical struggle between two concepts of culture that shape her identity at any point in her exilic journey. One concept of culture refers to a homogenous set of beliefs and practices and collective imaginary world particular to a nation or a community, which grounds identity, and in which she may find solace and protection, and which may have a specific religious and/or cultural code of behavior for women. The other concept is that of an unsettling, heterogeneous discontinuity open to new representations (Hall 1994: 395). Refugee women may find themselves living in multicultural contexts and different urban environments, which as a result, will affect family/social dynamics, as well as power relationships. Neither innocuous dialogue nor abstract and conciliatory dialectics, dialogism is at once an epistemology and an ethics of responsibility and difference, a way of being in the world which involves both learning and doing (Hajdukowski-Ahmed 1998).

A dialogical perspective recognizes that differences are embedded in relations of domination, subjugation, and resistance. Dialogism thus exposes and questions power relations concealed by the process of naturalization created by familiarity (Butler 1990; 1998c: 169; De Laureitis 1987; Foucault 1978). Unlike post–structuralism and postmodernism, however, it moves toward a teleological *open horizon* and does not stymie collective action and solidarity. Contrary to many discourses on development (Malkki 1995: 506), dialogism does not isolate "refugeeness" but grounds it in its historicopolitical context and in its root causes. Sexual violence is, for example, at once universal, but also gender and context-specific and culturally differentiated (Daenzer, chapter 14, this volume).

Dialogism is intensely at work when a refugee encounters a different location and environment, a different culture, different individuals, different circumstances, different worldviews, in crisis, in flight, and in resettlement. Each change is a source of identity transformation as it elicits questioning, reaction, repositioning on the part of the refugee woman who in turn, through her unique historical agency, affects her relationships and her environment. This is highlighted in the following section, which discusses the importance of naming, as well as in the subsequent section on the introduction of Gender Guidelines into the refugee determination process.

"Refugees"? "Uprooted"? "Forcibly Displaced"? The Politics of Naming and Its Implications

Definitions must be expanded and reconceptualized in order to accommodate the experiences of diverse populations and social categories as they occur and become known. "Refugee" as a specific social category emerged as a Eurocentric and gender-blind concept during the standardizing of legal and administrative processes for refugee settlements after the Second World War (Malkki 1995: 501). According to the most widely used definition, that of the 1951 UN Convention relating to the Status of Refugees, a refugee is a person residing outside his or her country of nationality, who is unable or unwilling to return there because of a "well-founded fear of persecution." Refugees thus experience "forced migration," in contrast to voluntary migrants who choose to leave one country in favor of another. In reality, however, the distinction between different types of migrants is not always clear (Newman 2003: 9). It may be difficult to ascertain whether asylum seekers, economic migrants, and those displaced by war and in need of protection are "voluntary" or "involuntary" migrants. Moreover, it is possible for individuals to become displaced within their own country, to be uprooted from their familiar environment by a natural disaster such as the 2004 tsunami, by civil strife as in Sri Lanka, or by the militarization of the economy conducted or facilitated by their own state, as in the case of the militarization of the oil industry in Sudan (Macklin 2004). The globalization of economy also turns farmers and/or indigenous populations into internally displaced people (Macklin 2004; Palay 2007), when a government expropriates them in order to allocate space—and offer financial "incentives"—to multinational companies or to developers, with little or no compensation to the evicted people. Such is presently the case in many parts of the world, including several states of India where the Special Economic Zone policy (SEZ) is creating a national controversy (Gupta et al. 2007; Srinivasaraju 2007). In the process of relocation, families and communities are dislocated and deprived of their livelihood; the relationship to land, work cycle, and to cultural/ religious practices is disrupted; men often become landless laborers and migrate to cities, leaving women to care for children and elderly relatives.

A new situation or a different way of looking at that situation dialogically challenges definitions and elicits new ones. The World Council of Churches (WCC), for example, now refers to "uprooted" people rather than to "refugees." According to the WCC, "Uprooted people are those who are forced to leave their communities: those who flee because of persecution and war, those who are forcibly displaced because of environmental devastation and those who are compelled to seek sustenance in a city or abroad because they cannot survive at home" (World Council of Churches policy statement 1995). The term "uprootedness" conveys the porosity of the boundaries between war zones and peace zones. In a dialogical reference to "refugee," it deconstructs the North-here-us / South-there-other dichotomies, reinforcing the idea that persons can be displaced without crossing national borders. It shifts the emphasis to the question of justice and to the contextual root causes and agency of the forced displacement, away from the essentializing individualization conveyed by the word "refugees" and from its initial narrow political connotation. Such root causes include regressive land reforms and policies, lack of development initiatives, civil strife, natural disasters, environmental destruction, foreign debt, urbanization, and a lack of conformity to human rights treaties and standards (Canadian Council of Churches Statement, http://www.web.ca/~iccr/docs/Cccunchr: 1998). The concept of uprootedness thus opens up a semantic space that allows us to expose the gendered effects of poverty and exploitation in countries that are not at war, for example the sexual trafficking of women in Central Europe (Malarek 2003, see chapter 3). The term "forced migration" conveys the same dialogical transformation.

The definition of a refugee has also been challenged on gender lines. Initially, the UN Convention defined "refugee" by the generic term "person," which obliterated gender differences in practices of oppression and their effects in the following ways. First, it artificially dichotomized the political refugee from the economic migrant (Giles et al. 1996: 16, 25), conferring more legitimacy on the first while in reality the two are often intertwined. Both the political situation and the economic situation affect women in specific ways; for example, a woman's poverty puts her more at risk of violence and exploitation (Valji 2003: 4). Second, the Convention separated the public sphere from the private sphere, concealing the violence that women may experience in their own home as well as the political activities they may undertake at home. In reality, there is a continuum in violence that affects women's identities and well being, as noted by de Alwis, "The public/private distinctions between battlefield and home, soldier and civilian, and state security and human security have broken down. Feminist analyses of conflict elucidate the intimate connections between war, political economy, nationalism, and human displacement and their various impacts across scale." (2004 a: 314). Third, "academics, other researchers, government policy makers, and international agencies from the North dominate much discussion and action involving forced migrants, and hence chiefly frame relevant institutions, agencies, programs and communities in virtually every part of the world" (Indra 1999a: 3), without fair attention paid to the gender factor, to the effect of power differentials and to the voices of "the South" (we should bear in mind that the meaning of "South" has shifted dialogically from a geographical to a more metaphorical, socioeconomic connotation).

Definitional discourses regarding refugee women have serious identity-related as well as policy implications, affecting decisions concerning refugee determination, detention and deportation, family reunification, and access to aid and services. A dialogical tension exists between the criminalization and the victimization of refugees (Giles et al. 1996: 19). Uprooted persons are sometimes dehumanized and depicted as burdens, undesirable, and even "bogus refugees," while at other times they are idealized as helpless victims and "genuine refugees." Trafficked women in particular face this duality. In the end, we must critically examine and deconstruct the names we use and reshape them in the light of new knowledge that emanates from new contexts (Indra 1996: 36). There is no universal "refugee woman." The above discussion has opened up the concept of refugee to include various forms of forced displacement that reflect the various contexts in which a woman becomes uprooted. What follows is a related illustration of dialogism as it pertains to gender-based persecution.

Dialogical Evolution at Work:
The Case of the Gender Guidelines

The creation of gender-based refugee guidelines has followed what Jo-anna N. Erdman and Andrea J. Sanchez, without referring to Bakhtin, called an "iterative and dialogic process" (2004: 69). At each stage of their development, the guidelines were transformed through historical contingencies by the voices of women who had previously felt excluded.

The notion of persecution for reasons of gender and sex was absent from the 1951 Convention on the Status of Refugees, whose drafters were focused on Soviet dissidents wanting to seek asylum during the Cold War. At the time of the 1951 Convention, women's rights were still marginalized and women's issues were considered to belong to the private sphere (Daenzer, chapter 14). This is somewhat surprising because it was known that "comfort women" had been used by the Japanese army, "Aryan" women had been used by Nazis for breeding purposes, and "non-Aryan" women—Jewish, Gypsies, Slavs—had been prevented from reproducing. As historical realities changed and women's movements grew, awareness of gender persecution and women's rights as human rights also increased. A standard legal definition had to be reformulated in order to accommodate those changes (Erdman and Sanchez 2004: 72), either in the form of a new category of persecution or new interpretive guidelines. The term "refugee" had to be reconceptualized through a transnational legal process to include gender.

Empowered by the UN's Women's Decade (1976–1985), women's groups such as the International Working Group on Refugee Women, the Young Women's Christian Association (YWCA), and the World Council of Churches were particularly instrumental in this respect. The European Parliament approved a resolution in 1984 asking states to recognize as a social group "women . . . who face harsh or inhuman treatment because they are considered to have transgressed the social mores of the country" (Erdman and Sanchez 2004: 74). Following direction from within the UNHCR, the United Nations released the Guidelines on the Protection of Refugee Women in 1991. In 1993, Canada became the first country to formally implement the Guidelines in response to the "concerted efforts of a coalition of feminist, human rights, refugee and immigration activists." (Macklin, quoted in Erdman and Sanchez 2004: 80). At first, Canada saw a slow increase in the numbers of women claiming asylum and relying on the Guidelines. Gradually, the concept of gender-based persecution filtered to different countries where it became more familiar and accepted.

Since then, new voices have emerged which criticized the guidelines and a new dialogical stage has been reached in this iterative process. Those new voices claimed that the guidelines follow a cultural relativist bias of the women's human rights movement (Erdman and Sanchez: 81). According to them, if violence against women is perceived as central for women of the North, women from the South view economic or educational disadvantages as a more important common denominator. Also, the interpretation of gender-based persecution tends to focus on persecutory practices in foreign countries of the South, thus constructing those countries as the "Other." Such dichotomization, which is also at the heart of racism and colonialism, conveys the image of cultures of the South as violent and misogynist, thus denying the reality of gender violence in the "more civilized" countries of the North and concealing their responsibility for the South's economic and social woes. It also leads to the creation of cultural stereotypes which obfuscate the diversity of cultures and experiences. One must also listen to the voices of refugee women claimants, who in effect, are the only ones who can adequately articulate their persecutory experience.

In these sections, we have seen the importance of definitions and naming to the lived experiences of refugee women. Next, we will explore in more depth how dialogism relates to the concept of the self and how, in turn, this affects refugee women as well.

The Dialogical Evolution of the Concept of the Self

The concept of the self has been constructed differently over time and across cultures, in a dialogical relationship with preceding discourses. In brief, the concept of the self has evolved from a monological understanding in which a person has a complete, unified, and essential self (e.g., in the Platonic-Christian and Cartesian traditions) to one in which the self is understood as being constructed and normalized by discourses of power (Foucault and poststructuralist theory). For Bakhtin and Taylor, the self is relational and constructed through a web of interlocution, and "selving" is a sociocultural process (Bakhtin 1980, 1981, 1986; Markus et al. 1997: 14; Taylor 1989).

Following Bakhtin and Charles Taylor, Hermans posits that (pseudo) dialogues precede the use of the pronoun "I," and that the self emerges from an I/Me relationship. The self is thus made of a multiplicity of transactional "Me" positions which cohabit in dialogical relationships, with the "I" position as an organizing center and a metaperspective that evolves in relation to the "Me's." The "I" is similar to the composer who writes a polyphonic score with the various "Me" voices/positions it encounters (Hermans and Kempen 1993: 6). Hermans defines the dialogical self as a self which "assumes the existence of an embodied, spatialized, extended, socialized and open system with dialogical relations between positions. It is further supposed that dialogical relations are always more or less asymmetrical and characterized by power differences." (Hermans and Kempen 2003:109). It is different from a postmodern view which rejects unifying principles (Hassan 1987). Dialogism is at work when the "I" encounters a new and different voice; a "Me" is then shaping, entering a lifelong process of reaction to the "I," which absorbs part of the new voice, or recoils from it, or rejects it, or reshapes it. Voices are imbued with collective meanings, cultural representations, and values, to which the "I" contributes her/his own voice, his/her active participation in history (Hermans and Kempen 1993: 167). The relation with others and between the "Me" positions is not immune to conflicts, disagreements, misunderstandings, or power play (Bhatia and Ram 2001: 301). Internal discourses and dreams are also filled with the voices of the others, which have created the "Me" positions.

In the course of her life and through her intensely dialogical experience, a refugee woman weaves her "I" through a web of many different voices, which she encounters and to which she reacts, creating "Me" voices that take up different pitches and differing intensities at various times in her life, like a composer creating a fugue, or a river receiving effluents that carve its banks, merge their currents, whirl into eddies, and continue their course toward the wide sea. As we shall see more specifically in a later part of this essay that will use examples from an array of forced displacement situations and refugee population groups, refugee women construct their identity through a nonlinear push-pull dialogical process. This process moves through "a constellation of practices" (Hyndman and de Alwis, chapter 4) in relationship to their historical and personal context, past "Me" identities, location, national and transnational legal systems, citizenship, social and cultural environment, all informed by gender. At different times and locations, a refugee woman may seek to retrieve a lost strand of her past identity, or reject it altogether, or practice "critical integration" when she bridges two worlds (McSpadden and Moussa 1996: 219, 235), or develop a transcultural identity. By transcultural identity we do not mean a synthesis of cultures but their relational coexistence, which translates into the coexistence of "Me's" within the same "I."

The "De-selving" of Refugee Women

In the process of their identity transformation, refugee women confront forces of "de-selving" which enter a dialogical relationship with experiences of "re-selving." "De-selving" does not mean a loss of identity and culture, but rather the gradual erosion of *agency* imposed by the organizations, spatial configurations, laws, and relationships they confront in their refugee experience. From the moment they are forcibly uprooted from their familiar environment, refugee women are situated within a constant process of "de-selving," of deprivation of their agency in various forms, extending even to the extreme of physical annihilation. They are shackled with the "de-selving" *dis* prefix or *less* suffix: dispossessed, disoriented, dislocated, dismembered; stateless, nameless, landless, homeless, and powerless.

This process of "de-selving" results from various forms of oppression to which men are also subjected, but the forms of oppression to which women are subjected take place within patriarchal power relationships that affect them differently. Refugee women are de-selved when "gender roles are affected in relocation by disruption of status and power hierarchies, geographical dispersal of kin and friendship networks, new residence patterns, loss of economic resources, differential access to new resources, shifts in work patterns, exposure to strangers with different lifestyles, and different expectations" (Colson 1993: 25). Overwhelmed by all those external pressures, tossed between locations, cultures, or services, they are led into passivity, and this further affects their sense of self, agency, and their mental health. Various gendered forms of objectification that refugee women encounter are intended to "de-selve" them. These predominantly target their body and include torture, sexual torture, female genital mutilation, forced pregnancy, forced abortion, or forced sterilization on them or other female family members (Agger 1992; Hajdukowski-Ahmed et al. 1999).

When in refugee camps, they are *under* the so-called protection of states and humanitarian organizations, which, in spite of some noted improvements, fail to include them in meaningful ways in their decision making, thus curtailing their agency (UNHCR 2006). When refugee boards reject an asylum claim to a woman on the basis that violence is inherent to society, and reduces rape to an act of "dreadful lust" (Sadoway, chapter 15) they also "de-selve" refugee women. In camps or in resettlement, access to food distribution, education and services, contraception and sexual care, control over their earnings or identity papers may be denied or limited. In her chapter entitled "Negotiating Masculinity in the Reconstruction of Social Place," L. McSpadden notes that the agency and sense of self of refugee women is reshaped by systems over which they have little control (1993: 244).

"De-selving" also occurs when the media and advocates for refugee women succumb to the cliché of grouping together women and children, as a result concealing and infantilizing the agency of women by association with children. War and poverty often separate women and children from men, a process which reinforces the tendency to construct "women and children" as a single entity in the popular press and scholarly works alike, even though the identities and needs of each group are vastly different. For example, in the second edition of S. Forbes-Martin's book on refugee women, women and children are lumped together in each recommendation (Forbes-Martin 2004 [1991]: 157). Nearly every article on refugee women (the present paper is no exception) perpetuates this association when it states like a mantra that "approximately 75 to 80 percent of the displaced are women and children." Television promotions for relief agencies and charities invariably portray limp, fly-covered children cradled in the arms of distraught and helpless mothers. Those representations commodify refugee women in their role as—failed—caregivers, depict them as helpless victims, thus allowing men and Western humanitarian organizations to play the role of saviors (Valji 2003: 9). Such imagery also conceals the specificity of the situation of children who have become orphans or of those separated from their families, such as boy soldiers, abducted girls, and children left behind while parents seek a better life.

When families make asylum claims in receiving countries, the "de-selving" continues when men make the decision to leave or are asked by refugee boards to give their account of events, denying women their own narratives and agency. A significant form of "de-selving" which refugee women face continually is their treatment as blank pages, as if they had no education, no occupation, or no life before, particularly when they interact with services, organizations, or institutions. In reality, uprooted women are anything but blank: their past and intense life experiences affect their identities every day.

Strategic Essentialism as *Faux* "Re-selving"

In the course of their refugee journey, refugee women also seize new circumstances as an opportunity for emancipation and self-affirmation. Sometimes, even when they seem to abide obediently by their community's norms and conventions, or when they appear to conform to mainstream stereotypes, they are merely using what is called "strategic essentialism" in order to protect themselves and their families without appearing to dispute those norms. The term "strategic essentialism," coined by Gayatry Spivak (1995), is a conscious and purposive verbal replication of an essentialist discourse on identity, which for example replicates cultural, racial, or gendered stereotypes. The users of strategic essentialism assume a temporary unified subject position in order to further a particular end. Such a practice has been documented among marginalized or disenfranchised groups when they experience a need in situations of asymmetrical power relationships. Strategic essentialism is a chosen essentialist positionality which is operational in specific contexts, amounting to role playing (Spivak 1995). Conscious and purposive imitation is in effect a strategic counterdiscourse; it creates a space in which refugee women reclaim their self and agency, as only *they* know that they are using essentialism as a strategy. In the case of refugee women, a whole public apparatus has created the stereotype of a powerless victim, "[b]ecause asylum officials assume that female asylum applicants are poor, uneducated, and incapable of confronting their oppression, women who do not fit this mould, (that is, most of the women who actually make it across borders), are viewed with suspicion" (Mertus 2003: 68). Strategic essentialism challenges that construct through *the conscious use* of such narratives which are tool boxes "marketed for consumption in the North. It is most tempting for asylum seekers—who are often informed by sympathetic lawyers—to create a narrative that fits the mould" (Razack 1998b: 99). Sometimes, researchers and NGO workers themselves practice strategic essentialism when they use gender more as an expected buzzword in development discourse and grant applications than as an operative concept in their work (Hyndman and de Alwis, chapter 4), and thus perpetuate a status quo that delays the process of empowerment of refugee women.

Experience shows that consistency is paramount in hearings; thus, recycling a stereotype that is familiar to authorities is more effective, because "it would be detrimental to their cause if their narratives were ambiguous, hesitant, complex and unprovable in the courts that make decisions on their status" (Murdocca, chapter 16). Authorities may not know that memory has its own complex organic life, particularly in the case of refugee women who have experienced sexual violence (Carruth 1995: 163; Sugiman, chapter 6).The genuine narrative of a refugee woman may therefore appear to be inconsistent and create suspicion, and she may be more effective in securing asylum if she uses a prepared coherent and familiar narrative with the appropriate and expected body language. Rather than claiming gender persecution, a woman from Somalia seeking asylum can more easily obtain refugee status if she claims to fear female genital mutilation, and a Middle Eastern woman if she claims to fear religious fundamentalism (Sadoway, chapter 15). The use of strategic essentialism opens up a space for a dialogical encounter between an ethics of care (saving herself or her family using a linear narrative of mimicry) and an ethics of authenticity (speaking the truth in a narrative that may be perceived as sketchy or inconsistent, thus jeopardizing her case). The use of strategic essentialism comes with costs, and in the end constitutes a *faux re-selving*. It can perpetuate racialized gender stereotypes and conceal gender issues. It silences narratives of strength and resilience and does not advance institutional knowledge or practices. It panders to conservatism and legitimizes misrepresentations and prejudices. Yet it has proven effective for refugee claimants. It is precisely these kinds of dilemmas and contradictions that refugee women face continually. More of these are discussed in the following section.

Dialogical Tensions in the "Re-selving" of Refugee Women

Tensions that arise from the refugee experience present themselves as challenges and should not be perceived negatively as contradictions, but should rather be perceived dialogically as different and competing world-views. They open up a space for agency, an inbetween standpoint and a vantage point from which critical questioning occurs and transforming opportunities emerge. We shall evoke several such life experiences that revolve around the notions of home and time, in different contexts of displacement that affect the identity of refugee women, with particular emphasis on their resettlement experience, which is more familiar to us.

From refugee camps to refugee determination boards and reception centers, the refugee service administration constitutes a whole apparatus that constructs the refugees as aliens and noncitizens, strangers and even enemies. Women still struggle to have their voices heard and their needs met (UNHCR 2006). As normal individuals confronting abnormal situations, they have to redefine themselves in relationship to those abnormal circumstances and to the whole apparatus that constructs them as "refugee women." Like refugee men, refugee women find themselves "inside-outsiders"—or "a part of and apart from cultural context"—which is conducive to sharpening critical thinking and to making them into potential agents of change (McSpadden, 245, in reference to her research conducted with Moussa and to Bennett's article, 1993). However, while both genders experience identity transformation, women experience it differently. First, a highly abnormal situation such as a war can present emancipating and identity transformative opportunities for women who felt stifled or oppressed in a patriarchal society (Gagnon, chapter 8; Hyndman and de Alwis, chapter 4). These may take the shape of employment opportunities, voting rights, or emancipation from cultural practices that have limited their potential. A refugee who leaves her country is not necessarily only a victim or disconnected from home. Those who stay are often more victimized and more vulnerable; they may be too poor or too sick or too emotionally attached to leave (Malkki 1995: 515). Such occurrences were made vividly painful by media coverage of the 2005 floods in New Orleans.

"Refugeeness" puts the notion of "home" into question and deconstructs its feminized connotation of "a safe place where women belong." Women who are traditionally defined by their belonging to a home find themselves particularly uprooted as homeless and stateless when they become refugees (Giles, chapter 2). But home can also be a dangerous place ruled by patriarchal, religious, and heterosexual norms, thus challenging the public sphere/private sphere divide as well as their safe/unsafe connotations. Furthermore, a woman can become a "refugee" in her own home or state, which leads to a rethinking of the notion of "refugeeness" which in turn would affect the Gender Guidelines. Policies can define, affirm, or deny identity and agency. Naming can demean or empower, and this greatly affects refugee women's identity and sense of self. For example, there is a vast difference between naming women "prostitutes" instead of "victims of trafficking" (Malarek 2003).

In the process of resettlement, refugee women often re-create the familiarity and protection of the lost home. They try to transplant some cultural roots using artifacts, food, music, or space for worshipping. A dialogical tension emerges between an idealization of the lost home and the new place, when life becomes difficult or uncertain in the host country, and when repatriation is not an option. However, while resettling, Sudanese women in our project felt they had less to lose and were more forward looking and resilient than men for the sake of their children, as one confided, "We are stronger than men. . . . Women can get humiliated, but they are still going" (Bhaloo et al. 2005: 22).

Refugee women often experience a dialogical tension between the physical and outer self (as expressed by physical traits, appearance, and demeanor, as well as language) and the inner self, in intense and multiple ways (Dufva 1998): in situations of violence and oppression such as torture; when refugee women use strategic essentialism in order to obtain what they need; when their inner self is different from the identity constructed by the community in which they live and to which they conform; or when their inner self is different from the way mainstream society portrays them in a given context (for example, when a woman *chooses* to wear a *hijab* in a society which views it as a sign of gender oppression). Assumptions constitute an important source of dialogical tensions.

Patriarchal control is regulated, particularly during national or anticolonial struggles, making women into bearers of authenticity, confining them to the kitchen, religion, and procreation. Refugee women themselves may prefer to uphold traditional values to seek security and a sense of community belonging, and they even fight along with their men (de Alwis 2004: 223). Refugee women who participate in such struggles are sometimes torn between their solidarity with their countrymen and indifference to men's struggles and to men's call for sacrifice, especially when they experience their solidarity as benefitting men only. For example, women who participated in the war of independence of Algeria in the early 1960s were sent back to their "private spheres" after the war was over in 1962. They were even threatened with death if they wanted to retain an emancipated lifestyle in the country they had helped to liberate and decolonize, one that became increasingly patriarchal and fundamentalist during the 1990s. Such was the case of the celebrated author Assia Djebar, herself a former freedom fighter and then refugee from Algeria during its fundamentalist phase, now a member of the Académie Française. Yet, Algeria, her culture, and the Arabic language are still very much part of her identity as she describes in her writings (1980, 1995). For refugee women who have lost everything else, their creativity can become the only safe home left that shelters their identity.

In contexts of resettlement, patriarchal control and opportunities for employment can be experienced as conflicting. The need for income offers opportunities for equality and emancipation, but it often undermines men's traditional function as breadwinners and their financial control. Some NGOs provide opportunities for women to learn skills that traditionally belong to the male sphere such as welding, which disrupts gender roles, identity, and relationships (Hyndman and de Alwis, chapter 4). It also subverts a traditional gendered form of development that is more grounded in capitalism, such as loan granting which eludes a gender analysis and does not pay attention to "who will benefit from the loan" and to the power dynamics of gender relations (Hyndman and de Alwis, chapter 4). Such initiatives also bring to light the importance of a feminist approach to development which is empowering and has a transformative impact on the relationship between men and women. However a feminist approach to development implemented by researchers/practitioners can also encounter the resisting discourse of women who hold a different worldview or a different concept of "emancipation," and for whom a national struggle—or simply physical survival—bears greater importance than women's emancipation as understood by many Western feminist researchers (Gorman and Mojab, chapter 7; Hyndman and de Alwis, chapter 4). Such encounters also contain the seeds of potential change.

Refugee women and men may feel pride when they see their daughters become more empowered, for example through educational achievements. But they also experience some anxiety when they fear that education could result in cultural alienation or estrangement, and that their parental authority will be contested and "normal" power relationships reversed (Coles 1992: 73). Refugee daughters bear the honor of their family, and they may experience conflict if they seek sexual emancipation. Displacement separates families, and refugee women can find themselves alone with their children, forced to repress their sexual desire to conform to gendered social mores (Bhaloo et al. 2005: 29).

Organized religions and places of worship are intensely dialogical spaces of struggle between faith and religion, between patriarchal hegemony and emancipation. Refugee women often rely on faith during their quest for healing and on places of worship as spaces where they regain hope and re-create social bonds. However, they may feel uncomfortable if leaders, who are predominantly male, assign a subjugated role to women or present a fatalistic worldview that prevent change and emancipation (Goździak, chapter 11). Under the A. Pinochet dictatorship in Chile, churches were used to organize consciousness raising, resistance, and social help, and women's activism found its place in the "communal kitch-ens" often maintained by liberation theology churches. We may have heard about "Red Olga," "the obstreperous, square-shouldered, white-haired Communist matriarch of La Victoria in Chile. Arrested in 1974 and held in the notorious Teja Verde concentration camp for two months, Olga re-turned to La Victoria and turned her tiny home into the "Olla Comun"—the community soup kitchen that not only fed two hundred families a day but also served as command-and-control center for the local anti-Pinochet resistance" (Cooper 1998). Such examples show the dialogical significance and emancipatory power of subversion of traditional spaces toward the horizon of human rights.

Finally, repatriation which is also perceived as "coming back home" (house and state) may mean coming back to a dangerous place (Malkki 1995: 509), or to a home that is not experienced as home anymore and es-trangement follows. Also, returnees may be "pushed" to return more than "pulled" by the desire to return, as they face new issues upon returning and reconfront abandoned gendered social constraints. They—particu-larly children and adolescents—may be forced to return to countries they have never seen, when their parents are forcibly repatriated. Such was the tragic case of Japanese-Canadian women who were internally displaced in camps during World War II and could no longer call Canada, where they were born, their home. Nor would they have felt at home in Japan (Sugiman, chapter 6).

The meaning of home, and the sense of identity and safety it procures is always precarious for refugee women. Subjectivities and power rela-tionships are thus continuously challenged and reformulated in relation-ship to ever changing contexts. Even citizenship, which is normally a stable identifier, ceases to anchor identities (Balibar 2006). Refugees, advo-cates, and researchers can also experience inner conflicts between think-ing and doing: "Challenging masculinist constructions of woman and nation is one thing; making daily decisions about that action to take in the context of war and personal safety is quite another" (Giles and Hyndman 2004b: 11). The same inner conflict can be experienced by researchers who are advocates for refugee women, and who become conscious of their own connection with the exploitation of refugee women's labor at the local or global level, or who feel indirectly responsible for their partici-pants' "refugeeness," while maintaining a comfortable status quo.

Refugee women also experience their relationship to their past and to the concept of time in a dialogical way that can be at once "de-selving" and "re-selving." For Stuart Hall, "[i]dentities are the names we give to the different ways we are positioned by, and position ourselves within, the narratives of the past" (Hall 1994: 397). Past experiences of refugee women are multiple, confusing, disturbing, painful, and deeply affect their identities (Chambon, chapter 5). Their personal past, which is grounded in the historical past of their communities and nation, is woven into their present in many ways. For example, Rachel Gorman and Sharzad Mojab describe how their past has affected the everyday experience of Kurdish women, who have acquired a highly historicized consciousness shaped by their national struggle. The effect of their past supersedes any wish for emancipation that the feminist field researchers had hoped for (Gorman and Mojab, chapter 7). The past is also present in the lives of traumatized women who can "relive" their trauma, not as a memory, but as a reactualization of the traumatic event. In contrast with narrative memory, which is re-membered, traumatic memory is an actual event that destabilizes their present (Carruth 1995: 163). A woman's voice may claim reconnection of the self, only to be contradicted by a body that is still struggling with its memories. The body of a refugee woman possesses its own memory and "speaks" its own language of somatization, particularly when the woman has experienced an unspeakable trauma, such as sexual violence (Agger 1992; Carruth 1995; Cockburn 1998: 36). In a previous study, a refugee encapsulated this unspoken voice in the powerful statement: "Nobody knows, but my body knows" (Hajdukowski-Ahmed et al. 1999: 25). In the studies we conducted, refugee women complained of headaches, backaches, painful menstruations, eating disorders, or fear of physical contact. Smells, colors, unwanted or unexpected touching, loud noises or bright lights could precipitate strong physical reactions in refugee women, alerting others to a damaged self. Refugee women also blamed themselves for enjoying life while their loved ones who still remained in their country were denied those pleasures. Their memory struggled dialogically with the healing forces of re-membering, relocating, and reconnecting. Conversely, their body could indulge in liberating pleasures (eating, drinking, dancing), and "speak" of reconnection and healing of the self (Hajdukowski-Ahmed 1999, 2003). In one participatory project, refugee women declined to speak of their past, but chose activities such as making clay masks of their faces that reconnected them with themselves, or planting herbs and baking bread that reconnected them with Earth and its elemental pleasures (Hajdukowski-Ahmed 2003).

Such profound encroachment of the past into the present elicits the question of *when* a woman becomes a refugee and invites us to reconsider the definition of *what* a refugee woman is. For example, can a woman who has already undergone female genital mutilation that had a traumatic effect on her still be considered a refugee and claim refugee status? Or, what if a woman claims asylum because of conflict-related gender persecution while conflict ceases in her country? Is she still a refugee? (Macklin 1996: 133). A refugee woman may offer different versions of the same traumatic events to decision-making authorities. Past and present narrations and interpretations of events and situations may be conflictual. New knowledge, new contexts, and new connections influence one's memory and may shed a different light on past experiences. Repressed memories may surface unexpectedly, and others may recede. A psychosocial dialogical approach acknowledges those fluctuations and does not dismiss them as inventions or pathologies (Agger 1992; Carruth 1995; Loughry, chapter 9).

When refugee women resettle in Western, fast-paced societies, time-related issues affect many aspects of their lives such as their interaction with mainstream institutions, the message perceived being something like, "You have the time; we have the clocks." The different experiences of time put the researcher/activist/service provider or therapist in a difficult dialogical in-between position in which they have to juggle two experiences of time and be answerable to both the refugee women and the institutions or granting agencies for whom they work. There is also often a contrast between the time mainstream institutions take to respond to their needs and the brief and scattered attention refugee women are given.

They need, for example, more listening time than doctors can or are willing to give before they are able to discuss their past trauma (Bhaloo et al. 2005: 33), particularly when they have experienced sexual violence. Refugee women (and men) often live in limbo and have to wait months—and even years—for their official status to be decided or for their spouse and children to be reunited with them. For example, in a participatory health promotion project (Hajdukowski-Ahmed et al. 2000), a refugee woman from El Salvador who had received asylum in Canada had to wait six years to be reunited with her child she had been forced to leave behind. Life was put on hold, shifting between hope and despair; Mother's Days were spent in grief and guilt. She was living in Canada, but her mind was in El Salvador. She felt "neither here nor there," in a situation of continuous crisis, of protracted "refugeeness." The fear of losing her child persisted even after reunion, and any interference by the child protection agency which sought to help her was experienced as a threat and as the reactualization of a nightmare. Living on an emotional and mental roller-coaster between "here" and "there" delays integration, affects the sense of self, identity, and mental health.

These dialogical tensions between situations and worldviews are not linear but are an ongoing gendered process of "to and fro movements" between here and there, between past and present. Refugees "change their predicament by using, adapting and mediating the social and cultural resources at their disposal" (Gomez 1993: 203). Amid this complex flux and reflux, their bodies and their dormant memories impose their own (dis)course.

The Dialogical Self and Language: Voice, Silence, and Translation

Dialogism starts with the concept of a self that is a unique historical agent, constructed through language as social interlocution and which can in turn transform language. Like the self, language is a living organism shaped by the people who interact in the sociohistorical context in which they are grounded (Bakhtin 1986: 75). Language is created at the border where the "I" encounters an "other." Dialogism does not attempt to conceal, subsume, or transcend the heterogeneity of verbal communication and of the worldviews it contains: it acknowledges and validates them. Similarly, the act of understanding or the act of translating is not reductionist but leaves intact the markers of difference. Any verbal communication touches upon thousands of live dialogical streams woven around its object and participates in the social dialogue around it, transforming its connotations, as we have seen in the case of the term *refugee* above. A foreign word or a new meaning penetrates us, persuades us, becomes ours, or is rejected by us (Bakhtine 1984: 386). Because our organism interacts with a social environment, even the biological has a social dimension; so does the individual unconscious, which absorbs the collective memory and rituals through language that penetrates into speech and dreams (Bakhtin 1986: 144). Feminist linguists have stressed the social dimension of language and communication and challenged its patriarchal ideological content (Cameron 1992; Yaguello 1979).

Verbal language also affects the body and is intensely related to the past experience of refugee women. Words can wound, and they can elicit flashbacks and provoke retraumatization. Refugee women who came from conflict zones have often experienced verbal communication in terms of life and death. Torture, rape, and intimidation were used to obtain information about male family members suspected of being activists. Words could have the same destructive power as land mines, making friends or neighbors into enemies, as refugee women from Rwanda or the former Yugoslavia explained (Hajdukowski-Ahmed et al. 2000). Silence can also be a choice and become self-silencing, a form of opposition or of resisting discourse, a means by which refugee women reclaim their agency and indicate their refusal to participate in a verbal exchange with their oppressors and later with authorities in the host country (Hajdukowski-Ahmed 2003; Goździak, chapter 11). An acquired culture of silence and secrecy often persists among displaced women in the host country.

Refugee women are often doubly silenced, first as refugees and secondly as women. Furthermore, because they have to juggle multiple employment and care-giving functions, they are socialized to silence their own experience, needs, and pain. Silence is imposed by power and by the necessity to survive, or it is self-imposed through an internalized gendered discourse which "seeks to produce subjects according to explicit and implicit norms" (Butler 1997: 133). In the host country, the status of a refugee instigates its own forms of silencing, such as language barriers, racism, discrimination, isolation, and fear of deportation. These further discourage survivors from sharing their past experiences, and compromise the process of reconnection of the self with the community and institutions.

Refugee women are often dependent upon the interpretation and translation services of service providers, administrators, or researchers. These services are offered within a context of power relations. When they seek asylum or come to a host country as spouses, it is often husbands who speak on their behalf and "translate" their situation and needs. Representation/translation by men exists in organizations such as refugee camps, which are predominantly male-staffed (UNHCR 2006). In translating, we speak for the other; we substitute our voice for hers; we frame her narrative. This constitutes in itself an act of appropriation (Hitchcock 1993: 186). Hence, the importance of a dialogical approach to translation, which resists the authoritarian representation of the other in "holding the strangeness of the other voice and the contingency of the exchange" (Hitchcock 1993: 188). In the act of translation, both voices—that of the translator and that of the translated individual—should remain visible and retain their agency. Translation should be looked at not as a means of control but as ethical dialogical coauthoring. The translation of nonverbal forms of communication such as silences and irony poses a specific challenge that requires time and cultural knowledge, as well as the will not to dismiss what one does not understand or chooses not to divulge. Dialogically understood, translation constitutes an act of recognition of the other's identity, culture, and agency. Translation, like participatory research or therapy, is a dialogical act in which the translator takes the position of an insider/ outsider, whether it is called "exotopy" by Bakhtin, or "rooting and shifting process," a phrase coined by the Women in Conflict Zones Network (WICZNET group), an interdisciplinary group of feminist scholars, activists, and policymakers founded in 1996 at York University, Canada (Giles and Hyndman 2004b: 7; Introduction, note 12). The position requires that "each participant in the dialogue brings with her the rooting in her own membership and identity, but at the same time tries to shift in order to put herself in a situation of exchange with women who have different memberships and identity" (Giles and Hyndman 2004b: 7). This rooting and shifting position/process leads to a concept of "cultural translation," which is of vital importance and significance for refugees. A cultural translator not only needs to have knowledge of and sensitivity for the context and the culture of the refugees, but also to be sensitive to the gender and power differential, and to the impact of words on interpretation and decision-making processes. For example, the narration of a dream may not bear the same significance for a mental health worker as for a refugee, for whom it may be a sacred experience. Translation is not a pragmatic act of photographic imitation, but it is an act of communication that requires interpretation and an ethical standpoint of listening and respect for the translated cultures. The cultural translator is a *passeur* or a connector who has a deeply dialogical function and occupies the interstitial space between two worldviews, which need to be communicated so that a mutual understanding is engendered that retains the notions of reciprocity and respect for difference (Bhabha 1994: 228–229; Budick and Iser 1996).

Rejecting Dichotomies in Identity Transformation: Toward an Ontology, an Epistemology, and an Ethics of Difference

Refugee women continually produce discourses to resist the identities that are imposed on them and generate their own "re-selving" narratives and strategies. In the course of our participatory projects with refugee women, those women who indicated a higher level of "re-selving" spoke of various factors that gave them faith in themselves and strength to take a firm command of their life and agency. Those factors included their life-giving capacity, their care-giving responsibilities, their faith, the various forms of support received and their participation in local places of worship, their adaptability, their sense of gendered safety through laws, the perception that having enjoyed less power, status, and agency than before, they have less to loose, and, above all, their hope (Bhaloo et al. 2005; Hajdukowski-Ahmed et al. 2000;). They reported a "re-selving" that was not linear, but the outcome of a constant struggle with "de-selving" factors they had experienced. In the process of their identity reconstruction, refugee women are engaged in a constant dialogical struggle between victimization and resistance, between being the helpless victim and the empowered survivor, between here "a present" and there "a past," between what they say and what they are silent about, and between grasping a situation as a challenge or perceiving it as an opportunity. They can take different "Me" subject positions that may appear antagonistic and contradictory in relationship to their context and their past. However, dialogically understood, contradiction becomes contiguity, and "Me" positions are considered as mere differences within a dynamic and organic process of transformation. Each new situation creates a contact zone with the "I" position that invites a new "Me" position, which can be an old position that resurfaces and/or is revised, a recent position that recedes, or a new one that emerges (Hermans 2003: 111).

Two or more seemingly incompatible positions can cohabit and function alternatively in different contexts, such as that of victim and survivor, traditionalist and emancipated. Refugee women express those positions in many ways: in verbal language, in body language, in social practices, and through artistic creativity and expression. A dialogical discourse analysis uncovers those positions and validates the agency of the refugee women at work, particularly when they resort to culturally-grounded nonverbal forms of communication, a frequent occurrence when verbal dialogue is not an option. In rejecting a system of oppositions and contradictions, a dialogical approach implies an ontology (a concept of being), an epistemology (a concept of knowing), and an ethics (a concept of valuing) of difference. To analyze such a level of complexity while foregrounding the identity and agency of refugee women requires the use of qualitative approaches.

Consequences for Research and Therapy

For researchers/practitioners, particularly if they work from a feminist perspective (Reinharz 1993), conceptualization cannot be separated from experience and practice; the field of research and the fieldwork are interconnected. Dialogism that links theory and practice prevents the reification of action when it is cut off from critical thought and helps in putting both of them in a situation of reciprocal critical evaluation. Practice (that is, through participatory action research or advocacy) breaks up the closed circuit of knowledge among scholars, and is thus more apt to inform social change.

Bakhtin's dialogical concepts and methods have been reformulated and made operational by Patricia Maguire, who has established a conceptual ground for feminist practitioners of Participatory Action Research (Maguire 1987). Dialogism is at the heart of Participatory Action Research (PAR) (Denton et al. 1999; Hajdukowski-Ahmed 1998: 646–47). PAR is a qualitative approach that privileges forms of dialogue that foregrounds the agency, the culture, and everyday life of participants through various methods and culturally-grounded forms of communication in order to reach a deep understanding of the researched question. The validity of the instrument of knowledge does not depend on its mathematical accuracy, but on its usefulness in transforming the situation according to the participants' experiential input. This methodology, in which the process is also a product, contributes to the "re-selving" of refugee women, as, for example, in the case of the silenced elderly Japanese women who were given a voice and a place in history by the feminist PAR practitioner who collected their stories (Sugiman, chapter 6). Conceptualization becomes then "the outcome of the connection of separate individual selves with others across spatial and temporal boundaries" (Gorman and Mojab, chapter 7). PAR also helps to grasp nuances, differences, and fluctuations in the process of identity construction and transformation. Two metaphors encapsulate the iterative complexity of a refugee woman's identity: that of a *journey*—"We don't know when the journey of a refugee woman starts and when it ends" (Daenzer, chapter 14); and that of an *eclipse*, which is never totally dark, and in which what appears to be hidden at first becomes increasingly visible and meaningful (Chambon, chapter 5). As an open-ended dialogical approach that validates the agency and worldviews of participants, PAR can lead to the destabilization of existing knowledge and open the space for new knowledge. It can destabilize and redefine power relationships between researchers and participants; the one questioned then becomes the questioner who reformulates the question and contributes to the reframing of conceptualization—even destabilizing the researchers' approach to feminism itself (Chambon, chapter 5; also Gorman and Mojab, chapter 7). PAR method and conceptualization are interrelated, in the same manner in which collective stories are linked with history (Gorman and Mojab, chapter 7). PAR is compatible with the Gender and Forced Migration approach (GAFM); it includes their common dialogism noted implicitly by Doreen Indra in her description of GAFM, which requires "both researchers and practitioners to articulate between a variety of different and not necessarily complementary ethical and cultural systems" (Indra 1999a: 20).

With PAR, tensions voiced between worldviews come to light, creating a space for awareness, for consciousness raising about the structures that construct women's identity, for example between a worldview in which abuse is interpreted as the fate or deserved punishment of women and abuse understood as a punishable crime. Approaches such as PAR prevent the commodification of dialogism into a fossilized and isolated academic field, cut off from the subjects themselves. As Nala Abdo has remarked, "While survey methods based on questionnaires can collect data, they fail to read lips, fail to capture feelings and fail to report true life experiences, all of which can only be gathered if research is gendered, focused and directed" (Abdo 1997: 96). The use of PAR has important educational implications. Students learn that knowledge is also generated by people in everyday situations; that like experience, it is a process in constant transformation; and that it reflects reality but also shapes it through the agency of each individual (Gomez 1993: 205). Educational institutions can validate the everyday experiences of refugee women by creating inclusive curricula in various departments and interdisciplinary programs of study. This in turn will have a positive effect on the self esteem and mental health of refugee women and that of their communities, while training future service providers and researchers to be culturally competent and practice inclusiveness in their professions.

Dialogism has implications for therapy as well as research. PAR is a method that includes the personal narratives of refugee women and experiential knowledge that helps understand "what the experiences of historical dislocation and uprootedness entails for psychological development" (Coles 1992: 7). Traditional Western therapists are trained to define the self in specific ways at the expense of more complex alternatives. They are taught to slice the self into categories that are rigid and static (i.e., passive, compulsive, type "A" personality, and so on). They are also trained in a Cartesian perspective to separate and dichotomize the real, the imaginary, and the parapsychological. For example, the checklist for Post Traumatic Stress Disorder includes symptoms such as nightmares, which are used to evaluate trauma but have different significance in non-Western cultures (Loughry, chapter 9). Suffering is *not* a mental disorder (Malkki 1995: 510). Unlike the psychosocial approach advocated by many refugee scholars, a psychological approach and therapy tend to essentialize and pathologize the refugee woman into a category, isolates her in her individual predicament, and disables her. It depoliticizes and dehistoricizes experience, thus moving away from root causes and collective responsibility. A dialogical relation between approaches would help refine therapies, which in turn would be more effective and create a wider space for resilience narratives.

Western therapies also focus principally on verbal language and tend to consider nonverbal forms of communication as supplementary, thus potentially reducing the significance of gender and cultural diversity. Furthermore, the often "rationalist" secular approach of many therapists may dismiss or overlook narratives of displaced women that convey their religious beliefs, their spirituality, and practices as insignificant or harmful superstitions. A dialogical questioning of this rationalist tendency has recently resulted in the inclusion of spirituality as an important focus in refugee studies and therapy (Goździak 2002). However, spirituality itself is dialogical; it can be at once an effective mental health coping strategy, but because it relies on transcendence and origin, it is also a form of dehistorization of the subject (Malkki 1995: 514). The purpose of dialogical participatory therapy is, with the participant as coinvestigator (Hermans and Hermans-Jansen 1995: 129), to validate all parts of the self ("Me's") and "re-establish the relationship to reality in a process where the person regains his or her history and the capacity to relate to other people, and where the person again has a vision of a meaningful future" (Agger and Jensen 1995: 105).

A dialogical approach considers contradictions or simultaneities "not as psychological flaws or illogical thinking, but as manifestations of the centripetal/centrifugal forces at work" in the life of the exiled individuals (Chambon, chapter 5; De Santis 2001: 1). To the subject, it returns her agency and normalcy by shifting responsibility for the pain and uprootedness experienced by the subject to what or who originally caused it.

Some questions remain difficult to answer and pose challenges to researchers and therapists, such as the following: What is the measure of well being? Who establishes it? Can we consider self-deception as a therapy? (Jopling 1997: 253). Are all cultural practices beneficial or acceptable? Cultural relativism can enter a dialogical conflict with a human rights approach. At this point, we can see the importance of a feminist analysis in the gender and forced migration field of study, and we concur with Lisa

Gilad who argues that a feminist analysis should fight cultural relativism when it affects the rights of women and acts "against the physical integrity of women's lives" (Gilad 1996: 75). Increasing the number of refugee women who become researchers and therapists and are engaged in a dialogical relationship with Western researchers can only enrich theories and perspectives through a cross-fertilization process.

Conclusion

The dialogical concept of identity has evolved in relationship to previous concepts, away from essentialism and toward a relational understanding. Dialogism enables a more comprehensive understanding of the specificity and complexity of the process of identity transformation of refugee women, of all factors that impact it, and of the power relationships that affect it. It helps question and eliminate assumptions, stereotypes, and dichotomies, accounts for variations and transformations. It does not stifle action but nourishes it; conceptualization and practice enter a dialogical relationship to inform and transform each other. A dialogical approach validates a refugee determination process that functions away from the individualization of cases and is thus better equipped to identify contextually systemic root causes of persecution, and to contribute to their eradication and to a fair determination process. The practice of a dialogical approach to research and therapy facilitates the empowerment and healing of refugee women. It is particularly effective in identifying and validating the existence and transformative power of agency in refugee women to the extent that, even in the most disempowering situations like torture, a dialogical perspective can uncover spaces of resistance and moments of agency that restore their agency and dignity. A dialogical approach makes us perceive refugee women "not as helpless victims but rather people who have been victimized and actors in their lives, resisting and taking the risks to change the situations in which they find themselves" (Moussa 2000: 32).

Dialogism creates an ontology of difference. In a sense, it questions the notion of theory itself because it is relational, multifactorial, and *iterative*, and therefore cannot be easily captured in a conceptualized form. It also invites us to wonder if conceptualizing an unacceptable situation might amount to "naturalizing it" and conferring on it a certain form of legitimacy. However, we must remain vigilant with regard to identity research and identity politics and ask ourselves with Seyla Benhabib, "What is the role of the state in encouraging identity politics, and in this process, what other options of social struggle and group solidarities are being precluded?" (Benhabib 1994, note 28). Gender is only one dimension of our identities and well being, particularly during times of economic, environmental, or political upheaval. Theorizing identity dialogically in relation to its impact on the lives of refugee women is indeed a crucial task, but it should not sideline the consideration of other struggles and solidarities, so that comprehensive and transformative knowledge is constructed with a view to eradicating all root causes of exploitation and degradation and in celebration of the spirit of renewal and justice.

2

The Gender Relations of Home, Security, and Transversal Feminism

REFUGEE WOMEN RECLAIMING THEIR IDENTITY

Wenona Giles

As I began to write this chapter,[1] people in Toronto came together to oppose the United States led war against Iraq. Many among the crowd were also opposing homelessness. The slogan in a leaflet that announced the Saturday march was "Homes, Not Bombs":

Saturday March 15th
STOP the WAR on IRAQ
12 noon US Consulate 360 University Ave.
followed by a march to join with housing activists of the Toronto
Disaster Relief Committee at the Moss Park Armory to demand homes not bombs.

The connection between war and homelessness continues to be stark. The organizers and participants associated with this peace demonstration perceive a continuum between homelessness in Toronto and militarization, enforced evictions, bombings of civilian homes, and the long-term transience and inadequacy of refugee camps in other parts of the world.[2]

This chapter questions the efficacy of citizenship for the homeless or for refugee women. The ambivalent relationship between homelessness and citizenship definitions is associated with the resistance of wealthy countries to address the root causes of militarized conflict, including the repatriation of refugees where possible, and the reconstruction of regions devastated by war. Citizenship, immigration, development aid, labor, and other state policies and practices are interwoven. Thus the gender, class, race, and North-South relationships in one area of state policy are part of a continuum that is reflected in the other policy areas. Examining the way in which a state defines its citizenship reveals much about its development/aid and North-South relations. Refugee women are particularly affected by the lack of long-term development aid. Humanitarian aid, which has been replacing development aid for many years, is closely tied to a vision of the refugee as a homeless victim, and women are particularly affected by this image.

Citizenship, Homelessness, and Refugee Development Aid

In most wealthy nation-states, homelessness and citizenship do not have an easy relationship. As Morley points out, "full citizenship has often historically implied not just rootedness in place, but property ownership and in many places the state has long demanded a fixed address in exchange for citizenship rights" (2000: 26). Manning argues that those inhabiting a home are regarded as citizens "in the citizen/nation/state triad" (2003: 32), whereas those who are homeless are more likely to be excluded from citizenship.

Refugees may indeed conclude that they need temporary housing and other assistance to support them while in exile. However, it is a mistake to think that refugees necessarily regard themselves as homeless. Most refugees try to remain very connected to their homeland: to the family and friends, land, material possessions, property, and culture they have left behind and to which they plan to return. However, normative conceptualizations of citizenship dictate that refugees are not citizens of their country of refuge and in many cases may lose citizenship in their homeland. They are thus akin to being homeless. Refugees are not only affected by the loss of citizenship in their own country, but also by the citizenship practices of wealthy countries, as I discuss below.

In this chapter I differentiate between definitions of citizenship and practices of citizenship. Although a definition of citizenship may *de jure* include all members of a national social group who are legally declared citizens, *de facto*, it may not. The definition of citizenship in Canada is still based on a statement of Liberal MP Paul Martin Sr. when he introduced the Citizenship Act to the House of Commons in 1946. He defined citizenship in the following way:

> Citizenship means more than the right to vote; more than the right to hold and transfer property; more than the right to move freely under the protection of the state; citizenship is the right to full partnership in the fortunes and in the future of the nation. (1:11)

This definition assumes that all who are citizens in Canada can practice or experience citizenship in the same way, in a "full partnership," and that the boundaries of national collectivism and civil society are the same and unchanging, or are "organically whole" as feminists have critiqued (Stasiulis and Yuval-Davis 1995; Yuval-Davis 1991). Citizenship practices reveal the extensiveness of the exclusionary aspects of citizenship that are dependent upon gender, "race," class, immigrant and refugee status, and other attributes. In addition, Morley points out that the problem with such conventional views of citizenship "is that the idea of the 'same for all' is often translated, in practice, into the requirement that all citizens should be the same" (2000: 124). Such an exclusionary form of citizenship is critiqued by Castles who argues for a "rejection of the conception of all citizens as equal individuals and its replacement by recognition of all citizens as having equal rights as individuals and different needs and wants as members of groups with specific characteristics and social situations" (Castles 1994 quoted in Morley 2000: 125). This revised definition of citizenship builds on Young's argument that there must be recognition of group differences and "that some groups are actually or potentially oppressed or disadvantaged" (Young 1989: 257 quoted in Morley 2000: 124). Such a definition contains an implicit activist agenda of social change toward addressing causes of oppression of particular groups such as, for example, refugee women in long-term refugee camps, as well as addressing their immediate concerns and needs.

In their present forms in Canada and other Western countries, citizenship definitions and policies cannot adequately address the plight of the homeless, because these policies do not challenge but rather reflect the inherent inequities toward, for example, homeless Canadians in Canada, and thus do not address the root causes of dislocation. Citizenship practices that exclude the homeless are reflected in the aid policies of Canada and other donor countries, which have also been remiss in addressing the root causes of homelessness and dislocation caused by war in other regions of the world.

It is well known that high-income countries, such as Canada, restrict the number of refugees who may enter through their borders through planned resettlement arrivals and the refugee determination processes for asylum seekers. Rather than receive large numbers of refugees, these countries prefer to provide financial assistance to less wealthy, refugee receiving countries through the UNHCR, other international agencies, and bilaterally. Wealthy regions of the world prefer that refugees—or those made homeless by wars or other disasters—should be cared for by their countries of origin or those neighboring countries to which they have fled—both of these sites usually located in poorer regions of the world.

The United Nations High Commissioner for Refugees (UNHCR) has pointed out that, "[l]ess-developed countries are both the major source and destination of refugees": 86 percent of refugees originated in these areas and 72 percent of the world's refugees are provided with asylum in these regions (2002: 24–25). However, the care of refugees in developing regions "implies a significant additional cost to an already fragile economy" (65). The economic effects of hosting refugees (numbers of refugees in relation to economic resources) "are mostly felt in Africa," in particular in Sierra Leone, the Democratic Republic of Congo, Tanzania, Ethiopia, Burundi, Rwanda, and Eritrea. Pakistan and Iran are the two principal countries outside Africa where "the economic impact of refugees on the local economy is significant" (65). Women refugees in these regions are especially vulnerable to serious human rights abuses as well as inadequate access to food, education, housing, and other basic needs.

In this period, defined in a recent popular press article as "the age of the refugee" (Rieff 2003: 36), the decision of wealthy countries to direct the flow of refugees away from their shores, while not sufficiently increasing aid and development funds to the countries of first asylum or the home countries of refugees, has resulted in a serious exacerbation of the existing political, economic, and social instability of these areas.

Over a decade ago (in 1992) an ILO (International Labor Organization) and UNHCR study argued that in order to reduce politically motivated migration by 2030, it is not enough for wealthy countries to provide *relief* and *resettlement* financial support—this type of support is myopic and has resulted in the creation of refugee camps as permanent living sites or as "displaced places" where the "camps have become worlds unto themselves" (Rieff 2003: 36). It is equally important to provide support for *repatriation* (which means support for the reconstruction of the homeland) and attention to the *root causes* of conflicts (Martin and Taylor 2001: 110–111). As the ILO/UNHCR study described by Martin and Taylor points out, this expansion of assistance to refugees requires more aid from industrial countries as well as other changes in the way aid is dispersed.

How are dislocation and the dislocated challenging normative definitions of citizenship, and how might these changes also affect North-South development aid relationships? I explore these issues below by first examining how the dislocation of refugee women is part of a continuum of dislocation from Canada and other wealthy Western countries to areas of militarized conflict. Second, I link transversal[3] ways of thinking about citizenship to new ways of defining the space called home. However, clarifying the connections between a lack of development aid for refugees and for their home countries is one thing; changing this situation is another and requires contextualization, activism, and lobbying.

Refugees and the Continuum of Dislocation

Elsewhere I have discussed the refugee camp-as-home and how women and homes are ideologized in refugee camps (Giles 1999: 90n). I argued that "[r]efugee camps are a deeply informative site for analysis of the ways that naturalized images of home are mapped onto representations of the state, the nation and international agencies" (90). In a related way, definitions of home, homelessness, and refugee camps are associated with the ways in which the state defines citizenship status. The manner in which dislocation is defined and acted upon by the state is part of a continuum of dislocation from, for example, the homeless woman in Toronto to the Somalian woman in a Kenyan refugee camp.

If the idea of home is associated with identity, homelessness has been equated in citizenship definitions with invisibility, lack of an identity/history, and being a problem. Homelessness among women is considered particularly damning/deviant—because the proper place for a woman is still thought by many to be in the home. Thus, refugee women and girls may be a particularly neglected group by virtue of their ascribed identity as homeless and their presence in refugee camps, which are often considered to be dangerous places for women (de Alwis 2004; Thiruchandran 2003). In addition, if they try to move beyond the status of victim to resisting their plight in some way, they may be regarded as neglecting, perhaps, even betraying, their homes (Morley 2000: 69) by their own ethnic group and also by aid workers and resettlement/emigration workers, whose policies are often wedded to a definition of women as victims (Andric-Ruzicic 2003; Helms 2003).

Alternatively, I challenge normative definitions of home and household thus also questioning practices vis-à-vis those in homes and the homeless. I argue that a home is in fact a complex set of ideas that may refer to a country of origin and an associated national identity; it may also correspond to a specific dwelling place/household, or to a family. The idea of home is a contradictory phenomenon: while it may confine women, it may also represent escape and freedom. For some it is a locus of resistance and struggle. Home is a gendered phenomenon and is the "location" from which many immigrant and refugee women begin to describe, defend, or justify themselves and their acts (Giles 1997: 387). Gender relations in immigrant or refugee households are influenced by traditional ideologies that involve a "remembering" on the part of immigrant or refugee women and of attachments to memories of home and thus also to household relations as experienced and remembered. I have also proposed a definition of households that lays a basis for challenging ideas of homelessness as well as concepts of citizenship which exclude the dislocated whether they are in Toronto, Colombo, or Sarajevo. As I have described elsewhere, households exist "for the survival of their members, across time and in the case of immigrants and migrants, across countries and continents. They are economic enterprises unto themselves, but linked to other households and always shaped by the larger economy and culture in which they are embedded" (Giles 1997: 388).

As I indicate in these definitions of home and household, and as Massey (in Morley 2002: 10) points out, it is important to remember that there are few instances in the daily lives of people in the world today that could be described as "simply local." Morley argues along with Marcus that "identity can no longer be mapped on to locality" (ibid.), but instead (as per Marcus 1992: 315), identity "is produced simultaneously in many different locales. One's identity, where one lives . . . is only one social context and perhaps not the most important one in which it is shaped" (Morley: 10). The "larger economy and culture" in which refugee women experience the household is shaped by policies of international agencies (e.g., the UNHCR), national state agencies in countries of resettlement (e.g., departments of citizenship, immigration/refugee determination, labor) as well as the effects of globalization in all its forms. An example of the way the state shapes households of immigrant/refugee women, is expressed in "masculinist definitions of 'work' and 'skill' in immigration policies, which have resulted in most immigrant women entering Canada in a contradictory way as dependents, rather than workers, because their work and education history have not measured up to the requirements demanded of the 'independent' class of immigrants" (Fincher et al. 1994; Giles 1997: 395). Host countries may reinforce naturalized images of women, positing that it is principally the "home [country of origin] culture" that prevents immigrant/migrant women from securing better jobs, more education, and fluency in the language of the country of immigration. As a result, these kinds of policies may lead to a privatization of immigrant and refugee women's lives, isolating them from a sense of the broader community in which they have resettled (Giles 1996a; 1997).

Bhattacharjee's (1997: 313–314) work demonstrates a broadly defined characterization of home. In research on South Asian immigrants in the United States, she shows how "homes" are defined at three different levels: first, "the (conventional) domestic sphere of the heterosexual and patriarchal family"; second, "as an extended ethnic community separate and distinct from other ethnic communities"; and third, "at the level of nations of origin, often shaped by nationalist movements and histories of colonialism." The analysis of women's overlapping and cross-cutting identities in these different homes can be used in studies of the situation of refugee women to challenge the notion that sharp boundaries exist around their identities, as well as the idea that they are homeless. This is not to say that immigrant and refugee women do not confront challenges in households/homes. Bhattacharjee points out that in the case of South Asian women in the United States, as in other cases, "women are in danger of being made invisible in all three homes." For example women may experience silencing in heterosexist and patriarchal homes; invisibility due to illegal status and a lack of documentation; dependency on men if they enter as sponsored immigrants (as in Canada) and thus invisibility beyond the home; and rejection and dismissal of abuse or violence against them by their own ethnic group, due to essentialist gendered definitions of national culture (1997: 322). Bhattacherjee thus presents a strong argument for more inclusive definitions of citizenship that will be attentive to immigrant and refugee women's experiences of inequality and asymmetrical power relations. This refers us back to Castles' call for a redefinition of citizenship, in which he refers to a recognition of the different needs and wants that groups may have and, I would add that groups within groups may have (Castles in Morley 2000: 125). In this regard, refugee women and girls often have different concerns and responsibilities than men and boys.

Contemporary analyses of immigrant and refugee women clearly necessitate a better understanding of households from the traditional anthropological (and state-defined) model of the household as a highly bounded functional entity. When traditional household analysis either neglects gender entirely or is associated with universalized gender relations, the result can be dangerously misleading, making it impossible to get beyond classical public/private characterizations of women's activities and commitments. The application of static, normative status and role constructions (that is, husband-father, wife-mother, and children) to studies of households are also profoundly limiting. If we accept the notion put forth by Indra (1999a: 15–16) and others, that households are dynamic structures that are always "in process," can we not then go further to describe homes as the meaning, structures attached to households by both those within and without "imagined communities" in the Andersonian sense? Approaching households as processual, allows a deeper comparison across communities, regions, or nations. It challenges exclusionary citizenship practices and has implications for our understanding of transversal practices and politics, and gendered relations of war and peace (Giles 1999: 86). This approach enables us to ask how citizenship practices in wealthy regions of the world affect the establishment and the shape of the households of refugees in camps and beyond. In addition, we are more easily able to hear the point of view of the refugee in his/her household regarding their immediate and long-term needs and wants.

There is thus also a continuum between normative definitions of citizenship and home with ideas about the security of the nation. The need to protect the home/self/nation has led to increased border security and the establishment of a state bureaucracy focusing on security, such as is evidenced in the United States by the recent establishment of the Department of Homeland Security. As Manning points out, "The link between security, the home, and the politics of inclusion informs a modern political imagination that rests on the assumption that state sovereignty offers the only viable form of political governance" (2003: 33). She argues that such a "state-centered discourse reinforces the notion that only homelike spaces provide the coherence necessary to understand and inhabit our worlds" (2003: 34).

Thomas draws a direct correlation between a lack of entitlement to *human* security and access to "conditions of existence in which basic material needs are met and in which human dignity, including meaningful participation in the life of the community, can be realized" (Thomas 1999: 3). She defines human security as requiring more than "simply material needs satisfaction, but attendance to nonmaterial aspects as well" (182), including engagement with democracy at all levels. She regards human security as having a different starting point than security of the individual (in the neoliberal sense), which refers to the extension of private power and activity based around property rights and choice in the marketplace (3). While we need further feminist critiques of human security, it is a useful concept and an important one to consider as it has a collective goal that is pursued for the household, village, and community (ibid. 2004 a: 307–312).

To what extent does a definition of home reflect exclusionary state practices that are bound up with ensuring the safety of the homed by excluding the other? In such an environment—more than ever—immigrants and refugees will feel the need to seek security in creating a protected space. Take for example the Vietnamese migrant who "sets up everything to look like back home"; or the Barbadian mother in the UK who places a small Barbadian flag on the front door and tells her children, "You can do whatever you want out there, but step into this house and you are in Barbados" (Morley 2000: 52). In the strange, new country, the migrant home is often a "bulwark against what is felt as the intrusion and undermining influences of the new host culture" (ibid.). In her discussion of transnational migration Mahler writes that while transnational actors (migrants, etc.), activities, and discourses can be agents of change, they can also contribute to the reproduction of "local, historically constructed social customs and power hierarchies. In age of the global, the local is not superseded" (1999: 713). Narrow definitions of citizenship are not only becoming more questionable but in particular are contributing to limitations on the access of refugees to basic human security.

Martin and Taylor point out that, today, most aid experts endorse the idea that the support of basic human needs (e.g., education and healthcare for women and girls), should supersede the funding of mega-infrastructural projects (e.g., irrigation dams). They caution, however, that it has been difficult to convince countries to increase their foreign development aid to poor regions. On the other hand, humanitarian relief aid has greatly increased. Loescher writes that in the decade between the early 1980s and the early 1990s, the amount of foreign aid spent on humanitarian relief efforts increased fivefold (Loescher 2001:190). These were funds diverted from development assistance for long-term development projects to an ever-increasing number of humanitarian crises. Thus "the underlying poverty and social inequalities that fuel conflict in the first place" (190–191) have taken second place or been ignored. There has been a continuous diminution of development aid to the poorest nations, as well as no new funds to address human rights problems that are also at the root of refugee disasters (191).

Manning writes that, "the stranger as racial other, migrant, or refugee is distinguished from the citizen insofar as he or she inhabits the placelessness of estrangement located between nations" (2003: 75). From this space, Manning argues, "the stranger as stranger than the state incites us to retheorize both the discourse of the other as stranger, refugee, or migrant and the discourse of state sovereignty" (2003: 75). In so doing, she continues, "we become aware of the ways in which the stranger is instrumental to the enabling of a certain version of citizenry based on the bounded subjectivities, relations and institutions of the modern territorial state . . . the stranger as racial other perpetuates a crisis of representation" (75–76). Likewise, Eschle writes that the homeless migrant and the *mestiza*, who are located in the borderlands between races and cultures, have recourse to postmodern strategies in reformulating subjectivity (Eschle 2001).

Homelessness and Transversal Feminist Practices

Through her interpretation of the novel *Fugitive Pieces* by Ann Michaels, Manning breaks down the binaries of security/insecurity and home/homelessness, arguing that the idea of homelessness arises as a "political gesture" (2003: 39) that challenges the connection between home, security, and nation—thus questioning and challenging home-based practices of exclusion. In Michaels's novel, home is a place that, while it may promise security, can also be a site of insecurity, destruction, and violence. Homelessness is often associated with mobility (or lack thereof in the case of female refugees), and its relationship with migrancy and refugee status opens up new ways of thinking about migration. Calloni (2002: 188) argues that "human mobility can help to establish new commonalities and new political perspectives for human society." She writes about a "cross-continental citizenship," giving the examples of a "Mediterranean citizenship" (that connects Europe, Asia, and Africa) and circumpolar identities that link eight countries in the Arctic zone (2002: 188). She argues that international relations can no longer be conceived of as "pure diplomatic relations" but have now evolved into "an overlapping composition of nations, international organizations, pressure groups and citizens"—and most importantly for my analysis here—that migration or human mobility has greatly contributed to this transformation, migration, in itself, "proposes" a notion of "social citizenship." How do transversal and comparative practices of networking demonstrate/play out/challenge the boundaries and borders—even moving us perhaps beyond the boundaries of cross-continental citizenship?

This brings me to the possibilities and place of transversal feminist politics for refugee women. Alexander and Mohanty argue for a theorization of feminism, central to which is a comparative analysis of feminist organizing, criticism, and self-reflection (Alexander and Mohanty 1997: xx). This is associated with a "comparative, relational feminist praxis that is transnational in its response to and engagement with global processes of colonization." Grewal and Kaplan (1994; see also Hyndman 1997: 17–18) regard feminist transnational and transversal practices as challenging purely locational politics, and as engaging and connecting rather than distinguishing and distancing people of different locations.

Indeed, while comparative research work is vulnerable to a static essentialism that denies difference and divergent histories of domination and dominance, we have argued (in the Women in Conflict Zones Network)[4] that it is also potentially an activist approach that incorporates social change toward the elimination of inequality and oppression. In our view, one of the outcomes of comparison can be to demonstrate difference, but this is not the central, nor the sole focus of an approach that is oriented toward activism. Brah's ideas have important implications for analyses of forced migration and gendered violence in the context of war. Her concept of "diaspora space" allows us to connect locations of violent conflict with people and places elsewhere, living "in peace." Likewise, gender relations are not fixed, but are produced unevenly across sites of violence and relative calm. The production and trade in military weapons, as well as resistance to banning landmines and other weapons of destruction, can no longer be viewed as issues that are located elsewhere, that is, in a "war zone" (Giles and Hyndman 2004: 39). Rather, "feminist work tends to represent war as a continuum of violence from the bedroom to the battlefield, traversing our bodies and our sense of self" (Cockburn 1998: 4).

Bhattacharjee's work on home also provides a basis on which it is possible to think about the relationship between comparative analysis and activisms. The three levels that she defines as the cornerstones for definitions of home among immigrants (the domestic sphere, the ethnic community, and the nation of origin) are interrelated in such a way that immigrants define and are defined through all three levels. She states that activism requires challenging the status quo in all three "homes" (Bhattacharjee 1987: 327):

It is not enough to fight the abuse in the family home alone. It is also necessary to fight the violence inherent in the community's use of the figure of the woman to construct its identity, and in its summoning up of essentialist and elitist national culture. It is important to fight the way definitions of the immigrant family, the immigrant community, and immigrants' national heritage conveniently work toward creating a privatized U.S. nation-state based on oppression. (ibid. 324)

Forms of activism, that parallel or are interwoven with these different notions of 'home' can be envisaged: that is, activisms that are rooted in local feminist politics and are informing and connected to national and global forms of feminist politics.

Arat-Koc's cautionary argument regarding the urgency of rethinking "the meaning, the mode and the relationships of 'global feminism'" (2002: 63) provides an instrumental link from this analysis of transversal politics to my earlier discussion regarding the continuum of citizenship practices, homelessness, and refugee development aid. She rightly argues that feminism as a political project must go beyond considerations of the need to ameliorate women's place in the world. Rather, we must rethink a number of issues in new ways, such as: "[c]ivil liberties, human rights, 'terrorism,' imperialism, internationalism and national sovereignty, among others" (2002: 63). It is the linkages between these phenomena that must also be constantly kept in mind in this feminist project. In others words, what is the relationship between citizenship practices that exclude the homeless in Canada and Canadian aid policies that will not address the root causes of homelessness and/or dislocation in poor regions of the world, except through the temporariness of humanitarian aid? A response to this question will go far in explaining the gender, race, and class relations of the refugee situation, which is one in which most refugee men and women are more likely to find themselves dislocated in a poor country rather than a wealthy one, and left to eke out an existence on humanitarian or "refugee" aid, rather than rebuilding better futures for themselves in their regions of origin, exile, or elsewhere. Women are more likely to be affected by the dearth of development aid, because they are less affluent and mobile than men, in every region of the world. As dislocated, poor, and racialized individuals whose identities become increasingly compromised once they are labeled as "strangers" or "homeless," and regardless of whether they have dependents or not, women stand to lose the most from this continuum of homelessness. But the very same ascriptions and the conditions under which they live in exile also challenge and create a "crisis" around normative definitions of citizenship, North-South inequality, and human rights as Manning (1976: 76), Eschle (2001), and others have pointed out. Herein lies the terrain of resistance and change that can point to interventions that will reveal the links between citizenship, homelessness, and forced migration and lead to change.

I conclude with two recommendations that arise from the issues raised in this chapter. First, an approach that links the provision of basic needs, such as good quality healthcare, education, housing, and employment, to civil rights in long-term refugee camps, must be explored and developed. This requires a regime change in refugee camps to one that will truly observe the *de jure* rights of refugees as laid down by the 1951 UN Convention Relating to the Status of Refugees. At present and in most camps, these rights are ignored or severely delimited (Chen 2004; Smith 2004). Secondly, it is crucial to rethink the links between the provision of humanitarian aid, the dearth of sustainable forms of development aid, and the existence of long-term refugee camps, or "refugee warehousing" as it is now called (Chen 2004). There is presently an opportunity for governments of developing and developed regions of the world and agencies working with refugees and in refugee camps to use the *Millenium Development Goals (MDG)* declaration announced by the United Nations in 2000, to seriously and substantively address the seven goals of this declaration regarding poverty and hunger, education and illiteracy, infant and maternal mortality, HIV/AIDS, environmental sustainability, targets for aid, trade, and debt relief by 2015 (United Nations October 2002) as these issues pertain specifically to refugees. Only when the root causes of conflict and exile are taken seriously, will the limitations of current definitions of citizenship for refugees be revealed.

Notes

1. An earlier version of this paper was presented at the conference: *Saying 'I' is Full of Consequences: Refugee Women Reclaim Their Identity,* Women's Studies, McMaster University, Hamilton, Ontario, 19–21 March 2003.

2. The alarming entrenchment of homelessness for refugees has recently been revealed in the World Refugee Survey 2004 which estimates that, of the twelve million refugees in the world, seven million have been sequestered for ten years or more in long-term refugee camps. This is now referred to as "refugee warehousing." See M. Smith, "Warehousing Refugee: A Denial of Rights, A Waste of Humanity," *US Committee for World Refugee Survey* (2004), 38.

3. According to Cockburn and Hunter, transversal politics is "the practice of creatively crossing (and redrawing) the borders that mark significant politicized difference. It means empathy without sameness, shifting without tearing out your roots. Italian women peace activists first used the term: *politica trasversale.*" C. Cockburn and L. Hunter, "Transversal Politics and Translating Practices" in *Soundings. A Journal of Politics and Culture* 12 (Summer), special issue on *Transversal Politics* (1999), 89.

4. The Women in Conflict Zones Network (WICZNET), is an international network of scholars, activists, and policymakers who have been involved in research on ethnicity, nationalism, and gender in militarized conflict zones. See Introduction, note 12.

3

Always "Natasha"

THE TRANSNATIONAL SEX TRAFFICKING OF WOMEN

Victor Malarek and Sarah V. Wayland

Nineteen-year-old Marika of Kharkiv, Ukraine, thought she was going to Tel Aviv to work as a waitress. Desperate for work, with a sick mother, an unemployed, alcoholic father, and two younger sisters who were wasting away, Marika seized the opportunity to earn some money for her family. Three days after leaving her home, she was brought to an apartment in Tel Aviv with four other women, two from Ukraine, one from Russia, and one from Moldova. A large, muscular man guarded the only door. After showering, the women were provided with sheer lingerie and told to put it on. The women then met their "owner." He had purchased them for $10,000 apiece, and they were to be his property until each of them paid off a $20,000 debt. He told them they would have to start working off the debt that evening by servicing clients. He warned the women that any refusal to do their job would be dealt with swiftly and painfully. The burly man at the door grinned menacingly at the women.

That first night, Marika was forced to have sex with eight men. Over the next four months, she had sexual relations with hundreds of Israeli men: soldiers, husbands, and religious men. If any of her clients complained, she received a slap in the face, a fine was added to the money she purportedly already owed, and she was given nothing to eat for the day. The windows were locked, and the door to the apartment was constantly guarded. Her thoughts turned to suicide. She prayed every day that someone would rescue her. But the days just passed.

Marika noticed that the clients did not distinguish between the women's ethnic backgrounds. Though Marika and the others came from different countries and spoke different languages, they were all Russian in the eyes of the men. Not only that, but many of the men addressed the women in the same way: "They called us Natasha. They never asked our real name.

To them, we were all Natashas." Marika continued, "We were their sexual fantasy. These fools would walk into the parlour and with a stupid grin on their face call out 'Natasha!' like we were some kind of Russian doll. And we were expected to smile and rush over to them" (Malarek 2003: xvi).[1]

Marika found it strange to be called by another name at first. But she soon accepted it as a form of escape:

> When I was alone in my thoughts and my dreams, I was Marika—free from this prison. But when I went with a man, I became this other woman—this prostitute called Natasha who was cold and dead inside me. Natasha was my nightmare. Marika was my salvation. I never told any of these men my real name (Malarek 2003: xvi).

And the men never asked.

Trafficking: A Global Problem

Marika's story of being trafficked into the sex trade is not unique. An estimated 250,000 women and children from Russia, the Newly Independent States, and Eastern Europe are trafficked into Western Europe, the Middle East, Japan, Canada, and the United States each year. Trafficked women and children from former Eastern bloc countries have been found in over forty countries worldwide.

In its 2004 Trafficking in Persons Report, the US Department of State conservatively estimates that approximately 600,000 to 800,000 people are trafficked across international borders each year (US Department of State Trafficking in Persons Report. June 2004: Introduction). Most international agencies and nongovernmental organizations place the figure much higher. According to the Trafficking in Persons Report, trafficking appears to be on the rise worldwide, and the overwhelming majority of victims are women and children. Trafficking is highly lucrative, traffickers are predominantly men, and organized crime elements use trafficking to consolidate their power and their wealth. As the International Labor Organization (ILO) reports, "Globally, forced labor—which includes sexual exploitation—generates thirty-one billion dollars, half of it in the industrialized world, a tenth in the transition countries" (2005).

The term "trafficking" has mostly referred to dealing in goods, especially illegal ones such as drugs or weapons. Its recent application to humans suggests that individuals too can be treated as commodities. The United Nations defines trafficking as follows:

> The recruitment, transportation, transfer, harbouring, or receipt of persons, by means of the threat or use of force or other forms of coercion, of abduction or fraud, of deception, of the abuse of power or a position of vulnerability or of

the giving or receiving of payment or benefits to achieve the consent of a person having control over another person, for the purpose of exploitation. Exploitation shall include, at a minimum, the exploitation of the prostitution of others or other forms of sexual exploitation, forced labour or services, slavery or practices similar to slavery, servitude or the removal of organs (UN Protocol Article 3, paragraph (a), in ILO Report 2005: 7).

Thus, trafficking involves coercion and exploitation as well as the objectification of persons, particularly women.

Trafficked persons are not refugees in the traditional sense of the word: they are not forced to flee their homeland from fear of persecution. However, the complexities of contemporary population movements have blurred the distinctions between "voluntary" and "forced" migration. Political, economic, social, and environmental factors may push people to leave their homes. They may flee because of persecution and war, be displaced as a result of natural disasters and environmental degradation, or simply because they cannot find the means to survive at home. As a result, scholars and activists have begun to prefer the more broadly conceptualized term "uprooted people" to "refugee" (World Council of Churches 1995a: 1, cited in Moussa 2000: 3). "Uprooted people" includes trafficked women who are pushed to leave their homes for economic survival. Indeed, many trafficked women never return home, either because they are held in confinement, have little earnings to bring with them, feel ashamed at having worked as prostitutes, or—if they have escaped from their traffickers—out of fear of being found.

Despite increased international awareness, trafficking in persons is on the rise. The reasons are simple. Trafficking is lucrative, enforcement mechanisms are inadequate, and penalties are mild. According to the United Nations, the global business of trafficking in persons is believed to generate revenue of US $12 billion per year for organized crime interests (Malarek 2003: 4). Trafficking in human beings is now the third largest money making venture in the world, after illegal weapons and drugs. Incredibly, most countries treat it as a lesser crime than trafficking in weapons or drugs.

In this chapter, we focus on the plight of uprooted women who are trafficked from Russia, the Newly Independent States, and Eastern Europe. We discuss the economic and political circumstances that give rise to the lucrative trade in women, the "othering" of women who work in the sex trades, the impact of trafficking on its victims, including the impact on their identity and well being, and, lastly, attempts to crack down on trafficking and to help its victims. In presenting this information, we draw on feminist theory to problematize the epistemological approach that is based on a dichotomous understanding of the world characteristic of a patriarchal social order (Jay 1992; de Beauvoir 1974 [1949]). This dichotomous division into oppositional categories also generates and justifies other forms of subjugation and inequities such as colonialism, racism, or homophobia. We challenge categorizations of women that encourage "othering" and stereotyping (e.g., subject/object, virgin/prostitute, legal/illegal, foreigner/citizen) and seek the inclusion of economic, racial, and postcolonial factors that help to blur the boundaries between oppositional terms. A gendered economic approach to women's bodies and thus to prostitution also helps to deconstruct these dichotomies and to overcome "othering."

Trafficked women such as Marika are silenced and resort to a splitting of their identities as a coping mechanism. We would like to see a world in which women are persons who have full control over their bodies, their subjecthood, their identities, their agencies, and their citizenship—women who can live within their selves as whole.

The Eastern European Connection: Recruitment to Slavery

Marika's story occurred within a broader environment of economic marginalization and desperation in the former Soviet Union. When the Soviet Union dissolved in 1991, people living there and in the Eastern European states previously controlled by the Soviet Union dreamed of a better life. Quickly it became apparent that market reforms were not generating economic opportunities for most citizens. Law and order were compromised by corruption, greed, and graft. Those with the means were taking their capital elsewhere. Social safety nets evaporated and tens of millions of persons were left without livelihoods or effective governments. Others became wealthy and organized crime grew. The black market economy, already well developed under communist rule, became even more important. It was in this context that organized crime gangs identified the most valuable assets of the newly independent states: beautiful, young, educated, well-mannered women and girls—desperate for money and with no future in sight.

Traffickers began to target these women and girls, painting attractive pictures of well-paying jobs abroad. They promised positions as nannies in Greece, domestics in Italy and France, maids in Austria and Spain, and models in North America and Japan. For this generation of young women, many of whom grew up nursing romantic fantasies of the West, these jobs were viewed as a dream come true. Some women naïvely answered advertisements in newspapers, such as the following one, which ran in Kyiv: "Girls: Must be single and very pretty. Young and tall. We invite you for work as models, secretaries, dancers, choreographers, gymnasts. Housing is supplied. Foreign posts available. Must apply in person" (Malarek 2003: 10). Women are not always recruited by strangers; they are often convinced by acquaintances, individuals of standing in the community, even family members. A nongovernmental organization in Kyiv that assists trafficked women from Ukraine has documented cases of recruitment into sexual slavery by teachers, a local psychologist, and the wife of a policeman. Women are sometimes recruited in groups. Thinking there is safety in numbers, they enthusiastically sign on. There are even cases of traffickers targeting teenage girls who are being released from state-run orphanages. Most frighteningly, women and girls have been abducted in broad daylight while walking down rural roads.

Miserable living conditions in the former state-controlled markets soon generated a ready supply of women. Before the 1990s, the number of women from Eastern Europe and the Soviet Union was insignificant in terms of trafficking. Today, they represent more than 25 percent of the trade (Malarek 2003: 6).

Some women do know they are being recruited to work in some aspect of the sex trade, such as massage parlors, strip clubs, peep shows, and escort agencies. Yet to call these victims "willing" is not fair. These women and girls are propelled by desperate economic circumstances, the belief that they will make good money, and maybe even meet Mr. Right, as in the film *Pretty Woman*. Instead, they end up in debt bondage where they are not free to leave, escape is all but impossible, and they are forced to have sex with dozens of clients a day. They do not get time off from work for illness or while they have their periods. In the end, the vast majority end up as nothing more than slaves—abused, used, and traded. And when they become too old or too sick, they are simply replaced with younger, fresher girls. In the words of Don Cesare, an Italian priest who works with victims of trafficking: "Most of them leave home without knowing. It is true that some know, but knowing does not mean wanting" (Malarek 2003: 111).

Work-related problems include various types of physical illness, alcohol and drug addiction, and other psychological and medical problems that come from constant abuse and gang rape. Laura Lederer of The Protection Project at the School of Advanced International Studies, Johns Hopkins University, classifies the consequences of commercial sexual exploitation into categories of harm (Lederer 2000). Health hazards include AIDS, PID (pelvic inflammatory disease), venereal disease, other sexually transmitted diseases, and infertility. Physical hazards include physical violence, battery, assault, rape, forced drugging, unwanted pregnancy, and drug addiction. Women have testified to being beaten across the back near the kidneys, incredibly painful but undamaging to their appearance. Others sport cigarette burns on their arms. Sometimes they are given drugs such as heroin or ecstasy to boost compliance. Women also face psychological hazards, such as mind/body separation, hatred of men, distrust, emotional impairment, loss of childhood, and drug addiction. Lastly, sexual exploitation gives rise to social problems for its victims, including discrimination, alienation, and ostracism. In addition to these harms suffered by the victims of trafficking, research shows that sex trafficking is a driving force in the global spread of AIDS.

The Global Sex Trade: A Question of Supply and Demand

The recruitment of women into the sex trade is driven by a single factor: the global demand for sex purchased by men. Overwhelmingly, men are the purchasers, and women are the goods or objects in the transaction. As Simone de Beauvoir stated in her discussion of how women have internalized their inferiority: "Woman has to learn that exchanges—it is a fundamental law of political economy—are based on the value the merchandise offered has for the buyer" (1992: 201). Today, women's labor and bodies are important goods in a globalized world economy. Within the European Union and other free trade zones, the fact that the free circulation of goods includes the movement of women's bodies reveals the extent to which women are treated as commodities. Even amid the heightened border security of the post-September 11 world, in which immigrants and refugees face more difficulties gaining access to the more economically advanced industrialized democracies, those who trade women across borders operate with relative impunity.

To the men who purchase their services, these women and girls are just bodies (Irigaray 1992: 210). It does not matter that they are enslaved; sex for money is a business transaction. This perspective is evident in Internet chat room discussions on sites such as the World Sex Guide. Website postings reveal how little thought is given to the women, their circumstances, and their rights. The right to sex is paramount and prostitution is a commodity exchange. On some websites, specific prostitutes are rated based on their bodies and their attitudes, that is, willingness to engage in various sex acts. The business of sex reflects broader trends in economic development. As a country's economy develops, native women are less likely to work in the sex trade, and a market emerges for women from abroad. In South Korea, for example, since the 1950s, dozens of bars and strip clubs have catered to American soldiers stationed in military bases there. As Korea's economy improved, Korean women had other economic opportunities, and fewer went to work in the sex trade. Bar owners became desperate for new women and appealed to government bureaucrats to import sex workers. Canada, facing similar shortages, had a special visa category for "exotic dancers" (Macklin 2003).

Imported sex workers come largely from developing countries, which includes countries from the former Soviet Bloc where few economic opportunities exist for women, destabilizing the First World/Third World and North/South dichotomies. In countries such as the Netherlands and

Germany where prostitution is legal, most sex workers are foreigners. In the Netherlands, prostitutes come from more than thirty-two countries, most trafficked in from Central and Eastern Europe. In Germany, 75 percent of the 400,000 women thought to be involved in prostitution are foreigners. Eighty percent of those women are from Central and Eastern European countries (Malarek 2003: 203). Critics claim that traffickers control most of the women in prostitution in these countries.

In addition to women being imported to rich countries, men travel the world in search of sex. With the Internet, travelers to any part of the world can access reviews of escort agencies, get directions to recommended brothels, and know how much to expect to pay for various sexual services. Men boast about their encounters in Web forums and exchange opinions about where to find the best sex. With this kind of information readily available, not to mention the tantalizing photos posted on the Web by pimps worldwide, sex tours are flourishing in dozens of countries. Men, who for a variety of reasons would not pay for sex at home, feel uninhibited when traveling to foreign lands. Some men go abroad seeking sex with teenagers or even children, actions considered criminal in their own countries.

A particular example of men going overseas for sex occurs when military forces and peacekeeping troops are stationed in a particular location. Bars and brothels spring up to cater to them, offering local and imported women for sexual services. Soldiers getting sex abroad is an old phenomenon, widely condoned by military officials. More disturbing is the connection to trafficking. The explosion of the sex trade in former Yugoslavia—largely due to the arrival of NATO forces, UN peacekeepers, and members of the UN International Police Task Force (IPTF)—is thought to have been supplied mainly by trafficked women from other parts of Eastern Europe and the former Soviet Union. Women brought into custody after their brothels were raided testified that these members of the international community were their main customers, and that they "regularly" had sex with IPTF policemen, usually without being paid as the IPTF were in positions of authority. Even worse, there is evidence that some of these men were actively promoting the trafficking of women and girls by forging identity documents, helping to smuggle them into Bosnia, and tipping off bar owners about impending raids. Most seriously, international police and soldiers actually bought and sold young women for as little as $800 and kept them locked in their own apartments for use as sex slaves.

Evidence of this has been brought to light in testimony before the US Congress as well as in wrongful dismissal lawsuits brought by whistle blowers against their former employers. One plaintiff testified that he had witnessed coworkers and supervisors "buying and selling women for their own personal enjoyment," some of whom even bragged about "the various ages and talents of the individual slaves they had purchased" (Malarek 2003: 173). Despite the evidence against them, none of the men who purchased women ever faced any criminal sanctions. That anyone would engage in the buying and selling of other human beings is appalling. That persons in positions of authority, who are ostensibly in the region to help the residents would carry out such conduct, is even worse.

In this section, we saw how the sex trade operates in a globalized world. Women from developing countries are brought to wealthier parts of the world. And men visit the Global South in search of cheap sex. The importation of sex workers and the exportation of wealthy clients seeking sex both foster trafficking. Traffickers see the demand and profit by providing the "supply." Sadly, the "supply" is considered by business owners as a commodity rather than as human beings with rights. Trafficking eliminates their voice and their agency, because trafficked persons are all but invisible in the wider societies in which they live. This invisibility is explored in the following section.

The Gendered Construction of the "Other" Woman: Forms of Silencing and Reification

To outsiders, trafficked women have been virtually invisible and their plight unheard. Their reification (or commodification) and their silencing are implemented through various strategies identified below.

Incarceration and Displacement

Except for the street trade, trafficked women are held behind locked doors in apartments, brothels, massage parlors, and bars. Even the street trade is under constant surveillance by pimps. As Michel Foucault demonstrated in his *History of Sexuality* (1978), the same technologies of power (i.e., the "panoptikon" and forms of surveillance) control the body of women for the purpose of reproduction, as well as for the purpose of their economic and sexual exploitation. Those technologies of power keep women under the watchful eye and punishing hand of the owner/trader. However, to the casual observer, trafficked women blend in seamlessly with the women who have "chosen" to exchange money for sex. Traffickers move the women frequently to prevent them from being detected, to keep them from developing attachments to clients who might become interested in their stories, and to provide customers with a "fresh" supply of women (Goodson 2003: 24).

Poverty and Deprivation

Clients of the sex trade seem oblivious to the plight of young women who are being held against their will. They may rationalize their behavior by claiming that they are paying money for services, providing an income to someone who might not otherwise have one. As one user of the World Sex Guide asserted when accused of using sex slaves: "These chicks are poor and I'm helping to feed their family" (accessed from World Sex Guide website 2 August 2004). Yet, for girls who have been trafficked into the sex trade, it is unlikely that they will keep much if any of the money they earn. Other users argue that men need sex—"it is how they are built"— even claiming that prostitution reduces the incidence of rape. Users of the sex trade also resort to "othering" to justify their behavior. Terms such as "whore," "hooker," and "slut" are used to objectify, commodify, and then dismiss the victims. Officers in Bosnia referred to trafficked women as "whores seeking a free ride home" (Malarek 2003: 164). In the bars in Bangkok women and girls do not have names; they have numbers pinned to their skimpy clothes. The men pick them by number. They are literally interchangeable sexual objects.

Religious and Patriarchal Constructs of Foreign Women

This "othering" is exacerbated by the fact that clients frequent prostitutes from foreign lands. Better to use other, foreign women than those who share an identity and a language with the user. In their arguments to the Korean government, club owners claimed that importing foreign women would help to keep American soldiers from sexually harassing innocent Korean women. An egregious example of the reliance on foreigners in the sex trade can be found in Israel. Leah Guenpeter-Gold, Co-Director of the Awareness Center, a nongovernmental organization focused on prostitution and trafficking of women in Israel, is particularly offended by the orthodox Jews who crowd into brothels on Fridays just before the Sabbath. She claims this practice has been widespread: "[b]ecause these women are not [viewed as] human beings. They are foreign women. The religious prefer it to be with foreign women because then they don't wrong Jewish women" (Malarek 2003: 78). Similarly, foreign women largely stock brothels in the Persian Gulf countries, because it is viewed as a crime to put Muslim women in the flesh trade.

In many societies, native women are perceived as the guardians of hereditary values, property, and racial purity, and the bearers and mothers of future generations. Religious teachings may prohibit certain sexual practices that are deemed "against nature" (i.e., masturbation, sodomy), particularly those which are not intended for procreation, such as when the semen is "wasted." For example in the Bible, the Book of Leviticus prohibits sexual relations with menstruating or pregnant women. However, fornication with a woman slave or a slave who is the concubine of a friend is not defined as a sin (Gerard 1989: 784–788). Following this logic, sex with foreign women and prohibited practices are seen as helping to maintain the purity of one's own women.

Patriarchal Construction of Exoticism and "Promiscuity" of Foreign Women

Foreigners are also constructed as exotic and promiscuous. Racialized and ethnic differences are critical components of the sex tourism industry. "Otherness" becomes a source of desire for clients (Kempadoo 1998). Within Europe, Slavonic women in particular are viewed as alluring and sexy, and also as having patience and low self-esteem. Agencies play on these stereotypes of Slavonic women, referring to all of them as Russian and calling them all "Natasha." According to the promotional literature from an Odessa agency that arranges sex tours for Western men, "Slavonic women have always been remarkable for their obedience and willingness to fulfil any wish. Time, spent with our girl, will stay in your mind and you will often remember it with satisfaction and pleasure" (Malarek 2003: 90). Such marketing promotes images of women who lack independence and the ability to think for themselves, just what clients wish to hear.

Patriarchal Global Complicities

The "otherness" is not limited to relations between user and victim. It is manifest in the enforcement, or lack thereof, against traffickers. Judges and police officers often identify more with the accused male than with the female victim. As a result, they may simply refuse to believe the victim. Consider the case of an Albanian judge ruling on an allegation against an Albanian bar owner whose accuser is a woman from Moldova who does not speak his language. From the judge's perspective, a young woman of the worst reputation is challenging his religion, his people, and his culture. Moreover, the bar owner is a wealthy, upstanding member of the community, whose profits are helping to finance the Kosovo Liberation Army (Malarek 2003: 133). What are the chances that the judge will side with the accuser?

For victims of trafficking, their chances for justice are all the more remote when, in addition to not being able to speak the local language, they are viewed by clients and authority figures as less than human. The rationalizations of the clients and the "othering" of the victims, combined with a level of misogyny still present in many parts of the world, helps to explain how men feel entitled to rape, kidnap, and torture young women, and why governments and police forces systematically turn a blind eye to these practices.

Combating Reification and Silencing:
Reclaiming Voice and Agency

Trafficking is an attractive crime because the profits are huge, and traffickers operate with relative impunity. If they are caught, they often get off with lighter sentences than if they had been transporting weapons or drugs. To add insult to injury, many women caught in police raids are usually treated as criminals rather than victims. They are often convicted on immigration charges and may be deported back to their country of origin. According to the Organization for Security and Cooperation in Europe (OSCE), significant numbers of women who are repatriated are subsequently retrafficked (OSCE 2004). Trafficking in human beings is a crime. It is a serious human rights' violation, not a question of illegal migration.

What can be done to reduce the incidences of trafficking in persons around the world? There is growing awareness of this transnational crime, but effective initiatives to combat it have been slow to emerge. Below, we briefly examine several initiatives against trafficking in persons, including international efforts, national level legislation, nongovernmental and individual actions.

On the international level, trafficking in persons has become an issue of global policy significance. Most notably, in November 2000, the United Nations passed the "Protocol to Prevent, Suppress and Punish Trafficking in Persons, Especially Women and Children." To date, 117 countries have signed the treaty, and ninety-seven have gone on to ratify it. It entered into force on 25 December 2003.[2] In September 2002, the European Conference on Preventing and Combating Trafficking in Human Beings was organized by the International Organization for Migration (IOM), in cooperation with the European Commission, European Parliament, and European Union Member States and Candidate Countries. The IOM is a key player in this area. In addition to research and dissemination about trafficking, it works with NGOs, international organizations, and government agencies to provide shelter and assistance for victims of trafficking, offers counselling and assistance to trafficked migrants in transit and receiving countries, and offers voluntary return and reintegration assistance to trafficked migrants.

Trafficking is a global problem, with victims and perpetrators moving across international borders. Yet enforcement is usually domestic, based on national laws and local policies. Laws regarding trafficking vary from country to country; some states lack specific trafficking laws altogether. In order to have any impact, international efforts must be supplemented by national level policies. It is beyond the scope of this paper to consider these in any detail, so we mention only the most prominent example. In October 2000, the passage of the Victims of Trafficking and Violence Protection Act by the United States Congress was a hopeful sign that the United States was going to crack down on trafficking. Under this law, the US Department of State publishes an annual report outlining how countries are dealing with trafficking issues.[3] These reports, while criticized for being an extension of US foreign policy interests, do at least draw significant attention to the problem of trafficking in persons.

In general, legislation should be based on two core principles: (1) criminalization of the act of trafficking and prosecution of the traffickers, and (2) protection of victims of trafficking. According to Michele Ann Clark, Co-Director of the Protection Project in Washington, D.C., "[t]he recognition of the trafficked person as a victim of a crime is a necessary step to ensuring their protection, as well as their entitlement to fundamental rights as set out by international law" (2004: 16). For example, in places where prostitution is illegal, trafficked women should not be prosecuted for engaging in the sex trades.

From Goods to Human Beings: Reclaiming Status as Subjects

Granting trafficked women residency status instead of deporting them would be a positive step. These are reasonable requirements, and governments are slowly adopting them. Italy has become the only country that does not require victims to testify against their alleged traffickers in court in order to receive a temporary residence permit.

International and national level initiatives are insufficient, but they represent a start. The real challenge is changing behavior on the ground. The international community can pass treaties, covenants, and protocols against trafficking, but traffickers and pimps will not change their behavior unless they are seriously punished for their actions. Traffickers bribe officials to look the other way, and sometimes the bribes are free sexual services. Not only does this guarantee impunity for the criminals, but also communicates to trafficked women that there is no way out. According to the US State Department Country Reports on Human Rights in 2002, police corruption is said to be particularly bad in Bulgaria, Belarus, Georgia, Moldova, Ukraine, and Russia, as well as in Greece and Israel. Corruption, complicity, complacency are all demonstrated by government officials, the police, border guards, and court officials in countries of origin, transit, and destination.

In brief, the financial incentives for trafficking must be reduced. In addition, attitudes must change on the ground. Even the best legislation will have limited impact if social discourse, norms of acceptability and customs do not evolve as well. In their testimony before the US Congress, the Co-Directors of the Protection Project asserted:

What is often overlooked in regard to successful enforcement of even the best pieces of legislation is that not only must the law itself be changed to impose liability on customers of sexual services and on patrons of places where trafficked women may be forced into prostitution; but, more importantly, to reform the functional equivalent of the law, that is, the customs, traditions, and acceptable behaviour. Countries that tolerate, accommodate, or normalize prostitution should review their policies and inquire into whether such tolerance, accommodation, and normalization contribute to the rising numbers of trafficking victims (Smith and Mattar 2004: 171–2).

Attitudes toward women in general must change, as well as toward a man's right to sex. The commodification of women stems from views that women are subservient, and that their bodies are expendable.

A comprehensive understanding of issues surrounding trafficking must be interdisciplinary. Interdisciplinarity requires the contextualization of the current situation in terms of historical, economic, political, and social factors, considering that traffickers operate within specific contexts. Interdisciplinarity requires that analysis be conducted from a gendered perspective, in which women themselves sometimes abet men in trafficking. An interdisciplinary approach to trafficking is conducive to the decriminalization of trafficked women and opens the way to their empowerment. Moreover, their trafficking experiences should be grounds for asylum in the countries where they reside. The practice of slotting/"slutting" women into oppositional categories such as "prostitute," or "refugee" must be overcome. Besides, differences do not necessarily entail oppositions (Jay 1992). Finally, as Mikhail Bakhtin forcefully argued: "A subject as such cannot be perceived and studied as a thing, for as a subject it cannot while remaining a subject, become voiceless, and consequently, cognition of it can only be dialogic" (1986a: 162), meaning that human beings are all subjects and under no circumstances could be treated as objects, therefore their voices which convey their worldviews have to be heard in all their complexity.

Reclaiming Voice and Identity at the Individual Level

National and international level anti-trafficking efforts seem but a drop in the ocean and leave one wondering why more is not being done. More hopeful signs can be found in the actions of nongovernmental organizations and individuals. Grassroots activists are working to improve women's rights by educating the public more broadly, counseling women who have been trafficked, and drawing attention to the costs of trafficking, not only to the victims but also to the wider communities whose young, productive members are lost. A number of nonprofit organizations exist solely to monitor issues of trafficking and human rights. Some of them, such as the Awareness Center in Tel Aviv and the Protection Project in Washington, have been mentioned in this chapter.

In addition, there are many cases of individual bravery and determination to help trafficked victims. People have risked their livelihoods and even their lives in trying to see justice brought to victims of trafficking. Take the case of Gordon Moon, an officer with the Ontario Provincial Police who enlisted with the UN for a stint in Kosovo. He established the first Trafficking in Prostitution Investigation Unit in Kosovo. Supported by peacekeeping troops, his unit raided brothels and rescued young women from appalling living conditions. Though he felt sorry not to have helped more people, in six short months his efforts enabled the rescue of close to three hundred women. Another inspiring example of courage is found in Don Cesare, a Roman Catholic priest who runs Regina Pacis, a safe house on the Adriatic coast of southern Italy, just forty-four nautical miles from Albania. Formerly a summer camp, the compound he runs is heavily guarded and houses about ninety women from various parts of Eastern Europe, all of whom were smuggled into Italy by Albanian traffickers. Over the past ten years, he estimates that he has helped more than one thousand women.

At all levels, it is important to create a forum for women who have suffered from trafficking to speak, to give them a voice and agency, to combat any form of reification of body and silencing of voice, to strive to eliminate any context that leads to abuse of power. Advocates are very important aids in helping the voices of victimized women slowly emerge from an abject silencing. Spurred by research for *The Natashas* and bolstered by the television and print publicity surrounding its publication, Victor Malarek's advocacy against trafficking has helped to create a space in which women can reclaim their voices, and ultimately, their identities.

Conclusion

In this chapter, we have focused specifically on the trafficking of women and girls from Eastern Europe, Russia, and parts of the former Soviet Union, particularly of Ukraine. Their plight is the result of particular socioeconomic circumstances of the region, but their victimization also stems directly from the demand for purchased sex by men who cause physical and emotional suffering to thousands of "Natashas" around the world. The psychological damage of involuntarily working in the sex trades is compounded by the denial of their individual and ethnic identities as well as by the isolation experienced by not being able to communicate in the local language.

Trafficking is a global problem, affecting women and children (including boys) from many parts of the world who are forced to work in intolerable conditions. Traffickers take advantage of desperation, preying on economic hardship as well as on humanitarian crises. The costs of trafficking are high, not only for the victims but also for the wider society. Trafficking deprives communities of human capital, contributes to the breakdown of social structures in communities, and increases the strength of organized crime interests.

Clearly, much remains to be done in terms of combating trafficking in persons. Increased global attention to trafficking in persons is an important first step. We know what actions must be taken to crack down on trafficking.[4] The challenge for international and national level actors is to find the means, *and the will*, to pursue them. The United States has generated a lot of attention toward the issue with its annual publication of the Trafficking in Persons reports, but reports should not become substitutes for action. At present, there is a gap between public discourse and action, with American political interests trumping the will to seriously combat trafficking. Research must lead to action, not merely create the illusion of action. Only then will trafficked women be able to take crucial steps toward reconstructing their own identities.

Notes

1. This chapter is largely based on Victor Malarek's book *The Natashas: The New Global Sex Trade* (Toronto: Viking 2003), with additional research added so as to better interpret the issue of trafficking from an interdisciplinary feminist perspective.

2. Further information about the "Protocol to Prevent, Suppress and Punish Trafficking in Persons, Especially Women and Children, supplementing the United Nations Convention against Transnational Organized Crime," can be found online.

3. The annual *Trafficking in Persons Reports* can be accessed on the website of the U.S. Department of State.

4. At its fifty-ninth session on 6 April 2006, the UNHCR issued "Guidelines on International Protection: Relating to the Status of Refugees to Victims of Trafficking and Persons at Risk of Being Trafficked" HCR/GIP/06/07. These guidelines, for the first time, recognize that forms of severe abuse inherent to trafficking (e.g., abduction, forcible or deceptive recruitment, rape, sexual enslavement, removal of organs) can be recognized as constituting serious human rights violations and are often a form of gender-related violence, which *"will generally amount to persecution"* (par. 15 and 19). The guidelines cover such areas as retrafficking, reprisals, or fear of reprisals inflicted on victims or a victim's family members as also amounting to persecution. The guidelines underline that states must also ensure that legal mechanisms are in place to ensure the accessibility of protection to the victims. While guidelines do not have legal enforcement powers, they provide crucial interpretative legal guidance for governments, decision makers, and legal practitioners as well as the judiciary, in addition to UNHCR's own fieldworkers (*Women's Asylum News* 59, April 2006, 6–7).

Significantly, on 13 May 2006, the Canadian Council of Refugees welcomed the announcement by the Canadian Government's Minister of Citizenship and Immigration of measures that would provide emergency protection to trafficked persons in Canada. The measures ensure trafficked persons will be treated as victims of crime rather than people who should be detained and deported.

4

Reconstituting the Subject

FEMINIST POLITICS OF HUMANITARIAN ASSISTANCE

Jennifer Hyndman and Malathi de Alwis

Introduction

This chapter examines specific ways in which gender relations and identities of displaced women are reshaped by humanitarian aid programs in
Sri Lanka. First, we explore the theoretical and practical stakes of focusing
on "women-based," "gender-based," or "feminist" approaches to conceptualizing humanitarian programs. Second, we illustrate how various forms
of humanitarian assistance by nongovernmental organizations conceive
of the displaced persons, either as beneficiaries of their programs or as
participants in training courses that aim to enhance employment prospects. Training programs in trades such as masonry, carpentry, and tractor repair for men displaced by the war in Sri Lanka reinforce gender
norms, but where offered to women, they destabilize existing gender relations, arguably opening up new spaces for women. In contrast, programs
that conceive of women as "beneficiaries" tend not to challenge existing
gender identities and, in one example, actually reinforce the stigma of
widowhood. The chapter is based on fieldwork and interviews in 1999
and 2000 with various staff at both national and international humanitarian agencies and with the people who received the training.

Reconstituting the Subject: Displaced Women
and Humanitarian Assistance in Sri Lanka

Assumptions about gender relations between men and women and gender identities (what it means to be a man or a woman) are woven through

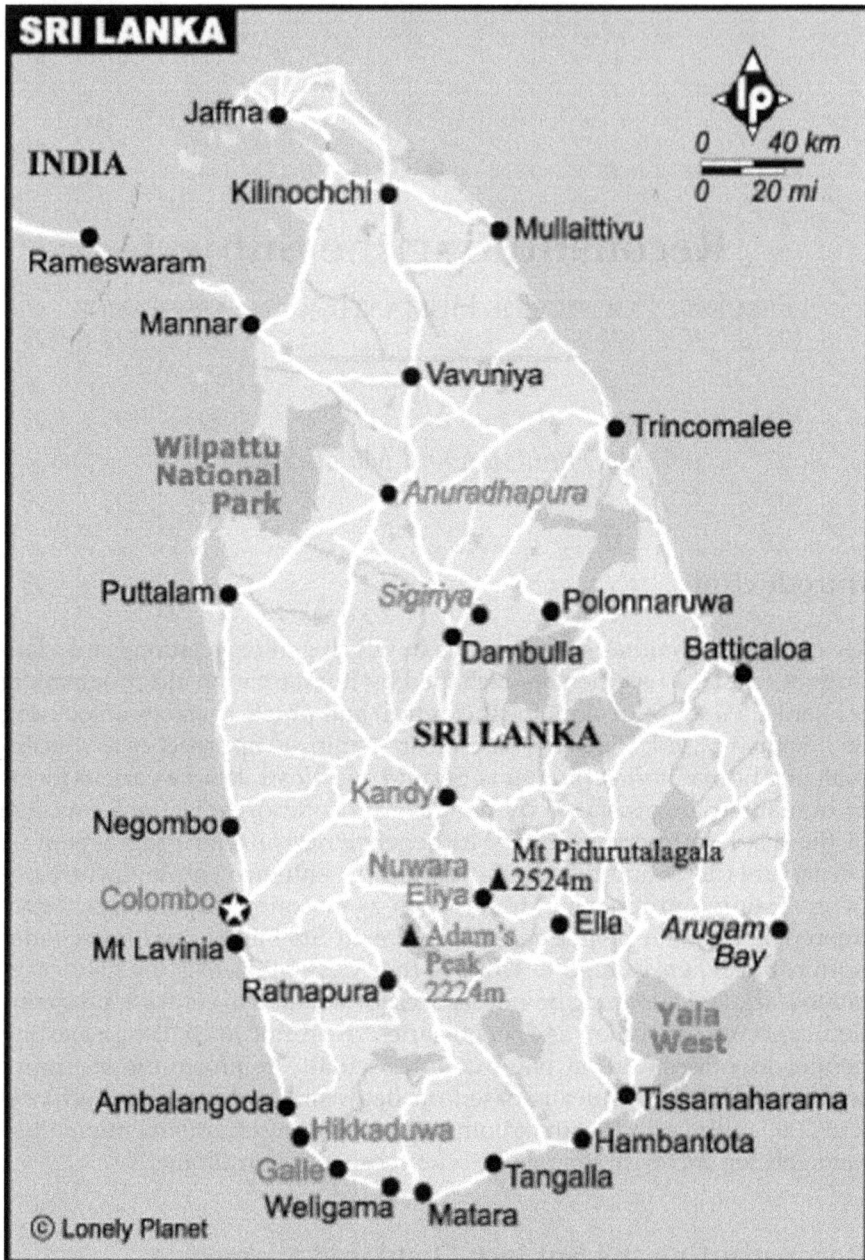

Map 4.1: *Map of Sri Lanka.*
Source: Lonely Planet http://www.lonelyplanet.com/
mapshells/indian_subcontinent/sri_lanka/sri_lanka.htm

the social fabric of a given place. Where people in a particular place are affected by violent conflict and displacement, these relationships are interrupted, changed, and adapted. Furthermore, where external aid for displaced persons is provided, it too introduces distinct gender norms, expectations, and relations that may vary from local ones. This chapter examines specific ways in which the gender identities of displaced women are shaped by humanitarian aid programs in Sri Lanka. Conflict and related human displacement in Sri Lanka tend to destabilize social relations, including those of gender. These conditions normally increase economic hardship for women (and men) and raise levels of vulnerability, particularly in relation to sexual assault against women. The destabilization of gender relations and identities, however, also opens up new spaces to transform gender relations.

Humanitarian and development assistance represent a matrix of practices, language, rules, and resources that often tacitly and unwittingly shape what it means to be a displaced woman by determining who fits into the category of "displaced," and how assistance will be provided to those within that group. Agencies delivering humanitarian programs can reinforce existing gender roles and conventional gender divisions of labor, or bend gender relations and identities by introducing alternatives through training programs and development initiatives. This chapter analyzes examples of both, arguing that the latter approach is feminist and provides a potentially less militarized option in the context of war.

After a brief note on methods and on the political context of Sri Lanka, we begin with a critique of the ways in which gender is employed within humanitarian and development circles in Sri Lanka. We reiterate our argument that gender has ceased to have much analytical meaning within the context of development and humanitarian organizations (Hyndman and de Alwis 2003). Instead, we contend, it has become part of a formula for successful funding applications and a tokenized requirement of humanitarian programs. One might consider this gender inclusion a sign of success for feminist politics, but we illustrate that only lip service is paid to the category "gender" with little recognition of the power relations to which it refers. A more comprehensive feminist approach to such programs takes gender into consideration but also attends to other bases of marginalization and/or displacement, such as ethnicity, ability, sexuality, caste, and age.

Displaced persons in Sri Lanka are not legally "refugees" as they are located in their home country, albeit one characterized by conflict over the past two decades. It is interesting to note, however, that people who are displaced are often referred to as "refugees" in Sri Lanka. In some cases, displaced persons in Sri Lanka were refugees in India and returned during a period of relative peace, only to be displaced again within the country. Hence the reference to refugees in the current context underscores a continuum of displacement across borders.[1]

Below, we illustrate the contrasting ways in which gender is deployed as a category for various "beneficiaries" and "trainees" in areas of Sri Lanka affected by conflict and chronic displacement. Specifically, we highlight two distinct approaches utilized by international nongovernmental organizations (NGOs) to assist displaced persons, especially women.

The Research: Methods and Context

The research was conducted by both authors over a period of two years, from January 1999 to December 2000. We concentrated on the districts of Trincomalee, Batticaloa, and Ampara, in the Eastern Province of Sri Lanka and on the Wanni region in the north. All these areas have been intensely affected by both conflict and widespread displacement.

We were unable to include the northern peninsula of Jaffna in our study due to high levels of insecurity at the time and no access to transportation to that location. In each of the regions, we met with people affected by displacement and assisted by community leaders, members of community-based organizations, and senior and junior staff in the branch offices of international, national, or local NGOs, working in development and humanitarian assistance. We visited each region at least twice over the research period. In Colombo, we conducted more formal interviews with country representatives and program officers in the head offices of international and national NGOs, while also engaging in extensive library and archival research at these offices where possible. Due to the instability of the political situation at the time and the sensitivity of issues addressed, we decided not to use a tape recorder or a formal questionnaire in our meetings. We nevertheless took detailed written notes, including specific information and quotes, gleaned from our conversations and meetings in order to preserve the accuracy of our information.

From February 2002 to January 2008, a precarious ceasefire between Tamil rebels and the Government of Sri Lanka held. War between the Liberation Tigers of Tamil Eelam (hereafter LTTE) and the Government of Sri Lanka's armed forces has, however, resumed and been waged for twenty-five years. The conflict has spawned large-scale displacement within the country and well beyond its borders, where a significant Tamil diaspora has emerged. The death toll now exceeds 70,000. Mass displacement, multiple displacements, long-term displacement, and attacks on communities of displaced persons amid intense militarization across the country, present massive challenges to both national and international organizations positioned to address the human needs they generate. Displaced persons include Tamil, Sinhalese, and Muslim groups, though the vast majority of displaced persons in Sri Lanka are Tamil. Although a ceasefire signed in 2002 is still in force, escalating violations have continuously prevented peace talks from reaching an effective resolution (United Nations Department of Public Information 2007).

Many Sri Lankans and Sri Lankan scholars, whose work spans several decades, have provided incisive analyses about developments within the country. Sri Lanka's present situation is an expression of a long history of conflict and struggle that cannot be covered in depth in this chapter (see Abeysekera and Gunasinghe 1987; Committee for Rational Development 1984; Jayawardena 1985; Jeganathan and Ismail 1995; Spencer 1990). Discriminatory measures in the fields of education, employment, and use of language were introduced after Sri Lanka's independence from Britain in 1948 and denied equal rights to the Tamil minority, giving rise to a fervent Tamil nationalism. "The failure of successive Sinhalese-dominated Sri Lankan governments to implement agreements with Tamil leaders saw the deterioration of relations between the two communities" (Refugee Council 2002: 4). Sinhalese nationalism has emerged just as ardently in Sri Lanka in response to the brutal violence and killing that the LTTE have waged upon civilians, both randomly and on strategic targets. Having provided this brief backdrop to contextualize our study, we now turn to theoretical and practical concerns related to assistance for displaced persons.

Beyond Gender, a Feminist Approach

Gender analysis alone is insufficient for theorizing power relations, identities, and experiences of men and women, especially in conflict affected areas. We contend that a thoroughly feminist analysis must incorporate *multiple* bases of identity and social relations, those related not exclusively to gender (Hyndman and de Alwis 2003). A feminist analysis provides a more powerful lens with which to examine the place of women and men, and a more compelling position from which to transform relations that provoke or perpetuate violence, hate, and inequality. The intersection of one's class, caste, religion, sexuality, nationality and/or race, and membership in social groups *produces* different gender relations across time and space. Gender is but one constitutive dimension of both men's and women's identities, their security, and their material well being under intense conditions of political instability. National identities are inevitably intertwined with gender, and prove to be at least as important as gender identities in analyzing relations of vulnerability and disparity among Sri Lankans. Insofar as gender has been integrated into development parlance, it has ceased to be a rigorous analytical concept within humanitarian and development organizations operating in Sri Lanka.

Gender has become something of a household word among development practitioners. Among those agencies and staff providing humanitarian assistance to people affected by conflict, gender is also a buzzword, but its integration into everyday operations is less apparent. In Sri Lanka, humanitarian agencies and development organizations work side by side in the country's northern and eastern provinces. Most people working in these organizations at senior levels know well that gender does not simply refer to women. They have come to understand that gender is a relational concept that juxtaposes femininity and masculinity, women's work and men's work, and varies across cultures. When it comes to integrating a gender analysis into humanitarian assistance, however, the ways in which gender relations and identities change in conjunction with the war economy and with competing Sinhalese and Tamil nationalisms, are rarely mentioned. The centers of prostitution that are generated around new army bases at the frontlines of the war and the mothers' movements that emerge as soldiers' lives are endangered by the war, do not fit inside the "gender box"; hence they are often ignored (de Alwis and Hyndman 2002). Gender is treated as a portable tool of analysis and empowerment that can be carried around in the back pockets of both international humanitarian and development staff. It has become part of the development and humanitarian aid lexicon, to be *included* in all proposals and evaluations, but without *analytical* integration of the power relations gender entails. Our objective in this chapter is to move beyond gender in this context and re-introduce a feminist analytical approach that engages disparate power relations inherent in both humanitarian and development work.

The ways in which gender has been conceived, practiced, and disseminated within development and humanitarian fields are a source of concern. In this analysis, we do not aim to criticize specific organizations or staff who participate in this pervasive lexicon and related practices. Rather, we have argued that a comprehensive and still portable feminist analytic approach or analysis provides a more sophisticated approach to understanding the *production* of gender identities and relations among displaced persons (Hyndman and de Alwis 2003). The idea that gender identities and relations are generated differently across space and time, and have no essential preordained qualities, is critical to changing them. This feminist analytic approach or analysis, then, is not only a tool for understanding social, economic, and political relations, but also for changing them.

We define "feminist" as analyses and political interventions that address the unequal and often violent relationships among people based on real or perceived social, economic, political, cultural, and sexual differences. The analysis and elimination of patriarchal or masculinist relations of power within each of these fields is a major, but not exclusive focus. There is more than one kind of feminism, and we do not wish to fix the category "feminist" in any singular manner nor to create a typology of feminisms. We contend that gender analysis has fallen prey to such rigidities, thus limiting its analytical strength (Hyndman and de Alwis 2003).

Gender remains a central concern of feminist politics and thought. However, its primacy over other social, economic, cultural, and political locations is not fixed across time and place. Daiva Stasiulis (1999: 194, 196) elaborates on the importance of relationship, position, and "relational positionality" to feminist politics, "They refer to the multiple relations of power that intersect in complex ways to position individuals and collectivities in shifting and often contradictory locations within geopolitical spaces, historical narratives, and movement politics. . . . Central to my interpretation of relational positionality is also a rejection of poststructuralist deconstructions that deny the material bases for power relations, however complicated their discursive representations." We agree with Stasiulis to an extent, though argue that poststructuralist analyses do not categorically deny the material bases of power relations. A poststructuralist analysis can reveal the very processes by which particular constellations of power are effaced or naturalized (Butler 1992). For example, Geraldine Pratt (2004) refutes the claim that poststructuralist theories immobilize feminism by arguing that they urge us toward concrete rather than metaphysical analyses:

> Whether feminism as a social movement is successful in articulating other liberation struggles within the category, woman, is something that is decided through political struggle and not only or finally through philosophical debate. . . . [W]e would expect the feminist movement to be increasingly emptied of its singular focus on woman, and possibly rethought around a broader critique of the production of social difference and the multiple exclusions enacted by dominant groups and institutions. (Pratt: 62)

She goes on to illustrate the ways in which Filipina migrant women admitted to Canada as caregivers are constructed in state discourse as compared to that of human rights and Canadian values, invoked by these same women to reposition themselves and unsettle dominant representations by the state and others. Likewise, a feminist poststructuralist analysis can expose the ways in which the refugee or displaced subject is constituted within particular constellations of practices, such as those employed by development and humanitarian organizations.

Gender policies in humanitarian organizations provide a *grid of intelligibility* for staff working with displaced populations. They furnish concepts and checklists to assist in the organization and functioning of camps, but they do not generally allow dimensions of gender or culture to change the assumptions of the overall planning framework in which field staff work. Historical context, regional geopolitics, cultural dynamics, and gender relations are left for field workers to "fill in" once in the field. Such policies are flawed because they do not take these "variables"—historical arrangements, proximate politics, and so on—as integral to all operations (Hyndman 1998).

In practice, gender policies and programs implemented by nongovernmental organizations or UN agencies produce specific gender relations and serve to reconstitute the refugee or displaced subject in specific ways. This is not to suggest that displaced women in Sri Lanka are without agency. In destabilizing social relations and conventional gender roles, conditions of conflict open up spaces that *change* societal expectations of women and men and transform gender norms. Such transformations rely in part upon the willingness of men and women to initiate and participate in such efforts and upon agencies that assist them. How humanitarian and development agencies conceive of and organize change creates specific subject positions that *situate* people, allowing them differing degrees of intention and constraint. Let us illustrate what we mean.

What's in a Name?: "Participants" versus "Beneficiaries"

In relation to income generation programs for displaced persons, we found basically two major humanitarian approaches to strengthening economic security. On the one hand, several international nongovernmental organizations (NGOs) provided small loans to targeted groups through microcredit projects. On the other, agencies offered skills training and on-the-job experience to specific groups (de Alwis and Hyndman 2002). The former approach allows NGOs to spend funds and implement the assistance more easily than the latter, especially in relation to gender goals. Our research also found that women, whose husbands were missing in action or away for extended periods, identified themselves as widows so that they could participate in such programs. Providing credit to widows for small business development or household food production that enhances self sufficiency is a much more straightforward task than, for example, changing societal perceptions about what kinds of work women can do and what kinds of places single women can occupy. We return to assistance for displaced "widows" later.

The work of skills training focuses on the transformation of gender norms and on the improvement of human capital, with the more practical aim of enhancing employment prospects. We found this approach to be the mainstay of one INGO, World University Services of Canada (hereafter WUSC). WUSC's four year plan outlines systematic efforts to improve gender equity—among other goals—and represents a systematic and long term strategy to invoke a gender analysis in all of its programming. WUSC (with funding from the Canadian International Development Agency, CIDA, and the United Nations High Commissioner for Refugees, UNHCR) has provided funds for courses in welding, bicycle repair, carpentry, and tractor repair in Trincomalee, Batticaloa, and Vavuniya. The courses are delivered in concert with local institutions that specialize in teaching these subjects. This kind of assistance is nothing particularly new, except that many of these classes are filled exclusively with young women. Other classes mix young men and women together, although our research found that women were less comfortable in mixed classrooms and less likely to finish their training if they represented a minority in the class.

One of the most productive aspects of WUSC's skills training program or "Project for Rehabilitation through Education and Training" (hereafter PRET) initiative, is the careful conceptualization and evaluation of every aspect of the program as well as the organization's commitment to learn from its mistakes and to constantly adapt to changing circumstances and needs. The PRET programs are divided into six months of classroom training and six months of on the job training, at the conclusion of which each participant is provided with a tool kit and financial incentives to start her/his own business or is helped to find employment in the region. The best students are frequently kept on at the workplaces in which they do their work experience, or hired as class instructors and demonstrators in the classes they once took. This form of skills training is also prefaced by a series of workshops that raise the gender consciousness of the program participants and supplemented by Parent Awareness Programs. Neighbor Awareness Programs have also been included at the request of some of the trainees, and Employer Awareness Programs also added, to introduce the idea of women in nontraditional sectors of the labor force. What is remarkable about this approach is its attempt to address the involvement of "unconventional" trainees and persuade a broad range of social groups that such training is beneficial. The training is not merely for the individual participants who take a particular course, but represents a broad effort to socialize and expose the immediate stakeholders to new ways of thinking about gender relations in the specific contexts of employment, family, and neighborhood. The comprehensive nature of such a strategy demonstrates a commitment to transforming social relations as well as upgrading the skills of individual men and women.

During our field work, the sight of three young Muslim women graduates of one course, welding iron gates in their home-based workshop, was indeed a concrete expression of changing attitudes about what women can do [see illustration 4.2].

In Eastern Sri Lanka, unmarried Muslim women are normally not allowed to work outside of the family home. In the case of these women, they told us that their families allowed them to take the training course, but insisted that they would have to work in a shop built onto the house of one of the young women's families after their course ended. They did just that and appeared to be patronized with considerable support by

Figure 4.2: *Muslim woman welder.*
Source: J. Hyndman

Muslim families in the area. This innovative integration of work and home spaces in order to maintain certain gender conventions, yet stretch others beyond societal expectations in Eastern Sri Lanka, is noteworthy.

We found, however, that most assistance to individuals and communities was done through microcredit schemes and associated loan programs. While this is no doubt an important component of humanitarian and/or development assistance, we find it questionable as the *main* strategy of addressing issues of gender in a context characterized by violent, ongoing conflict for at least two reasons. First, ongoing infusions of capital in actual currency can be and are diverted for other purposes by warring factions. This potentially fuels war rather than alleviating its consequences. Second, most microcredit programs do not address extant inequities and disparate gender relations.

Our research, however, found at least one promising practice of lending small amounts of money to "widows." Widows were a common group of beneficiaries, despite the heavy stigma that this term holds in Sri Lanka. On the one hand, some widows of the war are recognized and compensated by the state, making it beneficial to identify as such for purposes of securing income. In the Tamil language, however, the term widow "implies that which is inauspicious and pitiable" (Sachithanandam 1998: 191). Perhaps the most auspicious project involving widows was that implemented by the Association of Women for Action and Research (AWARE), a community-based organization in Killinochchi District where some women accepted loans from Oxfam and were able to undertake various enterprises that allowed them to earn a dowry to become marriageable again. Many women did this, though many others were afraid to take loans for fear of not being able to repay them. Already their mobility and moral integrity were questioned as "widows," they said. One might argue that using income generation programs to allow widowed women to pay dowries is a practice which runs counter to feminism. Yet, change is incremental. These women were castigated by the society in which they found themselves because they were women without socially condoned support, that is, husbands. The opportunity to recast themselves as "marriageable," however, enhanced their social status and acceptance considerably. The income earned had the potential to reintegrate them into society as more valuable members. While dowries may not be desirable from a feminist perspective, they remain socioeconomic practices which have social and material consequences for some groups of Sri Lankan women.

With the exception of AWARE, however, feminist or gender analysis in these credit schemes was absent. Our findings suggest that giving loans to women can cause resentment among men in the same community, who may not have similar access to credit. Many women took out loans on behalf of their male family members. Instead of empowering women, such loans to women can provoke a backlash among the men who want to avenge them, which in turn may exacerbate gender inequality and even generate fear within the household. Providing credit to women in and of itself is a gendered practice, but not a feminist one.

When asked directly what kinds of assistance they need, both men and women are positioned within a humanitarian (or development) discourse that shapes viable responses. That is, needs assessments and consultations are at once fraught exercises, where the universe of responses is highly conditioned by the practices and resources of humanitarian and development agencies. People predictably ask for things they know might be available in a relatively aid rich environment. Accordingly, we witnessed entire villages of women taking loans to rear goats, as an income generation strategy. In our meetings and interviews with both "beneficiaries" and NGO staff, we found that few other options were perceived to exist, despite the fact that many women had never reared goats before.

There was some evidence that microcredit programs rendered the International Nongovernmental Organizations (INGOs) that administered them susceptible to manipulation. "Beneficiaries," as they were usually called, were found to play one organization off against another, that, "CARE gave us this, so you Oxfam should also give us this." This has two potential effects: (1) that INGOs concede to groups in question without demonstrated need; and (2) that accountability is substantially reduced because funds from one organization can be used to "stand in for" funds from another organization when administrative checks and follow up is conducted. On several occasions, particularly in the Echelempattu area of Trincomalee District in Northeast Sri Lanka, no accounts or records of repayment were available for microcredit projects. Recordkeeping on loan repayments, we were told, was very difficult to obtain, especially in the LTTE controlled areas, raising the question of whether microcredit schemes were controlled by NGOs, "beneficiaries," or the LTTE authorities. The issue of sustainability also arises: to what extent does assistance create capacity for independent livelihoods? If job creation does not lead to increased economic independence after six months, does it serve to improve income security?

Clearly, microcredit schemes represent a well-intentioned attempt to relieve the symptoms of the war. At their best, they can restore self-sufficiency to those who lost it because of the war. At worst, they may serve to further fuel conflict, by infusing funds unwittingly into the war economy. It was only too apparent to us that only the resolution of the conflict in Sri Lanka could transform the structural impediments of mobility restrictions: repeated displacement, interrupted education, and related unemployment. Where such strategies may work well in peace time—when social relations of trust and stability exist—their efficacy appeared questionable in the northern and eastern parts of Sri Lanka in 1999–2000.

Our analysis calls for a rethinking of the impact of microcredit on income security initiatives, especially as they pertain to gender relations. Such initiatives cannot simply be counting exercises (i.e., how many women benefit?), but should attempt to change relationships between men and women, which remain inequitable or exhibit disparate power relations. Disparities may not be solely or even primarily based on gender. One's nation or ethnicity shapes political, economic, and social opportunities at least as much as gender. Skills training for women in tractor or bicycle repair goes a long way to transforming societal attitudes and perceptions. Their success cannot simply be counted, for example, by using employment placement after training as an indicator of achievement. If a woman completes the carpentry course but goes on to work in a garment factory (in a postwar scenario), her acquired skills and achievement serve to change perceptions of what can be done by women. We witnessed too many sewing programs for displaced women and not enough carpentry classes. The war represents a period of instability, displacement, and poverty for many of those affected, but it is also a space for potential changes in attitude, practice, and mores. Projects to improve income security cannot simply *include* a gender component in project design, implementation, and evaluation, but must begin to integrate *qualitative,* as well as quantitative measures of ascertaining project impact. Impact measurement is a buzzword in both humanitarian and development circles these days, but little discussion of the qualitative meaning of the term, if there is one, has occurred.

Concluding Note

We contend that a thoroughly feminist analysis incorporates *multiple* bases of identity and power relations, not gender exclusively. In the case of Sri Lanka, gender identity cannot be neatly separated from national identity; they are mutually constitutive. As argued elsewhere (Hyndman and de Alwis 2003), a feminist approach—one that combines multiple analytical axes contingent on time and place—provides a more powerful lens with which to examine the place of both women and men in society, and a more compelling position from which to transform relations that provoke or perpetuate violence, hate, and inequality. An abbreviated inventory of humanitarian and development practices pertaining to gender in the Sri Lankan context points to the professionalization of "gender" among development and humanitarian organizations in Sri Lanka. Nonetheless, "gender" still mistakenly stands in for "women" much of the time. Members of this category are often referred to paternalistically as "beneficiaries," a term that does not suggest transformation or change but a privatized welfare state, administered by nongovernmental organizations that stand in for government.

The understanding of gender relations and identities, introduced in the context of humanitarian and development work, does not necessarily serve displaced persons well, especially women.[2] Much of the current program initiatives need to be rethought, despite some constructive examples elucidated here. We seek, then, to reintroduce a feminist analytic approach to both humanitarian and development work, in an effort to understand and engage the displacement, insecurity, and trauma that shape people's lives.

Cross-cutting relations of gender, nation, geography, class, even birthplace, produce distinct patterns of dislocation and instability. The feminist analysis put forth here resists any one understanding of gender; instead, we highlight the ways in which gender identities and relations are produced differently through and by development and humanitarian discourses. Conflict destabilizes gender norms. While this may generate openings for women to take on new responsibilities, it also heightens uncertainty and insecurity for those displaced by war. Coupled with effective interventions and training to assist those affected, changes introduced during conflict can be transposed into a postconflict context where new notions of gender possibilities continue.

Note

1. There are some real differences between "internally displaced persons" (IDPs) and refugees, the main one being that displaced persons are still, in theory, protected by their government and refugees are not. In Sri Lanka, displaced persons do have basic rights, but many of the perks of citizenship, such as voting in an election, are suspended as long as people are away from their registered place of permanent residence. See C. Brun, "Finding a Place: Local Integration and Protracted Displacement in Sri Lanka." (Ph.D. diss., Norwegian University of Science and Technology, 2003).

2. We do not advocate the importation of Western feminist ideas of gender to replace those *in situ*. This arrogant approach suggests an orientalism that we have discussed elsewhere. See J. Hyndman and M. de Alwis, "Capacity Building, Accountability and Humanitarianism." *Forced Migration Review* 8 (2000): 16–19.

Section II

Challenging Methodologies
Challenging the Researcher

INTRODUCTION

The next four chapters analyze how theoretical assumptions are framed and reframed to take into account the context of refugee/displaced women's identities. The researchers' positioning and assumptions about uprooted women's agencies are also challenged.

Adrienne Chambon's study (chapter 5), which is grounded in a research project aimed at assessing a settlement program for refugees, reflects on what happens in the course of knowledge transmission between refugee women and researchers. Conversation and dialogue between a range of staff/volunteers and a group of women refugees was the method by which the staff/volunteers initially wanted to examine the structure of the one-on-one befriending encounters of the Canadian Center for Victims of Torture (CCVT) in Toronto. This methodology was chosen to enable them to assess and identify the less visible practices of the program. In agreement with Foucault and Bourdieu, Chambon shows how academic discipline and methodology influence the process and outcome of research. Reciprocal learning between and among staff/volunteers and refugee women was encouraged. One of the initial challenges was that the refugee participants did not have a vested interest in the objectives of the research *per se*. The research team, therefore, had to let go of their objectives and allow themselves to be engaged in conversations and dialogue that would lead to new understandings of themselves in the program and the perception of refugee women about their experience(s). Refugee women were thus given the space to shape and form the content of their experiences and points of view. In so doing, the researchers/staff were challenged as to their own feelings and "the absent presence that returns uninvited" as participants in the befriending process. Chambon traces the shifting positions and blurring of power relations, the "mirroring of emotions and experiences" in the course of the research, debunking assumptions in the process. The researchers/staff were challenged to recognize how women were appropriating the questions and reshaping their discourse when telling their stories. The use of the metaphor of the eclipse allows the reader to visualize the complexity of the learning process that the author investigates.

With the purpose of confronting historical amnesia and reclaiming women's social history, Pamela Sugiman (chapter 6) studies another form of state violence and its accompanying "cultural genocide." The context of her study is the enforced internment and geographic internal displacement in other parts of Canada of Japanese-Canadian citizens during the Second World War. The actual war did not take place on this land, and several Canadian-born individuals were "repatriated" to a land they had never seen. By using the narratives research method with thirty-eight second generation Japanese women of varying ages, class positions, sites of internment, and current residence, Sugiman explores with these women how identities were shaped in the prewar, war and the postwar period, the "ebb" and "flow" in the construction of a racialized "other," and the strategies of empowerment the women implemented to preserve their sense of self and their self dignity. Through multiple voices and vantage points, the author examines how state violence endured in the lives of these women and how it affected them and their daughters and even their granddaughters. The narratives illustrate how the wartime experience impacted the women in gendered and racialized ways even though some women were not conscious of this analysis, let alone of this language. How they dealt with emerging issues of citizenship, home, and homelessness reflected both the impact of state violence and women's agency, a connection that Wenona Giles also argued convincingly in chapter 2. While the Canadian state's redress of this violence gave a public understanding to Japanese-Canadian's feelings and restored a new cultural identity, the wartime experience clearly continues to shape who they are today. Similar to the situation of the women in the CCVT Befriending Program (chapter 5), the function of the narrative is essential in understanding the impact of state violence, in lending legitimacy to experiences and claims, in rebuilding identities and agency, and in bridging the past with the present.

Rachel Gorman and Shahrzad Mojab (chapter 7) use a dialectical approach to reflect critically on how theory and method are interwoven in research. The focus of this analysis is a critical feminist research project on the "learning" of Kurdish women in Europe and North America about their experience of uprooting. Feminist participatory research methodology and educational theory were almost immediately challenged in interviews and meetings they attended. Not unlike the women in the Chambon study (chapter 5), the refugee women participants challenged the researchers' assumptions, affirming their identities and agency in the research process. Through the process of dialogue, the activists' patriarchal subjugation was revealed and the historical consciousness of nonactivists raised. As a result, the research question changed in this process of dialogue. The chapter explores this appropriation of theory and methodology and shows how a relational/reflexive approach transformed the researchers' theoretical framework and saved it from a-historicism and empiricism. Similar to the Japanese-Canadian women in Sugiman's study (chapter 6), gender as well as historical context and their past has shaped who the Kurdish women are today. Their national identities and relationship with national associations were intricately interwoven with the uprooting experiences. This, in turn, revealed how the production of knowledge and social relations are ideologically rooted to the extent that the researchers had to "tone down [their] feminism . . . [and] internationalism . . ." (Gorman and Mojab, chapter 7). Gorman and Mojab learned to take into account the desire of Kurdish women to locate their stories in the Kurdish collective national consciousness. It is within this historical context that Kurdish women's agency and struggles can be understood.

Poet, writer, and feminist, Madeleine Gagnon (chapter 8) reflects on the genesis of her book, *Les femmes et la guerre* (2000). She travels back on the journey and field experience she and her colleague, Monique Durand, a journalist and then Director with Radio Canada, undertook in 1998. Each with her distinct professional skill and approach to the subject translated her experience into a very different final creation—a book for Gagnon and a series of ten documentary films for Durand—in which they set out to explore the experience of women in war situations. While they did not know what they were going to find, they started off with the intuitive assumption that two phenomena, namely, the wars that spanned throughout the century and the definitive leadership of women in the Women's Movement which marked the twentieth century, must be intertwined if they are to be fully understood. Gagnon and Durand were ready to listen to what women said about war, as well as to listen to the silence(s) on the subject. But they also dared as feminists to ask themselves: " [I]f war has existed since the beginning time . . . is it impossible that women be altogether absent or innocent?" (Gagnon chapter 8). The journey led them to Macedonia, Kosovo, Bosnia-Herzegovina, Israel, Palestine, Lebanon, Pakistan, and Sri Lanka. As a writer and poet, Gagnon elaborates on how she sought to go beyond geographical maps and sociological analysis. She wanted to delve into the unknown and become "an archaeologist of the souls," including her own (Gagnon chapter 8). She wanted to see with her own eyes, to hear with her own ears, to touch with her own hands "death at work during a state of war" (Gagnon chapter 8), and allow knowledge to emerge from the experience rather than *vice versa*. In the last section of her chapter, Gagnon reflects on the many lessons learned. One of the key lessons was that she became an active participant, and interviews turned into conversations and "dialogues of understanding with the protagonists" (Gagnon chapter 8). The one lesson which undergirded all the experiences, irrespective of location, culture, or country, is the "perennial war waged against women by the 'stronger sex,' by males . . . named in their words 'the war within the war'" (Gagnon chapter 8). From her sensitivity as a poet, perhaps Gagnon's most significant learning was how a world of massive destruction, grief, and suffering was re-created into beauty, as a celebration of the power of the imagination and creativity to heal and remake our lives. Gagnon gives two such poignant examples. The first was a visit to what is called by its residents the "Hiroshima" of Sarajevo. Observing the beauty of colors and shapes at sunset over a devastated medieval city was a sight that "neither an architect nor sculptor of genius could have planned or overlooked" (Gagnon chapter 8). The second example was a life-affirming ritual conducted by a woman from Bosnia whose loved ones were decimated by war. For Gagnon, retrieving beauty from horror is an act of love, resilience, and hope.

5

Befriending Refugee Women

REFRACTED KNOWLEDGE AND SHIFTING VIEWPOINTS

Adrienne Chambon

Research as Conversation

What happens to knowledge by way of refraction and through varied transmission? What can be known, told, and shown in conducting research regarding the life circumstances of refugee women? I wish to focus on research, as a practice of conversation and of dialogue, and to offer an account of what happens in the conduct of research when it is structured by a series of conversations with deliberate variations in the composition of the groups.

Grounding my reflections in a research project, I examine the structure of our encounters, our practices of talking and of telling, and the shaping of our emerging discourse, taking discourse in the Foucauldian sense to mean the way that we come to define the parameters of thought and action (Foucault 1969; Chambon 1999).

The Story of Research

The study on which this chapter is based, entitled *"Link By Link: Creating Community With Survivors Of Torture,"* was funded by the Center of Excellence for Research on Immigration and Settlement (CERIS). The research team was a partnership between the Canadian Center for Victims of Torture (hereafter CCVT), the University of Toronto's Faculty of Social Work, the School of Social Work at York University, and the School of Social Work at St. Thomas University.[1] The different phases of the work took place between 1996 and 2000. The initial aim of the project was a self-reflexive study of the Befriending Program, a core volunteer program of the Center that brings together clients and volunteers on a one-to-one basis to foster relations of friendship and integration in the community, and to facilitate links with organizations.

In its narrow definition, the study was an evaluation of a settlement program that aimed to document how the program was run and bring into view the less visible practices that sustained this service. The project was present oriented and bound to the local context of the agency. The Center is a major resource in Toronto, providing services to numerous groups. It has become a model for other agencies and provided guidance in setting up similar centers in Canada and abroad. It also provides consultations to settlement and mainstream agencies across the province. At the time of the project, the predominant source countries of emigration of clients were Ethiopia, Somalia, Iran, and former Yugoslavia.

Yet, our task was not an innocuous activity. The very material from which our study originated suggested a layered reading that could turn our inquiry into a more formidable quest. The challenge faced by the Befriending Program, as stated in the agency brochure, was to foster social links and reconnections for people whose social ties had been brutally severed and who had lost trust in society, and to facilitate their adaptation to their new surroundings. The actions mobilized by staff stemmed from a deeper understanding than practical knowledge on how to access resources, and owed their usefulness to a different kind of understanding. In becoming more acquainted with CCVT, it became apparent to us that the philosophy of human rights and world justice permeated the activities of the Center. The mandate of the organization, the traumatic circumstances of the lives of the refugee population it served, and its professional practices, all these factors opened up a space for a more fundamental questioning. Concerned about the activities of the program in relationship to our study, we started to wonder what could be shown, and what could be known.

In our study, the parameters of knowledge kept shifting, and along with them, the nature of the knowledge we developed. This kind of work induces a sense of confusion and instability. Along with destabilizing knowledge come destabilizing relationships between research participants and researchers, and uncertainties about who is to be "the knowing self." This leads me to raise a series of questions: What does it mean to know and to want to know in that context? What can be known, told, and/or shown? What cannot be known or shown? What might we not want to know? Some of the ideas I am working with in this chapter are "entering into conversations"; "the point(s) that stories make"; "changing configurations of participants in these conversations"; "reframing in the process of knowing"; and "not knowing what we are in the process of coming to know."

The agency operated largely through group activities, with the explicit objective of developing shared meanings. Our research reproduced this intent and engaged the groups that routinely operated within the agency.

Conversations were held between university researchers and agency staff researchers. Separate focus groups took place with refugee clients, volunteers, and staff, which were held in the context of those regular meeting times. There were also smaller group conversations. We invited triadic conversations among former client-volunteer-staff and university researchers, which replicated the client-volunteer (friend-befriender) exchanges, which are generally facilitated by a staff member.

In addition, we initiated unique formats of encounters for the purpose of the inquiry. Such forums were new to the participants and created alternative arenas for intergroup exchanges. The staging of such encounters is a common strategy in action research projects, which bring together groups which hold different views and that may be located across dividing lines of interests (Bradbury and Reason 2003). We thus set up an Advisory Committee, consisting of former clients, past and current volunteers, staff members and university researchers. During the concluding phase of the project—when outside staff were trained, we expanded the circle of conversations to include staff members from other agencies. Throughout all these various group exchanges, we tried to encourage the possibility of reciprocal learning from group to group and from person to person.

In the everyday running of the project, we talked to one another. We talked through one another. We met with each other, and we talked. We talked in different contexts and at different moments of the study. We talked about what we could talk about and what we could not talk about. Each time we engaged in such talk, the object of the study seemed to pivot, to take on new shapes, new colors. Each time we met, we pleated and folded new material, so to speak, we knitted and crocheted, we tore up and embroidered, we cut the cloth differently. Research was a way of circling around something important. Each separate conversation stemmed from a specific relational territory and led to a new understanding, a different unfolding of speech, a new space of reflection and of action.

In an earlier article entitled "If you ask me the right questions I could tell you!" (Chambon 1995), I argued that the question that guides the researcher is not necessarily meaningful to the participant. The participant does not know or much care about the object of the research. The two parties seldom have a converging stake in exchanging information, as Bourdieu (1993) eloquently underscored in presenting the vast interview project conducted by his team. Phenomenologist Steinar Kvale has argued (1996) that the dialogical and transformative nature of the diverse research conversations that routinely take place between researchers and participants, among researchers, and among participants, is a rarely uncovered phenomenon (Hajdukowski-Ahmed 1998). Yet, the various configurations of exchange can be thought of as so many different attempts at interpretation. They constitute various gestalts that are played out across positions and points of view.

A parallel image of a shifting cognitive landscape is the childhood game of folding paper napkins and cutting into the folds. Once flattened, the napkin displays rows of squares, circles, lozenges, and half-moons. Raising a question is like cutting into a fold; you can not quite predict what the overall schema will be. A comparable effect is achieved through the kaleidoscope. Rotation upsets the initial layout of the glass pieces. It shakes them noisily out of their place, they rattle and fall, and finally settle into their new arrangement, revealing a new colored pattern. Each twist and turn of a kaleidoscope is akin to a new question or comment that we make.

I will review some of the moments in the study, as so many shifts and turning points in our conversations. These were situations when we made room for surprises, we let go of a "point," we loosened our hold over the objectives of the study and let ourselves be moved on to new understanding. We reshaped what we came to know, and what this research would be about.

Knowledge at a Slant

One of the preconditions for starting the project was that the researchers would not inquire into the traumatic circumstances of torture or of war. Researchers would not ask about the past directly. They would avoid re-enacting past occurrences in their intolerable vividness and, instead, would concentrate on the present. However, it was clear to us that aspects of the past were filtered through the present. The past informed ways of being in the present. Talking about the present did not mean obliterating the past. The past could be read from traces in the present. We would address the present and the past through these traces. An initial series of conversations led us to refine our objectives and to state explicitly that we would engage with trauma indirectly. We would examine the strategies that refugees, staff, and volunteers devised to deal with its aftermath. We drafted a Research Ethics Protocol that specified this point. Focusing on the effects of events, rather than on their causes, is consistent with a Foucaltian approach to knowledge (Foucault 1979). The effects of disciplinary practices influence the strategies that persons invoke to address relations of power, and shape their strategies of knowledge. We deliberately shifted from a nonmediated evidential type of inquiry to a refracted form of inquiry.

The Question-Story Sequence

What did these conversations cover, and how did they take place? Initially we asked questions, and our research partners recounted events. They responded conspicuously with stories. They described situations, offered examples, and illustrations. It was exciting but also disconcerting. What were these stories telling us? What were these examples illustrating?

Stories are complex and multifaceted. A story is an elaborate way of re-framing a question. It is a way of appropriating it and reworking it. Compared to these stories, our questions seemed simple if not simplistic. We set our questions aside and started to perceive the texture of issues of which our questions were but an approximation. A story that is part of a conversation generates the unfolding of a second story. The participants told us many stories, and bits of stories. A second/third story is not a response to the first. It is a different response. It underscores a different point and sets up a different argument. One tale bounces off a feature of one story in a sequence of moves as an astute positioning, sometimes as a counterstory. Stories acted as strategies. Multiple stories tore apart the simple fabric of the question.

Some recurrent stories functioned like a collective painting. They were transmitted by several pairs of eyes and hands, each person adding a touch of color, insisting on certain features, and erasing certain aspects. At other times, we obtained several versions of the same event told in different groups, at different moments. Storytellers took up authoritative positions. We were invited to become familiar with a vocabulary of stories and with shared situations that were, at times, stark, and at other times, ornate. Whereas the question-answer sequence tended to solidify the dividing line between respondents and questioners—who started to resemble interrogators—the telling of stories was a way of drawing us in, a means of implicating us.

Staff Researcher and University Researcher

"Torture is social; it is a political act" was one of the early statements that the agency team members discussed in our preliminary research meetings. This statement seemed, on the surface, to be disconnected from our research objectives and was not explicitly articulated in such terms. However, it underscored that we were not to limit our understanding to mental health issues, nor to view the relations between clients and volunteers merely in psychological terms. This statement alerted us to the broader transnational dimension, which is the socioeconomic and political context of these migrations but falls outside the purview of particular social programs and resettlement activities, and therefore can easily remain unseen. These words raised a line of inquiry and constituted a challenge: how to maintain the background of this larger canvas in our minds and convey it in the project?

The conversations would move from one topic to the next, shifting easily across registers. In one such session, a staff member suddenly talked of how torture is silenced. Silence is maintained at the collective level, and equally at the interpersonal level. She spoke of this by giving a personal account. This is *not* a story that is easily told even between close friends, and therefore we cannot expect such disclosure to take place easily between strangers.

From the topic of friendship, the conversation evolved to discuss the sense of community life that refugee staff members had known in the countries they had grown up in, and they stated how much they missed that shared life in Canada. One staff person said: "We always did things together; we went to the market together." She added, "We often held hands as we went from place to place." Another added: "We visited friends together"; "celebrations meant bringing your friends along." Someone added: "If you had a problem, you could turn to people in the community. You wouldn't stay in the street without a roof above your head." They commented on a media story. It seemed an existential absurdity that a newly arrived refugee woman had found herself walking in the streets of a small town in Ontario, with nobody to turn to, to help her find a place to stay for the night. It was nobody's business, in some inexplicable way.

As we listened to these stories, the notion of *adaptation* took on a more complex meaning to include adaptation to a community-less society or to a different sense and way of being in the community. The juxtaposition of these stories and comments illuminated a paradox: a person who has been tortured has quite often been "turned in" by someone within the community. The systematic practice of torture is a mechanism for breaking up communities and dismembering solidarity. Simultaneously, people maintained cultural expectations of community closeness but combined with distrust about the nature of community relations (Chambon et al. 1998b). The sense and practice of togetherness, as well as deep and brutal disconnections, all take place inside the collective. These kind of jarred, apparently contradictory, or braided, findings were best conveyed through these stories and commentaries.

Researcher to Researcher

In the same series of conversations, we witnessed a form of bantering among group members that took as its source the intrusive, cumbersome, and profusely detailed bureaucratic demands made in Canada, specifically in processing refugees. These labyrinthine requirements invoked forms of *torture* (the word "torture" was actually used), or more precisely were reminiscent of routine acts used in military regimes and dictatorships that consist in individuals being constantly checked, documented, and observed. Such practices can take many forms, but they have in common a severe institutional violence and a dehumanizing effect. This comparison was uttered with intensity but in a markedly ironic tone of voice. And the words were left hanging there in the room as the participants looked at the rest of us, inviting our responses. And in a split-second, they shook their heads, dismissed their own comments, and moved on.

We were left speechless. We had not envisaged such direct comparisons. In the days following the meeting, uneasy, disturbing thoughts followed us and would not go away. I personally could not come to peace with this turmoil and asked a colleague to meet to talk about it. She too had experienced this intensity, and found herself reeling. We seemed to be going through a crisis, a crisis of learning, as Felman (1992) has so aptly described. A sense of cognitive dissonance and emotional disorganization. Something had taken place, an event of knowledge that could not be erased. Without warning, we had been shown how the transnational political realm can intersect with, and be transposed onto, the local, institutional culture of bureaucracy. We were confounded at the making of such abrupt parallels. We could make sense of it intellectually, somewhat, but the hiatus remained as we felt "outside" this specific experiential understanding. Importantly, though, we recognized that on this occasion the speakers had shared something new with us. They had let us "in." We had received not only the contour of the ideas but also the burden of the emotions. As a result, we could no longer maintain the stance of outsiders. We seemed to have suddenly shifted to what we came to call a more "witnessing" stance (Chambon et al. 1998a; Simon, Rosenberg, and Eppert 2000). We shared this realization with the tea, and came to redefine this kind of research as a mode of transmission.

Soon after, these findings became crystallized in the metaphoric image of the *eclipse*. This image seemed to capture the strangeness of our quest, the quality of its mystery, the tenor of unveiling and the intensity of our meetings. As a tool of inquiry, the eclipse conveyed several points. First of all, you cannot look at an eclipse directly, because it is dangerous; it will burn your eyes. Secondly, the shadow moves swiftly; it grows and fades at different moments. The "eclipsed" part is just as present as the more visible part. In watching an eclipse, the portion that is in dark appears voluminous and dense, whereas, by a strange contrast, the lit part of the disk seems surprisingly thin and flat. As you keep staring at the eclipsed portion, it seems to be staring back, as if in a challenge.

Indeed, experiences in daily living are more or less invaded and pierced by these returning images. The absent presence that returns uninvited. In later conversations with refugee women (clients) and with the volunteers, participants recounted how moments of memory and sharing by the refugees came up unexpectedly, and were often provoked by apparently innocuous incidents which held symbolic meaning. Lastly, during an eclipse, the world is strangely quiet, at a remove, as if at a standstill.

Women to Women

"We change from moment to moment," said one of the refugee women in the focus group. "That is something important that volunteers should be aware of." They then shared two story lines, or rather one and its opposite:

> My volunteer is patient with me. She is so patient! . . . I don't know if volunteers know that people . . . have mood swings. They know we have experienced a harsh change. But if I say, 'See you tomorrow for a movie!' and we schedule to go, but the next day I don't feel good, I don't want to go. Its important [that] volunteers should not take it personally or be offended. It is important to take pressure off us too.

Another woman started to speak, "Now I live in privacy, in my own apartment. Living in the rooming house was very hard. I am shy; I was hiding in the room." After a moment, she added: "It's good *not* to stay indoors, we need to go outside. Some days she [the befriender/volunteer] pushes me out. It's a good thing. There are so many places to see. Every day we go out. Then when you do it, you see others and you learn things."

These statements, thus counterposed, but shared in a single meeting, are not at odds with one another. The knowledge that is thus imparted is not contradictory. Together, these statements illuminate the complex relation that new refugees have with the outside world, with the city, its people, and its institutions. We can begin to understand the multiple movements between feeling *in place* and feeling *out of place*, to borrow Edward Said's autobiographical phrase (Said 1999). To initiate new steps, to go to a hospital, to access social programs, to seek housing for one's family or to feel caught in immigration procedures, these situations can be fraught with uncertainty, with fear, with various expectations. They can be *too much* to carry and to consider. But not necessarily always. They are also occasions for moving into new social spaces, with a growing sense of safety and accomplishment.

The group of women first talked about the need for "patience," a relational point of entry to talk, which they took up with great emotion. Women's talk often focuses on these important and difficult to name issues, the value of how to be in the relationship (Gilligan 1982). Feminist researchers have deliberately chosen to examine, amplify, and transmit everyday interactions, tasks, thoughts, and caring gestures. In talking this way, the quality of relating can be brought out as a philosophical stance. After speaking of their experiences, the participants went on to direct their point to the participant researchers and to the staff, providing guidance for the training of volunteers by translating their experience into learning. They worded their concerns within the framework of the agency and of the project, as we had described it to them—to explore, to name, and make recommendations for improving the workings of the Center and other such organizations. The women also gave examples of the meaningfulness of small gifts, the act of giving and receiving. One person mentioned a female volunteer who had given colorful hairpins to her granddaughter, and also helped her with a hospitalization procedure and came to visit her regularly. The act of being there in a relationship during moments of good living and in situations of illness.

The group explored the changing moods associated with staying at home and getting out of the house. They first named the home as a place of safety, contrasting this foothold with the external unknown realm of public and institutional spaces. Privileging the home as a place of refuge and grounding, in tension or in harmony with an outer community, is an important and complex issue in the gendered division of labor and relative attribution of space. This theme has been recurrently examined in feminist views of politics. A closely related example is Biddy Martin and Chandrah Mohanty's paper (1986) "Feminist Politics: What's Home Got to Do with it?" Martin and Mohanty have offered a rich account of the pursuit of safety, linked to notions of self, home, and community based on a literary autobiography written by Minnie Bruce Pratt, from the vantage point of their respective upbringings, growing up in Virginia (United States) and in Bombay (India).

Intergroup Conversations

The Advisory Committee meetings created a space for conversation between refugees and volunteers, in the presence of staff and researchers. We had unreflectively framed our questions as dichotomous sets of social relations, and we had started to inquire into the nature of helping and of *being helped*. This was problematic. These parameters anchored the respective positions and experiences of refugees and of volunteers as fundamentally distinct, though hopefully complementary. Such conventional categorical framing assumes that a unique, if not mutually exclusive, thoroughly distinct type of knowledge is *owned* by each of the groups. Suddenly, a female refugee participant abruptly broke the frame and interrupted the exchange by addressing herself directly to the volunteer participants. This former client leaned forward and, looking intensely into the eyes of the volunteers sitting across the table from her, asked them: "So what is it like *for you* to meet a refugee person at the Center? What is it like *for you* the day before the meeting? Is it like *for us* that we are nervous and wonder about what this will lead to? Do *you* wonder about calling it off?"

The rest of us were taken by surprise by her initiative, and even more so by its content—this sudden movement revealing our restricted assumptions. Thanks to her question, however, we were finally able to hear about a parallel set of worries and anticipations between the refugees and the volunteers. "I could not sleep that night," said a volunteer. "I tossed and turned in my bed, wondering: 'What do I want to know? What if they tell me the details of their lives? How will I react then? What am I doing this for? What should I know ahead of time about the circumstances of this person's life? Not the details of her experience, since the program does not give this information out in order to protect persons individually, and it is up to the refugee to share, or not, whatever he/she chooses to with her befriender. Do I have the responsibility to know of the region's socio-political situation before our meeting? What information do I need? What am I looking for?'"

Through this group-to-group exchange, we came to understand the strange nature of the artificial human connection that is fostered by the program, and the trepidations of the participants. The sudden discovery of a mirroring of emotions and experiences, which cut across the distinctiveness of the groups, revealed side-by-side a common query, and also deep social distances and disjunctures. The participants' (refugees and volunteers) expressions of anticipated fear of the burden of these encounters raised the question of the nature of these social ties. Indeed, how can strangers connect with an abyss of violence? How strange it is to meet someone you would not know unless for these horrific circumstances! What matters here? What is the nature of this social task?

Training, Transmission, and Representation

On this sensitive issue of transmission and representation (Gergen and Gergen 2000), we wondered how to find a good distance from the object of learning. How do training, or education, address the collective pain and destruction of history, and how to raise the question of responsibility? How to probe apparently stable knowledge (or lack thereof) and do it safely? This was the challenge of Felman's class, in which she grappled with transmitting experiences of the Holocaust based on archival testimonies (Felman 1992), the opposite challenge to coming up *too close* to the experiences.

The research project had a follow up in the form of a training program that staff and researchers developed with funding from the provincial arm of the Department of Citizenship and Immigration Canada (Canadian Center for Victims of Torture 2000). In planning the training sessions, we gave a great deal of thought to the question of the *distance* from which we wished to transmit what we had learned. We wanted to find a distance that would engage and disquiet all at once. In keeping with the nature of the project, we did not wish to throw the participants into a situation of vicarious transmission of social trauma (Herman 1997). On the other hand, we did not want them to learn *about* something from afar, looking at "the pain of others" at a distance, as Susan Sontag (2003) has argued in discussing photographs of war. Reifying or aestheticizing would perpetuate a divide between them and us. This concern has moved a number of artists of the third generation—who were at a distance from the historical experience—to work through what the Holocaust can mean for them and in engaging with *memory's edge* (Young 2000), to find ways of addressing an audience which moves them. We aimed to engage outside learners on the basis of traces, which could evoke *the touch of the real* (to quote a phrase from Geertz, as cited in Greenblatt 2000). Finally, in a wish to replicate the process of our learning, we hoped to foster an evolving posture of wanting to know (Chambon et al. 2000).

We therefore proposed certain forms of conversations, which seemed similar in their spirit to the ones we had held during the research phase of the project. "Holding" is a good word, as these conversations did not simply "take place," or "occur"; at their best, they were being *held* (Winnicott 1965). We designed a series of evocative exercises with this task in mind. In one of them, participants sat in a circle and looked at paintings, which had been made by refugee participants in the art therapy workshop of the Center. Some were images of a bridge linking (or not) the past and the present, and even the future. Another set of drawings represented a tree, as an image of one's life. In showing these pictorial works, no personal details were divulged about the lives of the people who had made them (similar to the way in which refugee stories are protected in the Center). But these pictures had been made by real people. We could not avoid that fact. One painting had a wooden frame. It was large and heavy, beautiful and cumbersome. Physically holding the picture, taking it in, relinquishing it, and entrusting it to another member of the group, meant feeling the weight of the story and the responsibility of the transmission. How long do you hold on to the image? How do you look at it? Do you glance at it quickly? Do you look away? Do you wish to speak to it? Are you afraid to drop it? How do you give it back? How do you let go of it? The group then debriefed.

We included an exercise based on the image of the eclipse, feeling our way with how to use it. As one of the trainees activated the source of light and shadow, as she cast the shape of the eclipse onto a space in which the others were invited to walk, she said forcefully, while moving her hand, "There is *always* a little bit of light that can be seen, it is *not* total darkness." Her voice was firm. Having appropriated the material metaphor for herself, she had come to this conclusion. She had reached a point of resolution. This was yet a new step in our learning.

Conclusion

We walked through a series of dialogues, of group conversations, which set up different occasions for speech and story. Unpremeditated words slipped out by chance, in the tension and excitement of the particular encounter. Each time, different things were told, and different things were withheld. The juxtaposition of stories, the changing groups of discussions, kept refining and redefining what the project was about, what we were learning, and the nature of the activity we were engaged in. Was this a program evaluation? Indeed it was, and so much more! How intricate was the knowledge that sustained it! How surprised we were in uncovering preconceived ideas!

Feminist scholarship has reflexively sought, and continues to seek, ways of multiplying voices and vantage points. In struggling to change the authoritative structure of narration, inventing new forms of knowledge transmission, to deflect established games of power by layering images and texts, straddling these uncomfortable lines between the framings made by the participants and those made by the researchers (Kaplan 1992; Lather and Smithies 1997; Reinharz 1992); all the while, documenting the interpersonal and interpositional moves, displacements, encounters, misunderstandings, with power still there.

The path that this project took was a continuous decentering of the "point" of the story, to the extent that participants could shape the form and content of what they transmitted from their many viewpoints. Something of their experiences was thrown at us. We learned by ways of knowledge interactions. The horizon of the project changed. There is much to learn in working carefully in this crab-like fashion. Overall, in the time spent together, trying to probe and loosen the ties of befriending with refugee women, in exploring the gestures of the everyday, what became more and more glaring is how immense and urgent the task of addressing state violence is.

Note

1. Team members were Mulugeta Abai, Teresa Dremetsikas, and Michele Millard from the Canadian Center for Victims of Torture, Toronto; Adrienne Chambon and Ben-Zion Shapiro from the University of Toronto; Susan McGrath from York University; Suzanne Dudziak, St. Thomas University; and Martha Kumsa, Wilfried Laurier University.

6

"Days You Remember"

JAPANESE CANADIAN WOMEN AND THE VIOLENCE OF INTERNMENT

Pamela Sugiman

"I have privilege. Yes that is true. But I also have memories. Of used-to-be-times." (Jo-ann Maria Vasconcellos cited in Childers 2002: 216)

Introduction

On 22 September 1988, after a concerted campaign led by the National Association of Japanese Canadians (NAJC), the Government of Canada formally acknowledged that its treatment of persons of Japanese ancestry during and after the Second World War was unjust and in violation of human rights' principles, as officially upheld in the contemporary period.[1] The Prime Minister of Canada pledged furthermore to ensure that such events not happen again, and publicly recognized the strength of Japanese Canadians in their steadfast commitment and loyalty to the nation (Miki and Kobayashi 1991: 138–39).[2] As a symbolic redress for past wrongs, the government also agreed to pay individual compensation packages to living internment survivors, in addition to making a financial contribution to various organizations whose goal was to promote cultural understanding and racial harmony.[3] Most significantly, the movement for redress touched the memory of the Japanese Canadian community, contributing to a liberation of feeling and thought among its people. Restored by a renewed sense of cultural identity, as well as legitimized feelings of anger and pain, many Japanese Canadians have recently been attempting to reclaim lost or stolen parts of themselves.

This project of reclamation has assumed various forms. Since the beginnings of the Redress Movement,[4] community leaders and activists have publicly narrated a collective memory of the internment, thereby challenging the longstanding silence of official history—the amnesia that has plagued our national memory.[5] Concurrent with this public campaign,[6] many other individuals, less centrally involved in the Redress struggle, have been contemplating their memories, too, ones that may be woven into the public narrative but ultimately claimed as uniquely their own. Some of these memories have been generated in private moments, in circles of friends and family. Others have been articulated among strangers in public forums. Some have been spoken of and preserved on paper. Selected memories have been stored safely in the hearts and minds of their holders. These personal memoirs have added to the existing narrative, but they have also produced different images than those that formerly made up our past. Notwithstanding the personal, political, and historical value of the collective redress narrative, it is important to keep in mind that our history is still very much a partial one.[7] It is complex and contradictory, fluid and ever changing.

In this paper, I add another layer to the ever-growing project of historical reconstruction by drawing on the narratives of thirty-eight Japanese Canadian *Nisei* (second-generation) women, varying in age, class-ranking, site of internment,[8] and current residence.[9] I sought these narratives with a particular interest in the enduring impact of state violence on women's lives. I listened to them, moreover, with attentiveness, honed over many years of feminist study and reflection, for the complex ways in which intersecting social processes of gender, "race," and class shape identities, relationships, and the institutional framework within which we carry out our lives.[10] My interpretation was guided by an understanding that the wartime actions taken by the state were gendered and racialized, and strongly directed by a capitalist logic.[11]

Though most never crossed a national border, these women may be described as refugees, internally displaced.[12] Rather than transnational, their flight and journey were from coast to coast, from Western Canada to parts of this nation located east of the Rocky Mountains. Though the Canadian state espoused a rhetorical commitment to the principles of liberal democracy, equality, and justice, the government in power blatantly violated the rights of this group, solely on the basis of "racial" origin. By definition, all *Nisei* were Canadian-born citizens. Yet they were denied citizenship rights and subjected to a host of violations and indignities.[13] Such violations were legitimized by the War Measures Act, an act that provided an opportunity for the blatant "abuse of power" (Miki and Kobayashi 1991: 25).[14] Through Orders in Council made under the War Measures Act, persons of Japanese descent were forced from their homes on the west coast of British Columbia (hereafter BC), placed in filthy detention centers, dispossessed of houses, businesses, automobiles and most personal belongings. Some were exiled to parts of the BC Interior; others were banished to "self-supporting camps," or put to work in family units on Alberta or Manitoba beet farms. After at least three years of such uncertain living, Prime Minister Mackenzie King completed his attempt to geographically disperse Japanese Canadians and obliterate the community. On 4 August 1944, the King Government forced persons of Japanese origin to "choose" to relocate either east of the Rockies (Ontario and Quebec) or across the Pacific Ocean to Japan, a country that was foreign to most. The official rationale for this order was national security. Never, however, has there been evidence that Japanese Canadians posed a security threat. It is these incongruities, the incredulity of this story that Japanese Canadians still grapple with. Though they never held an official refugee status, their treatment at the hands of the state suggests a refugee experience. Like many other people who have endured forced migration, Japanese Canadians have negotiated the trauma of displacement: uprooting, homelessness, forced movement, physical confinement, material loss, and disrupted identities, with a mixture of silence and telling, sharing and secrecy.[15] Though many of the women in this account have never before narrated these days of their lives, the experience has by no means faded with the passing of years.

What resonates throughout the women's testimonies is the theme of time, the relationship between past and present. Their stories do not only add to, confirm, or dispute the official historical record. Importantly, they also tell us something about the ways in which women currently remember and communicate indignities that happened many years ago. After all, attempts to reclaim identity and constitute oneself in the present are situated in projects to recover parts of one's past. As many of the women in this study have noted, such reclamation projects are mediated by memory (personal and collective). In presenting the women's stories of internment, I draw on the concept of memory to break down the dichotomy of past and present.[16] And in so doing, I explore the concept of passing time as a link between the two. While many women clearly demarcate the past (former selves, earlier events, and previous circumstances) from the present, at the same time their narratives suggest that the political events of years gone by have profoundly shaped who they are and how they live today. For many women, these long-ago times are indeed inescapable.

A Personal Memory: Ritsuko's Story

In 1944, a young woman named Ritsuko Sugiman traveled alone by train from her makeshift, tar papered "home" in Rosebery, a small ghost town surrounded by the mountainous splendor of the BC Interior. After spending several years at this internment site, Ritsuko was heading east of the Rockies. Her destination was Toronto, Ontario. She would soon be entering her first ever wage-earning job as a domestic for a prosperous *Haku-*

jin[17] family in Weston, a suburb of Toronto. She did not then realize that she would remain a domestic for several *Hakujin* families until she reached the ripe old age of seventy-seven.

Her first step was to meet and move in to the home of her new employers—a surgeon, his homemaker wife, and their four children. As she endured the long and uncomfortable train ride, Ritsuko thought about the ways in which her life was changing. She did not yet realize, however, that she would soon be working day and night, preparing meals, cleaning the house, doing laundry, ironing clothes, scrubbing floors, and polishing silverware, with little to no time off to see family or friends. Her immediate task was to carve out for herself a place in this new and foreign territory.

This arduous train trip is one of Ritsuko's most vivid memories of the wartime years. Ritsuko, my mother, was born and raised in Haney, BC, a small town near Vancouver. Before the war, she lived on her family's berry farm. In her girlhood, when not attending Alexander Public School, my mother helped to clear the land, harvest berries, perform household chores, and occasionally played baseball. She lived a simple life, characterized by exhausting physical labor. But as her train pulled into the downtown Toronto station in the wee hours of the morning, Ritsuko remembers being overcome with fear. No one was there to greet her.

Ritsuko and her family (mother, father, sister, and brothers) were forced by the Royal Canadian Mounted Police (RCMP) to leave their Haney farm shortly after Japan's attack on Pearl Harbor in 1941. After hurriedly packing their suitcases, giving away their pet dog, burying dishes and other personal possessions, they were shipped to Hastings Park, the Pacific National Exhibition horse stables that the government used as a holding center for Japanese Canadians. Ritsuko does not remember how long she lived in Hastings Park. She recalls only the timeless quality of her existence there, as well as the stench of manure and the loss of privacy. After Hastings Park, Ritsuko's family was sent on a long train trip through BC to Rosebery, one of the most northerly sites of internment. Her memories of Rosebery are vague, details eclipsed by uncertainty. She can offer fragments of memories but is frustrated as she attempts to give substance to years marked by nothing.

When Mackenzie King's Government forced Japanese Canadians out of BC entirely, my mother had little choice but to find work in Ontario. And domestic employment was one of the few options available to young working class women. By the time Ritsuko arrived east, the government had confiscated and sold all of her family's property, including ten acres of newly purchased, just-cleared land. What belongings remained, hidden underground, were most likely taken by looters. As Ritsuko moved to Weston, her eldest brother (the only one of five siblings not born in Canada), was settling with his wife and children in Japan. Angered by the government's actions, her brother decided that he could no longer call Canada home. None of the family saw him again. Ritsuko herself did not return to visit the remnants of her BC homeland until fifty-five years after her expulsion.

As this woman's narrative demonstrates, the political violence of the internment had many layers. Personal reflections touch the larger narrative in different ways. Ritsuko's testimony features all of the ingredients of the collective narrative; but the latter is not simply a compilation of the former.[18] Ritsuko, like others, weaves her own life and feelings in and out of official and public accounts. Frequently, the (official) collective story is used as a guide; but departure from it also brings relief. For some women, recounting their personal pasts is difficult, but not only because remembering is painful. In Ritsuko's words, the past is relived everyday. It brings on a familiar, not feared pain. The worry is about making their own stories, their snapshots, and their lapses of memory fit the official narrative. It is about the authority of a story that is consistent and accurate, and concern about the scrutiny of an audience that places greater value on official documented history than on diverse, sketchy, and mediated memories. Sensitive to these tensions in the process of social history, I now turn to the memories generated by the women who participated in this study. I will highlight just three of the many themes that emerge from their narratives: mother-daughter relationships, "race" and racialized identities, citizenship and homeland.

Crafting Identities in the Face of Political Violence: Then and Now

Mothers and Daughters

Nisei women experienced the internment within the context of family relationships as daughters, sisters, and, in a minority of cases, wives and mothers. Family relationships understandably were, and continue to be, important for the transmission of feelings, thoughts, and reflections on the war years. The widely-read published letters of Japanese Canadian journalist Muriel Kitagawa (1985) to her brother Wes, for instance, highlight the importance of close familial bonds in helping this brother and sister to endure the day-by-day injustices of war.[19] Likewise, analyses of government-censored letters written to and from Japanese Canadians reveal impassioned communication between wives and husbands, children and parents, sisters and brothers.[20] Much of this correspondence is dotted with uncertainty about their fate, melancholy, and despair. Furthermore, the letters highlight women's role in family decision-making, as well as the part they played in sustaining the family's emotional reserves.

Now elderly themselves, most having raised families of their own, *Nisei* women remember the internment not only through their own eyes, but through the eyes of mother, father, and less often, a husband. Thoughts about their parents' hardship and suffering in particular have shaped the ways in which the women present their own experiences and emotions. In remembering, Kay comments on age, retrospection, as well as an evolving framework for understanding political injustice. She stated:

> My parents struggled. When I recall now, and when you hear about these immigrants coming in to Canada, refugees . . . and through our Church helping them, I could see it. . . . I still remember . . . not too much about how we were living or anything like that because at that time it didn't dawn on me. But I've grown older too. And I read all these stories of people. And so on. They go through exactly what my parents went through.

The time that suddenly becomes available upon reaching old age in this culture opens up for Kay a space in which to reflect on the past. She continued: "When I think back . . . after the war and all that, we were so busy trying to make a living and helping our parents, you know, and having a family again, like togetherness, that I forgot a lot of the past. But it comes back to you, as you're getting older." While a "race" discourse often obscures the centrality of gender in internment narratives, the gendered nature of government policy, as well as the prewar sexual division of labor within families ensured that women and men experienced hardship in distinct ways. Women frequently bring up these differences, without making explicit reference to the function of gender. While many husbands, fathers, brothers, and boyfriends were incarcerated as prisoners of war in Ontario or forced to perform exhausting labor in road camps or lumber camps, women withstood their own hardships in the feminized sites of internment. Within these sites, *Nisei* daughters were most often in close physical proximity to their mothers. Mother seemed to be fixed in place, securely attached to home and family.

In thinking back, *Nisei* women express admiration for their mothers' initiative, resolve, and resourcefulness in the face of scarcity and adversity. Survival, the burden of familial responsibility, and making do on very little were themes recurrent in their testimonies. Their memories of mother not surprisingly produce enduring images of food in particular: *bologna*, rice, *shoyu*, *miso*, and chicken.[21] Sadako remembers her mother hiding such things under the floorboards, ingredients for cooking. "[I]n order to stretch the rice supply, Mom used to put barley in it," she recalls. In some cases, food imagery is embedded in an emotional response to effort on the one hand and waste on the other. Kay, for example, conjured up the sad image of her mother's futile attempts to feed her family on their voyage to the Interior:

I remember it [the trip from Hastings Park, Vancouver to the BC Interior] was at night and during the day, and at night. It was a long, dirty ride. And I remember you had to make our own food. And I remember some chicken that my mother had made. And it rotted because we didn't have any ice box or anything of that sort. And it got thrown out.

Some *Issei* (first-generation) mothers were also left with the responsibility of raising children in their husband's absence. This responsibility included both meeting their basic needs for food, clothing, and shelter, and providing moral guidance and protection. Some women now recognize that in this capacity, a mother was thrust into a "public" role for the first time in her life. With the departure of father and elder sons, the onus fell on mothers to negotiate for supplies with the BC Security Commission, or to seek permission from the RCMP guard to leave the internment site for the afternoon. In some cases, the *Issei* woman indeed became the family's representative. Kay further described her mother's efforts to provide:

My mother . . . she had it [money] all bound into a strap on her body. Would you believe it? During the night, I still remember because I was half awake. And you're kind of wary about everything, even at that age. And these guards, the [female] security guards [in Hastings Park] came along. . . . And you know what they were doing? They were looking for money. They all knew that the women had some money tied around them. . . . And I think a thing like that was happening to every, every . . . 'cause it's all women, mostly. . . . I distinctly remember it. It wasn't a dream. And to this day, you know. . . . I said to my mother, "I remember that." Because I jumped up too and they found me. . . . when I think of my mother going through all that though. You know, as you grow older and you have your own children, then you appreciate what your parents have done for you.

One of the strongest memories of mother is that of sacrifice. Mother was remembered as stoic and selfless, and primarily as maternal. Pauline stated, "Well, my mother. How do you explain your own mother? She was never complaining. She raised the six of us. I never heard mother complain about anything. And she was a good mother. She was always home." Likewise, Sue reflected: "My mother she was, let's see. My mother . . . everything is for the children. She sacrificed everything for the children." While these maternal images were no doubt the product of truly hard times, the memory of a selfless mother is accentuated by *Nisei* women's present day circumstances. The material comforts that many women (now retired) currently enjoy (the time and savings to travel, bowl, and enjoy cultural center events, restaurant lunches with friends, and trips to the zoo with grandchildren) stand in stark contrast to a mother's efforts to scavenge for pieces of coal to heat a leaky tarpaper shack in the cold of winter. The women tend to engage as well in what

Mona Oikawa (1999) terms the relational construction of memory. In remembering, they highlight differences in their own situation from that of
their *Issei* mothers. While many *Nisei*, then young women, had good
times, fun, carefree days, lacking in responsibility, their mothers did not.
Sadako commented:

> I think a lot of people had resentment by being moved away from the coast. At
> my age, I was too naïve for my age to know. So, I didn't know what was going
> on. My parents never talked about it. We never knew anything. But to me, I
> don't remember having any hardships because of the evacuation. . . . I thought,
> "Oh, this life is better than when I was in Vancouver" [with laughter].

On a similar note, Ruby remarked:

> Looking back now, it makes me feel terrible to think that all these people were
> chased out of their homes . . . put into camps or whatever. I mean, as a child,
> you don't . . . you know how kids are? You don't really think too much. But
> now when you know a little bit more. Living conditions must have been terri-
> ble for them. You think you had a terrible life. But then, "they" must have re-
> ally suffered.

The political violence toward Japanese Canadians produced many different kinds of losses. *Issei* parents lost property, livelihoods, years of hard
work, and savings. They bore the burden of caring for families while their
own freedoms were severely curtailed. And they suffered indignities in
full view of their offspring. As noted, many young men were forced to
perform demanding and unsafe physical labor on work projects in BC and
Ontario. Those men who voiced even a hint of resistance to government
officials faced emotional and physical penalties as Prisoners of War. Yet
Nisei women also suffered losses. As girls and young women, they lost opportunities and aspirations. Many of the women were never able to finish
high school. Some were just months from graduating when they were
moved from their homes. A few remember the kindness of high school
principals who issued them their diplomas, though they themselves could
not be physically present to graduate. Moreover, many were routed into
feminized and racialized jobs in which they had little interest, from which
they never moved. Says Gloria, "my dreams, I don't think I had hardly any
dreams to talk about." Those women, who remained in the ghost towns
long after their friends had moved to Ontario or Quebec, endured a sense
of timelessness, isolation, and sheer boredom. Other young females, whose
parents decided to relocate to Japan, followed them, contrary to their own
desires. Some *Nisei* daughters refused to abide by their parent's com-
mands and stayed in Canada, thereby jeopardizing close familial bonds.
Yet *Nisei* women tend to negate or at least downplay these costs. They
minimize their own suffering in relation to their mothers', fathers', and
husbands' painful stories.

Race and Racialized Identities

Many women speak also of another elusive cost—the psychic damage incurred by continued exposure to racism in its multiple guises.[22] In narrating their prewar lives, they offer various interpretations of "race." Some say that when they were young girls, they had little consciousness of the social process of racism and no sense of themselves as racialized. In their recollections, they were no different than the *Hakujin* children at school or in the neighborhood. Others remember instances of racist treatment, yet they normalize this racism. "Of course there was racism, but we didn't think much about it," remarked one woman. And yet others explain that while they were certainly aware of racial difference and discrimination, they could travel comfortably from one world to the other, from a Japanese world (home and family, community, language school) to a non-Japanese, typically *Hakujin* existence (public school, Canadian Girls in Training, public society at large). The women's understanding of "race" was shaped in large part by the demographic makeup of the community in which they resided. While some Japanese Canadians were numerically in the minority, others lived in areas that were heavily populated by persons of Japanese origin.[23] The latter group was least likely to remember racism as an issue in their early lives.

As the women situate their memories in the war years, however, there is a greater convergence of feeling.[24] The outbreak of war and the heightened anti-Japanese propaganda that followed gave new meaning to their "racial blood." The normalization of racism that some women had experienced previously was, as a result, severely disrupted. The two worlds, Japanese and *Hakujin*, could no longer be traversed. The government confined those of Japanese descent to just one world. Japanese Canadians became the "racialized other," with what to many seemed like a suddenness. According to Michiko: "We were well liked but when the war broke, all of a sudden we were dirty Japs." Likewise, Sachi remarked:

> Every major thing that have happened were created by the thought of racial prejudice. . . . See, when Japan caused Pearl Harbor, we thought it was terrible. . . . We hated Japan for doing that . . . we didn't see ourselves as Japanese, whereas the Occidentals saw us as Japanese.

Racialized images scar the women's memories of the war and immediate postwar years. Gloria remembers having to line up for food at Hastings Park, with people driving by gawking and pointing at "the Japs from the coast." Dorothy recalls trick-or-treating with her sister, only to discover the looks of alarm in people's eyes as they saw two "Japanese" faces staring back at them. And Sachi does not forget how the dean of a women's residence at McMaster University handed her a list of off-campus accommodation—denying her outright her space in the campus building. To the

Hakujin world, the Japanese face and body (black hair, "slanted eyes") conveyed meaning about the inner self. The physical markers of Japanese origin thus took on enhanced meaning for the women themselves. This externally imposed label prompted women to repeatedly underline the distinction between nationality and territoriality—between being Japanese living in Japan and being Japanese Canadian, born and raised in Canada. More importantly, this racialization resulted in a separation of the inner self from the physical self. The *Nisei* knew that inside they were Canadians, yet they were treated as though they were Japanese. As part of this dichotomization, many of the women ultimately attempted to deracialize themselves. It became imperative to escape the physical markers of racial difference.

Years later, Jean communicated a self-consciousness about her "Japanese looks." This was something that she experienced both in childhood and in the present. In her words: "There was discrimination and prejudice and even 'till now I feel that going into a strange place and . . . I'm Japanese. And they're looking at me. And I have that feeling where my kids don't have that." The psychic impact of racialization is enduring. Even women who are currently living in Toronto, a city that now boasts a high level of cultural diversity and an extremely large population of "Asians" in particular, expressed such thoughts. Jean spoke of a lingering sense of inferiority:

> Jean: I think one thing about the Japanese, when we came out here [East] we tried not to stay together.
>
> Interviewer: Were you conscious of that then? Trying not to draw attention to yourself?
>
> Jean: Oh, yes. Definitely. Even now and I'm not a shy person. . . . Yes, we have an inferiority complex.

Over time, the women adopted various strategies for achieving self-respect and preserving dignity in the face of a racially hostile nation. As Jean mentions, they have made concerted efforts to integrate themselves into the dominant society, largely by trying to "blend in" and not draw too much attention to themselves.[25] It is important to note that these strategies have been crafted within a coercive political context. While they reflect some agency on the part of the *Nisei*, they have also been developed with the clear understanding that the government aimed to destroy the Japanese Canadian community. Kim explained: "The government were sending, they sent the message. They said that we are not to congregate. We are to blend into the society. So, this is what we tried to do. So, they still didn't want us getting together." Yoshiye similarly remarked:

> The Government. . . . BC [British Columbia] wanted to get rid of all these black-haired people. And Ottawa said, "Alright." But the RCMP and the army said

there is no evidence to intern the whole group. But the politicians in BC were so vocal that they had convinced Ottawa. . . . It's interesting. It still goes on.

Some women note that during the war years, in an attempt to resist the essentialist category "Asian," Chinese Canadians would wear tags or other markers that distinguished them from those of Japanese origin. Ironically, in the decades following the Second World War, Japanese Canadian women and men tried to dissociate themselves from those of Chinese background. They related feeling embarrassment at how Chinese Canadians would not only speak in a "foreign" tongue on the public transit but that they would converse loudly. To this day, some women fear that they will be mistaken for a Chinese, Korean, or Vietnamese woman, commenting on the high visibility of such groups. Unlike the Chinese in Canada, says Sue, "We'd never speak Japanese in front of *Hakujin*." With the same fear of visible foreignness, most women did not teach their *Sansei* (third-generation) children the Japanese language or other Japanese cultural symbols. Furthermore, it became common practice to give *Sansei* children "English-sounding" first names, with a (seldom used) Japanese middle name. Sachi explained:

> When we were parenting, when my children came along, we refused to give them Japanese names . . . because of the cause of the rift and the problems we had at school. And we thought it was bad enough with the last name "Oye." So we just gave them English names.

Paradoxically, though, because the *Nisei* did not marry outside of the Japanese "race," their own children, too, bore the physical markers of "Japanese-ness," in spite of the erosion of culture and community. Consequently, *Sansei* daughters and sons faced racist sentiment as well while growing up in Canada. The face of racism endured by the *Sansei*, however, was different. Unlike their parents, they grew up in an era of equal opportunity. They did not experience the institutional discrimination (for example, in housing, employment, recreation, and formal education) that their parents and grandparents had known. The *Sansei* were more likely to confront racism face-to-face in the school playground or on the streets, especially as young children in the 1950s and early 1960s.

Nevertheless, a number of *Nisei* mothers deny that their children, now grown, ever suffered racism of any kind. They present the experiences of their offspring as dramatically different than their own. For instance, Amy stated:

> I don't really think my children felt any prejudice here [in Montreal]. I remember my daughter when she was going to McGill, she's always combing her hair, you know . . . she looked up and she said, "Mom, I look just like the Chinese kids." She didn't think she was Japanese. She always supposed she was English. I never let her know about any prejudice or anything like that.

Indeed, while my own childhood memories are vivid with recollections of schoolyard bullies and their taunts of "Jap" and "Chink," "off-the-cuff" racist remarks, and thoughtless questions about my "Japanese-ness," my own mother's testimony nullifies this experience. With sincerity, my mother maintains that her daughter did not encounter racism. One may speculate that mothers simply chose not to see that racism touched their children's lives. But it is also likely that their children, in turn, withheld information from their parents in an attempt to protect them from further grief in a society that was still very much racialized. Believing that she had already suffered too much and could bear no more, as a child I made a deliberate choice not to tell my mother about the racial slurs. It is significant though that the women's narratives do not address the intergenerational transmission of racism through memory. *Sansei* daughters and sons themselves experienced the internment through the memories of their parents, grandparents, aunts, and uncles.

Another shield of protection, as well as a strategy of empowerment among Japanese Canadians, has been the acquisition of formal education and entry into the professions, both of which have resulted in notable upward class mobility. From childhood, many *Nisei* recognized the importance of formal schooling. As they were growing up, some of the women repeatedly heard their *Issei* parents extol the values of educational success as a resource to help pave one's way in a racist society. Sue explained: "You know why our parents said, 'You got to do well?' Because you're Japanese, you've got to do better than the *Hakujin*—to prove yourself . . . Oh yes. They always say that."

However, as noted, the government's wartime policies presented the *Nisei* with formidable barriers. By the postwar years, many *Nisei* had lost years of regular public schooling or university/college training, their parents had been robbed of their savings, and aspirations had been dampened. In addition, the minority of women who did manage to further their post-secondary education were confronted with persistent discrimination in most Canadian universities and in the professions. In order to meet the needs of middle class *Hakujin* Canadian families, many *Nisei* women were directed by the BC Security Commission into low-paid domestic service. Others found employment in the needle trades, in the Jewish-owned textile factories of Montreal and Toronto. Women repeatedly told stories of kindness from Jewish employers in postwar Ontario and Quebec, one of the few groups who would hire them in other than domestic positions. In addition, many of the families that had relocated to the sugar beet farms in Alberta and Manitoba or to berry farms in Ontario remained in agricultural work long after the war's end.

Over time, a minority of the women became teachers, nurses, or social workers. Most, however, remained in clerical, secretarial, or manual working-class jobs. As they married and raised their own families with

working-class husbands, they experienced financial hardship and struggle. But over the course of these years, they also placed a strong emphasis on educational achievement in their *Sansei* children. In reflecting on
the war years, many women speak of their powerlessness. They explain
that without money, without political influence, they could do little formally to resist their treatment. But as mothers, in the postwar period, they
were intent on empowering their own children, thereby shielding them
from the violations and indignities to which they themselves had been subjected. While the *Sansei* today constitute a diverse socioeconomic group,
they demonstrate a higher than average level of formal education. Among
the mothers in this study, a striking number have sons or daughters who
are professionals: lawyers, professors, physicists, chemists, physicians,
teachers, and high-level computer programs.[26]

In some families, as a result, there is a significant contrast in the material circumstances of the *Nisei* and their children. Importantly, there is a
palpable difference in the life histories of mothers and now grown children. In narrating her story to me (and for my own daughter when she is
older), my mother repeatedly underscores the hard times of her life. She
conveys powerful images of labor, perseverance, and need. An important
part of her narrative is the sharp contrast between the scarcities of her
childhood and struggles as a mother and young wife, the comforts and
privileges that define my life, and the plenty in her granddaughter's.

Notwithstanding the many loving mother-child bonds, there is thus a
symbolic space between some *Nisei* women on the one hand and their
Sansei children and *Yonsei* (fourth-generation) grandchildren on the other.[27]
The *Sansei* and their children inhabit worlds that some *Nisei* mothers themselves still have mixed feelings about: a middle class world, a *Hakujin*
society. In our middle class existence, some mothers, moreover, reveal a
slight embarrassment about their working-class lives. It is curious that
while class interests unabashedly permeated the government's wartime
treatment of Japanese Canadians (much of it was about economic compet-
itiveness and the need for cheap labor), little has been spoken or written
about this dimension. One consequence is that in some families class tensions permeate intimate and loving bonds.

Citizenship and Home

The *Nisei* were displaced from their homes. Their national loyalties were
questioned. Their rights as citizens were breached. It is not surprising that
those who became mothers used their resources to make Canada a safe
place for their children. It is also not surprising that in reflecting on the
war years, the themes of belonging, citizenship, and national loyalty, remain prominent. Indeed, the distinction between the physical self and the

inner self (discussed above) was often drawn along the lines of national identity. The true inner self was a loyal Canadian, though the body may have looked Japanese and thereby like a dangerous, traitorous, "enemy alien." And while the popular view has long been that Japanese Canadians are a quiescent and forgiving people, many *Nisei* women today present a passionate critique of the government's wartime policy, condemning it as unjust, while at the same time declaring their unwavering allegiance to the nation. In some respects, these themes lie at the heart of the political analysis put forward by some women. Pat, for instance, stated:

> I'm sure we felt the anger. We were Canadian-born. Why were we being up-rooted and you know, our homes taken away from us? And they never found any signs of people trying to obstruct the Government. We were so law-abiding. . . . They accepted what the government said and they told us we'd be back in a few months. Well, that never was.

One recurring symbol of the violation of citizenship rights was the compulsory registration card that all persons of Japanese origin had to carry upon reaching the age of sixteen. While sharing their stories, a number of women paused to bring out their registration cards, now tattered and yellowed with age. They produced these cards, preserved through many moves, over the course of more than sixty years, as tangible proof of the injustices. Polly remembered:

> I turned sixteen in the camp. So there was a rule that we had to be registered with the Government as enemy aliens. I got my little registration card . . . you felt like a criminal. . . . But you didn't have to have a record like that, unless you did something bad . . . That's what it came down to. But we did it because we thought we had to do it. Anyways, I mean we had no choice. We were considered enemy aliens, not Canadian citizens. We were a non-status people. . . . Up until that time, we didn't have a care in the world. . . . All of a sudden, you have to grow up I guess and realize there are many evil things happening in this world.

Among a series of violations, another of the most unpardonable ones was the government's decision to force Japanese Canadians either to "repatriate" to Japan or move east of the Rockies. Sue commented on how the term "repatriation" was a misnomer, as very few *Nisei* had ever lived in Japan. To all of these women, Canada was home. And a rootedness in this country was most strongly articulated by the women who left it. At the war's end, obligated to comply with her parents' decision, for example, Chieko relocated to Japan. Ultimately, she married a Japanese man and gave birth to two daughters. However, Chieko says that, longing deeply to return to Canada, she cried every day. After residing in Japan for eleven years, Chieko decided to return to her homeland. Leaving her husband

and two young children behind, she traveled to Canada, found a home and a job, and later sent for the rest of her family:

> Chieko: I said, "You know, I want to come back to Canada. I don't care how poor I'm going to be in Canada." I said, "I'd rather be poor in Canada than be poor in Japan. Although I was doing well in Japan by then. But I never felt at home, I guess. I was always thinking of Canada. Canada. Some day when I go back to Canada, you know. . . I never thought of what I'd have to go through. I thought I could tackle anything. . . . So, I wasn't afraid." I said, "Okay, bye. I'm going to Canada." Leaving with two little suitcases.
>
> Interviewer: So what was it like once you stepped on Canadian soil again?
>
> Chieko: Oh, I was happy. I thought, "Oh God. I'm home now."

Upon returning, Chieko settled in Montreal. Not until 1949, four years after the war's end, however, could "cleared" Japanese Canadians again call British Columbia home. Throughout the 1950s and 1960s, some families returned to what remained of their homes on the West Coast, though many did not: British Columbia (7,169), Alberta (3,336), Saskatchewan (225), Manitoba (1,161), Ontario (8,581), Quebec (1,137), New Brunswick (7), Prince Edward Island (6), Nova Scotia (4), Newfoundland (2), Yukon and Northwest Territories (35). Source: Kobayashi (1989).[28] Those who now live in Ontario and Quebec, claim that they could no longer consider BC to be their homeland. With bitterness, some women explain their decision to remain in the East. It would be too difficult to return to the site of violence, they say. It is the following generations, the *Sansei* and *Yonsei*, who seek to return to the place of internment, in their own efforts to reclaim lost identities and a stolen history.

Conclusion: Bridging Past and Present

For *Nisei* women, the years of internment marked days to remember. These days were experienced in youth, within a cohesive ethnic and cultural community that would later be dispersed geographically and dismantled as a result of the government's act of cultural genocide (Miki and Kobayashi 1991). These days were also memorable because of their profound and enduring impact. These years of internment were momentous both in their material consequences and in their impact on individual subjectivities.

The women's narratives prompt us to think about the passing of time: day after day, year after year. And in doing so, we must reconsider the dichotomization of past and present. The past is not something that is over and complete; the present does not originate only in the current period. Women continue to experience events that happened many years ago. Their identities are strongly shaped by what they have already lived through. The current period mediates their memories. In order to understand the internment narratives of Japanese Canadian women, we must, then, think about the intermingling of past and present, and the sociological function of time in this process of mediation.

At first blush, it may seem that in the act of remembering the women themselves neatly demarcate junctures in time. Many women declare, for example, that what happened before is now over and done with. On close view, however, one wonders if this tidy temporal separation may serve a recuperative function. Like silence itself, it may represent an attempt to bring closure to a set of painful experiences. Sadako stated:

> So, you know, life on the whole, I mean I've hard a hard life but . . . like some people even to this day, resent the fact that they were moved away from the Coast. I don't have that. Past is past and forget about it. Think about the good days. And so nothing really bad. No. To me, that is, I don't know how my sisters felt.

The same theme of looking forward, leaving behind the tragedies of the past, is echoed by many women. We have moved on, and we have survived. We were naïve then, but we know better now. Such a gross injustice will not be repeated. But the complexity of these statements is apparent in the women's comments about the Redress Settlement and its implications for the wider political context in which they currently exist. In thinking about Redress, many narrators say that although the war years have long passed, on a personal level suffering continues, memories do not fade, and, in spite of monetary compensation, some wounds will never heal. Sachi expressed these feelings:

> Money didn't pay for all the suffering we went through. Suffering. I mean humiliation more. And then denial of our rights more than anything. I don't know that there was a just treatment that was ever compensated. . . . Because it was too much taken away from us at that point. Money will not pay for that.

Kim also commented that, "*Redress* does not make up. It does not make up for what we lost. What my mother had lost. And that's what I was sorry about." As these remarks suggest, many women believe that the most meaningful gain of the Redress Settlement has been the liberation of personal memories and the restoration of a collective memory. "At least it came out in public that it was a horrible thing," asserted Yoshiye. Polly likewise explained:

> In many ways I feel that people went through so much hardship. I'm sure they don't even want to talk about it. And maybe some people just—they might just come out freely because they feel more comfortable to talk about it now that more people know about it. . . . And more of the injustices that happen to minorities in a multicultural country like ours, I think, should be pointed out.

Pauline shared these sentiments, stating:

> I believe that is a good thing for children from the next generation to come along and see what can happen to people that lose their freedom. And let's hope that there'll be more of a tolerance. I don't think discrimination will ever be eradicated. There is some way or some thing that will come up. But at least, that we're more understanding about what discrimination can be and will be.

It is notable that, upon reflecting, some women contextualize their individual experiences, as well as those of the Japanese Canadian community, within the contemporary global setting. Though they are more likely to draw on a general concept of "injustice" rather than point to specific state policies and international political developments, they do lament the current plight of First Nations people, African-Canadians, and those of Arab background throughout North America. Linking personal subjectivity and biography to history, they caution that in spite of their own rootedness as citizens of Canada, somewhat shielded by the gains they have made in formal education and intergenerational upward social mobility, marginalized and vulnerable groups can still be found in this society. Thus, the line between past and present is mutable, and changes in individual lives remain distinct from fundamental social transformation.

These women have not left the past behind. They recognize that "small and fragile communities of memory matter in the overall picture of the dynamics of remembrance" (Irwin-Zarecka 1994: 55–56). In Irwin-Zarecka's words: "The 'realities of the past' as they pertain to individuals are not carbon copies of publicly available accounts. They are often worked out within smaller and larger communities of memory, their shape and texture reflecting a complex mixture of history and biography." The Redress Movement may have made it easier for *Nisei* women to speak by lending legitimacy to the very issue of political violence and its impact on people's lives, but also by providing a framework within which individual women may weave personal and unique stories. Few women contest the public or "master" narrative. Most are loyal to it. Indeed, they regard the publicized story of internment as *the* story, a product of their own community's struggle, their collective "face" to the wider *(Hakujin)* society. Yet this story is one that they themselves have not authored. Many women thereby intersperse personal vignettes with "historical events" and measure historical time with the milestones of their lives. In doing so, the women place themselves in history. Moreover, in reconstructing identities, in looking back, for example, at one's youth, in piecing together the fragments of a life, the narratives and the very act of narration unify an individual woman's life. The task and product of such an act is not typically neat nor is it objectively logical. But in the process of narrating, most women develop their own logic, one that transcends time, bridging past and present.[29]

Note

1. This project has been funded by the Social Sciences and Humanities Research Council of Canada and the National Association of Japanese Canadians. I wish to thank Robert Storey, Franca Iacovetta, Maroussia Hajdukowski-Ahmed, Nazilla Khanlou, and Helene Moussa for providing valuable critical insights on an earlier draft of this paper. Tomiko Robson, Gillian Anderson, and Candace Kemp offered skillful research assistance. My heartfelt appreciation also goes to the many women who generously agreed to share their memories with me. And to Ritsuko Sugiman and Tamura Sugiman-Storey; each continues to inspire this research in her own way.

2. On 22 September 1988, then Prime Minister Brian Mulroney stated in the House of Commons: "Mr. Speaker, I know I speak for members of all sides of the House in offering to Japanese Canadians the formal and sincere apology of this Parliament for those past injustices against them, their families, and their heritage, and our solemn commitment to Canadians of every origin that they will never again be countenanced or repeated." (R. Miki and C. Kobayashi, *Justice In Our Time. The Japanese Canadian Redress Settlement.* Vancouver, 1991: 9).

3. The Government of Canada agreed to pay, upon application, Canadian $21,000 of individual redress to those who had been interned, relocated, deported, or dispossessed of property, Canadian $12 million to the Japanese Canadian community for educational, social, and cultural programs aimed at building the community or promoting human rights, and Canadian $ 24 million endowment for the creation of the Canadian Race Relations Foundation (CRRF). Half of the endowment ($12 million) was provided on behalf of Japanese Canadians and in commemoration of injustices suffered by Japanese Canadians during and after World War II. Furthermore, it would again, subject to application, clear the names of those who were convicted of violations under the War Measures Act or the National Emergency Transitional Powers Act, grant Canadian citizenship to persons of Japanese ancestry who had been expelled from the country or whose citizenship had been revoked between the years 1941 and 1949 (and their descendants), and provide up to Canadian $3 million to the National Association of Japanese Canadians for their role in administration of redress through the implementation period (R. Miki and C. Kobayashi, 1991: 138–39).

4. Japanese Canadians have made various attempts to seek compensation for their wartime losses. In 1943, for example, a small group of *Nisei* in Toronto formed the Canadian Committee for Democracy, organized around efforts to secure full citizenship rights and to assess the economic losses of the wartime uprooting. In this discussion, I refer to the contemporary redress campaign that began in the late 1970s when the National Association of Japanese Canadians (then called the National Japanese Canadian Citizens' Association) established a Reparations Committee to look into the matter of redress (Miki and Kobayashi, 1991: 56, 64).

5. For an interesting discussion of the different ways in which individuals, governments, and societies deny political atrocities, see Stanley Cohen's (2001) book *States of Denial*.

6. During the mid–1980s, growing numbers of Japanese Canadians began to share openly their internment stories. These stories took on a more public quality as the media publicized them. This same point is expressed by Roy Miki in *Redress:*

Inside the Japanese Canadian Call for Justice, Vancouver: Raincoast Books 2005, 63–85. The NAJC, furthermore, launched an educational program on government records revealing that military leaders of the 1940s and the RCMP had recommended against the internment as a security measure. On 21 November 1984, the NAJC submitted to the government the brief, "Democracy Betrayed: The Case for Redress." In this brief, there were government documents, as well as the voices of Japanese Canadians. Miki refers to this brief as "an act of empowerment and a liberation," but also the first public challenge to the government since the internment.

7. For an insightful discussion of competing internment narratives, see K. E. McAllister on Japanese Canadians in "Remembering Political Violence. The Nikkei Internment Memorial Center." (Ph.D. diss., Department of Sociology 1999), and on Ukrainian Canadian experience, (F. Swyripa) "The Politics of Redress: The Contemporary Ukrainian-Canadian Campaign" (2000) in *Enemies Within. Italian and Other Internees in Canada and Abroad.* ed. F. Iacovetta, R. Perin, and A. Principe. (Toronto, 355–378).

8. I use the term "internment" loosely to refer to a broad range of violations including, for example, relocation to ghost towns of the Interior British Columbia, "self-supporting" projects, sugar beet farms, incarceration in Prisoner of War camps, "repatriation" to Japan, and government-regulated movement east of the Rockies. The Federal Government preferred to employ the euphemism "evacuation," restricting the use of the term "internment" to describe the incarceration of men in Prisoner of War sites.

9. In this chapter, I draw on the narratives of women who currently reside in Ontario, Quebec, or British Columbia. My larger study also includes women from Manitoba and Alberta. At the outset of the war, most of these women were adolescents or young adults. Only two were very young. Their fathers were farmers, agricultural laborers, fishermen, a printer, a physician, and small-scale entrepreneurs. Most mothers worked at home raising children, farming, sewing, cooking, and sporadically taking on agricultural labor or cannery work for cash. All of the women were born in British Columbia. At the outbreak of war, the women departed to various parts of the province: Lillooet, Bridge River, Tashme, Greenwood, Slocan (Slocan City, Lemon Creek, Popoff, Bay Farm, Rosebery), New Denver, Sandon, and Kaslo. All had at least one male relative (father, brother, uncle, husband) in a Prisoner of War camp or general road camp in Angler or Petawawa, Ontario.

10. This analysis has been informed by the writings of a number of scholars who have addressed the intersectionality of race, gender, and class over the past few decades. Among many, see in the bibliography: Agnew (1993), Anthias and Yuval-Davis (1993), Bannerji (1993), Brewer (1997), Glenn (2003), Jhappan (1996), Stasiulis (1987), Vorst et al. (1990), Wane et al. (2002). This study does not explore gender by offering a point-by-point comparison of women's and men's experiences. Rather, I am interested in exploring the *gendered assumptions* of government policy, and the experience of internment within a *social structure* that was clearly *gendered.* For a discussion of the need to "engender" analyzes of forced migration, see Doreen Indra (1999b). My methodological approach to the gathering of oral testimonies is closely linked to my theoretical assumptions. I approached the task of listening to women's narratives with a set of principles informed by various feminist researchers/oral historians including Behar (1996), Denton et al. (1994),

Fleishman (1998), Iacovetta (1999), Passerini (1989), Reinhartz (1992), Sangster (1998), and especially Portelli (1991; 1991a).

11. There is strong evidence to suggest that many of the policies and events of the internment were guided by the (gendered and racialized) economic interests of capital. For example, after confiscating the property and possessions (land, fishing boats, stores, houses, and so on) of Japanese Canadian families, the government sold the latter to *Hakujin* businessmen for a fraction of their market value. Many Japanese Canadians furthermore believe that *Hakujin* small business interests wished to eliminate the "Japanese" in Canada, whom they viewed as economic competitors. Importantly, during the war many prime age Japanese Canadian men were sent by the British Columbia Security Commission (BCSC) to work as cheap and "unfree" labor on road and lumber camps. Likewise, the Alberta and Manitoba sugar beet industry benefited tremendously from the exploitation of whole families of Japanese Canadians both during and after the war. The BCSC also directed *Nisei* women to fill low-wage positions as domestics in the homes of *Hakujin* families, largely in Montreal and Toronto. See K. Adachi, *The Enemy That Never Was. A History of the Japanese Canadians.* Toronto, 1991 and A. G. Sunahara, *The Politics of Racism. The Uprooting of Japanese Canadians During the Second World War,* 1980.

12. I wish to thank Maroussia Ahmed, Nazilla Khanlou, and Helene Moussa for offering this insight. Though the treatment of Japanese Canadians was in many ways unique, governments in various parts of the world have also interned other groups of people. For an excellent discussion of a range of internment experiences, see F. Iacovetta, R. Perin, and A. Principe's edited collection, *Enemies Within: Italian and Other Internees in Canada and Abroad.* Toronto, 2000.

13. In 1942, approximately twenty-two thousand persons of Japanese ancestry were exiled from their homes on the west coast of British Columbia. Seventy-five percent of these were naturalized or Canadian-born citizens. Many were given less than twenty-four hours notice.

14. Under the War Measures Act, the powers of Parliament were transferred to the Governor in council or to the cabinet, thereby exonerating then Prime Minister Mackenzie King's government from public accountability.

15. See M. Hajdukowski-Ahmed "On the Borders of Language, Language without Borders: Non-Verbal Forms of Communication of Women Survivors of Torture" in *Exile, Language and Identity,* eds.. M. Stroinska and V. Cecchetto. Frankfurt: Peter Lang, 213–229, for a thoughtful discussion of refugee women's experiences of violence and meanings of silence and non-verbal communication. Hajdukowski-Ahmed (2003: 217) claims that "silence also speaks." She writes that, "[d]uring the process of claiming refugee status, the Survivor is required to tell her/his story again and again at different junctures, thus forced to re-live a painful experience." This type of experience typically leads to Post-Traumatic Stress Disorder, which may be expressed through silence itself. In this sense, Hajdukowski-Ahmed explains, silence may be a "form of counter-discourse," permitting survivors to reclaim agency and assert a refusal to participate in a verbal exchange. They thus acquire "a culture of silence and secrecy," one which manifested itself in various aspects of everyday life. For an analysis of silence and telling among Japanese Canadian women, see Sugiman (2003), "Understanding Silence: Finding Meaning in the Oral Testimonies of *Nisei* Women in Canada."

16. For a fuller discussion of memory and women's experience, see for example in the bibliography, Epp (1997); Passerini (1989); Sangster, Sugiman (2004b). Also note the special edition on gender and memory in *Signs* (2002). In addition, there has recently been an abundance of important published works on the relationship between memory and history, generally. Among many others, see Connerton (1989); Irwin-Zawicki (1994); Portelli (1981, 1991, 1991a, 1997, 2003); S. Terkel (1986).

17. The term *Hakujin* is used loosely by Japanese Canadians to refer to "white" people or "Caucasians."

18. For a thought-provoking discussion of the relationship between personal memories and official history, see Yves Lequin's and J. Metral's study of the workers of Givors, France, "A la recherche d'une mémoire collective : les métallurgistes retraités de Givors," *Annales E.S.C.*, no. 1, 1980: 149–166, cited in N. Wachtel, "Introduction. Between Memory and History." *History and Anthropology* 2, no. 2, 1986: 207–224.

19. The letters that *Nisei* journalist Muriel Kitagawa wrote to her brother Wes during the war years have been published as *This Is My Own: Letters to Wes and Other Writings on Japanese Canadians* by Muriel Kitagawa, R. Miki, ed. (Vancouver, 1985).

20. These letters were censored by the Federal Government. Extracts from the letters are now housed in the National Archives of Canada. For a discussion of this correspondence, and the significance of family relationships, see P. Sugiman "Passing Time, Moving Memories: Interpreting the Wartime Narratives of Japanese Canadian Women" and "Unmaking a Transnational Community: Japanese Canadian Families in Wartime Canada." 52–68 in *Transnational Identities and Practices in Canada*, ed. V. Satzewich and L. Wong (Vancouver, 52–68).

21. For an excellent analysis of memories of war in the context of mother-daughter relationships, see for instance M. Epp, "The Memory of Violence: Soviet and East European Mennonite Refugees and Rape in the Second World War," *Journal of Women's History* 9, no. 1 (Spring, 1997), and M. Oikawa, "Cartographies of Violence. Women, Memory, and the Subject(s) of the `Internment'" (Ph.D diss. Ontario Institute for Studies in Education, University of Toronto, 1999). Writing about Mennonite women's memories of rape during the Second World War, M. Epp notes that narratives of wartime suffering typically depict women, particularly mothers, as "suffering quietly, submitting themselves to fate, or giving themselves into God's hands for protection" (75–76). Daughters and sons, she finds, often speak of their mother with reverence. Epp (2003) has also written about mothers, food, and tragedy.

22. There is now an abundant literature on the psychological impact of the internment on the *Nisei* and *Sansei*. In this paper, I only allude to the psychic costs from a sociological perspective. For a more complete discussion of the psychological impact, in the bibliography see Fujii, Fukushima, and Yamamoto (1993); Ina (1997); Loo (1993); Marsella (1993); and Nagata (1999).

23. Steveston and Vancouver, for instance, were locations in which there were Japanese communities (cultural, business, and residential).

24. I do not mean to suggest, however, that all of the women in this study related instances of racism during the war years and in the postwar period. Many of the women who were interned in ghost towns were segregated from *Hakujin*

and in the absence of direct face-to-face contact say (paradoxically) that they didn't experience racism while interned. In addition, a handful of women claim that once they settled in Ontario or Quebec, they never experienced racism. Here, what is most interesting is the women's definition of "racism." Many relate incidents in which they were told that they could not be hired or enter a recreational establishment because they were "Japanese," yet at other points in their narratives, they declare an absence of racism.

25. Many writers have commented on the high level of "assimilation" among Japanese Canadians. However, I do not use the term here insofar as it does not adequately convey the restrictions placed on Japanese Canadians. It implies a voluntarism that in this case is misleading.

26. As mentioned, this paper is based on the narratives of women who are currently residing in Ontario, Quebec, or British Columbia. In the latter phase of my research, I also gathered the stories of a small group of *Nisei* women in Manitoba. It is notable that the women narrators from Manitoba do not speak of the same upward class mobility on the part of offspring.

27. Because of the high rates of interracial marriage (over 90 percent) among the *Sansei*, the *Yonsei* are of mixed race. See A. Kobayashi, "A Demographic Profile of Japanese Canadians and Social Implications for the Future" Ottawa, 1989.

28. The concept of "master narrative" is introduced by M. Epp (1997) in "The Memory of Violence: Soviet and East European Mennonite Refugees and Rape in the Second World War." *Journal of Women's History* 9, no.1 (Spring): 69. Epp refers to master narratives as "stories or myths that structure meaning and that can in fact mask the particularities of an individual's situation." Master narratives shape personal life histories.

29. This insight was drawn from my reading of A. Portelli's essay "The Best Garbage Man in Town: Life and Times of Valtèro Peppoloni, Worker," in *The Death of Luigi Trastulli and Other Stories. Form and Meaning in Oral History.* Albany, 1991: 117–137.

7

War, Diaspora, Learning, and Women's Standpoint

Rachel Gorman and Shahrzad Mojab

Introduction

This chapter represents a first formal attempt to record theory and method developments of a critical feminist research project on the learning of Kurdish women—specifically women who have experienced war and national/political oppression and who have escaped the Kurdish region into Europe or North America.[1] This is a self-reflexive piece on our research process, thus representing more of our thinking than the Kurdish women's narratives of war and diaspora. Our research has shone a light on the point at which two of the major contributions of feminist research intersect—the project of revealing subjugated knowledge and the process of democratizing knowledge production. Recent writings on transnationality and diaspora have provided new tools for thinking about the impact of war and dispersal on women, but they also raise new challenges for researchers trying to explore the universal and the particular in women's experiences. In our attempts to highlight both *individual* stories of war and flight, and *collective* histories of struggle and resistance, our fundamental approach to feminist theory and method has been challenged. We found that trying to follow a liberatory research method forced the contradictions in our understanding of feminist theory into view. Rather than providing us with a set of examples of the subjugated learning of women who have experienced war and diaspora, our research did more to reveal problems in how we knit together theories of consciousness and feminist methodologies. The most important challenge we face in trying to understand the impact of war and diaspora on women's learning is how to continually (re)construct our reflections on learning and consciousness, and on feminist theory and method, within the context of historical and geographic movement.

In this chapter, using Marxist-feminist analysis, we will unravel some of the intertwined strands of method and theory that are threaded through our research process—for theory and method are dialectically related, but not identical. As we have stated elsewhere (Mojab and Gorman 2003: 231) by dialectical, we mean that we view social phenomena as relational, and as containing contradictions. We concur with Allman that, "[d]ialectical conceptualization involves apprehending a real phenomenon as either part of or the result of a relation, a unity of two opposites that could not have historically developed nor exist as they presently do outside the way in which they are related" (1999: 63).

Kurdish Transnationality, Diaspora, and Feminist Participatory Methodology

A major demographic and political trend of change since the latter part of the twentieth century has been transnationalization, that is, the breakup, displacement, and reconstitution of nations and ethnic peoples. The Kurds of the Middle East, now dispersed throughout the world from Canada to Australia, are one of the most complex cases of population movement in our times. Coming from "traditional" societies in the process of disintegration through war and state repression, Kurdish women face enormous challenges in the process of resettlement and through becoming citizens of the nation-states of the West. They have to learn about a whole universe that differs from their previous world—learning to live in different economic and social systems, acquiring different languages, coping with different gender relations, and integrating into different legal and political regimes. This is a universal experience of Kurdish women, despite varying immigration and refugee policy differences among the Western nations.

There are about twenty-five to thirty million Kurds now dispersed in the Middle East, Europe, North America, and Central Asia. Kurds are the fourth largest ethnic people in the Middle East, outnumbered only by the Arabs, the Turks, and the Persians. The Kurdish people were divided among the newly established nation-states of Turkey, Iran, Iraq, and Syria in the wake of the First World War. These centralist states did not allow the development of civil society in Kurdistan. Indeed, the policy of assimilating national minorities like the Kurds produces a situation of war and conflict, which continues to impact their lives even in diaspora. These wars destroyed the budding civil society in all parts of Kurdistan. Ethnic cleansing, genocide, and ethnocide have been the official policy of countries that rule over the Kurds.

The century-long plight of Kurdish people for sovereignty and self determination gained some international attention following the mass exodus of the Kurds from Iraq in the aftermath of the US-led Gulf War of 1991.

Since then, international human rights organizations have reported on-going internal and external conflicts leading to the massive dislocation of sizeable populations. The genocidal policies of Iraq and the internal war in Turkey have contributed to the endless migration of this people to the West.

In a research project entitled *War, Diaspora, and Learning: Kurdish Women in Canada, Britain, and Sweden,* one of our objectives was to study the impact of war and displacement on Kurdish women's learning. We chose a multiple feminist approach as our method, as we felt that such an approach would enable us to establish a relationship of trust and respect with research participants and would lead to a better qualitative study than if we based our work on a single source of information (Green-Powell 1997). We initially proposed the use of a feminist participatory research method in order to trace women's ideas and stories of war, diaspora, and learning. We used this method because of its promise of being *nonhierarchical,* of being able to converge *theory and practice,* and of being committed to *praxis,* that is, taking action or coming up with individual or collective solutions to the rising problems (Maguire 1987 and 1993; McDonald 2000; Reinharz, 1992; Vio Grossi et al. 1983; Weiler 1991). We also relied on feminist oral history and narrative approaches to enable us to examine the Kurdish community as a whole while locating the individual woman within her community. Reinharz suggests that through the individual we can understand culture, and culture can help us to understand the individual (1992). In other words, feminist oral narratives and life history methods permitted us to participate in the social systems in which Kurdish women were implicated (Clandinin and Connelly 1994; Freeman 1993; Okley and Callaway 1992; Thomson 1995).

From 1999–2002 we interviewed more than thirty Kurdish women in Canada, Britain, and Sweden, either individually or collectively. It is beyond the scope of this chapter to outline the details of our research process, for instance the discussion on the institutionalized, medicalized, and pathologized dimensions of an ethical review process that does not lend itself to a complex, multifeminist research methodology. Suffice it to add that the challenges we faced in order to acquire research authorization raised serious theoretical concerns with regard to the ways that institutional processes restrain feminist knowledge production. This is especially significant when we consider the fact that one of us, Mojab, has a long scholarly and activist connection with the Kurdish community both in the region as well as in the diaspora (Mojab 1997, 2000a, 2001a, 2001b). She is fluent in two languages of the region, which tremendously facilitated our feminist methodological approach.

Shortly after our first community meeting with Kurdish women in Britain, we realized that our methodological thinking required critical interrogation. The participating Kurdish women in our "research information session," in which we reviewed in detail our methodological approach and explained the theoretical significance of feminist methodology, were more interested in our ideas of the formation of a Kurdish state and women's role in nation-building, or in the debate on the tension between nationalism and feminism, or issues of denial of language rights as a means of national oppression, than in our insistence on the significance of participatory feminist methodology as a means of solidifying Kurdish feminist activism. These women were mainly Sorani-speaking Kurdish women from Iran and Iraq. Our feminist methodology workshop took place in an environment of hospitality and intimate women's bonding. The rigid theoretical and methodological tone of the gathering was replaced by a beautiful voice of a woman singer who invited all to join her. The warmth of her voice filled the room and as soon as she stopped, she said: "I always wanted to be a singer, but was not allowed, it is only now in my fifties that I have said enough is enough and I want to be a singer. This is the story of my life that you should write about. I have a lot to tell you." We were surrounded by enthusiastic Kurdish women who all wanted to be part of the research, and all we needed to do was to record their life history.

It soon became clear that our research inquiry in understanding the relationship between war, diaspora, and learning was only to be seen as what Himani Bannerji calls the "entry point." But, as she has suggested, the entry point "is not the end point, but the beginning of an exploration of the relationship between the personal and the social and therefore the political" (1995: 55). Therefore, we needed tools and mechanisms which could simultaneously unravel history and a whole set of other social relations, as well as being able to explain the coexistence of many contradictions in Kurdish women's lives: for example, the difference between Kurdish women's nationalist consciousness, which is highly developed and complex, and their feminist consciousness, which severely lags behind it. Even different migratory patterns for Kurdish women both reify the masculine and hierarchical nature of political organizations which they or their husbands belong to and expose the geopolitics of the region. For instance, women with a more direct access to the organizational hierarchical structure did not need to be displaced several times while fleeing war zones on their route to Europe or Canada. Women with the experience of feeling one oppressive regime (Iran) and being trapped in the borders of another oppressive neighboring regime (Iraq or Turkey) provided a complex analysis of the relationship between international organizations such as UNHCR and the state of Turkey.

Furthermore, as we continued interviewing women and participating in their public and private life, the shortcomings of feminist participatory methodology became more apparent. During long hours of interviews, these women told us about the significant historical moments and events that they remembered and how they wanted their stories to be located within those moments so present in the memory of the nation's collective consciousness. Our opening question of "What are you doing now?" was followed invariably with this answer: "In order for you to understand why I am here today and what I am doing, I have to begin with my life back home." It was this highly historicized consciousness of women which made the undialectical approach of the feminist participatory method apparent to us.

The feminist participatory method imposed its theoretical constraints on our attempt to remain attentive and faithful to each woman's individual narration as well as our ability to ground these narrations in the context of their collective and objective experience of patriarchy, militarization, capitalism, colonialism, or racism, for example. Our interviews made apparent that the past is present in the lives of Kurdish women, and it shapes their learning and living in the diaspora. Their past constitutes histories of war, conflict, forced assimilation, ethnocide, and suppression of language in the states (Turkey, Iran, Iraq, and Syria) that rule over them. This constant presence of overt violence is in sharp contrast with life in the West, where new, unfamiliar, and often invisible forms of conflict pose new challenges. Research has shown that women and children in warstricken areas are the most vulnerable population (Lorentzen and Turpin 1998). This is certainly true in the case of the Kurdish regions where war and other forms of oppression, including the use of chemical weapons, has devastated the life and property of millions of people in Iraq (since 1961) and in Turkey (since 1984). In addition to state restrictions on the rights of the Kurds, internal factors such as traditional and patriarchal relations contribute to the further marginalization of Kurdish women in all aspects of life.

Praxis and Further Complexities

In understanding the experience of women of war and displacement we needed a methodological approach which could address *praxis,* that is, the dialectical relation between thought and action, and between the subjective and the objective, or the particular and the universal. Bannerji calls this dialectical approach a relational/reflexive method, which:

> incorporates in it a theory of agency and direct representation based on our experience. As such I can directly express what happens to me. But my experience would only be the starting point of my politics. For a further politicization my experience must be recounted within a broader sociohistorical and cultural framework that signals the larger social organization and forms which contain and shape our lives. My expressive attempt at description can hold in itself the

seeds of an explanation and analysis. We need to go beyond expressive self-referentiality and connect with others in time and space (Bannerji 1995: 83–84).

Here is a methodology that can address the issue of women's desire to locate their own stories within the memory of the collective consciousness of the nation. Bannerji's relational/reflexive method has implications for the relationship between researchers and participants. Participatory feminist research methodology with its philosophical promise of breaking the hierarchical relations between researcher and participant was theoretically inadequate in responding to power relations between ourselves as researchers and the Kurdish women participants. Heshusius suggests that we need to apply a methodology which can replace an "alienated mode of consciousness" with that of "participatory mode of consciousness":

> Participatory consciousness is the awareness of a deeper level of kinship between the knower and the known. An inner desire to let go of perceived boundaries that constitute "self"—and that construct the perception of distance between self and other—must be present before a participatory mode of consciousness can be present. Participatory consciousness does not refer to activity as such, or verbal experience, nor does it refer to methodology or methodological strategies. . . . Rather, it refers to a mode of consciousness, a way of being in the world, that is characterized by what Schachtel (1995) calls "allocentric" knowing . . . a way of knowing that is concerned with both *the totality of the act of interest*" and with the "participation of the total person" (of the knower). [italics in original] (Heshusius 1994: 16)

She argues that methodological preoccupation by researchers with procedural objectivity and subjectivity "do not in their essential meaning refer to methodological problems. They point to how we understand the nature of our consciousness" (17).

We entered into this research as politically conscious Marxist-feminists. However, we feel that in many occasions during our fieldwork, we had to make uncomfortable political concessions. The issue of political compromise raises a significant question about collecting data on certain forms of social relations versus intervening in them. The original project, as was mentioned above, was to try to reveal the learning mechanisms and processes among Kurdish women in the diaspora. However, as we ended up collecting data on Kurdish women's experience of masculine party politics, patriarchal gender relations, state and family violence, our focus shifted to an attempt to document women's way of resisting and struggling against these relations. In this process, ironically, we found ourselves drawn into a tapestry of masculinity and patriarchal nationalism in a way that was debilitating to our research goals. For example, a well-connected and politically influential Kurdish man began interfering with our connection to Kurdish women. This was done through setting up meetings without consulting us, providing us with a selected list of women to be interviewed, and challenging some of our analysis based on previous fieldwork and contact within the community. The first interview which he arranged for us was with one of the first female *peshmargeh* (freedom fighter) whom he suggested "will be able to add much to your research because she is illiterate. A balance is needed in your research to be scientifically valid."

On another occasion, a husband was visibly disturbed when he heard his wife and children referring to the patriarchal behavior and attitude of some well-known male party members. We began the interview with two friends in one of their homes around mid morning. By early afternoon, the two teenage kids of the host arrived home from school. They had a snack and started watching television, which was located in the living room where we were gathered. Gradually, however, they turned their attention to their mother's story—a story which they were hearing for the first time. At this point our expanded circle was engaged in intense discussion, each contributing to another's stories by adding personal memories of people, events, and places. Then, the husband/father arrived. There was a short greeting followed by a long silence. We interrupted the silence by inviting our participants to continue. The host asked the husband to leave the room and help himself to the food in the kitchen. The husband reluctantly did so. But while in the kitchen, his attention was on the living room. The kids enthusiastically reminded their mother of the poor and often abusive treatment by their grandparents in the absence of their father in the mountains, and asked her to tell us this or that story. The husband suddenly reappeared and said: "Again a bunch of women and children are gathered and the gossip about reputable people (men) begins, and you call this research? Where is the objectivity in this research if you are collecting your information from a bunch of uninformed women and kids?"

Throughout this fieldwork, another source of aggravation for us was our seemingly docile participation in patriarchal nationalist relations. As a privileged woman of a dominant nation (Mojab) and a Western scholar (Gorman), both of us conscious of our class, gender, ethnic, and national location, we were committed to forge other political alliances, and cross these boundaries. However, the extremely dominant patriarchal nationalist relations continually sucked us into its vortex—in order to simply remain in the room, we had to "tone down" our feminism because we could not keep up with the continual reiteration of anti-feminist sentiments. We also had to "tone down" our internationalism in order to show solidarity with Kurdish nationalism, thereby leaving the door open to continual attempts to coopt us into revising our critique of violence committed against the Kurdish women. Overall, we felt that the deeper we went into this research, the more complexities we faced, which required further theorization. Kurdish women's lives are riddled with conflicting social and political agendas; capturing these contradictions and providing a powerful analysis is a difficult task ahead.

Women's Standpoint, Situated Knowledge, and Masculinist Theories of Learning

Since our research focuses on Kurdish women and *learning*, it is appropriate at this point to summarize our emerging critique of masculinist theories of learning, which we have developed through earlier projects we have worked on. We recognized that the way learning is theorized, even (or especially) new theories that seek to bring learning that is not formally organized or recognized into view, continues to exclude or obscure the experiences and learning of marginalized groups. We had also already detected problems with using the "learning" framework to describe elements of what goes on in social movements (Gorman 2001). In studies focusing on immigrant women in Toronto (see MacDonald 2000; Mojab and MacDonald, 2008), we set out to show that depoliticized and culturalized definitions of learning had been too narrow. We proceeded with the hypothesis that once more experiences of women were accounted for, theories of learning could be expanded to include experiences that had been marginalized. This strategy of expanding the definition of learning was easier to confront critically when the "learning" in question was explicitly organized as a political act.

In our project to undertake a comparative study of the learning of Kurdish women living in Canada, Britain, and Sweden, we did not start with this retheorization of learning in the context of a social movement, because we did not want to make *a priori* assumptions about the women as political activists. We began our study with a hypothesis that we should conceptualize learning for subjugated groups in terms of *survival, resistance*, and *struggle* (see Gorman 2002), with the intention of showing that the character of learning for women in the margins is different than that of learners in dominant groups. We did this, in part, as a first step toward a redefining of the concept of "learning," as a way of retheorizing learning in terms of a politicized understanding of consciousness. However, it seemed that the further we went into theorizing our work, the more we realized the impossibility of taking this "intermediary" step in critiquing learning theory. We were able to raise the conceptual category of learning only long enough to state two things: (1) that using the recognition of informal learning as a strategy for helping women gain credentials does not, on its own, provide a practical mechanism for overcoming labor market discrimination and exclusion; and (2) that the women with whom we were talking and thinking about were actually engaging in something else.

This discovery reflects Sandra Harding's (1987) description of the inherent theoretical instability of what she calls "successor science." Harding describes this as a process through which feminists use the definitions provided by a field of study (in our case, educational theory) in order to show that these definitions must be expanded and retheorized in order to accommodate the empirically observable experiences of women. Feminists who advocate for a method that pays attention to the experiences of women, and who argue that such a method will provide "greater empirical adequacy" (1987: 289), encounter three contradictions that refute empiricism itself. First, the identity of the observer is supposed to be irrelevant, but it is proven not to be; second, a bias is revealed in the way the topic of research has been selected and defined; and third, the fact that the process of following the original research agenda (in this case, to describe learning) will result in androcentric findings (1987: 290).

Dorothy Smith's (1997) standpoint method focuses on the mechanisms through which dominant groups organize social reality for everyone, and how as a corollary to this process certain knowledge becomes subjugated. Although Smith's method rightly reveals how people in general, and women in particular, participate in the solidifying of relations that structure their own subordination, it is not part of the scope of this conceptualization of social relations to look for women's agency, or consciousness in the active sense. As we proceeded with our research, it became clear to us that our project of looking at learning may be part of a quest for the "active side" of this subjugated knowledge. The relationship between learning, consciousness, and praxis is a historically determined process comprised of concrete, definite events that shape the relationship between the learner and her possibilities for learning, between the knower and what it is possible to know. From this perspective, feminist praxis exists as a definite historical set of knowledge and practices. Is it possible to see women's standpoint and feminist standpoint on a continuum? Only if we relate dialectically women's *consciousness* to women's standpoint—in other words, relate each woman's agency to the relations that organize her experiences. Without a concept of consciousness, feminist standpoint becomes simply a social subjectivity (or location) from which certain organized social relations are visible, while a "nonfeminist" woman's standpoint may reveal other/different social relations. It would be impossible to avoid multiplying these subjective possibilities indefinitely. The political position in a discourse and the subjectivity that is possible from that particular location become identical (rather than dialectically related) when there is no concept of consciousness.

Smith notes that she developed her notion of "ruling relations" by making an analogy to Marx's "specialization in the labour process" in the capitalist mode of production (1997: 17); Smith's resulting method is a very useful tool for articulating relations of oppression. The method is also, by extension, useful for articulating situated knowledge in so far as this is the knowledge of said relations from particular standpoints. In naming this aspect of social relations "relations of ruling," Smith argued that she was describing a new phenomenon that could not be captured by an existing Marxist concept. However, when feminist researchers *replace* the notion of consciousness with the notion of standpoint, a problem of historicity emerges. Abandoning the concept of consciousness disconnects the history of feminism from the present moment in which we are asking our question. Any social investigation must retain its sense of historicity—specifically one that does not stop before or during the research process. How else can we reconcile Bannerji's vision of a relational/reflexive method of social analysis, and her assertion that the structures that comprise our social universe are visible from any intersection of social relations, with the understanding that organizing or ruling relations can only be revealed from specific standpoints? It is precisely through the articulation of specific, situated knowledge that social relations can become visible to the researcher from any social intersection.

Situated Knowledge and the Interviews with Kurdish Women

To ask about situated knowledge in order to reveal in more detail the multiplications of structures that organize our social universe is one thing; however, to ask about situated knowledge when one wants to know what people in a certain location *think* about those structures is entirely another thing. This is not to say that the structures that organize our social universe are not related to what we know about them—they are dialectically related, not identical. This raises the notion of the relationship of *appearance* and essence, which is an indispensable aspect of a dialectical understanding of consciousness that describes the obscuring of the true character of social relations under capitalism. This is not the same thing as the positivist notion of true versus false consciousness, as Nancy Hartsock points out (1997). It is important to point out, however, that this obscuring does not apply to all social relations at all times, but rather is peculiar to capitalist relations—and not necessarily all relations under capital, but specifically the labor-capital relation. In Marxist theory this is said to arise from the separation—the alienation—of the worker from the product of labor, the simultaneous character of labor power as human attribute and commodity, and also (less fundamentally) from the separation of spheres of production and distribution. The process of alienation and the appearance of social relations have to be understood in a much broader sense in order to develop a deeper understanding of gender oppression. Although she does not employ the notion in her work, Dorothy Smith's relations of ruling can be used to reveal examples of how the process of alienation impacts women's lives in concrete ways. Thinking about gender relations and learning in terms of alienation can lead us to ask what knowledge has to be struggled for. It is unlikely that women are unaware of their particular *location* in terms of gender relations. The question therefore becomes what should/can be done about these relations.

For purpose of discussion here, we can identify two general types of Kurdish women participants in our interviews. One group was composed of women activists who had an official position or membership within a secular and socialist party. The other group was of women who showed political sympathy with a party based on the membership and activities of their male members of the family, that is, fathers, husbands, brothers, or uncles. In the eyes of the diaspora community, these women occupy hierarchically different positions. A *peshmerge* woman is more respected than *jin-e peshmerge* (a wife of a freedom fighter) or a *khushke peshmerge* (a sister of a freedom fighter). In our analysis of the life history of these women, we have been able to trace different situated knowledge of patriarchal social relations. For instance, one of our interviewees disclosed her unhappiness with her husband, a political activist. She told us that at one point she decided to reveal his abusive behavior, including battering her, to the political party. When we asked her what the party's response was, she said that they could not do much "except just lecture him." When we asked her how she felt about it, she gave the following explanation:

> I can't press him much. Reporting him to the party was a big punishment. I can't go further than this because I will create family feud. You see, I am bound by the *jin-be-jin-e* relation, which means myself and my sister-in-law were exchanged between our families. If I ask for divorce, it means that my brother should also return his wife to my in-laws. How can I ruin my brother's life?

Many of our participants, like the woman quoted above, unraveled a complex set of particular patriarchal relations without being able to make apparent the ideological and material basis for its (re)production. Wives of *peshmerges* talked about their abuse by the official government authorities, by their in-laws while their husbands were away in the mountains, or even by their own children for not having their father around (Mojab 2000b). Most, however, were reluctant to engage with our feminist analysis aimed at revealing the class, ethnic, ideological, and political positioning of the party. This, they argued, was only one story, "my story, my fate."

In interviewing two sisters, we realized that the women of this particular family had paid an unimaginable price for being affiliated with male *peshmerges,* in this case, their brothers. Both sisters served prison sentences and were tortured. For one of them, this began at age thirteen, and she had her first period under captivity. One of their sisters-in-law was executed after being severely tortured, not having revealed any information about the whereabouts of her brothers. Another sister committed suicide by self-immolation when life became unbearable for her due to the hardship of family dispersal and surveillance by the state. Their mother, after more than a decade, still mourns the death of her children and lives a socially and politically enforced/sanctioned "life of pride" of a *dayk-i shahidan* (mother of martyrs). The sisters stated emphatically that "we were not political," by which they meant that, unlike their brothers, they were not members of a particular political party, nor did they consider themselves feminists. However, by recounting their stories, they clearly exposed the patriarchal-feudal nature of the state. They were able to articulate the state use of female sexuality as a mechanism for silencing, breaking, controlling, and disciplining dissenting voices. A son in prison was a source of pride for families, a sacrifice to the cause of Kurdish nationalism. On the other hand, having a daughter in prison or even simply being taken for interrogation was a source of shame and a mechanism for the collective punishment for the family. The possibility of sexual torture and rape, and thereby a loss of one's chastity during police investigation, was the cause of much grief for a family with a female member in prison. The sisters attributed the premature death of their father to the stress they caused him, not to their brothers' political activism.

Under the condition of national oppression, another significant relation of ruling that these two sisters revealed was the use of the official language as a means of torture. The younger sister, who was not fluent in Farsi (the official language in Iran), was interrogated in that language. She said, "I told them (prison guards) that I did not understand them, and that made them even angrier and there were more lashes for me." Both sisters argued that their investigators made every effort to break them down by insulting their *kurdayti* (Kurdishness; Kurdish nationalism) and referred to them as savages and backward people; and they were especially contemptuous about the political parties which they believed their brothers were affiliated with. The stories of these two women clearly expose patriarchal and nationalist relations of ruling. They agreed with us on this point. The fact that these ruling relations manifest another deeper structure of oppression, that is, the politics of female sexuality as constructed by the state, Kurdish culture, and the masculinist notion of nationalism, remained unspoken. Even when we raised them, they were resisted.

In a dialectical approach, "human subjects" cannot be seen as passive depositories of the raw data that are indispensable for the researcher's analysis and theorization. They are, rather, human beings who understand the conditions of their life, reflect on their past, present, and future, and inform or teach the researcher, while at the same time learning from the research process. The knowledge produced in this process will not just be an interpretation of the world, but, at the same time, a consciousness that contributes to its transformation in the interest of the oppressed. The researchers engage in the research with the understanding that they themselves will be transformed by it. In this sense, there is no end to a research project; we have indeed developed relations of friendship and solidarity with our participants, and continue to learn from them and to contribute to their struggles to survive and thrive. Such an approach calls for continuity in the research effort; this continuity can be maintained if various research projects are interconnected through a commitment to resist relations of oppression. Obviously, there are political and economic restrictions on research (funding, institutional support, publishing, and so on) that run against such methodological and theoretical paradigms. Much research has supported, explicitly or implicitly, the nation-state, and its patriarchal and capitalist nation-building projects. We hope to contribute to the proliferation of a research tradition that is not centered on the state and the market.

History, Agency, and Consciousness

As Dorothy Smith (1997) reveals, relations organized by dominant groups come into being through the daily activity of human beings, including people in subordinated groups. Through the process of naming oppression, a subordinated group articulates the structures through which their oppression is organized. Once the people who can best see the contours of these relations have described them, these relations should/could be visible to everybody. Smith's method can be seen, along with the whole project of trying to develop feminist, anticolonial, antiracist research methods, as part of a move to make the *process of revealing social relations* conscious and intentional. Based on our attempt to truly engage in a participatory, relational/reflexive strategy, we argue that it is time now to make the way we engage with history conscious and intentional. This means we cannot proceed as feminists to study what women think, as though we have not *all* been impacted by the unfolding of history as it has already happened, and therefore do not have a consciousness of gender relations. We are aware of gender relations—however we describe them, whatever we think of them, whether we are for or against feminism, however we define it.

In our attempts to reconcile feminist method and theory, what to do with history, or how to conceptualize historicity, keeps emerging as a difficulty—and this difficulty has a context. It is tempting to speculate that this aversion to historical determination (which is not the same thing as historical determinism) may be related to what Ward Churchill (1998) describes as the pathological refusal of activists in the "comfort zone" of relative privilege to acknowledge the ongoing history of violence, uprising, and repression that characterizes the social reality of the Majority World.

Whether social theorists do indeed have an aversion to acknowledging the violence of imperialism, we can certainly trace the rejection of historicity in dominant strands of social theory. The move from structuralism to poststructuralism generally included a rejection of historical determination, and a number of theoretical maneuvers to prevent historicity from creeping back in.

When we think in terms of history and agency, it becomes impossible to think of consciousness in positivist terms, as something that can be correct or incorrect, true or false. Rather, consciousness should be understood dialectically. Bertell Ollman (1993) argues that in order to understand consciousness dialectically and as having historicity, it should be conceptualized as being always in motion. *Subjective* and *objective* indicates directions (or orientations) of consciousness about social relations—toward the particular, or toward the universal; toward one set of political actions, or another. Our earlier conceptualizations of learning *resistance* and learning *struggle* are analogous to subjective and objective consciousness, when understood this way. As in our discussions with our research participants, women often discuss certain social realities, and have different analyses about what to do about/in/with these social realities. When we understand certain concept categories as being dialectically related, such as subjective and objective consciousness, or structure and agency, this means we are not considering them separately, nor are we equating them as being identical. In other words, for there to be such a thing as true or false consciousness, subjective and objective consciousness would have to be pried apart—or to *achieve* true or false consciousness, subjective and objective consciousness would have to become identical.

Although Ollman provides an excellent description of a dialectical understanding of consciousness, the methods he outlines for studying it (which include group observation and media analysis) can lead us back into empiricism, if pursued in the absence of *dialogue.* This brings us full circle to the necessity of employing a participatory/emancipatory methodology—and of remaining true to it—that is, allowing the research question itself to change as the dialogue between researchers and participants reveals the "ideological account" of knowledge production. If we had refused to allow our question and conceptual framework to change during our research process, our original purpose of chronicling women's ways of learning would have led us in an empiricist, a-historical direction. Our original hypothesis that women's learning can be understood in terms of situated knowledge, or a standpoint, is useful only insofar as our purpose is to interrogate ways that social relations are organized. It does not reveal the active side of learning.

Conclusion

As discussed above, Himani Bannerji (1995) advocates a relational/reflex-ive method through which the *same* social relations can become visible from *different* intersections of social relations. To put things back in histor-ical order, we have to know what social relations to look for within these structures in order to locate them from a particular social intersection. It follows that an advantage of standpoint method is that the new knowl-edge it reveals (or more specifically, the articulation of situated knowledge) can be seen as *discoveries* of ways that exploitative and oppressive social relations are organized. Once these contours emerge, we can look for them from other social locations. In concrete terms, this is how situated knowl-edge has been used in the feminist movement. The process by which fem-inists come to recognize our location in relation to race, class, sexuality, and ability began with women articulating situated "knowledges from below." Consciousness raising, often accomplished in groups that perceived them-selves as subjugated, and organized around a particular oppression, had the function of articulating the contours of oppression—and once these are articulated, the privilege of women who are dominant in relation to a specific oppression also becomes visible.

As feminist researchers, whether we begin by trying to follow a political/ ethical commitment to participatory research, or by trying to (re)theorize social relations from a marginalized "standpoint," we will eventually have to deal with historicity, agency, and struggle. And this relational/re-flexive (or dialectical historical materialist) method is not only a thread that leads from the particular to the universal; it is also an integrated philo-sophical praxis. This means that whichever of these concepts we take as our starting point, we will eventually, as Bertell Ollman (1971) argues, be forced to grapple with the rest of them.

Note

1. Acknowledgment: This research has been supported by a grant from the Social Sciences and Humanities Research Council of Canada.

8

Being a Writer on Women, Violence, and War

Madeleine Gagnon
(Translated by Lori-Ann Moulton)

Genesis of the Book *Women in a World at War*

With the hindsight of some five years, if I want to accurately inform you of what the writing of the book *Women in a World at War* was for me, I must first discuss its genesis, as well as its conception and its realization.[1]

In 1998, with my colleague and friend Monique Durand, a journalist and director with Radio-Canada, the project was born, and it would soon become a *journey* and a field *experience*. I will address these two terms later. For both of us, it started as an intuition, what philosophers would call a hypothesis: if, as the second millennium closes, we believe that the twentieth century was marked by countless discoveries in every field of knowledge—be it physical or psychological—this century was also dominated by two fundamental phenomena: the wars that spanned it from beginning to end, but, also, for the first time in history, a groundswell, a vast Women's Liberation Movement, clearly led and driven by women. If these two phenomena, war and the Women's Movement, were in some sense temporarily intertwined in that century, which was also, incidentally, the one that marked our birth and our coming into symbolic life,[2] it seemed to us that in linking them in one single study, we could better understand them both, shed a better light on them. And who knows, by grasping them in light of each other, and each in our way, we could perhaps contribute to creating more peace on Earth if we could examine on site the role played by women in war.

Such was our initial intuition. For an intuition to bear fruit, it has to be generated by desire. For our part, it was a desire to explore; that is, to live the experience on site. Each human exploration, whether of love or knowledge, consists in risking a voyage into the unknown. We did not take the risk blindly, but rather imagined that the unknown would be tamed one way or another. Otherwise, one would have never become involved.

In French, knowledge and "co-birth" (or *co-naître, naître avec*) are etymologically linked in the word *connaître* (to know). For us, to be born with the other, whether a being or an event, would entail giving birth to a new and different self. To know the other—meaning to be born with the other, as the French language puts it, as in the case of women and war—inevitably leads to a better knowledge of oneself at the end of the journey. This is what the migrants of the world experience intimately, provided of course that they undertake their journey with open eyes, as the great writer and traveler Marguerite Yourcenar so beautifully expressed in her works (1951; 1968). Therefore within us, coupled with our initial intuition, was a desire to go elsewhere: to those places where we could meet women who had experienced, or who continue to experience, war. Whether they were victims or warriors (and there were many of the first and few of the second), what would those women have to say about war? For one thing, would they even want to speak to us? We were not psychologists, neither gurus nor missionaries. In no way did we wish to force anyone to share her testimony or to confide in us. Ready to meet with silence and accept it, we knew, however, that silence is not muteness. We knew how eloquent certain silences could be, and we both understood that these were translatable into each of our creative media: in the case of Monique Durand, writing a radio documentary, whereas for myself, writing a book. We both understood the word writing, not as a mystical or fantasy-bent experience, but rather as the last recourse we have if we want to understand the world of beings and of things; this when human sciences and philosophies, when all the rational discourses remain silent and give up when facing the absurdity of evil and the mystery of death, both our own death and the one we inflict on others during war.

Before leaving, we ventured to articulate what, through the vague understanding of the relational bond between women and war, seemed to us an obvious fact all the same, though tinged with uncertainty: that is, if war has existed since the beginning of the human world, it is impossible that women be altogether absent or innocent. If war has existed since the dawn of time throughout all civilizations, all cultures, all religions, and on every continent, we must dare to think, insofar as we would want to advance in the knowledge of this death drive in action—as we have both written about in our own way—we must risk this statement and put it at the forefront of our exploration: that is, women are also implicated in this unending history of human war. They also harbor a death drive, belligerence, hate, vengeance, and murder within them; and not only those women who take up arms, but also those who are victims. As far as we were concerned, we had to dare to acknowledge those intuitions. Both of us, and each and every one of the women we met—we had to dare not to exclude ourselves from the desire for war or violence. Such a desire is legitimate, as in the case of resisting an abusive enemy or in the case of self defence. But it can also be illegitimate, resembling what could be atavistic cobwebs that are tightly spun in our inner self, to the point of choking out into a spewing lava of blood and fire, almost as in the unconscious. This is what we told ourselves in a hushed voice, because these presuppositions were not commonplace in the feminist movement to which we otherwise wholeheartedly adhered. And, we were telling each other, if it was true that the women of the world had nothing to do with war, considering the inner strength with which they are endowed (a strength that the feminist movement publicly revealed from the second half of the twentieth century on), if women have always indeed been fundamentally and consubstantially opposed to war from all the fibers of their deepest being, there would not have been any war from as far back as memory allows.

So we had thought that, in spite of the fact that males have dominated females for thousands of years, in spite of all the economic, social, philosophical, and sexual subordination (and subjugation), women always possessed this formidable power to stop wars. But it did not happen. And consequently we could not agree with the feminist slogan of recent years, a thousand times repeated and invoked: "Women give life, men take it!" We knew that we had to move past this simplifying binarism. We had to go beyond these simplistic oppositions. We had to work within a relational framework, as Gilles Deleuze would say in *Mille Plateaux*, "*un esprit de conjonction*." Therefore, the project could not be described as either war *or* women. But rather as war *and* women. We thus understood that we had to descend into the furthest depths of the human soul. And our obstacle-filled journey was enlightened by the writings of those women who had dared to undertake the journey before us, however differently. There have been many such women. All the same, I would like to name a few: Colette, Gabrielle Roy, Anne Hébert, Virginia Woolf, Susan Sontag, Marguerite Duras, Luce Irigaray, Michèle Montrelay, Annie Leclerc, and Hélène Cixous. We wanted to acknowledge the contribution of women authors who have reflected and written on the relationship between women, violence, and war.

And so, it was in this frame of mind that we embarked on our adventure. And we were fortunate to discover that on site, despite all the adversity they had met, not only did the women want to answer our questions, but they frequently preceded our own with others in such a way that we advanced, feeling our way along together. In other words, they were driven by the same desire of co-birth and co-knowledge. They wanted out. In them was a burning desire to speak.

Conception and Organization of the Book

Given the geopolitical situation, the funding options, and our personal at-
traction to certain places on the planet, we finalized a program spread out
over some two years, which could be summarized as follows:

We looked for material support based on the needs of each project. The
list of countries was determined according to the chronological order of
each trip. In the Balkans: Macedonia, Kosovo, Bosnia-Herzegovina (I use
the word "country" to simplify, because at the time, Kosovo and Bosnia-
Herzegovina were protectorates run by the international community, NATO
first and the UN later). In the Near East: Israel, Palestine, Lebanon. In
South East Asia: Pakistan and Sri Lanka. It was quickly agreed upon that
we would set up in Paris before and after visiting each area, in order to
give ourselves time to think, to organize our material, and to write between
each destination. We also chose Paris because we had to work in French.
My colleague Monique Durand had undertaken the production of a series
of ten documentaries of one hour each for the French radio station, Radio-
Canada. The experts with whom we were going to meet were mostly located in Paris (apart from the sociologists, social workers, psychiatrists,
psychologists, psychoanalysts, lawyers, gynecologists, doctors, and NGO
field nurses). They are authorities on war and on the acts of violence committed against women in times of war. Those whom we thank in our book
or who speak in the radio documentaries include: Marie-Françoise Allain,
Hoda Barakat, Nalah Chahal, Véronique Nahum-Grappe, and Françoise
Héritier. Furthermore, all the field experts are present in the broadcast or
named in the book. As are the following organizations: CIDA (Canadian
International Development Agency), Oxfam-Québec, Doctors of the World,
Amnesty International, Centre Québécois du PEN Club International,
KFOR (the Kosovo Force is a NATO-led intervention force located in Mace-
donia and in Kosovo), and in particular, the Canadian, Hungarian, and
French militaries. Also included were the *Alliances françaises,* located in almost every nation, as well as the departments of language, literature, and
sociology of the universities in all of these countries.

Before discussing how I organized the book itself, I would like to mention the radio documentaries. My association with my colleague, who is a
radio journalist and director, has taught me a lot about her medium.
Among other things, I learned that a documentary is not the same as a report, that there is a fundamental difference between the two. A reporter,
including a war correspondent, works within the time-space context of
locality and immediacy, and directly relates what he or she sees or hears,
without the critical distance that separates the captured event from its
audio or video transcription. In other words, what is captured by the camera or the tape recorder is done so in a raw linear way: it is passed on as
is to the listener or the viewer. On the other hand, a documentary, be it

video or audio, introduces a critical distance between the raw data and their transcription. Barthes wrote that all true criticism is about "setting a text into crisis" (that is into questioning). In the same way, the documentary, by the distance it maintains between the object captured and the subject treated, sets into crisis what, in the case of the radio, is verbalized. The words of women in particular, but also those of men who have something to say on the subject of the war, as well as all kinds of reflections and analyses, feed this "setting into crisis." The latter is also nourished by the documentary maker's narration, as well as by appropriate quotations; for this series, Monique Durand drew excerpts from my book, read by an excellent voice professional, Danielle Bouchard. Finally, it is fed by music of all eras and genres, from both here and the yonder places to which we have traveled.

These ten documentaries are a true polyphony of thoughts, of testimonies, and of voices. In other words, they are what radio and television reports never are, but what writing is—that is, both text and its probing, simultaneously. With the purpose of clearing up any ambiguity, which, unfortunately, was frequently lingering among critics of the printed and electronic press, let me state that the radio documentaries are not an adaptation of the book *Women and War* (even if they do share the same title). And the book is not a literary transcription of the radio series either. We worked together, with the same fundamental objective and similar views. We labored together, in concert, and often on the same wavelength, so to speak. But, like all writing, each of our work remained entirely unique and individual or "solitary." It was, however, a "people-filled" solitude, to quote Deleuze (in his *Dialogues* with Claire Parnet). In other words, the writing of the documentary and of the book may have felicitously coincided, but they never merged. We have opted in our writing, as we did on site, for what Claude Lévi-Strauss calls the "appropriate distance": not too far, that is, not in a haughty and authoritative way with regard to the subject matter and ourselves, nor too close, that is, in a state of stifling symbiosis. In our opinion, it was the only way to undertake such an adventure if we did not want to collapse from the hardship and sorrow we encountered.

As regards the book, I will only comment on three of its aspects. First, its structure: it is divided into ten chapters, eight of which are on each of the countries visited and are written in such a way as to respect in the chapters the chronological itinerary of the trips, which took us to Macedonia, Kosovo, Bosnia-Herzegovina, Israel, Palestine, Lebanon, Pakistan, Sri Lanka. And of the other two chapters, "Pre-Voyage" was written in Paris before leaving, and "Return" in Montreal after completing all the trips. Secondly, it is a book of writing, in the way I have defined it for the documentary. In order to give all its dimension and scope to everything that I had the opportunity to feel, to dream and to understand through the testimonies heard, but also, in order to give meaning—that is, feeling, direction, significance—to the stone ruins and to the bodily and spiritual ruins of those interviewed, but also, in order to best render as accurately as possible, the absurd evil and calamity of death at work, I had to undertake, as it were, through the creation of my work, a re-creation. Otherwise, beware the perverse contemplation or voyeurism of the obscene, or in my case, the sterile atony or muteness that makes us barren, which is in other words what we call depression, or absence of creativity. The aesthetic approach that I chose, that is, to reach the world's beauty even when facing ruins or when standing above the abyss, was based on an ethical choice. It is my belief that the reporters who do not know this and who did not experience it in the very flesh of the work in process, only add fire to the destructive mills of war. Their books can be alluring, but they are perverse and lethal. This choice of writing means that *Women and War* remains hard to classify into a specific genre: essay or narrative. Too bad! Or so much the better! We could say that this writing is beyond genres, just as we say something is stateless or beyond borders, since the human complexity that it attempts to unravel and to translate, goes beyond territorial boundaries, whether religious, ethnic, or national. It goes beyond all borders and all nations. And sometimes only fiction can restore a dimension of truth to a reality which is torn, lacerated, and seemingly schizoid.

A Map Is Not a Territory

A map is not a territory, according to the historian Michel de Certeau. I have cited this sentence over and over again, first as early as in 1979 as an epigraph to my novel *Lueur*. I had wanted that novel to be a translation of the inner quest of the corporeal monument engraved with letters (tattoos), which are partly erased yet still present, letters that represent the return of the repressed, also called "drives" in psychoanalysis. I had called and still call this writing the archaeology of the inner self.

And this is how I had conceived writing *Women in a World at War*. After having unfolded and read the geographical maps of the countries where we were going to work, after having read numerous written works that broach the questions of war, human disasters, violence of all sorts, and the complex relationship maintained with death by those who kill or who are killed before their biological clocks inevitably stop, I wanted to explore further than the maps and sociological analyses. I wanted to go beyond all prescribed frameworks, and delve into the waters of the unknown. Like an archaeologist of souls—including my own—I wanted to survey the territories devastated by terror and death in action. I wanted to see with my own eyes, to hear with my own ears, to touch with my own hands, what the others had explored of death at work during the state of war, all the while maintaining the connection to the other within myself.

It seemed to me that the field experience was consubstantial with the book to come. It seemed to me, surging from the same flow of knowledge, that the writing of the book offered me the best lit path on which to proceed, hard as it would be, on that shady field littered with debris and remains. Writing, through its very qualities, which are at once reassuring and disconcerting, would know how to give the debris a voice. I knew this from a sustained lifelong practice of it. I had no scientific or philosophical proof. And still have none. If I had proof, I would no longer write.

And on site, writing was made possible thanks to the words spoken by the women, but also to those spoken by certain men who seemed to hold the same type of feminine intimacy with death—a sort of complicity made of tender gestures, of whispered sentences, of childlike laughter and sometimes even of tears, as though an archaic dance from deep within had resurfaced, an archaic dance learned from a loving mother and developed before the discourse of the law and of structured language set in. Those primal words and dance would have absolutely proscribed the violation of both life and bodies. Facing the horrors of war left them stupefied. Dumbfounded. They were left in the interstices of structured discourses. Like their sisters, they were abandoned on the shores of the unsaid. Of what still had not been said on the subject of war and on the death drive. Of words that want to come to life so that peace—and the joy to simply live one's life—become possible. That is to say: conceivable.

How many times did they come to us and put to us the following request: "Tell it. Write it. Tell your fellow citizens living in peaceful countries what we have lived. Bear witness to what we have seen." I am not making this up. These were their words. And we always answered, "We're here." After all, this was why we were there. In this location, in this multiple "over there," where people spoke to us in diverse languages—French, English, or vernacular languages translated by interpreters—beyond the request for testimony, we have learned and taken away lessons that we will never forget, and which I will attempt to synthesize in the final part of my essay. To summarize is somewhat frustrating if we concede that the lessons are to be found embedded in the writing of the book, as if *woven* into its very flesh. The metaphor of weaving conveys the notion of "textual fabric," which escapes mainstream discourse (*tissu* [fabric] and *texte* have the same Latin root: *textus*). To paraphrase Maurice Blanchot in *La Communauté inavouable*, only the "discourse of the text" has knowledge of what the text explores. Thus, the metaphor.

At the present time, I cannot convey to you what the vernacular languages—Bosnian, Arabic, Urdu, and so on—have taught me, since I do not know them. In the book, however, writing had the gift to translate the very musicality of their intonations, their breath, their cries, or their chants—and even their silences—because writing so much possesses its own network of musical scores. An ethnographic survey is necessary, if only to

capture the harmonies, melodies, tonalities (or atonalities) of the unknown and seemingly opaque local languages for what they can offer the
semantic field. For a better understanding of the other and of oneself.
"Over there where I am" as says so well the French radio series (and the
book) by journalist Daniel Mermet from the French station France-Inter.
Ideally, it would be best to learn all languages. The division of languages,
as that of religions and of territories, was born concomitantly with war. Initially, with languages, humans would have instituted, implemented, and
entirely created a challenge to death, a warding off of ill fortune before
they felt that death would fall upon them absurdly, blindly. "Let's keep
our eyes open, and let's inflict death," they would have stammered. Cyn-
ically, they would have thought: "Let's create death." And who knows,
short of being able to proclaim "Let there be light," such as a God of whom
they would be jealous, while chained to their rocks and unable to picture
themselves as happy Sisyphus, those humans would cyclically cry out
from the depth of their hellish entrails: "Let there be darkness." Then, tirelessly, out of rage and armed to the teeth, they would create this darkness,
staging death itself. From one war to the next, until the end of time.

The Lessons Learned

In the section "Pre-voyage," I explain to what extent we did not know
what we were going to find. Not anxious by nature, and having always
been fascinated by that which eludes me, I could feel the heavy weight of
doubt nonetheless. This is why I quickly stopped telling myself what was
a constraint and a form of censorship: "I am neither an ethnologist, nor a
sociologist, nor a war correspondent, or a specialist of whatever allows us
to access the various explorations of the planet. What am I doing, going
to these lands, and on what grounds?" A poet by profession, I chose doubt
as my fundamental basis for investigation. Pen and notebook as my only
compass, I would inhabit doubt. I would attend the interviews conducted
by my journalist colleague. I would listen. I would watch. I would take
notes. I would sketch faces and landscapes, note human words; I would
record the noises of the city and of the countryside, the birds' songs and
the animals' sounds. I would sketch the devastation and the beauty, the
burned crops and the rivers that continued to flow. I would be attentive
to madness and delirium—there have been a few experiences of these. I
would forget my knowledge, but would let my thoughts stemming from
that knowledge emerge. In other words, I would be present and maintain
an "appropriate distance." Receptiveness would be the host of this new
home built on doubt.

In this state of mind, very early on our path, thanks of course to a har-
monious understanding with my partner, the lessons learned came from

the site itself, from the people we had met, from the history and the geography that were theirs. From the moment I landed at the miserable and militarized airport in Skopje, Macedonia, my drifting attention became active, and all my senses sharpened. I was more than just a notebook of observations. I became an active participant in all the interviews, which soon turned into conversations, dialogues of mutual understanding with the protagonists, who, chosen by my colleague, naturally transformed into characters on the radio and in the book, all the while remaining persons in their own right. There lies the paradox of the documentary, whether oral or printed. This is also why, with regards to the book, many readers— both men and women—have asked themselves whether it is an essay or fiction. In the end, this categorization into genres is of little importance. I was well informed, and I wrote directly from life. And each person who will risk book will also read it directly from life.

If we can derive another general lesson from this writing and reading—I call it general because it was repeatedly formulated in every country and in every language—it is that the primordial war among humans, the one which is the foundational war, is indeed the perennial war waged against women by the "stronger sex," by the males. Through many testimonies, our field experience forced us to confront a reality that we were not expecting, at least one we believed to be constructed by our Western feminist thought, that is, what women (and some men), from one culture and language to another, named in their own words "the war within war," such as a type of transnational, transethnic, and transreligious war. A war that transcends all others and that would be, according to many, the origin of all wars. We did not put these words into their mouths. We have elected to use their incessant reminder, received as a universal lament, as a primordial motif into the framework of our respective writings. On the world stage of traditional wars, what we call "the war within war" reached its worst point with the war rapes, which, thanks to the work of on-site humanitarians, were recently declared by the United Nations as a war crime. Be it individual rapes or gang rapes, there are two things that could qualify these crimes (which are the outcome of all wars, as historical studies are starting to reveal): first, women's bodies are a territory to be conquered by the soldiering enemy in the same manner as all other physical and psychological territories; second, the male sex organ is used as a weapon in the same way as all other weapons. In the book, numerous examples are given of this concrete phallic power. The act of terror that is rape—which is the conquering of a weaker, open, and vulnerable body, of a woman or child, by a stronger body, armed with a gun/phallus—constitutes, through the obscene, the staging of the state of war in times of peace. And in times of war, this act expresses this explicitly: this raped, corporeal territory will be the sowing field of the conqueror, "in order to perpetuate the offspring of a pure and superior race," as it was often uttered in a state of orgasmic rage, and was so reported by numerous victims.

We knew that the state of war went against the law, that all the wars in the world allowed people to live outside the law. And we are beginning to understand, with the war waged against women (or children) through rape, that war also defies desire. Rape is the intrusion of death into desire itself. This is its perversion. It is this *jouissance* [pleasure] both in and from the death drive, which radically distinguishes pornography from eroticism. Such is the devastating effect of this war crime. And we have not yet grasped the psychological extent of devastation carved into the children born of this death, a fertile breeding ground for possible future wars waged from the instinct for vengeance, which comes from the same matrix of death and desire.

Working for world peace consists in grasping this frightening reality.

I should say that in addition to the strength of testimonies, given as though they themselves have the power to heal, we have learned about their strength of courage. I should have to put the word courage in the plural because from one region to another there have been so many examples of it which often took similar shapes. Further than terror, higher than pain, we found courage, which is, literally, putting one's heart into one's work. In spite of all the material deprivations caused by war, women have proven themselves to be of an astounding vitality: they bake bread, fetch water or wood for the fire, or continue to raise children and attend to various aspects of their education. With their men gone, killed at war or captured, they see to the essentials so that life can carry on. They told us that, in times of war, they learned the delights of the freedom to think and to act as they please. And for the first time in their lives, they experienced the satisfaction of using their authority and a certain power over a family or clan unit, to the extent that many feared a return to peace, which they considered devoid of meaning, or which meant for them the return of old hardships related to their situation as dominated and subjugated subjects once their men returned.

The war within war also includes the thousands of honor killings perpetrated by men against disobedient women who disobey them—their leaders—and their laws. These men are fathers, brothers, sons, or spouses. Women are murdered for having chosen to go against their code, the family, clan, or tribal honor code that they established. One day we must hope, as with the case of genital mutilations to which about 120 million are subjected per year, all this will be condemned by the international community as war crimes or crimes against humanity. The right of humanitarian interference, as defended some two decades ago by Bernard Kouchner and his colleagues from *Médecins Sans Frontières*, should eventually include honor killings and crimes of genital mutilation committed against women. Now let us imagine the opposite. Let us imagine that

men, by the thousands and millions, had been subjected to these violations from the beginning of the human world, and this because of the
wrath of women. Let us imagine that human males had, in great number
and since always, been deprived of their capacity to sexual pleasure and
sexual power, as well as their capacity to live. Had this been the case,
human laws would have long ago punished the perpetrators. In the face
of such injuries, no tradition or religion must stand in the way. It is our
duty to intervene in this war waged on women, on their bodies and on
their capacity to enjoy life. The entire planet is our garden. And in this
garden, all human bodies must be respected.

The last lesson learned, but not the least, touches on the beauty of the
world. Among those physically or psychologically wounded by war, we
have found an unfathomable aptitude for happiness, which can be translated only into art: music, dance, painting, and poetry. We have witnessed
an astonishing capacity for the contemplation of ruins, reminiscent of
what the postmodern critics have called "the aesthetics of lacerations or
the aesthetics of wounds." In my own writing, I have tried to remain true
to this way of re-creating the world, to make of it a re-creation from its
very disaster. I will provide two examples to illustrate this aesthetics, which
is based on an ethics of life when facing death in action, as I pointed out
at the beginning. The first is in Sarajevo, when some guides with whom
we had become friends and who had suffered from the endless siege of
their beloved and partly destroyed city brought us to a neighborhood
called "Hiroshima" by its residents, because it was the most devastated,
bombarded, and wounded place. They themselves had lost their house
and garden. And on this evening, with the sun falling into a thousand
vivid colors on the old medieval neighborhood recently turned into a museum of ruins, we saw our friends lost in the contemplation of those giant
sculptures, which were moving under the clear sky and under the shim-
mering of the rays of the setting sun. Neither an architect nor a sculptor
of genius could have planned or overlooked this setting. Only a horrible
accident of history had shaped this work of art, offered this Sarajevo
neighborhood to our admiring eyes. We could have been at the Acropolis
or even at the Coliseum in Rome. But it was the year 2000, and we were
facing Sarajevo's Hiroshima. In this exact space, time found itself multi-
plied, stratified, and our awareness of it came from this accidental work
of art. It was rebuilt by them, by us, as it always happens after human
tragedies; it was giving us this immutable lesson—that is, life goes on so
that it does not fall into idleness.

The other example is very simple. It is of a young woman in Bosnia
whose parents were killed and her lover missing, dead, or imprisoned,
but who, in her immense solitude, went to work every morning, even
though work did not exist anymore, since the building where she had
worked had been destroyed. But she went everyday nonetheless, walking

eight kilometers and, despite the danger, walked back the same distance to return home. What she told us was astonishing: everyday, she would put on her best clothes and fix her hair and makeup. Why? For whom? For nothing and for no one. "To stay alive," she plainly answered. This verse from an anonymous poet I had read a long time ago later came to mind, "The ultimate proof of love is to adorn oneself for a lover who is blind." This young woman, in her own particular way, was thus in the grip of love, the love of life. This is what kept her alive.

She had spontaneously contributed to the re-creation of the world. She had, in her own way, warded off the misfortune of worthlessness and of the pervading atmosphere of death. This is what writing signifies for me, whatever web on which it is woven, from the most insignificant to the most tragic. Writing, as understood by Elias Canetti in *La conscience des mots*, could be summarized into the expression of three gifts: the gift for compassion, the gift of metamorphosis, and that gift how much more difficult to understand, but which we have experienced daily during our peregrination, the gift of being able to stand up to the forces of death and nothingness with the force of life itself and of its re-creation.

The people we spoke to demonstrated that they fully possessed these gifts. All that remained was for us to put those gifts to work, each in our own way. This might explain why—being in the frame of mind in which we were—we came across very few women warriors, and not a single woman torturer. And this is also why we have dreamed about the world as much as we have reflected upon it. *Rêver l'Autre* [Dreaming the Other], which is the title of a book written by the psychoanalyst René Major, is an integral part of the process of co-birth and co-learning.

Notes

1. In 1999, Monique Durand and Madeleine Gagnon answered a call from Radio-Canada asking them to create a work that would mark the beginning of the new millennium. They set out to travel into seven war-torn countries and investigate the wars from a woman's perspective. Monique Durand produced a radio program and Madeleine Gagnon wrote a book. The book is divided into seven chapters: Macedonia, Kosovo, Bosnia-Herzegovina, Israel and Palestine, Lebanon, Pakistan, Sri Lanka. In her much acclaimed "poelitical" book, which is a magnificent example of political lyricism, Madeleine Gagnon gives a voice to women she met in those countries and records their stories, the horrors they have suffered, as well as their cries and silences. However, Madeleine Gagnon rejects the belief held by some feminists that women are inherently pacifists. In her book, women in war indeed suffer and grieve, but they also love, hate, give birth, work, sing, and heal.

2. Editor's Note: This paragraph refers to Jacques Lacan's theory, whereby the self normally evolves from the stage of the "Imaginary"—that is the stage of fusion with the maternal and of prelinguistic communication (babble) in infancy—

to the stage of symbolic order, social control, and organized language, in other words the stage of the "Law of the Father." The "stage of the mirror" when the infant perceives him/herself as a separate and distinct being—that is as an "other"— marks the entry into the Law of the Father, which for some feminist theoricians also corresponds to the entry into the patriarchal production of the "feminine" identity for girls.

Section III

Rethinking Practices
Creating Spaces for Agency

INTRODUCTION

In mental health literature the dominant paradigm for examining the effects of forced migration and displacement on populations has been psychiatry and to some extent psychology. Empirical studies conducted from these perspectives have provided us with valuable information on the human vulnerability and suffering experienced by refugee populations. This information has had direct relevance for those working with refugee men, women, and children in the healthcare and social services sectors. Such studies, often conducted in refugee receiving societies in the West, have also pointed toward the intersecting barriers for refugee populations in their new countries of settlement and the long-term impact of war, trauma, violence, and displacement on the mental health of refugees.

However, a growing number of theoretical and empirical works rooted in feminist critique is deconstructing the narrow, victimized image of refugee women. Instead, while recognizing the systemic barriers faced by refugee women at all phases of the displacement experience (including the country of refugee women's origin, transitional state of refugee camps, and resettlement society), the concept of *refugee women* is undergoing a deconstructive transformation. The multiple strategies for agency employed by refugee women and their resiliences are being explored and documented. In circumstances where refugee women's personal narratives are heard without fear of their persecution, the generic category of the refugee woman begins to break down, and instead we hear voices of individual women who have hopes and fears for their welfare, and especially that of their families and their communities. We learn about the strategies utilized by women to maintain their sense of self identity and their pragmatism in planning for and carrying out the tasks of everyday life for their families.

The chapters in this section of the book provide a complementary understanding of the mental health of refugee women. While recognizing women's agency, they also are cognizant of the daily challenges and systemic vulnerabilities faced by refugee women. Drawing from her work with refugee populations, in chapter 9 Maryanne Loughry explores gender, culture, and displacement in *The Representation of Refugee Women in our Research and Practice*. She examines the root causes for the dominance of trauma discourse in psychological and psychosocial research. Loughry also considers the multiple disciplinary bases to the conceptualization of refugees as resilient. While arguing that the gap between the trauma and resilience narratives is decreasing, Loughry also provides the reader with a helpful review of their strengths and weaknesses. She underscores the importance of involving refugees as partners in research and listening to their voices.

In the second chapter in this section, *Refugee Youth, Gender, and Identity: On the Margins of Mental Health Promotion*, Nazilla Khanlou and Sepali Guruge focus on youth, an understudied subgroup of refugees. They consider the concept of identity from a developmental psychological perspective and recognize it as an important aspect of mental well being. The effects of displacement on the mental health of female refugee youth are examined. In considering refugee youth identity and mental health promotion, the authors argue for the relevance of an ecosystemic approach and intersectional perspective. Recognizing the limited available theoretical and empirical literature that focuses on female refugee youth, the chapter concludes with guiding questions for future scholarship and practice.

Elźbieta Goździak makes a timely contribution to the field of refugee and religious studies in chapter 11, *Pray God and Keep Walking: Religion, Gender, Identity, and Refugee Women*. She argues that religion and spirituality can be an integral part of refugee women's personal and collective sense of identity and play an important role in their sense of well being. Goździak considers the lack of understanding among mainstream clinicians regarding the role of religion and spirituality for refugees. This neglect, she elaborates, overflows to public and scholarly discourse on forced migration. As in the other chapters, Goździak underscores the gendered experience of forced migration; she discusses how refugee women's religious engagement differs from that of refugee men and considers the "compelling, competing, and contradictory" ways religion influences refugee women's experiences.

A qualitative study conducted in their community by Lynda Hayward, Maroussia Hadjukowski-Ahmed, Jenny Ploeg, and Karen Trollope-Kumar on the experiences of the resettlement process of refugee women from Sudan is presented in chapter 12, *We Want to Talk, They Give Us Pills: Identity and Mental Health of Refugee Women from Sudan*. The researchers utilized purposive sampling to recruit participants in their study. The main themes of the study were related to dimensions of the participants' identity and their experience in the resettlement years in Canada. The participants reported that in Sudanese culture there was no equivalent name for mental health and discussed mental health promoting strategies that drew from interconnections, sense of collective identity, and self reliance. Gendered identity, as part of mental well being, was intertwined in the web of the participants' culture, history, and environment. The title conveys the silencing the women experienced, but also their self-affirming agency.

9

The Representation of Refugee Women in Our Research and Practice

Maryanne Loughry

In recent years, in my area of research and teaching, which is psychosocial work with refugees, there has been a split between those researchers and humanitarian workers who have conceptualized refugees as traumatized and needy, and those who have perceived the vast majority of refugees to be resilient and resourceful, with only a small proportion of the refugee population needing professional psychological assistance (should it be available). In one sense this is a simplistic characterization of psychosocial work with refugees, yet in another sense it is precisely these different conceptualizations that have shaped the various expressions of psychosocial work that are seen in the field. Each conceptualization sets up a different starting point for how refugees are "represented" in such work, how their experiences and needs are researched, what advocacy is done on their behalf, and certainly how programs are designed to assist them in humanitarian emergencies. In addition, refugee populations have most often been seen as homogenous groups. Scant attention has been paid to the influential role of gender, age, social class, and cultural background on the effects of displacement of populations, and yet clearly these are significant. Recently there has been a growing awareness of the importance of the local culture of the displaced population. Little advancement has been made however, in considering the significance of the gender of the individuals we are concerned with. This is surprising when it is now commonly acknowledged that in almost every aspect of life there is a clear differential power relationship between men and women. Even more surprising, when this is not considered in settings of conflict, disaster, and displacement, where this differential relationship is typically more pronounced than ever. In such settings both men's and women's access to resources, decision making, and information are radically altered and familiar roles renegotiated, all the more reason why the representation of refugees has to be gendered.

Issues surrounding contemporary conflict and displacement have become increasingly more complex in these recent years. The numbers of people forcibly displaced have increased, and there has been a blurring between the distinctions of migration and forced migration (Martin 2001). One result of this blurring has been the emergence of new categories of forced migrants: internally displaced persons (IDPs), asylum seekers, and undocumented people, to name but a few. A variety of responses have accompanied this proliferation of categories. These responses are evident in the constant reformulation of refugee policies, program interventions, and popular opinion. One thing that has not changed within this evolving scene is that overall about 70 percent of refugee populations are composed of women and dependent children (Forbes-Martin 2004). Within this complexity, psychosocial work has emerged in the last decade as a humanitarian response to the needs and experiences of refugees and other forced migrants. In some contexts—for example, post-genocide Rwanda or Kosovo—psychosocial programs abound. In other settings, such work is very scarce. In significant institutional initiatives such as the Sphere Project,[1] which formulated a humanitarian charter and minimum standards in disaster responses, psychosocial work is not addressed at all.

I will first address the range of psychosocial work. The term psychosocial is best understood as the influence of social factors on an individual's mind or behavior, and on the interrelation of behavioral and social factors. However, if one reviews the literature on the psychological and psychosocial research with refugees, one soon becomes very aware that it is the trauma discourse that dominates much of the literature that purports to be concerned with the psychological and social needs of refugees. This discourse, firmly grounded in the discipline of psychiatry and medicine, dominates for many reasons. It is a discourse that is comfortable with publication and statistics. Its research methodology is objective, evidence-based, and standardized. It quantifies fact and proves hypotheses. It also dominates because it conceptualizes suffering and distress in a manner that is at least a little familiar to many researchers and international humanitarian staff, and somewhat possible to relate to because it elicits comparisons from everyday psychiatric work. What it often does not tell is the refugees' own stories and how they conceptualize their experiences, how they feel they were affected and, possibly more importantly, what they think might be the best ways to address the consequences of the suffering. Trauma research is generally based on self-reported symptom checklist scales, such as the Harvard Trauma Questionnaire (Mollica et al. 1992), the Hopkins Symptom Checklist or the Impact of Events (IES) scale (Horowitz, Wilner, and Alvarez 1979). These self-reported checklists have been developed for use with groups rather than individuals, frequently in settings where there are insufficient numbers of trained professionals to make individual clinical assessments. The checklists attempt to identify and measure psychopathological responses. Based on the diagnostic criteria of the Diagnostic Statistical Manual of Mental Disorders (DSM IV), these checklists usually assess levels of post-traumatic stress disorder (PTSD), depression, and anxiety, and obtain an impression of the interviewees' perception of their ability to function in everyday life. While very well crafted, only some of these checklists have been culturally validated for a select few cultures (Mollica 1991). Many of the checklists have not been validated for the cultures in which they are being used. This is most often the case with refugee communities.

In a study of trauma in Sierra Leone in 2000, *Médecins Sans Frontières,* conducted a prevalence study of psychopathology in Freetown, Sierra Leone, using the IES checklist, and while acknowledging that the scale had not been validated for use in West Africa, applied European cut-off scores and reported that 99 percent of respondents had very high levels of disturbances indicative of severe PTSD (De Jong, Mulhern, Ford, Van Der Kam, and Kleber 2000). We know from anthropological studies, that the presence or absence of symptoms in different cultural settings is not always indicative of the same response to the stress or traumatic events encountered, and to assume the universality of these symptoms puts the researcher at risk of what Kleinman called "category fallacy" (Kleinman 1977, 1987), where we impose Western categories in societies for which they lack coherence and validity (Bracken 1998; Summerfield 1999). This could well account for the results in this study. Symptoms such as nightmares can be indicative of PTSD in some cultures and interpreted as messages from ancestral spirits in another (Eisenbruch 1991). Further, such research does not go out of its way to explore the people's own descriptions of their lived experience and the consequences of these experiences. Recent research seems to be showing that the refugees' interpretation of the events they have experienced and the context of these events are important for determining whether the symptoms they report are distressing or not (Jones and Kafetsios 2002). At the worst, if the research is simply limited to gathering prevalence data, it runs the risk of "pathologizing" whole populations (Pupavac 2002) or creating "vulnerable subgroups." Once pathologized, the needs of the population and the accompanying humanitarian response lend themselves to the justification for the creation of psychiatric and psychosocial services with a strong clinical focus. To return to Freetown, does this data mean that we now need to establish psychiatric clinics for 99 percent of the Freetown population in Sierra Leone, or is there another interpretation of the data that can inform policy and humanitarian program making?

The conceptualization of refugees as resilient people and "social agents" takes one down another research path, one that also has strengths and weaknesses. In the first instance, it is often more difficult to find this research literature. It is not as readily published and often resides in gray literature that by definition is either semipublished or to be found in nongovernment agencies' needs assessments, evaluation reports, and manuals. If published, the research reports are spread throughout a variety of journals and websites, often away from the mainstream view. The literature exists, but one of the reasons why the resilience narrative is not as familiar as the trauma narrative in refugee research, is that the resilience narrative draws on a variety of study areas and academic disciplines, including psychology, psychiatry, social work, community development, and anthropology, and often these disciplines do not communicate easily with each other.

Practitioners who are more comfortable with the resilience narrative tend also to be more comfortable with the term *psychosocial,* a term that is often not adequately defined in research literature and humanitarian programs. As a result, I have heard it said that psychosocial work can be presented as so all embracing of every aspect of humanitarian work, that it seems too diffuse and unfocused and possibly would be better understood as a "cross-cutting response" rather than one that seeks to "stand alone." Having said this, there are also a lot of strengths and insights in psychosocial research with refugees. In recent years there have been a number of initiatives focused on bringing what I have called the "gray literature" to light, as well as establishing research agendas to determine where the gaps are in psychosocial research. These include the development of a psychosocial framework (Ager 2002) and the identification of suitable research methodologies for psychosocial research, including the development of appropriate standards for psychosocial fieldwork (Aarts 2001). Many of these initiatives have brought psychosocial researchers into contact with each other and with the trauma researchers. The gap between the two groups has certainly been reduced. Independently of these initiatives, some researchers have chosen to approach refugee research through the use of a variety of methodologies, frequently employing both qualitative and quantitative methods and triangulating the data to check the validity and reliability of the research findings. This use of multiple forms of data and perspectives has reduced the reliance on just one form of evidence and has addressed some of the cross-cultural research concerns which I addressed above and which are so significant in our work. I wish to highlight the work of Dr. Lynne Jones, a psychiatrist from Cambridge, who has recently published a study on the adolescent understanding of political violence and psychology in Bosnia-Herzegovina (Jones 2002; Jones and Kafetsios 2002). Dr. Jones has employed both quantitative and qualitative methods, including symptom rating scales, participant observation, in-depth interviews, and other less conventional methods such as lifeline drawing. Her rich work has challenged previous findings in this area. In particular, I want to focus on her findings in relation to active political engagement and ideological commitment. Earlier work, particularly in the Palestinian territories (Qouta, Punamaki, and El Sarraj 1995), had indicated that active political involvement, especially once significant political gains were attained, had increased children's self esteem and decreased their symptomatology. Jones, on the other hand, found that disengagement, in the form of disinterest in the causes and consequences of the conflict, was associated with greater psychological well being and an increased sense of security. She explained this difference in findings, in the light of the nature and context of the conflict. What is significant here is that Jones, because of using a number of quantitative and qualitative research methods, has the data to explore in much greater depth the adolescents' own understanding.

In 1993, while in the Vietnamese camps in Hong Kong, I led a team of researchers in exploring women's perspective on detention. This research was a follow up to earlier research that had focused on the effects on children of living in detention (McCallin 1992). The detention centers in Hong Kong in the late 1980s and early 1990s were large prisons, made of concrete and surrounded by barbed wire. Movement was restricted both inside and out of the centers and many of them were characterized by violence and despair. In the Whitehead Detention Center, there was a population of twenty thousand Vietnamese asylum seekers. Women comprised approximately 40 percent of the population (Loughry, McCallin, and Bennett 1993). The children's study had led to new insights for the social service agencies that were working in the centers and had given the detention center population a sense that necessary questions were being asked, and that there was international concern for the children's well being. It was hoped that the women's study would do some of the same. The methodology employed in the research was both qualitative and quantitative. Over one thousand women participated in focus group discussions in five detention centers. Focus groups were used because this method was thought to be more culturally sensitive for the Vietnamese women. The research proved to be very popular and almost ran the risk of slipping into a series of afternoon tea meetings. The women expressed gratitude for being asked their opinions and being listened to. Eight themes emerged from the focus groups: joblessness, public and personal hygiene, medical care, stress, provisions, protection and safety, leisure and recreation, and education of children. These results emerged in a setting characterized by riots and threats of forced repatriation. The emerging themes reflected more the everyday concerns of the women in the context of a violent setting. They would not have been easy to predict without hearing from the women. They also gave the women, and the nongovernment agencies that were accompanying them, something to work with.

In subsequent years, I also conducted a collaborative study on children in Gaza City designed to elicit the concerns of refugee children and adolescents. Gaza City is also a setting that could be characterized as one of prolonged violence and deprivation. We employed a similar method of focus group work, as well as developing with the children a "worries" scale. This scale was constructed using items contributed by Palestinian children. Initially the questionnaire had thirty-seven items that children had said they or others worry about. When the children's responses to this questionnaire were ranked, their number one worry was "dirty streets." This was followed by "Israeli occupation" as number two (MacMullin and Odeh 1999). A repeat of this study in a West Bank town produced the same result. Again, who could have predicted this, and was this something that could now be addressed? The results do not negate the concerns of the children with regards to the conflict that was totally influencing their lives, but it does reflect refugee children actively getting on with their daily chores and activities in the midst of the conflict. Interestingly, when we looked at gender difference in worries, the girls reported a greater degree of worry than the boys. They also worried more about different things than the boys. We discovered again that to ignore the factor of gender was a sure way not to fully understand the concerns of the children we were researching.

The above two studies, and there are many others, reveal the consequences of engaging refugees as partners in research. In my experience the results of this engagement are unexpected and very revealing. I believe this is particularly so when we work with refugee women.

One thing that seems to remain constant in all of the categorizing, recategorizing and responding to refugees is the significant proportion of refugees who are women. This fact, I will argue, is often readily acknowledged in literature but is today not fully taken into account in refugee policy and refugee research. Some years ago, there was a great deal of focus on refugee women. There was the pioneer work of Susan Forbes-Martin (1991) and the People Oriented Planning initiative of UNHCR (Anderson 1994), both in the early 1990s. Those particularly concerned with refugee women, advocated for the creation of programs and initiatives that were for refugee women alone. Discussions ranged across the field and in various headquarters about the appropriateness of such programs with many fearful they could further marginalize women. Later, gender mainstreaming was accepted as the appropriate alternative (Crewe and Harrison 1998), particularly in agencies such as UNHCR. However, like many other gender mainstreaming initiatives, it would now seem that the necessary focus on the needs of differing groups of refugees has been swamped by the dominant paradigm of the mainstream itself. It would appear that these earlier discussions have now faded into the background, and many assumptions have been made about the psychosocial needs of refugees without considering the population along gender lines. To give an example, while preparing this chapter I did a search on PsycInfo for recent psychological research on refugees. From 1996 there were 763 research articles related to refugees, seventy-five referred specifically to refugee children and only thirty-seven were particularly focused on refugee women. In recent years, we have often come to know the concerns of refugee women through knowing their children. We have only recently started to have a literature that looks at the needs of young refugee men (Turner 2000).

In the area of mental health, we know that women have very different prevalence rates for specific disorders to those of men (Ramsay, Welch, and Youard 2001). We also know that women tend to present their symptoms differently and require different management. These factors should require us to ask how best to interpret symptom rating checklists when they are done across adult populations without disaggregating the population for gender. When we work with refugee women from various cultural groups, gender differences can partly account for what is reported as under recognition of mental health problems, or even the opposite.

I want to come back to the question of research methodology. Our starting points in the area of the psychosocial needs of refugees will in many senses determine our endpoints: what it is we have to say, or in many instances to publish? The consequences are significant. The starting points determine how the refugees are represented in the research, whether their perspectives are fairly taken into account, and whether the results of the research have gender validity. In the recent era of evidence-based medicine, narratives, or the opportunity to tell the story of the experience, has been somewhat sidelined. I am led to believe that this trend is slowly being reversed (Roberts 2000). It is argued that postmodernism has played a significant role in this reversal.

Whatever the reason, in the area of refugee studies, an area replete with different cultures and profound experiences that are outside of the ordinary, it is important that we researchers work to ensure that it is the refugees' voices and experiences that are at the forefront of our work and the cornerstone of our research methodology. Not to do this is to contribute to the negative consequences of forced migration. For those of us who want to ensure that our research is not only culturally valid but also gender valid, the incentive is to engage refugee women at every level of the research process.

Note

1. The Sphere Project was launched in 1997 by a group of humanitarian Nongovernmental Organizations (NGOs) and the Red Cross and Red Crescent movement to establish standards for humanitarian response to environmental disasters and conflict situations. www.sphereproject.org

10

Refugee Youth, Gender, and Identity

ON THE MARGINS OF MENTAL HEALTH PROMOTION

Nazilla Khanlou and Sepali Guruge

In this chapter we explore the identity and mental health of refugee female youth. Specifically we consider identity as an aspect of mental well being and approach the topic of identity from a developmental psychological perspective within the resettlement context. While we recognize the importance of the social and geopolitical dimensions of identity, we argue that its psychological dimension also has particular relevance to mental health promotion initiatives. Our focus of inquiry in this chapter is on youth. We distinguish this group from children and consider it as the psychosocial period between childhood and adulthood. As these stages of human development (childhood, youth, and adulthood) are historically and culturally bound, we hesitate to provide a specific age range for this period. In our work with youth in the North American context this phase is often recognized as "adolescence" or the "teenage" years.

This chapter begins with statistics on the size of refugee youth globally and in Canada, followed by the effects of displacement on the mental health of refugee youth. An overview of theoretical literature on adolescent identity and our theoretical position regarding refugee youth identity are elaborated next in the chapter. We argue for the relevance of identity in mental health promotion initiatives, and propose questions for future scholarship and practice in the field of refugee youth identity and mental health promotion.

Refugee Youth Global Population

Refugee youth are a significant size of the global refugee population. Over the last decade or so, millions of children and youth have been killed, wounded, or orphaned due to political, ethnic, or religious conflict, war, and ecological disasters. According to the United Nations High Commissioner for Refugees (UNHCR), in 2003 the global refugee population was around 9.7 million (UNHCR 2004). Among the 17.1 million persons of concern to UNHCR, which includes internally displaced and stateless persons, 7.3 million (43 percent) were school aged children and youth. During the same year, Canada had 25,984 refugees, of which close to half were children and youth (female: 48.3 percent; male: 51.7 percent) (Citizenship and Immigration Canada 2003). In light of the significant numbers of refugee youth both at the global level and at the national level in Canada, we propose that addressing the mental health promotion needs of refugee youth must take center place in mental health promotion theory, research, and practice.

Displacement and the Mental Health of Refugee Youth

To understand the effects of displacement on the mental health of refugee youth, a literature search of the National Library of Medicine's database (MEDLINE) and Cumulative Index to Nursing and Allied Health Literature (CINAHL) was conducted. The following combination of key words was applied in searching articles that were written in English and published from 1990 to 2004: youth/adolescence/children *and* refugee *and* mental health/psychiatry. The search resulted in twenty articles. In addition, articles and book chapters that were available to us through our work and communications with colleagues were also reviewed. While there has been a growing recognition and interest in the health of refugee children and youth, published literature on the psychological identity of refugee youth is limited. We searched for this topic and came across two scenarios: (1) little or no focus on youth, or (2) the experiences of youth were grouped with those of women or children. Provided next is a summary of retrieved literature on the topic of mental health of refugee youth.

Migration, whether planned or not, is a stressful process. For refugees who are forced to leave their countries of origin and have not had time to create a sense of closure with their past (to say their goodbyes), to plan the practicalities of travel and resettlement, the migration process can be even more stressful (Berman 2001; Fazel and Stein 2002). Recent studies have explored the effects of war and war trauma on the physical, mental, and emotional health and well being of refugee children and youth (e.g., Ackerman 1997; Barnes 2001); while other studies (e.g., Phan 2003) have noted their resilience, strength, and motivation in overcoming these challenges.

According to a number of authors (Barnes 2001; Berman 2001; Fazel and Stein 2002), the stresses children and youth are exposed to can be understood as occurring at three stages: premigration, migration, and postmigration stages. Others such as Lustig et al. (2004) noted these stages as preflight, flight, and settlement phases. These chronological phases of refugee experiences have been used here to outline the effects of displacement on the mental health of refugee youth.

In the *premigration* context, youth may experience chaos and trauma, even though the amount, the intensity, and the length of this experience may vary. In general, they may have been exposed to physical harm, intimidation, threat, deprivation, separation, and isolation, and have experienced or witnessed torture, trauma, assaults, murder, and unexpected deaths of their family members, friends, and neighbors (Berman 2001; Fazel and Stein 2002; Miller 1994; UNHCR 1994). Such experiences may accompany loss of their cultural and social systems and structures, and access to education, training, and healthcare (UNHCR 1994). In addition, incidences of random, purposeful, or systematic sexual violence are often committed against adolescent girls during periods of conflict, war, and their aftermath (UNHCR 1994). Adolescent girls, in particular, may be subjected to any of the following: sexual abuse or rape, early or forced marriage, forced or coerced prostitution, and trafficking (Ward 2002). In addition, they may have had to live in camps and other temporary shelters that did not include adequate living and sanitary conditions (UNHCR 1994). Such experiences may lead to difficulty in achieving the milestones in their transition from childhood to youth to adulthood. These difficulties may be experienced differently by youth based on their gender and age, as well as the social, cultural, political, and economic environment within which they live.

For refugee youth, *migration* to a safe country can be a lengthy process, and may involve poverty, loss of security, and isolation that may create significant threats to their mental health and well being. During this period youth may be separated from their family, at times as a strategy to get them to safety when it is difficult to travel as a family (Ayott and Willamson 2001; Fazel and Stein 2002). In addition to the stress, anxiety, and fear they may experience due to separation from loved ones, and the uncertainty about how and when they might reach a safe country, youth may continue to endure trauma and violence (Fazel and Stein 2002). During migration to another country, they may be exposed to cross-border attacks, labor exploitation, physical abuse, and sexual violence and exploitation (Human Rights Watch 1999; Thomas et al. 2004).

The number of *postmigration* stresses that youth have to endure once they reach a safe country is also significant. According to Fazel and Stein (2002), the adjustment period in a new country is often referred to as a period of "secondary trauma." During this period youth may continue to experience multiple stressors including racism at large, financial difficulties, cultural and linguistic differences, and loss of familiar support systems (Fazel and Stein 2002; Lipson and Omidian 1997). Referring to previous work by other scholars, Berman (2001) stated: "Separation from family members after migrating to a new country has consistently been identified as a threat to the health and well being of refugee youth" (245). On the other hand, differential rates of acculturation among family members (Williams and Westermeyer 1983) can result in, among other challenges, intergenerational conflicts (Birman 1998; Handa 2004; Rick and Forward 1992). Berman (2001) elaborated: "As children and adolescents become skilled in the language and customs of the new country, their parents may need to depend on their children for help with language and social skills. The resulting role reversal is seen as a threat to the parents' authority" (246). Balancing and negotiating competing expectations of their peers and parents at times can create significant stress for refugee youth. Youth also experience stress as part of their parents' and extended family's post-migration challenges and anxieties. A number of publications (e.g., *Of Silk Saris and Mini Skirts* by Handa 2004) describe the struggle youth, and adolescent girls in particular, may experience in their search for a "cultural" identity and desire to "fit in" their new society.

Identity as Part of Mental Well Being

In providing an overview of theoretical literature on adolescent identity formation, we refer to Erik Erikson's influential work as the starting point. Close to four decades ago, in his seminal work on youth and identity, Erikson observed that "in the social jungle of human existence there is no feeling of being alive without a sense of identity" (1968: 130). To date much of the psychological developmental literature has focused on mainstream youth. While recently more attention is being given to the identity experiences of immigrant youth (for example, Khanlou, Siemiatycki, and Anisef 2003; and Khanlou et al. 2002), theoretical and empirical literature related to refugee youth identity is sparse.

Across the Western context, the period of adolescence is recognized as a key stage in identity development. Erikson's (1963, 1968) particular focus on adolescence and identity as part of the human life cycle led to its recognition as an important construct. Youth's ability to resolve the psychosocial dilemma of identity crisis continues to be regarded as an indication of mental well being. While identity is experienced as a psychological experience, Erikson regarded identity within youth's historical and social context. However, research conducted among youth subsequent to Erikson's work often focused on the psychological dimension and less heeded its social aspect. This resulted in psychological developmental literature focusing predominantly on mainstream youth and considering their experiences as the developmental norm (Khanlou 2006).

In addition to an *a-contextual* construction of identity, earlier classical work in the field of identity and adolescent psychosocial development assumed that male developmental pathways were the norm for both genders (Khanlou 2007). Feminist scholarship critiqued the male bias embedded in Eriksonian developmental theory (e.g., Gilligan 1982). More recently, mainstream feminist discourse on gender in general as well as on health and youth identity in particular has been critiqued to represent dominant viewpoints (Guruge and Khanlou 2004; Ohye and Henderson Daniel 1999). Only recently are researchers beginning to explore the relationship between adolescent refugee status and self image (e.g., Begovac et al. 2004). "The uprooting, disruption and insecurity inherent in refugee situations can harm children's [and youth's] physical, intellectual, psychological, cultural and social development" (UNHCR 1994: 38). It is also important to explore the relevance of culture in mental health promotion. "Culture provides children [and youth] with identity and continuity. By learning the values and traditions of their culture, [they] learn how to fit into their family, community and the larger society" (UNHCR 1994: 29).

In arguing for the important role of identity as part of mental well being, and the influence of family, community, and the society at large on identity development and mental health and well being, we apply an ecosystemic approach. A visual representation of an ecosystemic framework, a modified version of Heise's (1998) as noted in Guruge (2004), is provided in Figure 10.1.

This approach, which recognizes that human development is influenced by the continual interaction between the individual and her/his environment, is congruent with evolving mental health promotion concepts (Khanlou 2005). Also given the complex and multiple dimensions of identity, an ecosystemic approach provides us with an intersectional view on the

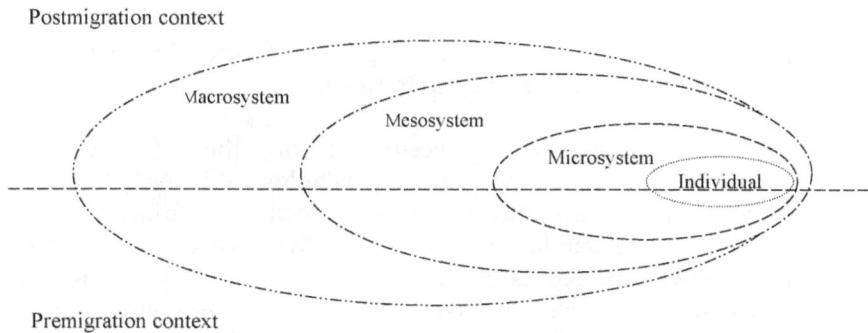

Postmigration context

Macrosystem

Mesosystem

Microsystem

Individual

Premigration context

Figure 10.1 *Visual representation of an ecosystemic framework (Source: Guruge 2004)*

mental health of refugee youth. Thus, mental health promotion is recognized to occur at multiple levels, including the individual, familial, community, national, and international levels. This approach implies that mental health promotion initiatives are not confined to the domain of healthcare or social service providers. While these providers can, and do, play a paramount role in dealing with the psychosocial outcomes of displacement and promoting the mental health of refugee youth at the individual level, initiatives taking place in systems such as justice and law, education, and immigration and resettlement can have consequences on the individual identity development and mental health of youth and their families. Furthermore, the ecosystemic approach recognizes that when efforts are made to promote global peace, support human rights, and reduce international economic disparities, the mental health of individuals including refugee youth is also promoted.

Toward New Directions in Mental Health Promotion with Refugee Youth

In this chapter, we have explored the identity of refugee youth from a psychological perspective, and argued that refugee youth are not fully considered in mainstream youth identity theoretical and empirical scholarship. This limitation has translated into the lack of appropriate lifestage and gender-specific initiatives, as well as educational, health, and social services, and immigration and resettlement policies for this group in resettlement societies. The effectiveness of mental health promotion polices and initiatives for refugee youth relies on considering the intersections of youth identities across gender, race, ethnicity, culture, and class within specific personal and familial contexts, and alongside community and larger social systems of the host country (e.g., immigration, employment, and education) (Khanlou and Crawford 2006).

We propose the following questions to guide future scholarship and practice and to further bridge the gap in this field:

1. How does the sense of displacement during the critical years of human development affect youth's psychological identity?
2. How do the presence of fear and stress resulting from persecution, violence, social instability affect female youth's psychological identity?
3. How do the experiences of refugee female youth living in refugee camps differ from those granted refugee status in a receiving country?
4. How does the sense of space (e.g., confined physical space, restricted mobility, living in constant close proximity to others) affect youth's psychological identity?

5. How do the transformations in refugee laws and general political context affect refugee youth?
6. What protective factors provide a buffer for refugee youth dealing with postmigration and settlement stresses and challenges?
7. How do female refugee youth build resiliency and maintain their hope for the future? How is this related to their sense of mental well being?
8. How do the social markers of identity (gender, ethnicity, in-group/out-group membership) and lifestage intersect in youth' psychological identity in the postmigration and resettlement context?

In conclusion, with growing globalization of the teenage period in human development and domination of mainstream representations of youth in the resettlement context for refugee youth, we believe scholars, practitioners, and policymakers must urgently pay close attention to the intersections of gender, lifestage, and identity. We call for imminent attention because we recognize identity as an important aspect of the mental health and well being of refugee youth.

11

Pray God and Keep Walking

RELIGION, GENDER, IDENTITY, AND REFUGEE WOMEN

Elżbieta M. Goździak

The title of my chapter, *Pray God and Keep Walking*, comes from a book by the late Bea Hackett (Hackett 1996). Bea's volume includes narratives by twenty-eight refugee women who discuss how their lives have been shaped and rearranged by flight and loss, by refugee camps, by resettlement policies, and by their own individual responses, skills, and initiatives. Although spirituality and religion are not the main focus of Hackett's book, many of the narratives are testimonies to the strength refugee women derive from prayer and faith. The phrase *Pray God and keep walking* comes from a story by a Haitian woman, Marie Claire, who came to the United States in 1989. The subtitle, *Religion, Gender, Identity and Refugee Women*, enumerates the issues I examine in this chapter and evokes the complex interplay of religion, gender, and identity, including the often contradictory status spirituality and religion play in refugee women's lives and the ways religion affects their identity.[1]

Throughout this chapter, I will discuss these and related points—such as the difficulty of separating religion and spirituality when it comes to gender issues and the challenges refugee women face when they seek solace and assistance from spiritual leaders. I will begin by making a few observations about the state of affairs when it comes to the issues of religion, gender, and identity in the forced migration discourse and practice. In my capacity as a political dissident and a refugee woman from Poland who found safe haven in the United States in the mid 1980s, and as a researcher and policymaker with two decades of experience in research and policy analysis on various aspects of forced migration, I have dealt with issues related to the role of religion, gender, and identity in refugee women's lives both personally and professionally. I will draw on both of these experiences.

My conceptualization of religion encompasses both the sociopolitical and spiritual dimensions of the term. In addition to "religion," I also use the term "spirituality." Spirituality used to be a "predominantly Roman Catholic term applied chiefly to certain practices of prayer within a traditional institutional church framework" (Muldoon and King 1995: 331). In recent decades, however, there has been an expansion of both the meaning and the application of the term spirituality; both Christian and non-Christian traditions began to use the term. References to spirituality are also made in social movements such as Marxism, feminism, or even the environmental movement. "The term has broadened to connote the whole of the life of faith and even the life of the person as a whole; including its bodily, psychological, social and political dimensions" (Schneiders 1989: 679). No matter what definition of spirituality one adopts, it is nearly impossible to separate spirituality from religion. Nonsectarian understanding of spirituality is only applicable to philosophical discourse. In the real world of human experience, spirituality is never exhibited in a nonsectarian manner. I use both terms to indicate the very close relationship of these two concepts.

The Role of Religion and Spirituality in Forced Migration

I have known for a long time that religion and spirituality play a major role in the lives of many refugees, including refugee women. The Catholic Church provided spiritual and material support to many political dissidents in my native Poland, and the Catholic faith sustained many Polish women and men in the difficult times of living under a totalitarian regime, enduring detention in internment camps, suffering maltreatment by the state security force, and surviving the dark days of martial law. But those were personal experiences. As a social scientist, I have been searching for validation of these anecdotal data.

I first began studying the role of religion and spirituality in refugee lives after the Gulf War of 1991, when the federal Office of Refugee Resettlement (ORR) assisted the first cohorts of the 7,761 Kurdish and 30,392[2] Iraqi refugees resettled in the United States. The latter group included many young, single males who did most of their social development either in Saddam's army or in the refugee camp in Saudi Arabia, and were experiencing numerous adjustment problems upon resettlement in the United States. The group also included a smaller number of devout Muslim women whose clothing, *hijab* in particular, made them very visible in local communities and often impeded their integration process.

At that time I was working as a Senior Public Health Advisor in the federal Refugee Mental Health Program (RMHP), an intra-agency agreement between the Office of Refugee Resettlement (ORR) and the Substance Abuse and Mental Health Services Administration (SAMHSA). The RMHP and ORR team was looking for ways to ease the Iraqi refugees' integration into the secular American society. In fact, it was the secular nature of the resettlement services, particularly psychosocial and mental health programs that seemed to be the major stumbling block in providing culturally appropriate services and developing rapport between Iraqi refugees and service providers. Many a time, an Iraqi told me "Elźbieta, how can I trust somebody that does not believe in God?" Contrary to popular belief, the Iraqis had a great appreciation of religious diversity, but found it difficult to relate to "people without God."

Indeed, although polls indicate that 90 percent of Americans profess a belief in God, a much smaller fraction of mental health clinicians share this belief (Larson, Milano, and Lu 1998). Sevensky (1984) observed that some psychiatrists, for example, are suspicious of religion because of their lack of knowledge or practice of religion and because psychiatrists may observe radical differences between themselves and their patients in regard to religious matters. A study conducted by Galanter and colleagues indicates that 56 percent of psychiatrists identify themselves as agnostic or atheist, while only 5 percent of the general US population identifies with these categories (Galanter et al. 1991). Bergin (1980) also noted the disparity between the low levels of religious sensitivity of therapists in contrast to their patients.

However, one does not necessarily need to be religious in order to incorporate spiritual and religious beliefs into treatment modalities. Meitzen et al. (1998) studied clinicians' knowledge of religious issues and their willingness to utilize such knowledge in clinical practice. The study's results support a low level of religious knowledge on the part of mental health clinicians whose self rating of religious knowledge averaged 2.85 on a scale of 1 (low) to 5 (high). The researchers concluded that "This level of religious knowledge would not, in many instances, suffice to comprehend the beliefs and presuppositions about life and the world which shape the inner dynamics of an authentically religious patient" (Meitzen et al. 1998: 7). Indeed, many of the Muslim refugee women I worked with commented that they felt misunderstood by the mainstream service providers, who did not understand their beliefs and did not see the person behind the *hijab*, or did not understand the many reasons why women veiled. A young Somali woman once told me: "I never veiled when I was growing up. Actually, I was a T-shirt and jeans kind of girl for most of my life. But here I use my clothing to protect myself from being ogled and to clearly identify myself." Interestingly, 61 percent of the surveyed clinicians reported that they used religious knowledge in their practice and only 33 percent consistently refrained from initiating discussions of religious and spiritual matters with their patients even if they considered themselves knowledgeable about these issues.

I gathered further data supporting the importance of religion and spirituality in forced migration in the course of a needs assessment of thirty-two thousand Cambodian refugees residing in Long Beach, California, and a three-month field assignment at Fort Dix during Operation Provide Refuge (OPR). Elsewhere, I have written about Operation Provide Refuge, a US resettlement program for some 4,200 Kosovar Albanians expelled by the Serbian authorities during the wave of violence that swept Kosovo in late February and early March of 1998, and displaced by the seventy-eight–day bombing campaign launched by NATO a year later (Goździak and Tuskan 2000; Goździak 2002); highlighting the role of religion and spirituality in ameliorating the suffering of ethnic Albanians and arguing that the spiritual context of human suffering should provide the foundation of understanding and responding to the suffering of refugees. In these articles I underscored the intersection of refugees' suffering and resulting trauma with spirituality and religion and juxtaposed the *emic* perspective of the Kosovars, who conceptualized their suffering as a spiritual experience and turned to Islam to recover from war trauma, with the *etic* perspective of the Western service providers, who tended to secularize the suffering of the Kosovar Albanians and shied away from interventions incorporating religious ritual and spiritual beliefs.

Although my research with Iraqi, Cambodian, Kosovar, and, later on, Bosnian and Somali refugees, confirmed the diversity of religious and spiritual beliefs and practices that sustain many refugees and forced migrants in their processes of displacement, migration, and integration to the host society, I have noticed that contemporary considerations among both researchers and policymakers, tend to neglect the role of religion and spirituality as a source of emotional and cognitive support, a form of social and political expression and mobilization, and a vehicle for community building and group identity. Virtually no scholars examine the different roles religion plays in the lives of refugee women. Despite the fact that religious persecution figures prominently in the UN definition of a refugee, and faith-based organizations which provide emergency relief to refugees facilitate the settlement of refugees and provide them with a wide range of social services, policy debates about migration and displacement on the international and national levels have tended to ignore religious issues.

In the United States, eight of the ten major resettlement agencies are faith-based, but religion and spirituality have been absent in the public discourse on refugee resettlement and integration. It is difficult to elucidate this contradiction with any certainty. I have heard many different explanations. Most of them invoked separation of State and Church as well as federal funding that bars recipients from proselytizing. All US voluntary agencies receive federal funding to resettle refugees and are fearful that activities aimed at utilizing refugees' spiritual and religious beliefs to enhance their resiliency might be perceived as proselytizing while using taxpayers' money. A number of agencies serving refugees of different faiths seemed ill prepared to deal with religious diversity: they lacked knowledge of other religions or commitment to interfaith dialogue. Other explanations were reminiscent of an increasingly secularized nature of mainstream, institutional religions in the West. Some pointed out strong secularizing currents among new immigrants, who come to the United States from traditional Muslim, Hindu, or Buddhist societies to "breathe a sigh of relief, cherishing not only the freedom to practice religion but also the freedom not to, the freedom to be secular in their life and thought" (Eck 2002: 30).

The neglect of the role of religion and spirituality in the lives of many refugee women and men can also be seen in the scholarly discourse on forced migration. When Dianna Shandy of Macalester College and I (Goździak and Shandy 2002b) issued a call for papers seeking submissions to a thematic volume of the *Journal of Refugee Studies* on religion and forced migration, we received numerous emails from researchers and policymakers encouraging us to proceed with the planned volume, but expressing regret that they never pursued these topics in any systematic way and had only anecdotal information confirming the significance of religious beliefs and practices in refugees' journeys. Most authors who did submit manuscripts indicated a dearth of research on this issue and struggled to place their own studies in a broader analytical context. These experiences appeared to reflect a more widespread state of affairs. For instance, the Social Science Research Council (SSRC) and the International Center for Migration, Ethnicity, and Citizenship (ICMEC) (see www.newschool.edu/icmec) located at the New School for Social Research, both in New York City, launched preliminary efforts in recent years to encourage research among scholars to understand the many intersections between religion and migration. It is not yet clear whether these seed initiatives will develop into any sort of systematic or enduring inquiry. Incidentally, only one of the projects supported by SSRC focused on gender and religion; Marie Friedmann Marquardt received a SSRC fellowship to conduct a research project titled *Changing Landscapes, Revising Selves: Gender, Transnational Migration, and Religion among Mexicans in the New South.*

When religion is considered in studies of refugees, it most often receives attention for its role in conflict settings and the politicization of religious identity. This approach can be seen in examples as geographically diverse as Ireland and the Sudan, and is exemplified by Sells' (1996) attempt to prove the religious character of the Serbian and Croatian campaigns against the Bosnian Muslims as he explores the religious dimension of the Bosnian war, in particular the role of Christian religious mythology in preparing the ground for genocide. The relationship between religious persecution and refugee is central to the definition of a refugee and has long been considered of importance as a root cause of flight and should be of equal importance in protection of refugees. It plays a key role in the global triage of refugee cases and forms a basis for admission to resettlement countries (Zolberg, Suhrke, and Aguayo 1989). The connections between religion and identity, as discussed by E. Valentine Daniel (1996) in his study of nationalist violence and refugees in Sri Lanka, are often essentialized in ways that mask the construction of ethnic categories.

Another emergent theme within the study of spirituality and refugees is the role of religion in coping with trauma. Welaratna (1993), for instance, documents the experience of Cambodian refugees, including a story of a middle-aged woman and her young daughter, who survived Pol Pot's "killing fields" and have begun new lives in America. She underscores the importance of interpreting Cambodians' holocaust experiences within the context of Theravada Buddhism. The role of religion in coping with trauma becomes particularly significant in the current debate between trauma-based Western behavioral science and indigenous approaches to human suffering, including religious and spiritual beliefs and practices (Goździak and Tuskan 2000; Goździak 2002). Discussing Mozambican refugees in Tongogara Refugee Camp in Zimbabwe, Ann Mabe observes that the most neglected component of culture in the refugee camp is the spiritual well being of the people (Mabe 1994). Mabe discusses very eloquently the importance of ancestor spirits for the well being of Mozambican refugees; without the spirits a lineage is adrift, for the ancestors of the spirit realm are an integral part of daily life as mediators between the people and the creator, and as protectors of and counselors for the lineage's living members. Unfortunately, the discussion does not illuminate the role religious beliefs play in refugee women's lives; for example, Mabe's description of the process of choosing a medium for an ancestor spirit does not indicate whether women can play the role of a medium.

The importance of spiritual beliefs in coping with transition extends beyond the refugee camp to integration into the country of settlement. Writing about the differences in values, expected behaviors, language, and economic subsistence that were the sources of stress for Lao refugees arriving in the United States, De Voe (1997) discusses religion as one of the sources of support. Krulfeld (1994) points out that having access to a Lao Buddhist temple (*wat*) gives the community not only a sense of ethnic maintenance, but also psychological support. Moreover, establishment of permanent religious institutions is a sign of enduring, committed presence of newcomer religious communities in their new homelands.

Religion operates in compelling, competing, and contradictory ways as it shapes the experiences of refugee women, serving as a source of resiliency, facilitating and sometimes impeding integration processes. Being a refugee—the suffering in wartime, loss of homeland and family members, and the challenges of life in a new country—is for many forced migrants, a spiritual crisis of unparalleled severity. The basic spiritual needs—hope, meaning, relatedness, forgiveness or acceptance, and transcendence—are threatened in the forced migration process. The impact of being uprooted is particularly poignant and often very traumatic for refugee women, especially when rape and sexual abuse become commonplace. Unmet spiritual needs put refugee women's integration and well being at risk. Supporting refugee women's faith is therefore important at every stage of the migration process. It is important that refugee women not only pray, but also keep walking.

Incorporating Gender into Forced Migration Discourse and Practice

The refugee field has struggled for many years with the issue of incorporating gender into the forced migration discourse and practice. Refugee women have been an "invisible" majority for many years, both internationally and in the United States. The situation is changing, albeit slowly. In the past decade, the United Nations High Commissioner for Refugees (UNHCR) has promulgated *Guidelines on the Protection of Refugee Women*, as well as more specific guidance in addressing sexual and gender-based violence targeted at refugee women and children. The United Nations has also promoted *Guiding Principles on Internal Displacement*, which emphasize both the special vulnerabilities and strengths of women displaced within their own countries (Martin 2004). However, despite the increased awareness and understanding of the vulnerabilities of refugee women, major problems remain in protecting and assisting them, including protecting refugee women from gender-based violence, sexual exploitation by armed forces, government officials, and even aid workers, and providing access to reproductive health services and prenatal care, to name but a few examples.

The situation in the United States has not been much different. It took over a decade after the passage of the Refugee Act of 1980 before the federal Office of Refugee Resettlement (ORR) focused its attention on refugee women. Today, many speculate that without Lavinia Limon, the first and so far the only woman at the helm of ORR, that might never have happened. The first activity that Lavinia Limon initiated upon arrival in Washington, D.C. to assume the ORR directorship in the first Clinton administration was to organize a conference, *Mission Refocused: Focus on Women*. Conference participants—representing grassroots refugee women's leadership, service providers, policymakers, refugee advocates, and researchers—discussed ways to establish policies and programs that would provide equitable treatment of refugee women and men, instead of focusing predominantly on young, employable males. Funding for domestic violence programs as well as grants to strengthen gender balance in refugee families followed. Unfortunately, under the current Bush Administration, ORR is paying much more attention to the male leadership of faith-based and ethnic community organizations than to gender issues and gender relations in refugee communities.

In any case, the amount of attention policymakers pay to refugee women does not necessarily mean that gender issues are being incorporated into their discourse. Moreover, with few notable exceptions, policymakers, researchers, and advocates alike have been equating "gender" solely with women, women's activities, and women's special needs, at best adding refugee women's voices to their agendas. Here I use the term "gender" rather than "sex" deliberately since "gender" explicitly rejects biological explanations for hierarchies of inequality and power that privilege men and disadvantage women. Rather than being a fixed trait, invariant over time, gender is constructed through social and cultural ideals, practices, and displays of masculinity and femininity (Scott 1986 and Hondagneou-Sotelo 1994). Embodied in gender roles, relations, and hierarchies, gender is a core organizing principle of social relations and opportunities (Boyd 1999: 8).

Moreover, as Indra points out:

> [N]either in talk, research, policy analysis, nor programming can "gender" be equated solely with women, nor solely with women's activities, beliefs, goals, or needs; . . . "gender" is a key relational dimension of human activity and thought—activity and thought informed by cultural and individual notions of men and women—having consequences for their social or cultural positioning and the ways in which they experience and live their lives. (Indra 1999 a: 2)

It is not sufficient to just "add women's voices" (Lamphere et al. 1997) to the discussion about refugee women. Any formulation about women—all women, not just refugee women—has to include men, since gender is constructed socially and produced rationally (Collier and Yanagisako 1987; Ortner and Whitehead 1981; Rubin 1975, 1984). And as Lamphere suggests:

> These relations are now understood to be constituted within a cultural, economic, and political system that is also historically situated. Such systems involve race, ethnicity, class, and other forms of inequality that must be integrally incorporated into any gender analysis (Lamphere et al. 1997: 4).

The benefits of engendering forced migration discourse and praxis are many. Let me highlight a couple. Making gender an integral part of the forced migration discourse allows both identifying the vulnerability and emphasizing the agency of refugee women. We are all aware of gender-specific vulnerabilities that exist in emergency situations caused by forced migration that often render women more susceptible to different dangers, including sexual assault and increased rates of mortality and morbidity.

However, these vulnerabilities do not stem solely from biological differences between women and men. They are also affected by social factors. Gender morbidity differences, for example, are strongly influenced by social context, by the position women and men occupy in society, the access each gets to services, and the kind of medical care each receives (Boelaret et al. 1999: 166).

On one hand refugee women experience increased vulnerabilities, but on another hand refugee women and girls, even the very young ones, "often have well-developed moral, political, and philosophical understandings of the events in their lives and worlds" (Nordstrom 1999: 78). Refugee women make important, life-and-death decisions at every stage of their migration process, but rarely get asked to be involved in political solutions or peace building activities. Conceptualizing gender as a relational dimension of human activity and thought allows us also to pay attention to refugee women in different positions within the same society (female heads of refugee households, orphaned girls, rural or urban refugee women, etc.) and in relation to different categories of men (husbands, fathers, brothers, spiritual leaders, clan leaders, etc.). Furthermore, the variations among refugee women within the same category—heir individual voices and personalities, the strategies they forged vis-à-vis husbands, kinsmen, ritual practitioners—are also central to the engendered forced migration discourse. The engendered discourse is particularly important when in a discussion of the role of religion and spirituality in forced migration.

The Nexus of Gender and Religion in Refugee Women's Lives

Religion affects the lives of all refugees. I have observed firsthand the importance of religious ritual and the beneficial presence of spiritual leaders on the Kosovar Albanians at Fort Dix. Arriving in the camp, the weary refugees, so far away from their homeland and tired after a long flight from Macedonia, were searching for a spiritual respite. Upon entry to the welcome center, they felt safe, often for the first time in many months, and able to shed a tear for the loss of loved ones, for their devastated homes, and for their war-ridden homeland. Their spirits soared as they were greeted by the US Army Chaplain Captain Mohammed Khan, a Muslim chaplain assigned to Operation Provide Refuge for most of its duration. Chaplain Khan in his scull cap, a crescent emblem on his battle dress uniform's lapel, warm smile, and *Salaam Aleykum* (May God be with you), an Arabic greeting understood by all Muslims, was the embodiment of religious freedom in the United States, and a panacea for the Kosovars' suffering. He alleviated their suffering better than an army of doctors in any emergency room.

Friday prayers (*Jumah*), held at 1:00 PM in an open field, also played an important role in healing war wounds. Approximately eighty people, on average, attended Friday prayers every week. Albanian speaking imams were available to lead the community in the prayer. Christian army chaplains helped to arrange prayer rugs and distribute skullcaps and head scarves to those who needed them. A local mosque donated dozens of white caps and colorful scarves. Young women, who arrived at Fort Dix in fashionable urban clothes, eagerly looked for matching scarves and often asked me to take pictures of them getting ready or returning from prayer service. Kneeling on prayer rugs—men and boys in the front and women and girls at the back—the Kosovars listened intently to the imam, who prayed in Arabic: "God is compassionate. God is merciful."

Refugee women's engagement with religion is often very different from the experiences of refugee men. Research indicates that faced with similar adverse circumstances men and women react differently. A study of prisoners in a Russian labor camp showed that women observed religious rituals and celebrated birthdays, while men fantasized about escape, solved chess problems, and talked incessantly about politics (Weinberg 1992). Indeed, while the men at Fort Dix lingered after *Jumah* prayers to talk to the imam about their guilt associated with leaving the KLA fighters behind and made predictions about the outcomes of the war, the women stayed together to discuss opportunities available to their children in the United States, to plan for resettlement in US communities, to organize a wedding or to plan a naming ceremony for the seven babies born in the camp. The men prayed and looked back, while the women prayed and kept walking forward.

And yet while refugee women may find solace in religious ritual, their relationship with religion, particularly organized religion is not simple. I am reminded about this issue whenever I speak to audiences of refugee women, female community leaders, and victim advocates working on behalf of battered refugee women. When I first presented my research on religion in forced migration to the Refugee Women's Network, a grassroots network of some seven hundred refugee women resettled throughout the United States, and asked them about the role religion plays in their own lives and how they incorporate religious rituals and spiritual beliefs into the many programs they run all over the country, the answers were very complex. I was told:

> Elżbieta, it is not so simple. While many of us are deeply spiritual and religious, our lives and behaviours are often regulated by male religious leaders. The solace we derive from our faith is one thing, the unequal treatment and oppression experienced at the hands of an imam, a batiushka or a priest is something else.

Religion operates in compelling, competing, and contradictory ways as it shapes the experiences of refugee women, serving as a source of resiliency

as it both facilitates and impedes integration processes. It can have a particularly contradictory status in refugee women's lives. The close relationship between core religious beliefs and religious institutions, with their
associated rituals and customs, means that the distinction between these
is often overlooked. Religious institutions both at the family and community levels regulate refugee women's position within societies. Custom and
tradition, often justified on religious grounds, ensure refugee women's conformity to conventional gender roles, which can be sources of powerlessness and pain. In particular, notions of fatalism which are integral to many
religions, from Hinduism to Orthodox Christianity, can offer comfort to
the powerless and an explanation for suffering, while at the same time
constrain women (and men) from seeking change.

Let us look at the intersection of gender and religion when it comes to
suffering and resulting trauma. Suffering has been an inseparable element
of many refugees' lives. Religion is thought to help people cope with life's
experiences by assigning meaning to events (Kelley 1972; Roberts and Davidson 1984). Both Eastern and Western religions may help refugees cope
spiritually, cognitively, and emotionally with what has become known as
the "survivorship syndrome" (Fraser and Pecora 1985–86; Haines, Rutherford and Thomas 1981; Hendricks and Skinner 1979). Research also indicates that religious rituals play an instrumental role in trauma healing.
One of the recognized effects of religious ritual is to create both sacred
time and sacred space:

> [A] moment out-of-time and a place apart, nearer to the supernatural and the
> center of the universe than to the streets and neighborhoods of everyday. Rit-
> ual renews the world by offering an opportunity for participants to step out-
> side of it; it renews time by bringing the past, the present, and the future
> together. (Wellmeier 1994: 17)

However, in some cultures women are often denied both the knowledge
and the practical skills required to initiate rituals. In fact, most human religions, from tribal to dominant religions, have treated women's body, in
its gender-specific sexual functions, as impure and polluted and thus to
be distanced from sacred spaces and rites dominated by males (Radford
Ruether 1990: 7). In many denominations, women are officially barred
from ordination and men run the spiritual and administrative affairs of
the congregations. Nancy Donelly in her book *Changing Lives of Refugee
Hmong Women* (1994) writes about the importance assigned to ritual by
Hmong in Southeast Asia and the difficulty of maintaining many spiritual
practices in urban America:

> Hmong women's lives in Southeast Asia generally, and in Laos particularly,
> may have been inadvertently secular as few of the women I spoke with seemed
> to have any systematic knowledge of traditional cosmology or ritual practices.

... Most of my subjects were afraid of spirits, but drew a blank when asked how beliefs fit together. The extensive spiritual understanding and practice described by Chindarsi (1976), and Tapp (1988), and others was the province mainly of Hmong men (Donelly 1994: 86).

No wonder so many Hmong women are searching for a "room of their own" in Christian churches while often maintaining traditional beliefs. Daphne Winland (1994) explored the role of Christian conversion in the early adjustment experiences of forty-three Lao Hmong women in Ontario. Her study demonstrated that this transition from a traditionally animist and preliterate past did not result in the wholesale abandonment of Hmong practices and beliefs, but rather in a dynamic relationship of custom and innovation. Women turned to the Hmong Christian church (Mennonite) as a resource of empowerment, but also to maintain key Hmong social practices and values. The church proved to be a valuable resource in helping these women cope more effectively with the constraints of gender and minority status.

Aihwa Ong (2003) identified similar trends among Cambodian refugees. In her recent volume, *Buddha is Hiding,* she discusses the loss of Buddhism and the search for a spiritual compass in the Church of Jesus Christ of Latter-Day Saints. She points out that for the young Cambodian converts:

Mormonism provided the means to create some kind of combined religion and to serve eschatological needs. It was also a path to higher education, and to assimilation into white middle-class society. American churches came to provide moral discipline and community in exchange for an ambivalent salvation in which the inward search for the self was inseparable from racial subordination (Ong 2003: 20).

Mormonism has a special appeal to some Cambodian women. As Ong indicates:

Older women, stripped of family support, turned to the church for material and social resources. But women in their late teens and early twenties who joined the Mormon Church sought something less tangible. They wanted to be Mormon Young Women. By surrendering themselves to church discipline, they learned to manage their own subjectivity as clean-living young women, to develop a new status that commanded respect and facilitated hypergamous unions with white Mormons (Ong 2003: 222).

The role of refugee women in formal and informal religious spheres is complicated and calls for a careful analysis of the conditions and ways in which religion both promotes and lowers status of women compared to men and helps to empower women. There is a body of research indicating that organized religions discriminate against women, both theologically (Carr 1982; Fiorenza 1992 [1983]; Himmelstein 1986; Weaver 1986) and institutionally, especially in opportunities for formal leadership (Chavez 1997; Lehman 1985; Nason-Clark 1987; Swidler and Swidler 1977; Wallace 1975, 1992).

However, most of these studies focused on mainstream women. Despite the fact that substantial research has been done recently on women and religion in the United States, few studies take note of, much less focus on, women within refugee/immigrant congregations. While there is some evidence that migrant religious institutions play a central role in helping newcomers adapt to US society and in recreating and reproducing traditional culture (Ebaugh et al. 1999: 585), the study of the religious institutions of recent migrants is still in the early stages and the literature concerning women's roles within them even sparser (Ebaugh et al. 1999: 586). The few studies of religious institutions among newcomers that do exist (Christiano 1991; Diaz-Stevens 1993; Dolan 1988; Haddad and Smith 1994; Min 1992; Numrich 1996; Warner and Wittner 1998; Williams 1988) demonstrate clearly the role they play in the settlement process. Yet, few studies describe the specific impact of religious participation and practice on the status of immigrant/refugee women.

A.R. Kim's (1996) research on Korean Christian women shows that the church strongly reinforces the traditional Confucian ideal of the submissive and selfless woman. J.H. Kim's (1996) research, on the other hand, shows how "churched" Korean women used their "learned silence" and seemingly oppressive experience in a male-dominated church as a form of passive resistance. Luis Leon (1998) in his study of a Hispanic Pentecostal church in Los Angeles shows that women's role in food preparation at the church gives them a way to participate in religious ritual and provides them power in the reproduction of ethnic identity.

According to McCloud:

> [I]n the conservative mosques serving the South Asian immigrant community, women are more or less out of sight, holding no leadership positions, although they may teach in the Islamic schools, and generally the mosque administration is not welcoming, either to non-Muslims or to other Muslims of different ethnicity. [In] the more liberal community mosques, on the other hand, ... while women may be separated in the prayer areas, they often play active roles in the running of the mosque (2003: 163).

Other research suggests that women use religion and religious institutions to argue for equality (Briggs 1987; Charlton 1987; Daly 1973; Ice 1987; Royle 1984; Weaver 1986; Weidman 1985); as social and physical spaces in which to network with other women and built feminist consciousness (Ammerman 1997; Hargrove 1987; Kaufman 1991; Winter, Lummis and Stokes 1994; Weaver 1986; Wuthnow 1994); and to assert informal power in the practice of unofficial, domestic religion (Brown 1991; Diaz-Stevens 1993;

Dougherty 1978; Jacobs 1996; Neitz 1995). But again, these findings pertain primarily to US-born women. There is little empirical evidence that these processes apply to refugee women.

The Nexus of Religion, Gender, and Identity in Forced Migration

Throughout time and space, religion has defined and divided people—Protestants against Catholics, Christians against Muslims, and Hindus against Sikhs. For most refugees and immigrants, religion helps define their identity. It provides a place where people can gather with each other and offer emotional and material support. And yet, these issues are discussed only in passing in studies of forced migration (see Portes and Rumbaut's [1996] discussion of the Catholic Church as a defining institution around which Vietnamese families in the United States have organized, and Stepick's [1998] description of the contribution religion makes to the identity of Haitian refugees settled in Miami). Religion often also plays a prominent role in defining individual and group identity. In the forced migration field, identity is equated both with ethical/religious affiliation and "refugee identity."

Discussing identity is not easy. For example, when people ask me how I identify myself, I often give them my "narrative" answer. It is a long story, I tell them, and if they show they are interested to hear it, I go on to say that I was born, raised, and educated in Poznań, Poland, but while in graduate school spent part of each academic year in the United States doing library research. I sometimes add a few sentences about my involvement in the Solidarity movement in the 1980s and my forced displacement to the United States with a one-way passport and little hope that I would ever be able to go back to Poland. I tell them how I struggled to reestablish my professional career, ultimately succeeded, and worked for a research and policy analysis center, for an historically black university, the federal government, and that I am now working as a research director at the Institute for the Study of International Migration at Georgetown University, a private Jesuit college.

But my answer is not always delivered in a narrative form. Sometimes I simply say that I am a political refugee from Poland. The reactions to this statement differ depending on who my interlocutor is. Many of my colleagues say, "Oh, Elżbieta, you are not a refugee, you don't look like one"; or "How long are you going to be calling yourself a refugee? You have been in the US almost 20 years." On the other hand, many of the refugee women I work with just smile a knowing smile, and we proceed from there. I have to confess that when I first came to the United States, I never identified as a refugee woman. My identity was strongly connected to my ethnic and professional roots. As I said before, discussing identity is not easy.

The forced migration discourse both cautions against generalizations about defining the term "refugee" (Zetter 1988, Malkki 1995) and argues that there is such a thing as "the refugee experience" (Stein 1980). I agree with Stuart Hall that:

> Cultural identities come from somewhere, have histories. But like everything historical, they undergo constant transformation. Far from being eternally fixed in some essentialized past, they are subjects to the continuous "play" of history, culture, and power. Far from being grounded in a mere "recovery" of the past, which is waiting to be found, and which, when found, will secure our sense of ourselves into eternity, identities are the names we give to the different ways we are positioned by, and position ourselves within, the narratives of the past (1994: 397).

Identity, particularly ethnic self-identity is a gendered process. Rumbaut's research (1994) on the second generation shows that gender was a significant predictor of virtually every type of ethnic self-identity, suggesting that issues of gender and ethnic identity may be connected. For example, girls were more likely to choose additive or hyphenated identities as well as Hispanic pan-ethnic self labels. The refugee women I studied often simultaneously acted in ways that both reproduced traditional culture and began to change the structures in which they lived as they accommodated to their new settings. Many uniformly "did gender" in their congregations by preparing and serving ethnic foods and by being major contributors to the formal ethnoreligious education of the second generation, thereby simultaneously re-creating gender, ethnicity, and religious faith. In many cases, they contributed further to the reproduction of traditional culture through their practice of "domestic religion." Many congregations included formal women's groups, in addition to informal ones. These existed for purposes of spiritual expression and/or social service delivery. Within these groups, refugee women supported one another, especially newcomers, and shared everyday problems and solutions within a context where traditional language, values, and customs were also shared.

Research suggests that the role of ethnoreligious educator is the single most frequent, and in some cases virtually the only, formal one that refugee and immigrant women play within their congregations, and it is therefore very important to them. Women play an active role in imparting both religious and ethnic traditions to second generation and immigrant children through their involvement in formally organized classes. Women are reproducing gendered expectations that link members of their sex to children's education and well being and to the supervision of their social networks.

However, in their struggle for self-identity, many refugee women are often at odds with the male leadership's desire to strongly uphold claims for the maintenance of "traditional" cultures "imagined" by them that proscribe particular roles and identities for women. Some comply, but are rarely nostalgic for the way that life was back at home. The struggle to reconcile one's self-identity with that proscribed by the male spiritual leadership is particularly difficult when conservative spiritual leaders invoke religious texts in order to maintain the "imagined" pre-refugee status, ethnic identity, and social and gender equilibrium.

While most religious movements have their roots in transformatory visions, which focus on the inner ethical motivations of the person and respect for all individuals, regardless of gender or ethnicity, in reality there is an abundance of oppressive interpretations of religious texts promoted by male-dominated religious institutions. Obviously, these interpretations can be challenged by alternative interpretations of religious writings. In fact, that is what many feminists are attempting to do. Feminist theologies reclaim the egalitarian spirit of many religious texts to counter the current life-and-death threat presented to women in many contexts by religious extremists. For example, Iman Hashim and Fatima Miernissi argue that the practices of veiling and *purdah* (seclusion) have no foundation in the Qur'an and discuss the manner in which patriarchy has circumvented the Qur'an's essentially egalitarian message. Hashim also talks eloquently about reasons for feminist engagement with Islam. However, as Sadia Ahmed (1998) describes in her article on religious extremism in Somalia, feminist engagement with religion and gendered reinterpretation of religious texts are only useful for the majority of women *if* women at the grassroots can gain access to these arguments. It is they whose bodies become the battlegrounds for competing interpretations of religious texts, and they who require both basic education and knowledge of religious texts and arguments as weapons against fundamentalist interpretations of their religion.

Otherwise, we can only pray God and keep walking.

Notes

1. A shorter version of this chapter was presented at a conference, "Saying 'I' is Full of Consequences. Refugee Women Reclaim their Identity," held 19–21 March 2003 at McMaster University, Hamilton, Ontario, Canada. I am grateful to Doreen Indra who first suggested that my work on the role of religion and spirituality in forced migration might be of interest to the conference participants and to the readers of this volume.

2. Data provided by the Office of Refugee Resettlement, arrivals as of December 2003.

12

"We Want to Talk, They Give Us Pills"

IDENTITY AND MENTAL HEALTH OF REFUGEE WOMEN FROM SUDAN

Lynda Hayward, Maroussia Hajdukowski-Ahmed, Jenny Ploeg, Karen Trollope-Kumar

Africa has been one of the two top sources of refugees to Canada since 1999. The number of refugees from Sudan has tripled from 1999 to 2004. Due to ongoing conflicts in Sudan, this trend is expected to continue, particularly with the tragedy of Darfur. However, studies on the issues faced by African women refugees are scarce (Cleaver and Wallace 1990).

Although refugee women are normal people who are forced to deal with abnormal and traumatic situations, they tend to be socially constructed as victims and needy. Refugee women experience many of the hardships of men, but they also experience gender-specific forms of presettlement violence such as sexual violence and intimidation (Cleaver and Wallace 1990; Cutrufelli 2004; Moghissi 1999; Rousseau et al. 1997). They face specific postsettlement challenges (e.g., changes in roles, isolation, cultural tensions, and barriers to accessing mental health services) that undermine the foundation of their identities and position them as vulnerable to mental health problems (Allodi et al.1986; Blair 2001). Generally, when refugee women arrive in Canada, they experience a sense of relief as their physical safety and basic needs are met. The state of their mental health remains a hidden but serious issue. The stigma attached to mental illness and the fear of deportation may lead women to refrain from disclosing their problems (Chappel and Morrow 2000). However, refugee women have culturally specific ways of expressing their strengths and resolving their problems, which transform in the new context of their host country. The concepts of mental health and healing are also culturally and socially constructed, and need to be conceptualized broadly.

This chapter presents research findings based on a participatory project conducted by a university-community interdisciplinary team which included researchers in the fields of Nursing, Medical Anthropology, Public Health, Women's Studies, and from the regional Settlement Services.[1] The team's objectives were to further understand factors that contribute to a refugee woman's well being, and how she copes with her past experiences and current situations as she reconstructs her identity. This chapter reflects upon the complex relationship between refugee women's identity transformation and mental well being as exemplified by a group of refugee women from Sudan. Authors also record how, because of their unsettling experience with mainstream organizations, refugee women from Sudan were led to construct a collective identity as a wall of protection from the outside mainstream world. The chapter title is in effect a metaphor for the various forms of silencing the refugee women encountered, particularly when they resettled in Canada, and the need and will for self expression they communicated in the course of the project.

The Need for Further Understanding

Research on the mental health of refugees is weighted toward studies that evaluate levels of psychopathology. The Harvard Trauma Scale is a standardized tool used to evaluate mental health that has been validated cross culturally (Silove et al. 2002; Sondergaard et al. 2001; Loughry, chapter 10). It has been used for comparative purposes among different refugee populations (Redwood-Campbell et al. 2003). However, this tool is based on the assessment of symptoms related to post-traumatic stress disorder and was particularly used among male Vietnam War veterans in North America. Its epistemological basis lies in Western psychiatric models of mental health, and thus has been called into question by medical anthropologists and cross cultural psychiatrists, who point out that there are deep cultural differences in the way that mental health issues are experienced and expressed. The meaning of symptoms is culturally shaped, and symptoms may have different metaphorical meanings cross culturally. As Helman states, "each culture has its own language of distress" (1990: 94). A Sudanese refugee woman experiencing mental distress may complain that her "head is not together," while one in Latin America might complain of "nervios," with entirely different sets of symptoms (Low 1985). To develop a gender-sensitive and culturally appropriate understanding of the mental health issues among refugee women requires an understanding of the perception of the women themselves about mental health (Guarnaccia and Rogler 1999).

Information about refugees' own definitions and perceptions of mental health services is limited in the literature on refugee mental health (Li 2000; Redwood-Campbell et al. 2003; Williams 2001). Canadian studies on mental health seldom use an interpretive approach with a focus on refugee personal experience; rather they focus on factors such as the process of integration examining services provided, and tend to target subpopulations by race rather than culture (i.e., Black or Native). Often Canadian research studies the integration experiences of immigrants and refugees, without distinguishing between the two. Gender-specific studies of refugees from Africa are rare (Cleaver and Wallace 1990). In order to implement effective and culturally sensitive mental health services, it is imperative to explore further how refugee women perceive mental health issues and how their culturally grounded healing practices contribute to positive mental health practices. A review of the literature suggests that fully understanding the unique cultural characteristics of refugee women is critical in treating mental health problems they may incur (Watters 2001). This can be achieved by examining help seeking behaviors (Foss 2002; Phan 2000; Weine et al. 2000) and culturally bound syndromes, while remaining focused on the perceptions and knowledge of the refugee women (Guarnaccia and Rogler 1999; Lock 1993). There also needs to be an understanding of the cultural variations in somatization (Foss 2002; Kirmayer and Young 1998; Li 2000), in the clinical presentations of depression and anxiety (Kirmayer 2001), and in cultural differences in the expression of emotional states (Foss 2002; Stevens 2001).

A Study of Sudanese Refugee Women

To address these gaps in our understanding, we conducted a study with Sudanese refugee women (Bhaloo et al. 2005). The objectives were: (1) to explore how mental health is understood, experienced, and constructed by refugee women from Sudan; (2) to describe their experiences with mainstream, community, and mental health services in Canada; (3) to explore culturally grounded healing practices that contribute to resilience and positive mental health; (4) to explore the process of identity transformation and the generation of informal support networks in the postmigration context.

A grounded theory approach was used for this research, which uses an inductive, from the ground up method to generate theoretical explanations when little is known about the topic (Glaser and Strauss 1967; Strauss and Corbin 1990). This is a fitting method for the exploration of the unique worldview, social context, social relations, social action experiences, and cultural constructs of refugee women's mental health, healing practices, and informal support system (Crooks 2001). A purposive sample of a diverse group of eleven refugee women from Sudan who have settled in Hamilton was recruited for this study. Two focus groups were conducted: one to collect the data and a second to validate the results. The initial focus group was followed by in-depth interviews with three participants from different regions and subcultures of Sudan. The transcriptions of narratives were analyzed collaboratively to develop consensual understanding. A constant comparative method of analysis, which looks for recurrent themes, was used to interpret the participants' responses to the questions (Glaser and Strauss 1967; Strauss and Corbin 1990). The eleven Sudanese refugee women participating in the study ranged from twenty-four to fifty years of age, and most have been in Canada less than seven years. They came from north and south Sudan, and belong to different cultures, religions (Christian and Muslim), and language groups. These women are survivors with strong voices and much to share that can be of benefit to their community, other refugee groups, and mental health professionals.

Identity Is Contextual and Relational

We have learned that a Sudanese woman's identity, self esteem, and mental well being is closely linked with her role in the community as a wife and mother, and the value placed on children and family in their close-knit communities. As one participant in the study said: " A woman has to know what is the meaning to be a 'woman,' and is prepared by her mother for the role of wife and mother." She further pointed out: "You are to be proud and concerned about your family. . . . You as a mother, as a woman, you are not like men. You are different and you have to understand that. . . . We have love and we have to take a big part of the responsibility" (Bhaloo et al. 2005: 24).[2]

Extended kin, elders, and the community provide support to women in this role. These women identified themselves as strong individuals who were prepared to make sacrifices for their families and be positive role models for their children: "I love my family and I can do what it takes to help them" (35). To be perceived as complete, a Sudanese woman has to get married and have children, for "[s]he feels if she has no man, she has no value"(29). As another participant stated: "Having children helps mental health—[you] needs to marry a man who will have kids with you otherwise no point" (30).

Family name is also a source of pride and respect in their community, for "in Africa it's very shameful to have a bad reputation in the family" (45). Family reputation is also associated with how well their children do in life, which reflects directly back on mothers. With such a high value placed on family and Sudanese women's role of wife and mother, it is not surprising that, "[i]f they are happy in family, they feel everything is okay" (43). Family stability is the main contributor to a Sudanese woman's emotional well being and positive mental health. The majority of these refugee women demonstrated great strength and resilience as they coped with very challenging circumstances that made them vulnerable and affected their mental well being.

Experiences Undermining the Identity of Refugee Women

Our findings indicate that four common experiences particularly undermined the identity and mental well being of refugee women: loss, life in limbo, economic hardship, and raising children in Canada.

The Impact of Loss

Perhaps the most profound experience affecting the women's identity and mental well being has been the war-related forced displacement, and dismemberment of their families and support networks. Women who had never traveled outside of their village had to flee to new communities and had to mask their identity by adopting local customs in order to protect themselves from violent attacks. Sometimes, they had to undergo new scarifications—as local identifiers—on their face in order to blend with local ethnocultural groups. Many lost their fathers, husbands, children, and other relatives. Girls without a father to protect them socially became very vulnerable to rape and sexual exploitation: "They have no skills, no education and can't get a job so [they] go to people who take them in. They do whatever to get money" (24). Often women's husbands and young sons were forcibly taken away to fight in the war. Men who came back to their families alive often were traumatized, wounded, or disabled. Other men fled leaving their families behind. Some women had to leave their children behind and grieved their absence in Canada. Describing circumstances affecting their mental well being, the focus group participants told us that:

> Women are affected more by kids taken to war and a lot of them became widows. Husbands disappeared sometimes. Husbands live far away for many years. Here in Canada, we face the problem of women coming alone, leaving kids back at home, and dreaming of getting kids together. This really makes a woman crazy (26).

As a result of the forced displacement, their families were dispersed around the world and in refugee camps (i.e., in Yemen, Egypt, Kenya, or Uganda). Many were on the road for years: "I was born in a village. Village is not safe. I was in camps since 1984—since war started. The army was always bombarding. We moved around until we found a camp" (25). As one woman explained, these losses have a lasting impact on their mental well being: "So we are getting well but not very well. . . . I lost my father and it was very hard, and my grandfather. . . . I lost everything because of the war" (26). War has widowed them, separated them from their husbands, or left them without news of their relatives and friends. The original identity markers have disappeared, official identity papers lost, markers carved on the flesh changed, and new markers are constantly being negotiated.

Living a Life in Limbo

When new environments are forced upon refugees whose identity derives from their belonging to a specific community, identity becomes intensely conflictual and stress-inducing. Moreover, this forced mobility has created insecurity, mistrust, fear of the future and of growing new roots, which makes refugees less likely to seek help and give priority to their own needs (Bowen 1999; Cole et al. 1992).

Time is experienced as fractured or "in limbo"; refugees are always waiting for someone or something, whether it is lost relatives or official papers. The Sudanese women felt that their life was spent in a waiting room. They had to wait for everything, and the uncertainty, temporariness, and precariousness of their refugee situation was taking a toll on them. Time was an issue when waiting to claim status, for family reunion, for their health card. The procedure for applying for refugee status was "a very long procedure . . . The time they call you to the hearing, you don't know when. . . . Then when you go, you don't receive the decision" (Bhaloo et al. 2005: 30). When one woman was asked how long she had to wait for her husband to join her, she said: "Nobody knows. Nobody knows anything, not even Immigration says anything" (30).

Economic Hardship

Most of these women experienced economic hardship—a circumstance that has affected their self esteem. Those trying to support their families found that the role of a Sudanese working woman had changed, both in Sudan and Canada. In Sudan, they found it increasingly difficult to survive with the restrictions imposed upon them by Islamic Law, which discouraged them from working outside the home. Suitable work was difficult to find, especially if a woman was not a "Muslim Sister" (active in Islamic movements). As one participant observed: "I think most of the Muslim Sisters now are not real Muslim Sisters, but for economic purpose, they act like that to get a job." The situation was even worse for Christians to the extent that, "some change[d] religion to get a position"

(24). This undermined the reinforcement of their identity provided by a securely rooted religion.

Upon arrival in Canada, the skills, degrees, qualifications, and experiences of refugees are devalued and not recognized. A Canadian education is expensive, and as one participant said, "There is no guarantee if you go to school that you will find a job here" (29), due to a lack of Canadian experience and English language proficiency. A sense of loss of social status and having to beg for a job was felt as humiliating and stressful. Sudanese women experience difficult working conditions and occupational instability in Canada. Some women had no choice but to accept low paying jobs and resort to working at several small jobs, leaving little time to care for their families or themselves. Because occupational and financial stability is considered necessary for a marriage to take place, marriages were fewer and at a later age. Perceived as having an incomplete identity without a husband and children, Sudanese women confided that this stage was prolonged by their exilic circumstances, making them more vulnerable socially and affecting their mental health.

Raising Children in a New Environment

Sudanese women found "the Canadian system about the process of taking care of kids difficult" (30). Dealing with mainstream child-centered institutions such as the school system, the Children's Aid Society, and the police was very challenging, creating fear, anxiety, and anger in adults and children alike. For example, "[the children] are put in [a] class; they don't know how to read or how to learn. They are angry and stressed and that's why kids are getting in trouble now" (33). Many of the women did not understand the school system and were concerned that schools did not make the effort to get acquainted with newcomers' culture and history. Moreover, working conditions such as night shifts or juggling part time jobs, coupled with a lack of personal transportation, made it difficult for refugee women to attend meetings with teachers or pick up children on time. Educators who are unaware of these situations may label refugee women as "bad parents," and such misunderstandings are extremely stressful.

Sudanese women felt that their children's behavior was misunderstood and too often sanctioned. The women feared the police in Canada because they perceive that they treat teenagers like adults, and incarcerate them, whereas in Sudan the police treat teenagers like children. Thus, the women looked for help from their community, "trying not to talk to police because children become the victims" (32). Sudanese women expressed the fear that when they or their teenaged children did not comply with norms of the land, their children would be taken away from them. They also claimed that agencies that protect children did not understand certain occupation-related or family-related situations the women faced. After the research project had ended, women felt freer to talk about the negative aspects of their experience with mainstream organizations, particularly with law enforcement. Criticism became sharper, and women spoke up, wondering why their adolescent sons were thrown in jail with hardened criminals for petty crimes that would have deserved only strong scolding and punishment by community elders. They felt that helping with education and employment would have been a more constructive approach.

All came to a tragic climax when one participant, who had spent her life in refugee camps, had her children removed—including her newborn who was "apprehended" right after delivery—by the local organization "for their protection." There was a high level of cultural misunderstanding involved when the social worker had felt compelled to act, after identifying as "child abuse" what was perceived by the community as different rearing practices. Eventually, the court returned all children to the mother and father. This tragic case revealed the risk involved when one does not know the new language, the new laws and legal system, does not know the local communication style. The sense of alienation was again perceptible in court, where legal jargon entrenches power differences—"I don't understand what they say, and it is my life and that of my children they are talking about"—the young mother lamented (51). Men and women from the community rallied around the distraught parents and attended court proceedings in a show of solidarity. As the mother later poignantly conveyed: "In our country, it is the army that kidnaps our children. We came here hoping to find safety for them, but here they are kidnapped by the organization that is supposed to protect them" (29). The mainstream organization had reenacted the family dismemberment experienced during the war, and unwittingly retraumatized the family and the community. A social gathering was organized by the community, at which time painful stories were shared, tears shed. Criticizing and mocking the institutions released the tension. Interviews or focus groups had a somewhat more inhibiting effect on women's voicing than a spontaneous and congenial social gathering. It became clear why refugee women chose to stay clear of those organizations, and why they portrayed their community as ideal for problem solving.

Mental Health and Healing

Although their mental energies were weakened by their circumstances, Sudanese refugee women drew upon their strengths to assist them in coping with the resettlement process, and in reconstructing their identities in a new host country, as one of them emphasized, "I feel strong because I love my family" (36). To quote a participant: "For women, they can get humiliated but they are still going. They cannot give up easily" (29). A belief in their own strength was a foundation to their mental health. These women had a built-in resilience and relied a lot on themselves, as one of them explained, "Nothing will keep me down" (29). They tried to work in order to keep their dignity, and they emphasized the importance of educating themselves and learning.

Study participants told us that there was no specific name for mental health in the Sudanese culture, explained then: "We don't give name because name makes a person more sick so we don't want to tell that person she is sick" (20). Sudanese women believed that to label a woman as mentally ill would "mark" her and as a result she would feel more isolated and upset. Rather, they had a culturally grounded functional definition and could easily identify members of their community who were in distress and needed their help. The Sudanese community watched for behavioral changes in their members, as did family members. For example, they observed: "She's doing nothing for herself. She just stays like that. Some of them refuse to take a shower. . . . She just leaves all her duties. She looks as someone who is not aware" (23). Changes in explicit behavior such as self care, communication, household duties, and responsibilities were signs of something wrong in their friends' life and alerted community members, giving them a pretext to contact women who appeared unwell to offer help.

Sudanese women said that they were not shy about going to doctors for physical ailments, but still preferred to follow their own way, looking for support from family, elders, and members of their community who could relate to their problems. The Canadian healthcare system posed major challenges for them, both in terms of securing healthcare coverage and receiving the care they needed in a timely fashion. Eligibility issues, the financial costs of healthcare, and difficulties accessing community-based psychiatric services represented major barriers for refugees. Professionals often did not have the time or the expertise to go beyond the physiological signs of mental health problems. Interpreters were too expensive for the service providers and often unavailable when needed. Mental health providers were too few and overworked with too many patients. The women described the system of referrals as frustrating, too long, and too bureaucratic. As one participant said, doctors "put you on waiting list to meet the specialist after 3 or 4 months. By that time, I have already become crazy or have become okay!" (35).

The women asserted that "Canadians [doctors] are really useless with us because they don't know our thing" (35). They claimed that doctors only treated the symptoms with medication. As one participant explained, "the doctor will give you tablets and counsel you but this is not the solution" (35). In essence, their difficulties with the medical profession can be summed up in the phrase: "We want to talk, they give us pills." For Sudanese women, the healthcare system in Canada does not take into account the fact that changes, transitions, and healing are a gradual process, which integrates past experience and the knowledge of self in context. As a result, in keeping with the nature of their self-regulating and self-help community, they drew upon a number of culturally grounded coping strategies or healing practices, which included: reliance on family; reliance on elders and community mediation for family conflicts; reliance on close friends; strength in community participation; culturally grounded beliefs and practices (e.g., storytelling, rituals); mocking the system and collective laughter; reliance on self and self-help activities; and participation in community activism.

Reliance on Family

The primary source of support for all Sudanese women was the family. As one participant said: "I feel comfortable when I am with my family. If there is a problem, family helps. Both sides of family help out when there is a problem" (37). Sudanese women also relied on elderly family members who acted as counsellors and mediated using stories and examples from their experiences to guide and advise.

Elder and Community Mediation

Elders were highly respected and provided mediation for family problems. People often called elders to ask them to help someone in the community, and to visit the person. When the elders went, they would "sit down and listen to the person who wants to complain . . . , so they can address the reasons [for the complaint]" (40). In the process, the elders' social usefulness, self esteem and identity were strengthened. As one elderly participant stated, she was "very happy because they accept me to be an elder. . . . All of them respect me" (40).

Mediation by community members (i.e., elders, family, friends, respected couples) to pacify, to scold, and to advise was highly valued in the local community. One participant gave an example of community mediation with a husband who drank to illustrate how the community dealt with this problem: "Back home they [women] cannot get very miserable because if [the] husband is a drunkard, people come [and] talk to him. . . . 'You have to change and leave the beer and have to start your life'" (40). A second participant expanded this illustration saying, "We will find old people to talk to him to, and even men. We try to find men who are close friend to him" (40).

Strength in Community Life

Many refugee women arrive in the new country without their husbands or extended family and have to readjust their lives accordingly (Champassak 1995; Ellis 1994). A cohesive and welcoming Sudanese community often becomes a woman's primary source of support. Through their sense of community, the Sudanese refugee women followed each other's news and helped each other out. As a focus group participant said: "The community is so related to each other, so if you have any problem you speak openly." (38). The Sudanese community members enjoyed doing things together such as picnics, communal celebrations, giving presents, and cooking food for community members who were unwell. They even set up a small micro-credit system for families with special needs. The community essentially acted as observer, regulator, and helper to identify and resolve problems.

Later on, community tensions emerged that stemmed from the political situation in Sudan, and had been concealed by an idealized construct of an "imagined community." In reality, Northern Sudanese and Southern Sudanese were still suspicious of each other and not interacting much. Rivalries simmered, and some women were resentful of others who they thought received more help from local settlement organizations. However, they rallied together to organize a demonstration that called for public support for the Darfur refugees. It gradually became apparent why immigrant and refugee communities take pride in caring for their public image of unity and solidarity, which they construct for the consumption of the "outside world." They construct walls that protect them from mainstream institutions which they fear, and tend to keep their problems confined within those walls.

The Role of Friends

Women who had no family in Canada also tried to re-create an extended family with trustworthy friends, primarily women in the Sudanese community. They sought support and help from these friends saying: "To talk to our friend is easier than to talk to a counsellor" (39). They felt that other women understood their past and current situation. This was particularly true of teenage girls who faced specific issues and did not want to add to their parents' worries. As one of the participants said: "Girls share problems, support each other. Talk to solve problems. No need to go to parents for small problems" (41). But some women remained cautious and kept problems to themselves. Suspicion, but also human compassion, had been sharpened in refugee camps and during flights.

Special Beliefs and Practices

Certain cultural beliefs and practices facilitate adaptation, particularly the use of storytelling. Storytelling was often used by elders to mediate problems. By narrating successful examples, elders helped women who were unwell feel better. For example, one elder told a person a happy ending story about someone back home and concluded that the person was "[n]ow fine" (41). Sometimes, constructive deceptions in the form of stories were necessary to make unwell women feel good: "I lied to encourage her. . . . In seven days she changed and she took a shower, fed her children, dressed well. So, I healed her" (41). Laughing about what was happening to them and poking fun at the mainstream organizations provided a temporary healthy release of tension. The practice of *zar* in certain groups was also mentioned:

> In Sudan, some women solve their problems through Zar (Boddy 1989), a complex social ritual which seems to have a positive influence on mental health. During the Zar ceremony, female family and friends gather together to express and vent their feelings and problems. Through drumming, singing, and dancing, women enter a trance state in which they can speak the secrets in their hearts. This "letting go" of inhibitions has a healing effect on women who have repressed inner conflicts and tensions in order to focus on their family's needs (39).

When researchers probed them further on that question, Sudanese refugee women in our project did not give much importance to the practice of *zar*, claiming that "mostly uneducated rural women do it" (41). Retrospectively, one could ask: were the academic researchers more attracted to the creation of "an exotic other"? Or were the refugee women themselves dismissing the practice of *zar* in order to deflect potential "othering" and criticism? The answer here is less important than the question.

Reliance on Self

Using leisure and pleasurable activities such as singing, taking a walk, and even eating helped refugee women cope. Muslim Sudanese women also turned to their holy book, the Qur'an, for help. Some said that: "This kind of problem is for myself. If nobody consoles me I just go and pray. This is a kind of solution" (37). Sudanese women also tried to avoid thinking about their problems, reduced their expectations, or gave up. Avoidance may have led to withdrawal, isolation, and silence, but it was considered the best solution in certain contexts. For example, women feared that open discussions of family problems in the broader community would have attracted unwarranted attention from mainstream organizations such as agencies for child protection.

Activism

Sudanese women who had taken on leadership roles in their community had come to recognize the importance of citizenship and responsibility;

they had become vocal and organizing. As one participant declared: "We have to participate at all levels, take the decision itself, not just obey and listen. . . . I participate in . . . election campaigns. . . . I am not keeping silent" (43). Seeing a positive effect through political activism helped Sudanese women deal with their own issues, and built confidence and self esteem. For example, one participant said: "I help newcomers. I know things now and I can help them to use facilities here" (40). Activism increased sharply after the "crisis" with the child protection agency; the experience empowered women and fostered leadership in several.

Hope and Optimism

As also found in other studies (i.e., McSpadden and Moussa 1993: 221), refugee women emphasized the energizing effect hope and optimism had on their mental health. They cultivated hope and optimism between themselves: in their terms, being "positive and hopeful," or "seeing the glass half full." They used various strategies to help each other, and to help their husbands and their children to overcome moments of discouragement and pessimism. They offered positive "examples to learn by," emphasized the importance of "giving a chance," encouraged "patience for gradual changes" (Bhaloo et al. 2005).

Tensions in Identity Reconstruction

For this group of Sudanese women, mental well being was closely linked with identity perception and transformation in the new host society. As new experiences were reshaping their identity, they met with a number of challenges both within their own community and within the Canadian mainstream society—linguistic, cultural, generational, and gender-based.

Learning Yet Another Language

Language is a major barrier that many refugee women have to deal with in their new host country (Ellis 1994)—a barrier in finding employment, locating a school for children, doing day-to-day activities, accessing healthcare, or describing health symptoms. It can be a great source of frustration and tension for newly arrived refugees. As one participant said: "I have to study the language first, because language is the first barrier. To find a job is not difficult, but language is the problem" (Bhaloo et al. 2005: 43). Language is one of the most serious difficulties refugee women encounter when interacting with mainstream healthcare services (Li 2000). The most recently arrived participant confided that, "[c]ommunication is number one, especially for women. I was advised to go to school and learn the language and about the Canadian system a lot so I can know the good and bad sides of it" (42). She firmly believed that learning the language will make the transition less confusing and scary.

Cultural and Intergenerational Tensions

Due to the weakening of family support, refugee women face numerous cultural and intergenerational tensions in Canada. Those who arrive alone as single mothers or widows find it more difficult to be accepted by the Sudanese community. In our study, Sudanese women who were single or did not fit the cultural "norms" claimed that members of the community observed their behaviors more carefully and were more prompt to judge them. One focus group participant lamented:

> I am married to a foreigner and in the Sudanese community this is not acceptable. So, when I introduced myself to the Hamilton community, I had a lot of questions asked about me. You want to be active, join the community but they feel there is something behind this story. Imagine how this affects you. You are already alone. You miss the family because in my town everybody knows who I am (45).

This lack of acceptance frustrated women who had adjusted to a different lifestyle—be it by marrying a foreigner, refusing to wear a *hijab,* or drinking and smoking. As a participant told us: "The most difficult pain I get in Canada is from my own people. . . . The same traditional beliefs follow me here. We have to mend that" (46).

Associated with cultural transformations, Sudanese women also noted that they experienced generational challenges in Canada. An example would be when the elderly "want to give advice to young women and some of them ignore them and they don't want to listen. . . . They lose respect" (46). A major cause of this challenge is the framing of what is reality in Canada. Television creates illusions and expectations in the minds of younger Sudanese, who think that what happens on television is real and the norm. This results in problems and misunderstandings. For example, the public expression of affection is different in Sudan; it is particularly discreet between men and women. In addition, young Sudanese women feel pressure to rely more on their physical appearance, on brand name clothing or make-up, in order to increase their chances of finding a job, a husband, or just to feel part of the new society. This can result in a lack of communication between mothers and young girls who are reframing their culture, as a mother complained: "They want to copy what they see on TV . . . this may confuse elder people; . . . girls are now doing things in secret" (46).

New Gender Roles

Generational and cultural challenges arise in part due to the new gender roles all generations of Sudanese women experience in Canada. The reversal of traditional gender and generational roles constitutes a major component of their identity transformation. In the study, some Sudanese women had to provide for themselves and their children because they came alone or had male family members who were unemployed or disabled by the war. They had more responsibilities inside and outside of the home than in Sudan, and their tasks were more fragmented. In addition to playing the role of wife and mother, women strove to continue their education. One participant noted that: "They started to go to different places to develop themselves. They are changing" (47).

The Sudanese women demonstrated considerable ability to take on multiple roles and be self reliant in Canada. As one participant said: "I go for shopping, drive kids to school, go to emergency, and do everything here by myself" (47). Most were grateful to have more autonomy, but also felt tired by the workload and responsibilities they had in Canada: "Since I have been here in Canada, I'm not tired, I'm exhausted!" Without the family support system they had in Sudan, they found their roles to be overwhelming at times. They claimed they did not have time for themselves like they did in Sudan. As one participant exclaimed: "The only messy thing here is me!" (47). Yet the women equated Canada with education and freedom. When asked what has changed for young Sudanese women in Canada, one participant responded: "Education . . . We are allowed to go to school. We can go shopping alone, do things freely, even when we are married" (47).

The focus group participants were more aware of their rights as women. As one participant told us: "Husbands think women are changed" (47). As a result, Sudanese men felt more vulnerable as they had lost their traditional control and their role as main wager earners, and felt threatened by the fact that women enjoyed more freedom, financial independence, and rights. Participants recommended that all newcomers learn the laws that protect women in Canada, and their rights and duties.

Role adjustments in the new country differed for each woman based on her socioeconomic status back home. The higher their status in Sudan, the more difficult the change and risk to their self esteem and mental well being. For example, one participant, who had practiced medicine and had domestic help in Sudan, was jobless and found it challenging to take on the responsibilities of the house by herself. Women from lower socioeconomic backgrounds remarked that they benefited from learning about the Canadian system and enjoyed their independence in Canada: "I've been here one year in Canada, a single mom and do all things alone. I can do bills, go to bank and sit in a group to discuss my problems and I like that.

I learned from friends. I'm more independent and even if my husband comes later, I'll depend on myself more" (49).

Throughout this process of identity transformation, they continued to view themselves as important positive role models within their families and community. As a focus group participant said: "We came to Canada as a second home. It's an independent world where you need to be strong . . . I develop my skills and although I find it more difficult I like it" (49).

Identity Transformations: Questions Arising

Refugee women come with a past that continuously threads its way into their present, permeates it, and affects it. Their mental well being is intimately connected with gendered identity, and both are influenced by their historical context, their culture, and their human environment. It is particularly the case for Sudanese women, who do not experience their identity as autonomous, rather as dependent on family and community. To be recognized, respected, and have self respect at every stage of their life is important for women in the Sudanese community. The experience of displacement and relocation creates ruptures in the continuity of identity formation and mental well being, which affects their identity reconstruction in Canada. The prefix "dis" precedes every facet of their experience: *dis*-placement, *dis*-memberment, *dis*-location, *dis*-connection, and *dis*-ruption. It is what rips them away from their body, their self, their family, their community, their country, the continuity of cultural values held dear from one generation to the other—what for them used to be and should be safe spaces. Sudanese women, like other women in the world, were constructed to nurture and protect those spaces and feel safe in them.

In transforming their identity, the issues associated with their mental well being are complex, interrelated, and permeate all aspects of their lives. The process of identity transformation not only follows the temporal course of their life, it is deeply affected by the changing locations and the new contexts. It is affected by the nature, extent, and impact of their trauma, the level of resilience and family/community support, by the different social environments in which they are sent to live, by the memory of their past, the circumstances of their present, and their hopes for the future. A caring ethnocultural community has both a protective function and a regulatory function. It can build self esteem and mental health but also harm them, particularly when these women are perceived as "changing too fast," or not abiding by cultural norms.

Over the duration of the project, researchers realized that Sudanese women felt the need to protect the good reputation of their community— out of pride, out of fear of mainstream institutions, fear of losing their refugee status, and to ensure positive attention and good services. The women also communicated the need to continue transforming tensions and rivalries into celebrations of strengths and respect for differences. One cannot stress enough the importance of time and trust when developing dialogue in research. Dialogue helped to nuance narratives, because narratives can be constructed by participants who may have their own agenda. It uncovered factors such as racism, which had not been discussed with researchers at first. What was true, constructed, or concealed in their narratives? When meaningful information was obtained outside of the research process, such as during a social gathering or during a car ride offered to the participants, researchers also faced an ethical dilemma on whether that information could be included in the findings. Finally, given the relatively small sample size, one cannot affirm that the findings presented are representative of the mental health situation of refugee women from Sudan in general. As a result of the researchers' dialogue on research methods, a Participatory Action Research (PAR) process well suited to future research with refugee women was initiated. The researchers also had to rethink their concept of mental health and coping strategies, reflect on the continuous presence of the women's past, and on the inclusion of cultural representations and practices. Frequently, refugee women and their community tend to idealize a home and a life to which they cannot return, and in which they had a specific role. A gender-based tension exists between this idealization and their new life with its new challenges and freedoms. Questions arise that reveal the complexity of what could be construed as mental health: is retreating into this idealized life a healing coping strategy, a survival instinct, a necessary transition, or a harmful regression? What is a measure of mental healing—the subject's "feel good" declaration, or the therapist's pronouncement, which is also imbued with her own cultural representations? Who defines norms of mental wellness and decides when it is attained? In Western therapies there is a danger in "premature unification" (Hermans and Hermans-Jansen 1995: 143). Still indebted to a Cartesian frame of thought, they separate the real, the dreams, and the imaginary, whereas these are all part of the same living experience in many cultures, including in the Sudanese culture. A Cartesian approach also tends to individualize and isolate experience, while individuals and factors are interconnected. Rather than seeking to label them under known diagnoses, mental health specialists should investigate the self of refugee women (and men) as complex, layered, and transcultural. This leads to a "depathologization" of the self, which not only enriches our understanding of mental health, but respects the identity and the agency of women, and, in and of itself, has a positive effect on mental health.

Participatory therapy, which is based on the same principles as Participatory Action Research, offers an approach that is conducive to the enhancement of mental health. An interdisciplinary practice, it promotes a holistic understanding and is suspicious of categories and assumptions.

In the process, it looks at the root causes of mental health issues, removing responsibility and guilt from the individual. Colearning, the validation of identity, agency, knowledge, culture, and context, the inclusion of all forms of communication, contribute to rebuild identities that integrate and make sense of past and present experience (Hermans and Hermans-Jansen 1995). Rather than rely on pills, participatory therapy relies on dialogue and connectivity, and strengthens the sense of self of refugee women.

Each stage in the lives of refugee women from Sudan represents at once both challenges and opportunities. Sudanese women expressed the need to find solutions to their challenges, but also to help mainstream organizations and society at large communicate appropriately with culturally diverse individuals and communities. They had a strong interest in reaching out to various mainstream organizations to educate them and befriend them, such as the Children's Aid Society, the police force, schools, churches, healthcare providers, and so on. Sharing their experience and suggestions with the researchers and the community at large enhanced the awareness of, and respect for, the Sudanese culture and women among non-Sudanese, which in turn enhanced the women's sense of self and self esteem. They felt useful to their community, and were eager to see concrete results. The Sudanese women strongly advocated the use of community mental health workers who would be familiar with the cultural context, language, and specific mental health issues faced by refugees from their country.

For the members of the research team, the research process proved to be both enriching and unsettling. Researchers held a variety of roles related to refugee women—a community board member, a program director for a settlement service, a physician, a public health nurse. As we began to engage with the Sudanese women, hearing their stories, we began to reflect on our professional roles with refugee women. The women had been silenced or had constructed narratives because of a lack of interest and ethnocultural sensitivity in mainstream organizations, because of a lack of time, because they were racialized, mostly poor, and women. We learned to listen and to appreciate the importance of time and bonding, in the common pursuit of knowledge. Pills are just a camouflage for what we do not find the time to hear, or do not want to know. It was humbling to see ourselves and the Canadian institutions for which we work reflected through their eyes. Their challenge to each of us is to strive to make the services available for refugees more relevant, accessible, and culturally appropriate.

Notes

1. We would like to sincerely thank all the Sudanese refugee women who participated in this project and shared their knowledge, their wisdom, their pain, and

their laughter. They have taught us, touched us, and inspired us. Our gratitude also goes to the Settlement and Integration Services Organization (SISO) and to Madina Wasuge, its Program Manager, for facilitating this project in so many ways. In addition, we would like to extend our thanks to Cindy Escobar, Karen Henderson, Kathy King, Claudia Montan, and Maria Sarmiento for their many contributions to this project, and to the Community Care Research Center and the Arts Research Board at McMaster University for their financial support.

2. Quotations from the participants originate from the report *Refugee Women from Sudan and Their Mental Health*, by S. Bhaloo, A. Carias, M. Hadjukowski-Ahmed, L. Hayward, J. Ploeg, and K.Trollope-Kumar. 2005. Hamilton, Ontario, Community Care Research Center, McMaster University.

Section IV

Reviewing Policies

<small></small>

TAKING RESPONSIBILITY FOR THE RIGHTS OF REFUGEE WOMEN

Introduction

The double bind for refugee women is that the word "refugee" has come to mean powerlessness and subjugation while ostensibly conveying the need for protection under international law. Once they flee their countries, refugees have no rights *per se*. In contrast, internally displaced persons (IDPs) are not even protected under international law because they remain in their own countries and are subject to the laws of the state. While international guidelines for the protection of IDPs were developed in 1996, these guidelines have no international legal enforcement power since they cannot supersede the laws of a sovereign state.[1] Trafficked women's position is still more ambiguous (Wayland and Malarek, chapter 3).

The chapters in this section take a critical look at the implementation of refugee policies and law, as they apply to the protection of refugee women internationally and in Canada. Together, authors draw from their professional location and analytical framework a comprehensive picture of the limitations and possibilities of policies aimed at protecting the rights of refugee women. They elaborate on the challenges and responsibility which come with the recognition of the agency of women as social actors in the refugee situation and beyond.

Judith Kumin (chapter 13) evaluates the progress of the UNHCR with respect to the inclusion of gender in its operational programs and policies. She points out that while a great deal has been achieved by the UNHCR with the establishment of policies to protect refugee women, and of gender-related guidelines for staff in the field, refugee women as a constructive force are still not fully recognized. The gap that separates policies and their implementation remains the biggest challenge. Yet countless examples are available today to demonstrate that in responding to needs that emerge from uprooting, refugee women have taken on the responsibility to improve their social and economic situation, to engage in peace building actions and the refugee return processes. Kumin offers eight structural and attitudinal actions, to overcome policy implementation gaps and barriers.

Hyndman's and de Alwis' (chapter 4) evaluation of international and NGO program implementation in Sri Lanka contribute additional critical insights related to gender policy and practice. The authors argue that "gender" has been used as a way for successful funding applications programming without attention being paid to gender power relations. We have to move beyond the concept of gender *per se* and implement a rigorous intersectional feminist framework which will position gender issues and power relations within interlocking systems of class, caste, religion, sexuality, nationality, and membership in social groups. Such a framework will also enable a more compelling position from which to transform relations that provoke or perpetuate violence, discrimination, and injustice.

After reviewing the development of "gendered refugee policy gap" of the 1951 Convention relating to the Status of Refugees, and the 1967 Protocol Relating to the Status of Refugees from an international perspective, Patricia Daenzer (chapter 14) examines Canada's policy responses to the Woman at Risk Program and the refugee determination process for women seeking refugee asylum through the Immigration and Refugee Board from 1988 to 2002. One of the positive outcomes of these policies has been that more women have "risked their lives to seek asylum in allegedly safe countries" (Daenzer chapter 14). Statistics also indicate that in the late 1990s a significant number of women have been processed through the Women at Risk Program. This program, however, has not been able to fast-track women in urgent need of being lifted out of areas of danger because they also have to fulfil medical and security requirements, and criminal background checks. In addition, they have to prove that they can become self sufficient (similar to immigrants), which defeats the purpose of the program: clearly, women who are actually at risk would not be able to wait for such a process. Daenzer argues that Canadian refugee policy in general and with respect to women has been characterized by moments of "indifference, generosity, racism or ambivalence" (Daenzer chapter 14). The challenge, she concludes, is to go beyond statistics, definitions of gender persecution, and bureaucratic obstacles to clearly demonstrate that Canadian policy and practice stands solidly behind the full expression of human rights of displaced and persecuted women.

From the perspective of a lawyer advocating for refugee women's claims for asylum, Geraldine Sadoway reviews the implementation of the Canadian "Guidelines on Women Refugees Fearing Gender-Related Persecution," together with similar policies in the United States and the U.K. (Sadoway chapter 15). Supporting her arguments with case law decisions,

Sadoway argues that the Guidelines have, on the one hand, offered greater possibilities for women securing protection from gender-related persecution. On the other hand, their application has had adverse effects on the rights of these women. For example, advocates and responsible persons for the determination of these claims have been known to have internalized stereotypes about women from Eastern European and Third World countries portrayed as living in excessively patriarchal societies. They also continue to adhere to the myth that rape is a private criminal act of lust. This approach has either placed the rights of women claimants in jeopardy or revictimized them, in an attempt to present them as helpless victims needing Canada's protection. At the same time, the views of neo-orientalists and cultural relativists about Arab countries and Islam have also denied women the right to having their claims heard as political acts of resistance. Furthermore, Sadoway forewarns that the growing trend of neoconservative and antifeminist attitudes on refugee determination boards and society in general is a phenomenon that needs to be monitored, as it will become a barrier to the full implementation of the rights of refugee women.

In the final chapter (chapter 16), Carmela Murdocca takes the discourse on refugee women's rights and as social agents a step further. Murdocca discusses the 1998 work of Sherene Razack, which explored gender persecution asylum laws as they were applied in refugee hearings of the Canadian Immigration and Refugee Board. Murdocca first argues that Canada's recognition of gender-based asylum is an important antiracist feminist legal "incentive" (Murdocca chapter 16). She reviews Razack's explanation that the refugee hearing is an encounter between the (superior) white First World and the racialized Third World. Razack ascertains that the refugee hearing is a "profoundly racialized event" in which Third World women relate their experiences "outside of, and at the expense of their realities as colonized people" (Murdocca chapter 16). Thus First World complicity in this colonization process as well as the causes for uprooting do not feature in the hearing process but affect its outcome. Furthermore, when refugee women affirm their agency in the context of their histories, in effect, they challenge the stereotype of vulnerability and in so doing jeopardize their chances of being granted asylum. The critical question is whether legal instruments of human rights can bring about social justice for Third World women, when "the law functions as the *locus* of racialization and a primary site for policing racial, sexual, and cultural membership in Canada" (Murdocca chapter 16).

The second section of Murdocca's discussion consists of an interview with Sherene Razack. Together, they revisit Razack's work in the context of the post-11 September 2001 tragedy and its aftermath, as it impacts Muslims and people of Arab descent. Razack explores how the refugee determination process has the responsibility of finding ways of going beyond stereotypes about Arabs and Muslims and racialized scripts that allow them to "rescue" women from these communities. She stresses the importance of developing a feminist strategy, which will achieve women's rights by offering women options that will strengthen their position as social actors rather than victims.

Note

1. While the UNHCR has, under special circumstances been given special authority by the United Nations Assembly to care for the protection of internally displaced persons, this mandate is that of the United Nations High Commissioner for Human Rights (UNHCR). "Guiding Principles on Internal Displacement" [on the situation of and for the protection of IDPs] were developed in 1996 by the Special Representative on IDPs of the UN Secretary General. International law cannot be applied to IDPs since it would infringe on the national sovereignty. For full text of the Guiding Principles see: www.unhchr.ch/htm/menu2/7/b/principles.htm

13

Protecting Refugee Women

UNHCR AND THE GENDER EQUITY CHALLENGE

Judith Kumin

In preparing this chapter, I tried to remember the first time I thought consciously about how refugee women perceive themselves.[1] I can remember the occasion, even though it was more than twenty years ago, because it was on my first field assignment for UNHCR. I was sent to a beach in southern Thailand, near Songkhla. It was at the height of the Vietnamese "boat people" crisis, and I was expected to look into the needs of some refugees who were reported to be sheltering on the beach. It turned out to be a group of young women, none older than eighteen or nineteen, who had been abducted by pirates during their journey from Vietnam. They had been raped and mistreated over many days and weeks, and then dumped unceremoniously in the shallow waters off the Thai coast.

We sat on the beach and, with the help of a Vietnamese-speaking colleague, the refugee women and girls told me what had happened to them. As a new UNHCR recruit, I had little idea of how to react to what I was hearing. But I learned a number of things that day, which have stood me in good stead over the years. I learned to listen to the testimony of refugees and not to dismiss it as not credible, simply because it was too horrible for us to believe. I learned about the courage and resilience of refugee women. And I learned how important it is for refugees that justice be done—the women I met wanted the pirates tracked down and were willing to appear in court as witnesses. And I learned about the determination of refugee women to take the future into their own hands.

This was more than twenty years ago. At that time, UNHCR did not have a policy on refugee women. The agency only had a handful of female staff and there were no guidelines on sexual and gender-based violence. No one in UNHCR talked about gender-based persecution, or gender equity, and if the term "gender mainstreaming" had been invented, it had not yet reached the UN.

Needless to say, times have changed. Today, if you type the words "gender mainstreaming" into an Internet search engine you get four million hits. The words "refugee women" yield a million. Even the more technical term "gender-based persecution" yields over thirty thousand. Today, UNHCR has a clear policy on the protection of refugee women. It has published detailed guidelines on gender-related persecution, and all UNHCR field offices are expected to involve refugee women in the planning and delivery of their programs.[2]

Canada can take considerable credit for the advances that have been made in protecting refugee women. Canada was the first country to develop a resettlement program for refugee women at risk.[3] The Canadian Immigration and Refugee Board's 1993 Gender Guidelines[4] were the first of their kind; Canada was a driving force behind the UN Security Council's adoption of Resolution 1325 on Women, Peace and Security,[5] and Canada collaborated with the UK to develop a Gender and Peace Support Operations training initiative for military and civilian personnel, and a Website to house relevant materials.[6] Canada has been relentless in reminding UNHCR—at all levels—of the agency's fundamental obligation to protect and assist refugee women.

Most observers will admit that UNHCR has made a lot of progress. Not enough, perhaps, but still a lot. Whether the glass is half full or half empty depends on one's perspective. The issue of refugee women reclaiming their identity is of vital importance to the UNHCR since, in my opinion, the bigger the bureaucracy, the greater the effort which needs to be made not to lose sight of the individuals for whom one works.

The challenge is to hear the specific voices of refugee women. This is why, in 2001, UNHCR organized a dialogue with refugee women from around the world, which involved more than twenty-five local and regional consultations including one held here in Canada, as well as a large-scale consultation in Geneva.[7] A refugee woman addressed UNHCR's Executive Committee that year—the very first time the states which constitute UNHCR's governing board had heard from a refugee, much less from a refugee woman. The High Commissioner has publicly announced the organization's commitments to refugee women, and expects all of his staff to honor these commitments.[8]

But, how do we ensure that these efforts are more than just lip service? After all, the ultimate objective of understanding the experiences of refugee women, and how they perceive themselves, is so that we can develop appropriate policies and initiatives to support, and more importantly, to empower them.

I am looking at international issues, in order to provide an overview of the areas in which UNHCR is concentrating its efforts, to make sure that the experience of refugee women *does* actually influence policy responses. I will focus on eight areas that we consider to be of primary importance.

First, we need to continue to advocate for a gender sensitive application of refugee law and procedures. Canada blazed the trail in making clear that there are forms of persecution which are unique to women, and that—even though the 1951 Refugee Convention does not make specific reference to gender—gender-related persecution can fall squarely under one or more of the five grounds for asylum enumerated in the Convention. The Immigration and Refugee Board's Gender Guidelines[9] are now over ten years old, and they impelled a number of other countries to issue gender guidelines of their own.[10] Some states have even included reference to gender-based persecution in their legislation.[11]

Still, in many countries, decision makers fail to understand how to analyze asylum claims involving gender persecution, which often takes place at the hands of private actors rather than state officials. In Germany, for instance, persecution by nonstate agents was until recently not recognized as giving rise to refugee status—though the new German immigration law brought a long awaited change in policy. In the United States, the case of Rodi Alvarado Pena, known as the Matter of R.A., gave rise to considerable debate. This case involved a Guatemalan woman who had suffered a decade of violence at the hands of her abusive husband, an ·ex-soldier. The police and the courts in Guatemala ignored her appeals for help. She fled to the US, where she was initially granted asylum (in 1996); the Board of Immigration Appeals overturned that decision in 1999.[12] Attorney General Janet Reno, on the last day of her tenure in 2001, vacated the Board's decision, but her successor, Attorney General Ashcroft remanded the decision back to the BIA in January 2005. Appointed in February 2005, Attorney General Alberto Gonzales did not respond to Senators' questions on the issue of protecting women refugees during his confirmation hearings. I raise the issue because I do not think we can afford to be complacent. Here in Canada, there is broad recognition that women can be refugees in their own right, but at the same time there is a real effort elsewhere to limit the number of persons to whom the label "refugee" is attached. As a result, in many countries, women with a well founded fear of persecution may find themselves granted diminished levels of protection, or no protection at all. This is why UNHCR recently updated its *Guidelines on Gender-Related Persecution*,[13] and why partners are encouraged to disseminate these *Guidelines* as widely as possible.

Along with the issue of gender-based persecution, there is the emerging question of the protection needs of women who have been trafficked, in particular for sexual exploitation. While this is not necessarily best dealt with in the refugee context, it is an important human rights question, which also deserves attention.

A second area where we need to concentrate our efforts is in making sure that refugees and women returning to their home countries not only have equal access to humanitarian assistance, but are themselves involved in the design and implementation of aid programs and policies. When NGOs and UNHCR held the first consultation with refugee women in 1988, the prevailing view expressed by these refugees was (and I quote one refugee speaker): "Women are left out of everything. We do not participate in planning or designing programs that are aimed at us. We are second class citizens when it comes to food, water, and shelter distributions. We remain the world's invisible refugees."[14]

Indeed, a veteran UNHCR official, Christine Mougne, recently remembered working in 1980 in what was then Zaire, when thousands of terrified Angolans trudged across the border. Food was distributed and large plots of land earmarked for the Angolans. The criteria for assistance were simple: aid was allocated to all "able-bodied male heads of household." Christine was appaled. "Aren't there any refugee women here?" she recalls asking her colleagues. It had not entered anybody's mind that more than half of the adult refugees were women.[15]

Even ten years later, when a million Kurds fled Iraq in the wake of the Gulf War in 1991, little had changed. A former UNHCR emergency officer, John Telford, remembers that when a food distribution system was finally set up for the displaced civilians, all the appointed food marshals were local men, and little aid reached any women. Designating women as food marshals, he says, "didn't even occur to us."[16]

Over the past decade, the fight to give refugee women a better deal has resulted in considerable progress. The former High Commissioner for Refugees, Ruud Lubbers, instructed all UNHCR field offices to make sure that refugee women participate in management and planning of activities. But we constantly need to ask, what more needs to be done?

One of the keys to further progress will require a real effort on the part of many aid agencies—including UNHCR—to change the mindset which underlies our thinking. We need to stop concentrating on programs that prolong the stereotype of refugee women as "vulnerable." This stereotype results, I think, in underplaying "empowerment" projects that can provide women with better educational, economic, and leadership skills, and in turn enhance women's roles in a camp or when they return home.

There is a great deal of positive experience to build on. For instance, in Kosovo, the Women's Economic Empowerment Project is designed to give women access to credit. In the refugee camps in southern Algeria, women are responsible for reception and distribution of humanitarian aid. In Guinea, a program has been launched to provide alternative jobs for refugee women practitioners of female genital mutilation. But much more needs to be done to shift the paradigm, and to think of women as a powerful force in their communities, rather than as passive recipients of the world's largesse.

A third vital area concerns the safety and security of refugee women and girls. We need to intensify our effort to ensure their security and especially to address the problem of sexual and gender-based violence. It was not long ago that the shocking allegations of sexual exploitation of refugee women and girls surfaced in West Africa. Since then there have been similar reports from Zimbabwe, Tanzania, and Nepal. As a result, a taboo has been lifted and this difficult issue is finally out in the open. There is now a UN Inter-Agency Task Force on Protection from Sexual Exploitation and Abuse in Humanitarian Crises. UNHCR has committed itself to strengthening awareness of sexual and gender-based violence through staff training and by ensuring that refugees are informed of their rights. We are also committed to addressing conditions in the field that make women and children vulnerable to abuse, to working to put an end to harmful traditional practices, especially to female genital mutilation. And we are committed to ensuring the accountability of all staff members in carrying out their duties on behalf of refugees.

There are numerous actions underway to meet these commitments. These include deploying more female staff, establishing a reporting mechanism through which refugees can raise complaints, ensuring refugee access to legal systems for the prosecution of violators, and reviewing camp layout to ensure security and privacy, to name just a few. And new UNHCR Guidelines on the prevention of sexual and gender-based violence against refugees have recently been issued.[17]

But the underlying fact of life is that so long as assistance is scarce, refugees will be vulnerable to exploitation. So long as refugee women have to walk long distances in isolated areas to collect firewood or water, they will be at risk of attack and rape. So long as adequate food, shelter, water, and medical care are lacking, agencies will find it difficult to invest in programs to combat sexual and gender-based violence.

A fourth area in need of dramatically reinforced efforts is that of education. More refugee girls need to attend school. Education and literacy are key to empowering women, and preparing girls for future roles. Last year, girls made up 39 percent of refugee children attending UNHCR assisted primary schools worldwide, but comprised only 29 percent at the secondary school level. In some locations the disparity is much greater. In Dimma, a remote refugee camp on Ethiopia's border with Sudan, out of 570 refugees attending secondary school, only six are girls.

There are, of course, many sides to this issue. Girls' education is influenced by parental attitudes, dependence on the labor of girls, sexual and other types of harassment of girls in school, and early marriage. We will need to work harder to remove obstacles to girls' education. Among other measures, we need to push for the recruitment of more female teachers and classroom assistants, to ensure that girls receive sanitary supplies so that they can attend school without embarrassment, and to raise awareness among parents about the benefits of sending daughters to school. More refugee girls need to be targeted for scholarship opportunities.

Fifth, it is essential that refugees and women returning to their home countries are properly registered, and have their own personal documentation. The need for some form of personal documentation is a feature of daily life in nearly every society. As a refugee, establishing one's identity can be essential for a wide range of reasons—to register births and deaths, to contract marriages, to obtain housing or employment, to qualify for food rations or medical care or social benefits. Adequate registration is a prerequisite for the legal and physical protection of refugees. It may even be essential to prevent *refoulement*.

Looking back, this is another area where progress has been made. In July 1984, when UNHCR issued a note on "Identity Documents for Refugees," it made no mention of the importance of making sure that refugee women have their own documents. The document on registration prepared in 2001 for UNHCR's Global Consultations stresses the importance of making sure that each family member is independently registered—including women and children. Indeed, this should be standard practice in every refugee situation.[18]

Sixth, and this is primarily relevant in the context of repatriation, we need to promote recognition of women's right to own property. In recent repatriation operations, a large proportion of returning households have been headed by women. If rural women cannot hold title to land, they have little prospect of being able to look after their families.

In Guatemala, returning women were directly involved in repatriation negotiations and among the concessions they won was recognition, for the first time, of the principle of equal ownership of both private and communal property. Although it took a decade of work, it is now enshrined in Guatemalan law and jurisprudence, benefiting the entire population. A similar law was enacted in Rwanda in the aftermath of that country's 1994 genocide.

Seventh, and most importantly, we need to promote the inclusion of women in conflict resolution and peace building efforts. The international community is slowly recognizing the role that women play in preventing war and sustaining peace. A major benchmark was the adoption by the UN Security Council on 31 October 2000, of Resolution 1325.[19] This was the first time in its history that the Security Council had dealt with the issue of women, peace, and security.

Sceptics might say that this is just another piece of paper, another UN Resolution to be filed away and ignored. I believe this resolution is different, because unlike most Security Council Resolutions, 1325 has an active constituency of organizations and individuals who are going to demand that governments and international organizations implement it.

Swanee Hunt, at Harvard University's *Women in Public Policy Program,* insists that the idea of women as peacemakers is not just political correctness. She points out that there is plenty of research to support the stereotype of women as more collaborative than men and more inclined toward consensus and compromise.[20] Indeed, former US President Bill Clinton is reported to have said in exasperation in July 2000, after the failed talks between Israelis and Palestinians that, "if we'd had women at Camp David, we'd have an agreement."[21] Also, Hunt notes that, since women have usually not been the ones holding the guns or dropping the bombs, they often have less psychological distance to cover in order to reach across a conflict line. Women's roles as mothers and family nurturers cut across international borders and ethnic divisions. Women have a huge investment in the stability of their communities. When Resolution 1325 came before the Security Council, Secretary General Kofi Annan reminded the Council: "For generations, women have served as peace educators, both in their families and in their societies. They have proved instrumental in building bridges rather than walls."[22]

This is all the more important, since women are no longer just the random victims of war but, increasingly, are specifically targeted. For this reason the International Criminal Tribunal for the Former Yugoslavia has handed down a conviction for rape used as a weapon of war, and the Statute of the new International Criminal Court recognizes rape as a crime of war.

With these positive developments, it is all the more disappointing that Bosnian women were not invited to participate in the Dayton Peace Conference, which finally put an end to the war in Bosnia. Nonetheless, during the conflict, dozens of women's associations remained active across ethnic lines, and women—one needs only to think of the women of Srebrenica—were among those most profoundly affected by the conflict. More recently, even after the Security Council had passed Resolution 1325, the demobilization and reintegration program jointly planned by the World Bank and the Government of Angola limited assistance to UNITA and government soldiers, excluding those women and girls forced to serve as "wives" of the combatants. Also since passage of Resolution 1325, peace negotiations in the Middle East, Burundi, and in Sudan, either did not include women at all or did not do so at a high level. Sima Simar was initially given a ministerial portfolio in Afghanistan and then lost it. At the time of this writing (2003), the UN's Department of Peacekeeping Operations has a gender advisor who is based in the Peacekeeping Best Practices Unit. There is still just one woman acting in the capacity of Special Representative of the Secretary General. In other words, we clearly have a lot more work to do—even if we have come a long way.

My eighth point is that we still need to achieve gender equity within our own organizations. I do not believe that only women can militate for women's rights. Nor do I believe that men and women have to be equally represented in all departments at all times. Nonetheless, I am persuaded that ensuring a fair representation of women within UNHCR and other UN organizations, and especially at the highest level of decision making, will serve refugee women and girls better. At present, only 25 percent of staff at senior management levels in UNHCR are women. Virtually every evaluation of UNHCR's activities on behalf of refugee women over the years, including the one done in 2002 by the US-based Women's Commission on Refugee Women and Children, has highlighted the relative absence of female staff as an obstacle to obtaining information from refugee women and addressing the protection issues they face.[23]

Life as a refugee or a displaced person is disempowering—for men and women, boys and girls alike. Refugees live not only with a myriad of practical problems, but with the constant mental torment of their uprooting. Yet it is important to recognize that refugee women are an extraordinarily constructive force. We are well armed with policies, guidelines, and other tools to protect refugees and assist women, and to advocate for their rights. Now it is time to concentrate on translating these policies into action in the field, and on marshalling the contribution of refugee women to building lasting peace. The UNHCR is counting on those interested academics to hold us accountable for this.

Notes

1. This chapter was first prepared for the March 2003 Conference, "Saying 'I' is Full of Consequences, Refugee Women Reclaim their Identity," at McMaster University, Hamilton Ontario. The author was then the UNHCR's Representative in Canada. Developments since 2003 are not necessarily reflected in the text.

2. See UNHCR, *Guidelines on the Protection of Refugee Women* (Geneva, July 1991); *Guidelines on International Protection No. 1: Gender-Related Persecution within the context of Article 1A(2) of the 1951 Convention and/or its 1967 Protocol relating to the Status of Refugees*, (HCR/GIP/02/01) (Geneva, May 2002); UNHCR *Good Practices on Gender Equality Mainstreaming: A Practical Guide to Empowerment* (Geneva, 2001); *Sexual and Gender-Based Violence against Refugees, Returnees and Internally Displaced Persons* (Geneva, May 2003b). These documents are available online at http://www.unhcr.org.

3. Canada established its *Women at Risk Program* in February 1988. Background information is on the Web site of Citizenship and Immigration Canada at http://www.cic.gc.ca/english/refugees/women-1.html.

4. Immigration and Refugee Board, *Women Refugee Claimants Fearing Gender-Related Persecution*," Guidelines issued by the Chairperson, March 1993 (updated November 1996). Available at: http://www.irb-cisr.gc.ca/en/notices/cgi_e.htm

5. UN Doc. S/Res/1325 (2000) of 31 October 2000.

6. The *Gender and Peacekeeping Training Course* produced by Canada's Department of Foreign Affairs and International Trade and the UK's Department for International Development is available online at http://www.genderandpeacekeeping .org/participant-e.asp

7. See 2002b: UNHCR, *Respect our Rights: Partnership for Equality. Report on the Dialogue with Refugee Women* (Geneva, 20–22 June 2001). Geneva (December). http:// www.womenscommission.org/pdf/unhcr_w.ref.pdf. Accessed 10 April 2007.

8. Ibid., 38.

9. See supra, note 4.

10. The United States issued guidelines on adjudicating asylum claims from women in 1995, Australia did so in 1996, the U.K. in 2000, and Sweden in 2001. For an online compendium of governmental gender guidelines for asylum adjudicators, see http://www.uhastings.edu/cgrs/law/guidelines/html.

11. Ireland's *Refugee Act* (1996, available at www.ris.ie/legislation/) defines membership in a particular social group to include "persons whose defining characteristic is their belonging to the female or the male sex or having a particular sexual orientation."

12. See K. Musalo, "Matter of R-A-: An Analysis of the Decision and its Implications," 76 *Interpreter Releases* 1177, 9 August 1999.

13. See supra, note 2.

14. Quoted in UNHCR, *Refugees* 126, 2002: 7.

15. Ibid. p. 6.

16. Ibid.

17. See supra, note 2.

18. UNHCR, *Practical Aspects of Physical and Legal Protection with Regard to Registration*, UN Doc. EC/GC/01/6, 19 February 2001.

19. See supra, note 5.

20. S. Hunt and C. Posa, "Women Waging Peace: Inclusive Security," *Foreign Policy* 2001 (May–June): 38–47.

21. Ibid. 42.

22. UN Press Release SG/SM/7598 of 24 October 2000.

23. Women's Commission for Refugee Women and Children, *UNHCR's Policy on Refugee Women and Guidelines on their Protection: An Assessment after 10 years of Implementation* May 2002: 3. Available at www.unhcr.org/cgi-bin/texis/vtx/research/opendoc.pdf

14

Social Protection of Refugee Women

PARADOXES, TENSIONS, AND DIRECTIONS

Patricia M. Daenzer

"They may be living in a refugee camp or trying to survive in a country where they have no status and few, if any, rights. They may even be in detention or facing a risk of forced return to persecution. For them, resettlement to a third country represents the only available solution" (Canadian Council of Refugees: State of Refugees in Canada 2002).

Introduction

The 1951 Geneva Convention on Refugees incorporates no recognition of the gender-specific persecutions endured by women asylum seekers. Scholars and advocates persisted for decades in attempts to broaden the conventional definition of the term "refugee," and to differentiate and thus illuminate experiences of women asylum seekers. Resettlement guidelines, issued by the United Nations High Commissioner for Refugees (hereafter UNHCR), finally changed direction and tone in 1985, through cautious endorsement of policy focus on women asylum seekers, followed by clear guidelines in 1991. Canada and other nations responded to the UNHCR policy priority on women by introducing pilot programs aimed at fair and swifter resettlement of women asylum seekers whose lives were in imminent danger. Other nations opted for policy modifications, which broadly included recognition of the needs of refugee women without changing the basic principles of their resettlement and migration statutes. This chapter examines Canada's policy response to women asylum seekers during the period 1988 to 2002 and compares gendered refugee policy trends in Canada with selected nations. It concludes that, although resettlement policy directions have created new visibility for women asylum seekers, the purported protections do not necessarily lead to full expression of rights for forcibly displaced and persecuted women.

Gendering Refugee Policy Gaps

The absence of reasonable policy protection for women within the 1951 United Nations Convention Relating to the Status of Refugees (hereafter referred to as the 51 Convention), and the 1967 Protocol Relating to the Status of Refugees, should be understood in a larger context of the nullification of gendered rights and flawed analysis of social affairs. In the 1950s women had fewer rights, and violence against women was still unmitigated in many nations. In the case of Canada, shortly preceding the period during which the 51 Convention was crafted, questions had only recently been settled uneasily (1940) about whether all Canadian women were entitled to the right to vote, and entitled to keep the jobs they performed during wartime (1940–45) in the absence of men who were at war (Daenzer 1993). Canada had not yet settled questions about the right of women to be treated as equal partners at marriage dissolution (Chambers 1997). The 51 Convention was crafted at a time when, at least in Canada, women's rights were discretional in public policy.

Also, in the 1950s, few other countries had enshrined rights for women consistent with their equal entitlement as citizens of nations owing appropriate protection for all members. Those who collaborated in the crafting of the 51 Convention reflected political norms of nations, which had not yet come to terms with women as citizens owed inherent rights.

Not surprisingly, the 51 Convention embodied conceptual gaps and problematic language. Key related concepts—"persecution," "torture," and "well founded fear"—were either theorized as male phenomena (Valji and De La Hunt 1999) or were contested, especially with regard to the experiences of women (Greely 1996; Mathew, Hathaway, and Foster 2003; Pearce 2003). For those who supported the gender neutral tone of the Convention, "refugee" was understood to be a political condition encompassing temporary statelessness and usually flight from imprisonment and torture. Torture was understood to mean what military rulers inflicted upon dissenters. Since women were expected to be politically invisible and silenced within the private domain, they were not seen as victims of persecution nor worthy of special consideration in refugee law (Camus-Jacques 1981; Swedish Migration Board 2001; Valji and De La Hunt 1991). Forced marriages, genital mutilation, rape, and forced abortions, for example, were understood to be private domain matters (Pearce 2003; Swedish Migration Board 2001), and seldom subject to state interference. Women often existed outside the scope of protection owed by their states and were ineligible for sanctuary according to the terms of the asylum agreement shared by nations.

In deliberations of refugee law, the House of Lords in the United Kingdom dwelt on that very issue of "existence outside of state protection." Debates there, which led to inaction, focused on the distinction between the state's ability to protect and the state's unwillingness to protect. For example, if women could prove that persecution by non-state actors (family members) was ignored by the state, then they could become eligible for the surrogate protection afforded by the 51 Convention—they would be considered legitimate refugees.

But the behavior of states would have to suggest that they were complicit with non-state actors in the persecution of women. In addition, there would need to be legal agreement on the concept of "persecution" (Pearce 2003; Wilsher 2003). So, in principle, women in a given state who are subject to persecution by non-state actors, and receive no protection by their states, would be recognized as members of a "particular social group" with well grounded fears for their lives. Sex and national affiliation would be included as grounds for protection. These deliberations were really about how to include women under the provisions of the 1951 Convention because they are women.

Sweden took the position that, ". . . identity as a woman is not within the purview of the convention's ground. . . . [of] membership in a particular social group . . . ." Women were not to be given special consideration because they were women. According to Swedish law, it was irrelevant that women as a whole group endured similar persecution because of their sex. However, gender-specific persecution *per se* was not ignored. The individual circumstances that led to the asylum claim were to be appreciated, with special attention to the difficulties women faced in defending their claims. Sweden was prepared to hear women's cases as individuals but not to suggest that they are persecuted because they are women. Their program guidelines are clear that "each person" may have a credible claim for asylum, and that women's experiences may be quite different from men's.

From 1951 to 1985 these debates emerged and expanded; the focus and question was about if and how to include women under the guidelines of the Geneva Convention—if international law could supersede domestic customs. What seemed lost in the analysis of states' responses to questions about the protection of women seeking asylum was that the deliberations and forays into semantics meant that women needing protection were trapped by linguistic ambiguity. States were complicit in permitting the ongoing persecution of women while they advanced and perfected arguments and language. There had to be, it seems, robust justification for lifting women out of persecution and rewarding them with sanctuary—for allowing women to become political actors in their own defense.

There was no agreement on definitions and action in the United Kingdom until 2004. Canada took action in 1988, and Sweden introduced clarifications in 2001. Between the 1980s and 2000, a number of wars and political uprisings around the world had displaced and thrown into harm's way millions of women. Additionally, millions of other women fled to nations that they hoped would give them sanctuary, because they were members of that "particular social group." Wars, political uprisings, international bureaucracies, and social customs limited women's lives and freedoms.

Instructively, the 51 Convention was inspired by the war that defended freedoms; the document aimed to rescue men who were trapped on the wrong side of the battle lines, and to protect and provide sanctuary for those who might become victims of future episodes of faith, or ethnically-based persecutions. During that war, which defended freedoms, women were used as sexual slaves, labeled as "comfort women": they were a wartime commodity at the discretion of men. (It took fifty years to somewhat settle those claims made by the "comfort women" victims.) Yet nowhere does the 51 Convention embody an understanding of everyday social persecutions endured by women because of their sex. The 51 Convention addresses the similarities of men's and women's political experiences and ignores the specific differences that shape the nature of women's exile. Prior to changes introduced in 1991 by the Executive Committee of the UNHCR, women benefited only if they shared the experiences of men.

Indeed, in many cases, though certainly not all cases, men and women begin the journey into exile driven by the need for political safety and sanctuary. The 51 Geneva Convention responds to this need for safety from well founded fear of political and social persecution due to one's race, faith, affiliation, or politics. Women's social and political reality is much more complicated and less linear than the parameters conveyed by the Convention. In many cases, for example, women asylum seekers flee to safety from the very men who are considered to be their legal protectors, guardians, and economic providers. They flee from persecution due to unequal protection under domiciliary laws and enter a domain of statelessness, where men still have power over their destinies. While men generally, not always, flee from political persecutions to havens, women find it more difficult to find sanctuary from men who are in positions of power, throughout their flight in search of safety. Resettlement policies have therefore had the effect of transferring many women from certain violence and persecution to a potential of violence and persecution.

This has been so because when nations finally began to consider the asylum claims of women, there was disagreement about whether women's domicile nations had indeed failed to render protection consistent with their state's obligation and capacity (Mathew, Hathaway, and Foster 2003).

The question was—did states really fail to protect their women citizens? Cultural norms acceptable to the domicile nations of women asylum seekers complicated these considerations. The persecution endured by women was often not seen as rights violations; these were customs and practices of cultural groups and often occurred in the "private sphere."

The 51 Convention offered guidelines for the protection of persons who were members of a "particular social group," and thus had well founded fears of persecution due to their membership in such groups. Between 1951 and 1984 there was no consensus that women, because of their sex, could or should be considered as members of a "particular social group." Women asylum seekers were therefore victims of an enduring paradox: they faced persecution because they were women; they were unprotected by refugee laws because they were women. Consequently, they fell in between gaps in international law, which obliged receiving states to prove that home states refused them normal protection from persecution, and the laws of home states which defined persecution and their obligations to citizens in ways which transgressed women's rights (2003).

The experiences of women and girls who are asylum seekers, then, include more than waiting in refugee camps and yearning for a safe haven. The process of seeking asylum removes women from legal and civil protection, in principle, and predictably renders them vulnerable to even more acts of violence. Rape, sexual slavery, death, violence by partners and spouses, violence by border guards and those exercising military might, and loss of rights and protection have been variously reported as some of the most violent crimes against women asylum seekers (Camus-Jacques 1989; Forbes-Martin 2004; Mtango 1989; Mertus 2003; Valji and De La Hunt 1999; UNHCR Executive Committee 1990). But the violence endured by women asylum seekers is part of a universal sociocultural phenomenon. Additionally, violent crimes in asylum transit are not the only challenges faced by women asylum seekers. Nor is violence the unique experience only of women who are seeking asylum. Violence against women is structurally vertical; it occurs up and down the economic and ethnoracial class scales. It is universally hierarchical but differentiated; it occurs in every nation regardless of the strength of civil and legal protections. The persistence of violence against women could be attributed to the resilience of notions defining women as chattel, and by the complicating and erroneous public/private debates, which legitimate the subordination of women. In the latter, women's experiences (reproduction, labor, violence) belong within a private sphere beyond the reach of laws and rights protection (Crawley 1997, cited in Harvey 2001). Not surprisingly, until the 1980s women were strategically invisible or ignored in refugee laws. The incremental policy of visibility of women and girls as asylum seekers developed over a recent period of ten years (Executive Committee UNHCR 1990) and is coterminous with political change to the general and universal condition of women. The 1979 Convention on the Elimination of all Forms of Discrimination against Women (CEDAW) can be credited with influencing the inclusion and visibility of women in public policy and in asylum laws. More women were emboldened to become actors in their own liberation.

In the 1980s and 1990s greater numbers of women began risking their lives to seek asylum in allegedly safe nations. Increasingly it was difficult for nations to ignore the plight of women, especially since many, Canada included, were positioning human rights on the international economic agenda and calling nations to accountability on their record of human rights. Nations began asking not if, but how to integrate women's concerns into refugee law. Europe took the first official step. In 1984 both the European Parliament and the Dutch Refugee Council passed resolutions stating that:

> The concept of *"a particular social group"* [cited in the 1951 definition of Convention Refugee] could also be applied to "groups of women who transgressed moral and ethical principles in their society and who were victims of cruel and degrading treatment as a result" (Forbes-Martin 2004; Valji and De La Hunt 1999).

The UNHCR voiced agreement in 1985 (through Conclusion 39, 36th Session), which stated that:

> states are free to adopt the interpretation that women asylum seekers who face harsh or inhuman treatment due to their having transgressed the social mores of the society in which they live may be considered as a "particular social group" within the meaning of Article 1 A(2) of the 1951 United Nations Refugee Convention (Valji and De La Hunt 1999).

It took the UNHCR six additional years to develop guidelines to support its conclusion put forward in 1985. By the time it had tabled its 1991 Guidelines on the Protection of Refugee Women (UNHCR, Executive Committee 1991), Canada had already established its pilot Women at Risk Program. Women had finally been incorporated into both refugee processes and given tenuous acknowledgement in the 51 Convention.

In the final analysis, the integration of women's issues into refugee law appeared to rest on two points. Firstly, were crimes by non-state actors (partners, spouses, family) admissible as persecution? (Nijhoff 2002; Wilsher 2003). Secondly, could women be considered as members of a "particular social group" as defined in the 51 Convention? Canadian jurisprudence contributed to clarification of the latter in 1993 and again in 1995 by defining what membership in a "particular social group" should encompass (Canada vs. Ward, cited in Daley and Kelley 2000). Women who were discriminatingly persecuted and subjected to cruel cultural norms were clearly admissible under the 51Convention.

By 1988 Canada had already bought into the idea that women asylum seekers needed gender-specific processes and protections. And, not surprisingly, Canada was the first nation to issue Guidelines on Women Refugee Claimants Fearing Gender-related Persecution, which conformed to the UNHCR 1991 guidelines (Canada 1993, 1996b). The Women at Risk Program was the starting point for the proactive inclusion of women in international refugee law.

Refugee Women in Canadian Law and International Policy Guidelines

The Women at Risk Program was developed to address special needs of those refugee women: (1) whose safety could not be ensured where they were; (2) who often did not have family or friends to support or protect them; (3) who were vulnerable to the threat of rape and other forms of violence due to lack of protection; (4) or whose situations were so critical that urgent protection was required (Citizenship and Immigration Canada 2002 a, b, c, d). The program was operationally vulnerable since it predated the document Guidelines on Women Refugee Claimants Fearing Gender-Based Persecutions, which was introduced five years later in 1993. The paradox of this program was that it emerged out of, and was made possible by, clarification of concepts such as membership in particular social groups, persecution, and torture. However, definitional vagueness in the brief guidelines issued for the AWR (Association for the Study of the World Refugee Problem) encouraged discretions and limited its capacity for generosity. Field personnel and frontline gatekeepers could apply their own cultural definitions of concepts such as desperate circumstances, critical situations, and urgent protection, all cited in the explanation of AWR.

In spite of Canada's recognition that women needed to be rescued from precarious and life threatening circumstances, it approached the AWR imperative with a dual focus: the aim was to save some women who were in danger and simultaneously to bring only "suitable" persons into Canada. Instead, there should have been sequential aims of the AWR program. The first urgent task should have been to lift women out of all areas of danger. The second, less urgent task should have been to process women according to revised procedures. However, potential AWR candidates were required to pass medical, security, and criminal record investigations before being selected to enter Canada through the AWR program. Also, all women selected under this program were expected to attain self sufficiency in due course. The problematic concept of self sufficiency had the potential to encourage subjective cultural biases during the hearing process. Yet the operational notes to the program suggest that "women at risk" were not required to meet admissibility criteria prior to being admitted to Canada.

So Canada's choice to structure this contradiction into the AWR program must undoubtedly have been an attempt to avoid the complications of *refoulement*. Having to return persecuted women to domains in which their lives were endangered would have created unwanted international attention and criticism. But, the criticism that the AWR program subordinated women's safety to rules, which privileged healthy applicants, was one that Citizenship and Immigration may have been prepared to live with for the duration of the pilot AWR program.

Between 1988 and 2002 when the Immigration and Refugee Protection Act 2002 came into effect, Citizenship and Immigration Canada tells us that the AWR program resettled 2,250 women and children into Canada (CIC, Canada's Program for Women at Risk). The United Kingdom tracked approximately 3 percent of total refugees defined as women requiring special protection. Sweden does not publicly disaggregate statistics by issue, since their focus is on integrating all newcomers on the same but equitable grounds.

Data also shows that during the years 2000 to 2002 female refugees outnumbered male refugees to Canada by significant numbers. And refugee women have considerably less education than refugee men, a fact which becomes important in analyses of the post-settlement experiences of women (Canada, Facts and Figures 2002).

In spite of anecdotal criticisms of the 1988 AWR program, Canada led the international community in the response to women asylum seekers who were in grave danger. In 1993 the Immigration and Refugee Board issued guidelines to maximize the potential and streamline the operations of the AWR program. In 1995 the United States issued similar guidelines and Australia followed in 1996. The U.K. issued its guidelines in 2000. Sweden also issued carefully worded guidelines in 2001 but refrained from interpreting women as members of a particular group. All those guidelines share the following aims:

> Jurisprudence: to ensure that women's asylum claims are fully considered under the Refugee Convention so that jurisprudence properly reflects the experiences of both females and males

> Procedures: to ensure that the asylum determination process is accessible to both women and men and that the procedures used do not compromise or prejudice women in the process

> Evidential Requirements: to ensure that the judiciary are aware of the particular evidential problems which women asylum seekers may face and that appropriate steps are taken to overcome them (Immigration Appellate Authority of the U.K. 2000)

The strength of Sweden's approach to women refugees is the emphasis on integration instead of on granting asylum. Sweden has linked integration

Table 14.1 *Refugee Class by Gender and Category*

Refugee Class by Gender and Category 2002 (Dependents)

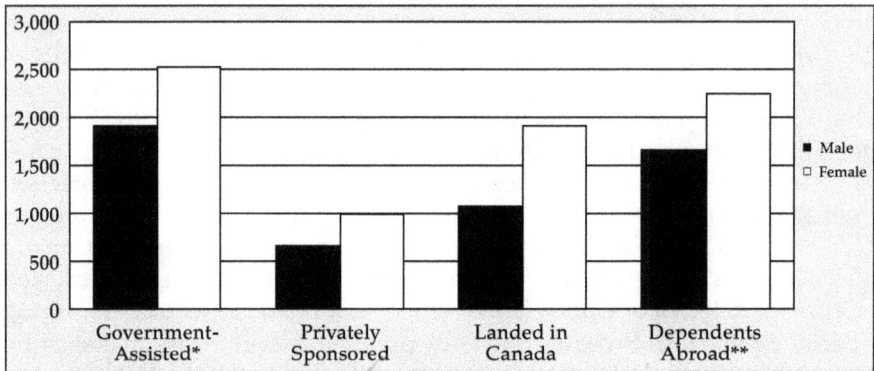

Refugee Class by Gender and Category (Dependents)

GENDER	CATEGORY	2000		2001		2002	
		Num.	Percent	Num.	Percent	Num.	Percent
Male	Government-Assisted*	2,547	40.35	2,136	36.00	1,935	35.15
	Privately Sponsored	649	10.28	801	13.50	703	12.77
	Landed in Canada	1,624	25.72	1,354	22.82	1,155	20.98
	Dependents Abroad**	1,493	23.65	1,642	27.68	1,712	31.10
	Subtotal	**6,313**	**100**	**5,933**	**100**	**5,505**	**100**
Female	Government-Assisted*	3,842	42.11	3,169	37.10	2,548	32.79
	Privately Sponsored	862	9.45	1,121	13.12	1,008	12.97
	Landed in Canada	2,419	26.51	2,151	25.18	1,907	24.54
	Dependents Abroad**	2,001	21.93	2,100	24.59	2,307	29.69
	Subtotal	**9,124**	**100**	**8,541**	**100**	**7,770**	**100**
	Total	15,437		14,474		13,275	

*Includes Kosovo refugees who arrived in 1999 as part of a special movement and who obtained permanent resident status in 2000.
** Dependents (of a refugee landed in Canada) who live abroad.
Note: The table for Refugee Class by Gender and Category (Principal Applicants) excludes principal applicants who were admitted as Dependents Abroad because it attempts to give a more faithful representation of the family unit. Even though principal applicants are processed in the Dependents Abroad category by administrative convention, they are in fact dependents. Therefore, principal applicants who are admitted into Canada under the Dependents Abroad category for administrative reasons are included in this table. Source: Citizenship and Immigration Canada: Facts and Figures 2002. www.cig.gc.ca/english/pub/facts2002/refugee/refugee_3.html

Table 14.2 *Refugee Class by Gender and Level of Education (Principal Applicants)*

Refugee Class by Gender and Level of Education - 15 Years of Age or Older, 2002

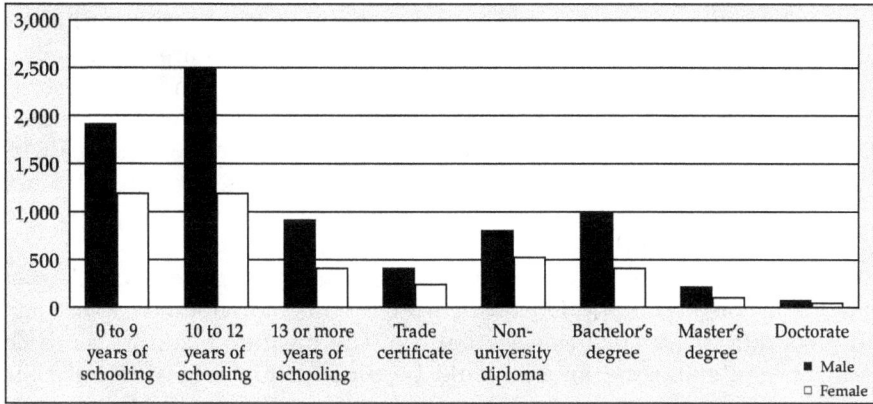

Refugee Class by Gender and Level of Education - 15 Years of Age or Older, 2002

GENDER	EDUCATION	2000		2001		2002	
		Num.	Percent	Num.	Percent	Num.	Percent
Male	0 to 9 years of schooling	1,846	18.97	1,782	20.05	1,861	24.30
	10 to 12 years of schooling	3,469	35.65	3,102	34.90	2,519	32.89
	13 or more years of schooling	1,254	12.89	990	11.14	865	11.29
	Trade certificate	807	8.29	587	6.60	390	5.09
	Non-university diploma	928	9.54	1,000	11.25	803	10.48
	Bachelor's degree	1,173	12.05	1,150	12.94	975	12.73
	Master's degree	203	2.09	218	2.45	175	2.28
	Doctorate	51	0.52	59	0.66	71	0.93
	Subtotal	**9,731**	**100**	**8,888**	**100**	**7,659**	**100**
Female	0 to 9 years of schooling	1,385	29.15	1,257	28.79	1,246	30.77
	10 to 12 years of schooling	1,524	32.08	1,329	30.44	1,254	30.96
	13 or more years of schooling	514	10.82	435	9.96	383	9.46
	Trade certificate	345	7.26	241	5.52	200	4.94
	Non-university diploma	493	10.38	562	12.87	485	11.98
	Bachelor's degree	416	8.76	462	10.58	411	10.15
	Master's degree	49	1.03	58	1.33	59	1.46
	Doctorate	25	0.53	22	0.50	12	0.30
	Subtotal	**4,751**	**100**	**4,366**	**100**	**4,050**	**100**
	Total	**14,482**		**13,254**		**11,709**	

Note: This table excludes principal applicants who were admitted as Dependents Abroad because it attempts to give a more faithful representation of the family unit. Even though principal applicants are processed in the Dependents Abroad category by administrative convention, they are in fact dependents. Therefore, principal applicants who are admitted into Canada under the Dependents Abroad category for administrative reasons are included in the table for Refugee Class by Gender and Level of Education (Dependents). Source: Citizenship and Immigration Canada: Facts and Figures 2002. www.cig.gc.ca/english/pub/facts2002/refugee/refugee_3.html

of newcomers to broader social welfare through immigration and refugee policies. Refugees are both central to and subordinated to the broader Swedish Integration Policy for the 21st Century (Government of Sweden 2002). Admitting newcomers (refugees and immigrants) is a joint process with one anticipated outcome. Emphasis and resources are dedicated to stabilizing refugees and immigrants into the labor force and social fabric, regardless of sex (Government of Sweden 2002). However, for Sweden this is workable since Swedish labor market policies are the most egalitarian and women friendly among the Western nations. In contrast, Canada's women refugee post-resettlement program is not fully responsive to social integration and maximization of human rights.

Swedish gender-based persecution guidelines are governed by other favorable considerations. During hearings, women do not have to explain or elaborate issues such as sexual abuse. The position taken by Swedish lawyers is that sexual abuse would be difficult to discuss because the abuse itself produces an inability to elaborate on the details. Such sensitivity is both thoughtful and protective, elements not normally found in public policy.

Canada's Guidelines specify four distinct critical issues:

1. To what extent can women making a gender-related claim of fear of persecution, successfully rely on any one, or a combination, of the five enumerated grounds of the Convention's refugee definition?

2. Under what circumstances does sexual violence, or the threat thereof, or any other prejudicial treatment of women, constitute persecution as that term is understood in jurisprudence terms?

3. What are the key evidentiary elements which decision makers have to look at when considering a gender-related claim?

4. What special problems do women face when called upon to state their claim at refugee determination hearings, particularly when they have had experiences that are difficult and often humiliating to speak about? (Canada, Immigration and Refugee Board, Update 1996)

These guidelines encourage sensitivity in programmatic details. Questions persist about accountability and progress in creating racism-free administrative environments. Racism and cultural stereotypes have been liabilities in immigration policy advancement for many years. The strength of the Canadian guidelines is its articulation and focus on just distribution of privileges and rights to refugee women.

For the most part, women's journeys as refugees to an ostensibly safe nation is still an underexplored experience. There is still only scant knowledge about when and how women begin their journeys, and when and if they end. This chapter takes the position that arrival in a safe country begins a new phase of a journey toward personal safety, which is often mired in obstacles. It questions assumptions made by current settlement programs and public policy, that integration, adaptation, and settlement flow in sync following arrival in safer countries when settlement services are provided. That assumption suggests poor understanding of the social relations of women in Canada.

The perilous nature of the refugee process and the uncertainties associated with women's attempts to become permanent members of safer nations, their statelessness and outsider status in the nations where they seek refuge, combined with their gender, make their position more politically risky than those who enjoy selective protection as immigrants. Gender imposes a number of invisible barriers to full citizenship attainment for women. Nevertheless, refugee women are increasingly becoming "creative and dynamic actors in their own histories" (Camus-Jacques 1981). Their self advocacy helps shape and improve public policy and the quality of settlement programs. Immigration and refugee legislation is no longer a document and process removed from public influence and untouched by the opinions of women. For example, Canada's Immigration and Refugee Protection Act 2002, benefited from public hearings and expert input from a variety of stakeholders. No doubt, in the future, it will be modified by the strength of women's advocacy and public input.

Canada's Immigration and Refugee Protection Act 2002, Bill C-11: Impact on Women Refugees

Canada's Immigration and Refugee Protection Act, Bill C-11, was legislated in 2001 and came into force in 2002. It includes clear statements about the protection of refugees, clarified and expanded definitions, and has been supplemented by new emphasis that aims to stop the flow of refugees between Canada and the United States.

The new legislation focuses on the following main areas of reform:

- creating a simpler, more coherent legislative framework, with objectives that reflect Canadian values and are responsive to current realities, including strengthening human rights commitments
- strengthening family reunification
- modernizing the selection system for skilled workers and business immigrants and facilitating the entry of skilled temporary foreign workers
- introducing transparent criteria for permanent resident status and enhancing the rights of permanent residents

- strengthening refugee protection through a faster, fair process

- streamlining the immigration appeal system

- maintaining the safety of Canadian society and respect for Canadian norms of social responsibility (CIC CIRPA: Citizenship and Immigration Canada, Canadian Independent Record Production Association An Overview 2002)

The "Safe Third Country Agreement" (2004) between Canada and the United States permit border guards to refuse entry to refugees who are either crossing from Canada to the United States or from the United States to Canada. This agreement assumes that both Canada and the United States are considered equally "safe" or "desirable" countries by asylum seekers. The element of choice for refugees has been eliminated by this agreement. For women who have been persecuted by family members or by spouses or partners, crossing from the United Sates to Canada or Canada to the United States may well be the last resort for sanctuary away from persecution. Or, women might wish to settle where they have family or friends, which might not have been the first port of disembarkation.

What necessitates special exemptions for women in this case, also, is that often women are trapped in layers of persecution. Their home states might be in turmoil and their lives may be in danger from political upheaval. In addition, they may have been living with political upheaval in fearful family relations, referred to in the Guidelines as "fear of persecution for reasons of kinship." Obtaining refugee status in a new nation while still trapped in fearful and oppressive relations does not constitute asylum. The Canada/United States Safe Third Country Agreement [Canada ruled against it in November 2007] may provide no safety for these women refugees.

The Guidelines for *Women* Refugee Claimants Fearing Gender-Related Persecutions should supersede the Safe Third Country Agreement between Canada and the United States for women who are persecuted. The procedures outlined in the Guidelines, pertaining to process and context, are adequate for screening out security risks.

Bill C-11 also tightened entry regulations that apply to immigrants and refugees at the same time that political violence increased in many parts of the world. Women are doubly at risk during these episodes of violence and persecution; rape, sexual enslavement, the cultural nullification of status and rights, and the loss of children are some issues faced by women who are trapped in regions of violence and persecution. Current estimates suggest that political, religious, and social violence within nations has created an estimated 14.5 million asylum seekers worldwide (Canadian Council of Refugees 2002). The silenced and invisible women are not included in those statistics and are likely to become collateral damage of stringent immigration policy born out of fear. This is, of course, a hidden gendered consequence of the era of heightened security. Another paradox for refugee women is that emphasis on heightened security in Western nations lessens the protection and security of women asylum seekers in poorer nations.

The emphasis on refugee protection in the new legislation, Bill C-11, includes the following:

(*a*) to recognize that the refugee program is in the first instance about saving lives and offering protection to the displaced and persecuted;

(*b*) to fulfill Canada's international legal obligations with respect to refugees and affirm Canada's commitment to international efforts to provide assistance to those in need of resettlement;

(*c*) to grant, as a fundamental expression of Canada's humanitarian ideals, fair consideration to those who come to Canada claiming persecution;

(*d*) to offer safe haven to persons with a well founded fear of persecution based on race, religion, nationality, political opinion, or membership in a particular social group, as well as those at risk of torture, or cruel and unusual treatment or punishment;

(*e*) to establish fair and efficient procedures that will maintain the integrity of the Canadian refugee protection system, while upholding Canada's respect for the human rights and fundamental freedoms of all human beings;

(*f*) to support the self sufficiency and the social and economic well being of refugees by facilitating reunification with their family members in Canada;

(*g*) to protect the health and safety of Canadians and to maintain the security of Canadian society;

(*h*) to promote international justice and security by denying access to Canadian territory to persons, including refugee claimants, who are security risks or serious criminals (Canadian Statutes 2001).

Unlike the 51 Convention, there is less room in Bill C-11 for discretions and competing interpretations. For example, with reference to (*a*), there are now sufficient international agreements about definitions of "displaced and persecuted." Rape is considered persecution: it is either persecution in the political sense (rape by invading soldiers), or persecution in the absence of defined protection (state withholds protection by indifference and knowingly) (Pearce 2003; Swedish Migration Board 2001; Wilsher 2003). The Guidelines acknowledge specific women's issues, which were previously excluded from definitions applied to aspects of the 51

Convention. Because the Guidelines work in tandem to buttress the Urgent Need of Protection protocol derived from Bill C-11, and focus on issues, such as women who are subjected to forced marriages and treated as chattel when found undesirable, and women who endure body burns and other torture if husbands are not satisfied with their material worth, they are clearly understood to be covered by the 51 Convention and the new Guidelines. But, in spite of carefully crafted regulations and guidelines which buttress the Act, the historical tendency of compartmentalizing women's public and private lives for political expediency is likely to persist. Tenacious history is difficult to untangle from old administrative practices, and professional discretion (such as that of refugee gatekeepers) often has the potential to defeat the sound policy intentions of policymakers. This means that it will be unlikely that violence in the home, and torture linked to marriages in some cultures, will result in boatloads of female asylum seekers being welcomed on Canadian shores.

In section (b) above, where the following seems to refer to a policy point other than Bill C-11 points a to h above, there is scant evidence to date to support the Canadian objective or priority of providing assistance to those in need of resettlement. The latter would comprise far greater numbers than are currently estimated, and could easily be the majority of many nations of the developing world. Section (b) more accurately refers to those successful in seeking asylum rather than those "in need" of resettlement. However, if Canada intended to expand women's refugee resettlement to those in need of resettlement, this would entail new international agreements and less emphasis on sovereignty. The UNHCR does not currently have this authority; nations working together could improve resettlements with mutual benefits to both receiving and dispatching nations.

In section (c) "fair consideration" would be a useful guideline if women's issues were not only well understood, but also if serious international collaboration were aimed at defending the rights of women. The recent inclusion of women in considerations of the 51 Convention has created a framework complete with legal arguments, advocacy, and public education. It is possible to move forward in the interest of persecuted women.

Section (d) could be made more specific by citing women without hope of rights and protection in their homelands as potential asylum seekers and guaranteeing "fair" access to such a process. Section (e) speaks of human rights and fundamental freedoms; women's rights and fundamental freedoms are rarely well understood or articulated in public policy.

In conclusion, Canada comes to this historical moment of the Immigration and Refugee Protection Act through decades of inconsistencies. Historically, Canada's inclination to absorb refugees may have been more generous than that of the United States, but still Canadian history shows that refugee policy has, at times, been characterized by spurts of indifference, generosity, racism, or ambivalence. Canadian policy responses to refugees have generally been influenced by world events and driven by reciprocal agreements with other nations. This is not unreasonable since Canadian migration flows are also influenced by economic social trends and close interrelationships with the United States.

The 1993 and 1996 updated Guidelines on Women Refugee Claimants Fearing Gender-Related Persecution is the most progressive document in the interest of women asylum seekers in Canada's history. The document provides new context and new voicing or representative opportunity for women. But Canada should not rest on these achievements.

15

The Gender Factor in Refugee Determination and the Effect of "Gender Guidelines"

Geraldine Sadoway

The Context

In July 1991, the United Nations High Commissioner for Refugees (UNHCR) published *Guidelines on the Protection of Refugee Women*, drawing attention to the fact that, while the Refugee Convention[1] forms the basic legal instrument for the protection of all refugees, "refugee women and girls have special protection needs that reflect their gender" and "special efforts may be needed to resolve problems faced specifically by refugee women."[2] In March of 1993 the Chair of the Immigration and Refugee Board of Canada (IRB), Nurjehan Mawani, issued the Chairperson's *Guidelines on Women Refugee Claimants Fearing Gender-Related Persecution* (hereafter referred to as the Gender Guidelines). These were the first guidelines ever issued by a chair of the IRB and were the first guidelines on gender-related persecution issued by any adjudicative body dealing with refugee status determination, in the various countries that have signed the Refugee Convention. The Canadian Gender Guidelines were subsequently updated and reissued in November 1996 as Guideline 4: Women Refugee Claimants Fearing Gender-Related Persecution.[3] Since the Canadian Gender Guidelines were published, refugee adjudication bodies in a number of other countries have issued similar Gender Guidelines[4] and in the past ten years considerable jurisprudence has developed in different countries in which the application of the Gender Guidelines can be observed and analyzed.[5]

Do Gender Guidelines Help Refugee Women?

Despite (or, perhaps, because of) the prevalence of gender inequality and violence against women throughout the world, the individualized method of determination of refugee status under the Refugee Convention has often failed to protect women who face very serious harm and are not adequately protected by the states in which they live. The very ubiquitousness of gender discrimination, and the fact that many forms of gender oppression are common to the refugee receiving countries, as well as to the refugee producing countries, tend to make some of the specific forms of persecution of refugee women almost invisible. Thus while a woman fearing female genital mutilation (FGM) or bride burning might readily be seen as having a well founded fear of persecution in most Western countries, a woman fleeing rape or domestic violence may be less easily distinguished from women in the country of refuge, and her plight is more likely to be minimized.[6] The reaction to news that women might be accepted as refugees due to these more universal forms of gendered oppression might get the following response: "Women are battered and raped in Canada too, but that doesn't mean they should qualify as refugees!" On the other hand, forms of oppression of women that are less well known in the West (or relegated to history)—child brides and forced marriage, female infanticide, honor killing, forced sterilization, and so on—tend to be hidden under the cloak of "culture," and refugee decision makers may be influenced by theories of cultural relativism and wary of applying a Western standard to the perceived cultural norm in the country from which the claimant has fled.[7]

The Gender Guidelines help to overcome these two barriers for women refugees, because they are firmly rooted in various international human rights instruments.[8] According to the Gender Guidelines:

> [T]he fact that violence, including sexual and domestic violence, against women is universal is *irrelevant* when determining whether rape, and other gender-specific crimes constitute "persecution" and the decision-maker is advised to focus on whether the risk of that violence is the result of "a failure of state protection."

With respect to cultural relativism, the Gender Guidelines state that:

> [S]ocial, cultural, traditional and religious norms and the laws affecting women in the claimant's country of origin ought to be assessed *by reference to human rights instruments which provide a framework of international standards for recognizing the protection needs of women.*[9]

The international instruments referred to, include the *Convention on the Elimination of All Forms of Discrimination Against Women*, the *Convention on the Political Rights of Women,* the *Convention on the Nationality of Married Women,* and the *Declaration on the Elimination of Violence Against Women.*

Stating the forms of oppression of women, including the universal ones of rape and battering, in the Gender Guidelines brings the reality of gendered persecution into focus for the decision makers and locates these forms of oppression squarely within the context of human rights: women's rights are human rights. In fact, the Gender Guidelines make it easier to protect women through the Refugee Convention. Some simple examples come to mind. In 1986, I represented a woman whose husband, a wealthy businessman, had abused her for years including having broken her arm in the same place *seven* times (we had X-ray evidence of these repeated fractures). She fled her country on a visitor visa to Canada, even leaving her children behind, because she was so terrified of this continuing brutality, and knew that she would not receive any protection from the police in her country. We initiated a refugee claim for this woman but also filed a "humanitarian" application because we had no hope that, at that time, the Refugee Board would accept her claim based on domestic violence. (In fact, the "humanitarian" application was successful, and the refugee claim was then withdrawn). Ten years later, after the Gender Guidelines had been adopted in Canada and after the *Ward* decision in the Supreme Court, another client who was in a very similar situation—fearing her abusive spouse and unable to rely on state protection—was accepted as a Convention refugee.[10] A review of the Compendium of Decisions relating to Guideline 4, published by the IRB in February 2003, provides a clear indication of the much greater possibilities of securing refugee protection for women since the Gender Guidelines came into effect.[11]

Stereotyping, "Neo-Orientalism," and Reactionary Backlash

One danger of the Gender Guidelines is the tendency of advocates to simplify and stereotype the claimant to easily fit the categories of the Gender Guidelines. Thus an advocate may present the claimant as a passive victim fleeing the stereotypical patriarchal or "macho" Eastern or Southern state, asking the Board members to buy into both stereotypes, when in fact the reality of both the claimant and the country she comes from is more complex. It may appear easier and safer, for example, to base the claim on fear of FGM even when this may be only one aspect of the case, and the claimant is actually opposing the practice of FGM as part of a more sophisticated resistance to discrimination and inequality within her social environment. If the case is argued only on the issue of FGM, the claim might be denied because the woman has already been subjected to this practice (in the Board's view, if it has already taken place, she no longer has any reason to fear it), or because new laws have been passed condemning the practice of FGM, even though the laws are not being enforced.

In a compelling critique of the stereotyping of Islam by advocates and academics through use of the Gender Guidelines in refugee claims by Arab and Muslim women, Susan Musarrat Akram gives examples of how the use of Gender Guidelines has actually hurt some refugee claimants and resulted in the denial of their claims. In describing asylum claims of three Iranian women in the United States, she demonstrates how the women were "silenced" by the decision to base their claims on the social group of Iranian women who opposed the dress code, imposed by the theocratic regime in Iran, when in fact the cases could have been based on fear of persecution due to religious and political opinion. All of the women were Muslim, but they disagreed with the "Islam" practiced by the government of Iran. Their nonconformity was not merely a preference for Western dress and culture, but a positive expression of their own Islamic beliefs and their political opinions, in opposition to the Iranian regime. Akram concludes that the "new Orientalism emerging from feminist perspectives on human rights advocacy in the asylum and refugee context, threatens accurate presentations of human rights violations and victimization."[12]

In the context of refugee claims based on sexual orientation, failure to look and act like the stereotype might result in a refusal of refugee status. In a perceptive article describing the situation of gay Chinese men seeking refugee status in Australia, Kristen Walker suggests that refugee status may be a "violent gift," requiring those who seek it to stereotype themselves, doing violence to the individual with complex subidentities.[13] The Gender Guidelines may be a "violent gift" that sacrifices the more nuanced complexity of women refugees, especially when they do not readily fit the stereotype expected by the Refugee Board.

However, a more serious problem is the backlash against the Gender Guidelines, based on reactionary, neoconservative and antifeminist attitudes toward women. This is seen particularly in cases involving the more universal forms of oppression of women, such as domestic violence and sexual assault. In the case of domestic violence, Board members have been quick to applaud any efforts by a particular state to remedy the protection issue, so that the passage of a new domestic violence act might be enough to satisfy the Board member that the situation has changed, and the claimant may now obtain effective state protection in her home country. High profile cases, highlighting the failure of state protection in Canada as revealed by the inquests into the murders of Arlene May and Gilian Hadley by their respective partners,[14] encourage the Board to refuse claims by women who have fled to Canada to escape an abusive partner, on the grounds that no state can guarantee protection.

Furthermore, Board members must be continually educated on the basics of "battered wife syndrome" and the nature of sexual violence. Despite the Gender Guidelines, some Board members are still prone to make the same kind of assumptions that some lower court judges in Canada make about women who are victims of domestic violence or rape. In overturning a lower court decision in the case of *R. v. Lavallee*, the Canadian Supreme Court Judge Bertha Wilson described the "myth" about domestic violence as follows: "[E]ither she was not as badly beaten as she claims, or she would have left the man long ago. Or, if she was battered that severely, she must have stayed out of some masochistic enjoyment of it."[15] Despite the fact that the Gender Guidelines specifically cite the Supreme Court decision of *R. v. Lavallee* to draw attention to inaccurate myths about wife battering,[16] some Board members still do not find it plausible that a well educated and intelligent woman would remain in a situation of spousal abuse. In a 1998 decision refusing the claim of a woman subjected to several years of severe domestic violence, the Board members found that this claimant was "assertive," "intelligent," and resourceful in acquiring an education and employment and in getting to Canada, and that she demonstrated "a certain degree of independence, organizational ability and competence." These characteristics did not fit in with her alleged "helplessness" and her claim that for a long time she was "powerless" to leave her abusive partner. The Board therefore concluded that her story of abuse was "exaggerated," and her evidence was "fabricated."[17]

Some decisions on refugee claims involving sexual violence reveal the persistence of myths about rape as a private, criminal act of lust, outside the scope of the Refugee Convention.[18] In a US case that was decided after the adoption of US Gender Guidelines by the Immigration and Naturalization Service, the Federal Board of Immigration Appeals determined that the claimant's gang rape by soldiers in the Guatemalan military was "a random criminal act, unconnected to the government." Fortunately, the Ninth US Circuit Court of Appeals overturned this decision on appeal.[19] In a U.K. case of a woman raped by state agents, the Adjudicator of the Immigration Appeal Tribunal refused the claim on the basis that it was "simple and dreadful lust" rather than persecution.[20] The appeal was also unsuccessful, but a public campaign was launched to prevent this claimant from being deported to her country of nationality.

The Gender Guidelines, Refugee Protection, and International Human Rights Law

In spite of the setbacks, the development of Gender Guidelines in Canada and other countries has made a dramatic improvement in the protection of women who have fled their countries and has raised the profile of the continuing oppression and inequality of women worldwide. The Gender Guidelines have also opened up the possibilities of refugee protection for other vulnerable social groups: children,[21] the elderly, gays and lesbians, persons living with HIV/AIDS, and persons with disabilities. At the same time, there is tremendous resistance to recognizing these "nontraditional" grounds of persecution under the Refugee Convention, nourished by the antirefugee bias in the dominant media. Guidelines alone will not ensure good decision making if the refugee determination system itself lacks appropriate safeguards, and if the selection of Board members continues to be affected by political patronage.

Tragically, refugee determination is becoming more and more "the luck of the draw" in Canada. Under the *Immigration and Refugee Protection Act*, only one member of the Refugee Protection Division of the IRB hears a refugee claim, and a claimant can make only one refugee claim in her lifetime.[22] Although an appeal process was included with the new legislation, it was not implemented when the Act came into effect in June 2002 and has still not been implemented. We have many excellent and well-qualified Refugee Board members, however the lack of an appeal on the merits to catch the mistakes of less competent members is a very serious flaw. New guidelines to increase the efficiency of decision making at the IRB—including hearings by video conference, strict rules on extensions of time and adjournments, and "reverse order" questioning[23] of the claimants—all have a disparate, adverse impact on the most vulnerable refugees, including women, children, and survivors of torture.[24] Judicial review on narrow legal grounds does not constitute an appeal and is out of reach for most refused refugees because of the legal complexity and cost. The "pre-removal risk assessment" [PRRA]—available to all refused refugees—is not an appeal either, as the PRRA officers may only consider new evidence that could not have been presented at the hearing before the RPD. The current 2 to 3 percent success rate of PRRA applications is clear evidence of the failure of this process as a safety net. Although a refused refugee claimant may submit a "humanitarian and compassionate" application to be landed in Canada, filing such an application (with payment of a $550 filing fee) does not delay removal from Canada, and the current processing times for these applications is two to three years. When the "Safe Third Country Agreement"[25] comes into effect, women fleeing to Canada through the United States will also be denied the opportunity of even making a refugee claim in Canada, as they will be ineligible.

It is the most vulnerable and traumatized refugees—women, children, survivors of torture, persons with disabilities, and so on—who are the principal victims of this seriously flawed refugee determination system. The Gender Guidelines are needed more than ever, and similar guidelines should be developed to assist in the determination of claims by other particularly vulnerable groups. But if the claimant has the bad luck to draw one of the more reactionary or less competent Board members, or if she is simply unable to recount her history of abuse when she first comes to Canada, her chances of rectifying the situation and securing protection are very poor.

At the same time, the potential to use positive Refugee Board decisions based on gendered persecution to improve the human rights of women internationally is not yet being fully exploited. Deborah Anker (2002) makes the point that the "parallel disciplines" of international human rights law and refugee law, traditionally have not had much to do with each other; but they are becoming increasingly interconnected, and this is a useful development. Refugee claims are fact based and provide for individual remedies in a procedure that is private and confidential. However, the individual cases grouped together could lead to actions to publicize and denounce the failure of state protection before international human rights bodies, such as the Human Rights Committee of the United Nations, the European Court of Human Rights, the Inter-American Commission of Human Rights, the Court of Human and Peoples Rights of the Organization of African States, etc.[26]

Furthermore, international human rights tribunals that seek to prosecute war crimes and crimes against humanity have had to develop procedures for receiving victims' evidence, which accommodate the particular difficulties and vulnerabilities of such witnesses, and the evidentiary guidelines used by these tribunals can inform the procedures followed by refugee claims adjudicators. For example, the international criminal tribunals on Yugoslavia and Rwanda (the ICTY and ICTR) have made allowances for the effect of Post-Traumatic Stress Disorder (PTSD) on a victim's ability to testify consistently.[27] The same principle should apply in the hearing of a refugee claim if the claimant is suffering from PTSD. The Gender Guidelines provide some assistance, but more comprehensive guidelines, describing the effect of head trauma and PTSD, are needed to assist in the determination of claims by survivors of torture.[28] It is also of note that the recognition by the ICTY and ICTR that rape is a war crime and a crime against humanity has helped to counteract the myth of sexual assault as an act of passion rather than an act of violence.

Now more than at any time in history, human rights activists, refugee advocates, and the academic community have the opportunity to work together to call states to account for the treatment of women and other vulnerable social groups. By mainstreaming women's rights as human rights, the Gender Guidelines have enhanced the possibilities for valuable exchange and mutual reinforcement between refugee law and international human rights law. It is important to build on the progress that has been made. The fabric of international human rights law can be strengthened as it is interwoven with the testimonies of women refugees. The granting of refugee protection based on gendered persecution is a positive step in the direction of greater recognition of economic, social, and cultural rights as human rights and toward a feminist "reconstruction"[29] of international human rights discourse.

Notes

1. The United Nations Convention Relating to the Status of Refugees of 1951 and the Protocol of 1967. www.unhcr.org/cgi-bin/texis/vtx/protect?id=3c0762ea4

2. *Guidelines on the Protection of Refugee Women,* United Nations High Commissioner for Refugees, Geneva, July 1991. www.icva.ch/doc00000822.html

3. *Guideline 4: Women Refugee Claimants Fearing Gender-Related Persecution,* 13 November 1996, Immigration and Refugee Board, Canada. The major change in the updated guidelines was to reflect the Supreme Court of Canada decision *Canada (Attorney General) v. Ward,* [1993] 2 S.C.R. 689, which provided a basic framework for analysis of refugee claims based on the Convention ground of membership in a "particular social group"; and also some guidance to applying the Convention definition in situations of non state "agents of persecution" in which, although the state is not directly complicit in the persecution, the person may be found to be in need of international protection due to the failure of the state to provide "effective" protection. See Policy—Chairperson's Guidelines at www.irb-cisr.gc.ca/en.

4. *Considerations for Asylum Officers Adjudicating Asylum Claims From Women,* United States Immigration and Nationality Service (INS), 1995; *Guidelines on Gender Issues for Decision-Makers,* Australian Department of Immigration and Multicultural Affairs (ADIMA); *What Does this Stand for?,* Position Paper on Asylum Seeking and Refugee Women, July 1996; European Council on Refugees and Exiles (ECRE), December 1997; *Gender Guidelines for the Determination of Asylum Claims in the UK,* Refugee Women's Legal Group, UK, 1998; and *Asylum Gender Guidelines,* Immigration Appellate Authority, UK, November 2000. *Refugees and Gender: Law and Process,* Heaven Crawley, Jordan Publishing Lt., Bristol, 2001.

5. N. Kelley, "The Convention Refugee Definition and Gender-Based Persecution: A Decade's Progress" *International Journal of Refugee Law* 13, no. 4 (2002).

6. See A. Macklin, "Refugee Women and the Imperative Categories," *Human Rights Quarterly* 17 (1995): 213–277.

7. See H. Crawley (supra, note 4) at pages 10 to 12 for a review of the debate on the relationship of women's human rights and the issue of cultural relativism in the context of refugee law. See also J. Bhabha, "Embodied Rights: Gender Persecution, State Sovereignty and Refugees, *Public Culture* 9 (1996): 3–32.

8. K. Daley and N. Kelley, "Particular Social Group: A Human Rights Based Approach in Canadian Jurisprudence," *International Journal of Refugee Law* 12, no. 2 (2000): 148–174.

9. *Guideline 4: Women Refugee Claimants Fearing Gender-Related Persecution,* 13 November 1996, Immigration and Refugee Board, Canada. Section B. Assessing Feared Harm.

10. C. Kentridge, "Victim of Spousal Abuse Granted Refugee Status," *Law Times* 28 June–4 July, 1993; M. Clayton, "Afflicted Women Find Hope In Canada's Refugee Rules," *Christian Science Monitor,* 9 March, 1994.

11. *Guideline 4: Women Refugee Claimants Fearing Gender-Related Persecution: Update,* Immigration and Refugee Board, Canada, February 2003, www.irb-cisr.gc.ca/en/about/tribunals/rpd/compendium/index_e.htm

12. S. Musarrat Akram, "Orientalism Revisited in Asylum and Refugee Claims," *International Journal of Refugee Law* 12, no. 1 (2000): 7–40.

13. K. Walker, "The Importance of Being Out: Sexuality and Refugee Status," *Sydney Law Review* 18 (1996): 598.

14. For the jury recommendations of the coroner's inquests concerning A. May and G. Hadley, see the Ontario Women's Justice Network website: owjn@web.ca.

15. *Guideline 4: Women Refugee Claimants Fearing Gender-Related Persecution: Update,* Immigration and Refugee Board, Canada, 1996, at Endnote 31.

16. ibid.

17. IRB File No. U97-00088, 9 September 1998.

18. J.R. Castel, "Rape, Sexual Assault and the Meaning of Persecution," *International Journal of Refugee Law* 4, no. 1 (1992): 39–56.

19. Garcia-Marquez v. Ashcroft, 02-74068. United States Courts of Appeals for the Ninth Circuit www.ca9.uscourts.gov/.../8a3d80c334dc875f882572930000957b/$FILE/npa04_07.pdf

20. The case of Rose Najjemba, referred to in *Women's Asylum News*, Issue number 44, August 2004, at page 2, and fully described in WAN Issue No. 31, April 2003.

21. The Chair of the IRB issued *Guideline 3: Child Refugee Claimants: Procedural and Evidentiary Issues,* September 30, 1996. Unfortunately these guidelines do not deal with substantive law issues of what constitutes persecution of children. The U.S. *INS Guidelines for Children's Asylum Claims,* 10 December 1998, go much further in this regard.

22. *Immigration and Refugee Protection Act,* S.C., see 27, 2001, implemented on 28 June 2002. Under the former *Immigration Act,* two Board members heard a refugee claim and a split decision resulted in the granting of refugee status to the claimant. There was no appeal but a repeat claim was possible if the refused claimant left Canada for three months and then returned. This served as an appeal in some cases and, according to anecdotal evidence, about 40 percent of repeat claims were successful.

23. Rather than being examined first by her counsel, the new standard procedure is for the Refugee Protection Officer to examine the claimant and then allow counsel to ask questions. This is the reverse of the traditional trial procedure in which the person who bears the burden of proof has the opportunity to present her case first, with the assistance of counsel. "Reverse order" questioning was instituted by IRB Guideline 7 in 2003.

24. IRB Chairperson, Jean-Guy Fleury, introduced Guidelines 5, 6 and 7 in 2003, all designed to increase the efficiency of the Refugee Protection Division (RPD) of the Immigration and Refugee Board.

25. Canada and the United States agreed, following the events of 11 September 2001, to implement the "safe third country" arrangement, denying access to the refugee determination system to claimants who passed through the "safe third country" before reaching the country in which they wanted to claim refugee status: thus refugees passing through the United States on their way to claim protection in Canada (about 40 percent of Canada's refugee claimants), will be found

ineligible to make a claim in Canada. Similarly, any refugee claimants arriving first in Canada and then attempting to travel to the U.S. to claim asylum (currently a tiny percentage), will be returned to Canada. For an excellent discussion of the failure of similar "safe third country" agreements in Europe, the "Dublin agreement," see Macklin, "The Value(s) of the Canada-US Safe Third Country Agreement," Caledon Institute of Social Policy, December 2003, www.caledoninst.org. [The *Safe Third Country Agreement* between Canada and the U.S. came into effect on Dec. 29, 2004. In November 2007, the Canadian Federal Court ruled that it violated the Canadian Charter of Rights and Freedoms.]

26. D. E. Anker, "Refugee Law, Gender, and the Human Rights Paradigm," *Harvard Human Rights Journal* 15 (Spring 2002): 133–155. Anker describes how this was done in a complaint to the Inter-American Commission on Human Rights of the Organization of American States [OAS] by Haitian refugee women in the U.S. who had been raped in Haiti during the struggle against the dictatorship. This effort was a crucial first step in recognizing rape as torture and as a crime against humanity.

27. See the decisions of the ICTY on Tadic and of the ICTR on Akayesu: Prosecutor v. Tadic, IT-94-1, Trial Chamber, Judgment, 7 May 1997; Prosecutor v. Akayesu, ICTR-96-4, Trial Chamber, Judgment, 2 September 1998.

28. J. Cohen, "Questions of Credibility: Omissions, Discrepancies and Errors of Recall in the Testimony of Asylum Seeker," *International Journal of Refugee Law* 13, no. 3 (2002): 293–309. The Canadian Council for Refugees, the Canadian Center for Victims of Torture and other groups have repeatedly asked for IRB guidelines to assist in the determination of refugee claims by victims of torture and trauma. [On Dec. 15, 2006 the Chair of the Immigration and Refugee Board published Guideline 8: *Guideline on Procedures With Respect to Vulnerable Persons Appearing Before the I.R.B.*]

29. H. Charlesworth and C. Chinkin, *The Boundaries of International Law: A Feminist Analysis,* (Manchester, 2000).

16

Pursuing National Responsibility in a Post–9/11 World

Seeking Asylum in Canada from Gender Persecution

Carmela Murdocca
In Conversation with Sherene H. Razack

Introduction

In 1993 Canada became the first country to issue guidelines on refugee women claimants fleeing gender-related persecution. Since then other countries, following Canada's lead (the United States, Australia, and Sweden, for example), have adopted their own guidelines, or have changed legislation to recognize gender-based persecution and asylum or have advanced the issue through the law.[1]

Beyond the fact that Canada has become a world leader in implementing human rights measures to protect women from gender-based persecution, thinking critically and acting legally in response to violations against women has emerged as a central component of national and international responsibility. The fact that states have been seeking to protect women's rights, or imposing sanctions on nations that fail to do so, however, has not been straightforwardly about social justice. In a post–9/11 context, responding to violence against women, both nationally and globally has enabled Canada to position itself as a moral arbiter of the values of democracy and human rights. The ideological consequence for Canada and the West has been to exonerate our own accountability in current global relations and, specifically, our own implications in the perpetuation of violence against women. Canada's recognition of gender-based asylum is an antiracist feminist legal incentive, and as such it is necessary to examine the national effects of what appears to be an important and urgent feminist measure.

Sherene Razack first explored the Canadian implications of asylum laws pertaining to gender persecution when she began to explore how gender asylum guidelines were operating in the practice of the law.[2] Researching empirical data from refugee hearings, Razack found that the process of "culturalization" that operates in a refugee hearing (the legal operation of cultural difference as a marker of inferiority) requires a disavowal of the ways in which capitalism and racism work to sustain patriarchal violence. This led her to argue that it is imperative to historicize gender persecution in order to better account for relations between women and nations, each as subjects in history across and within national and international lines. What is required, Razack argues, "is a theory of difference that accounts for the violence in the lives of women and our complicity in it."[3]

This interview with Sherene Razack revisits her work on gender persecution and attempts to highlight some of the elements required to uncover and trace the historical, political, and racial relations that underlie a politics of national responsibility in the context of race and the law. The interview is preceded by my analysis, which attempts to identify the elements of a methodology of national responsibility that Razack invokes through her work on gender-based asylum. Utilizing the recognition of gender-based asylum as our point of reference, this discussion highlights that any examination of the relationship between race and the law should not operate through a mode of inquiry that merely assesses individual subjects before the court. Instead, investigating legal claims to social/national responsibility, as evidenced in asylum claims based on gender persecution, requires an examination that is cognizant of the impact of what appear to be antiracist and/or anticolonial legal incentives (incentives that identify a nation's own role and complicity in global injustice) and how they ultimately work to consolidate a particular version of the nation that is upheld by the implementation of individual and group justice. As Razack suggests, gender-based asylum discourse "is one of pity and respect . . . it is not one of justice and responsibility."[4] Thus, this discussion examines the analytic move required to consider a politics of national responsibility in the context of gender-based asylum law.

Gender-Based Asylum and National Responsibility

In her analysis of the implementation of Canadian measures to combat gender persecution, Razack highlights that it is *only* useful to speak of women's rights (or "human rights" as it is often legally codified and organized) as a concept that has wider potential use when being attendant to such issues of historicity and social justice as they pertain to the variety of ways in which "Third World women" are made (or are not made) into subject/citizens in inter/national contexts.[5] In particular, Razack urges us to consider the refugee hearing as a "profoundly racialized event" that is implicated in the production of a "discursive apparatus that entrenches notions of Western superiority and Third World inferiority."[6] She further argues that "gender persecution, as it is deployed in refugee discourse, can function as a deeply racialized concept in that it requires that Third World women speak of their realities of sexual violence outside, and at the expense, of their realities as colonized people."[7] Razack maintains: "When histories of imperialism, colonialism, and racism are left out of sexual violence, we are unable to see how these systems of domination produce and maintain violence against women," and, more critically, we are unable to determine how the "First World is complicit in both the sexual and racial persecution of Third World women."[8]

In order to adequately historicize gender persecution in Canada, it is imperative to show how particular subjects emerge through the discourse of gender persecution and show how "imperial stories" get (re)produced through codifying the contours of permissible racial/cultural narratives that invite a consideration of gender-related asylum in the Canadian context.

The analytical move in Western feminism that ultimately produced the concept of gender persecution utilizes a universal woman, and a similar erasure of histories of genocide and exploitation has sometimes ensued. For the most part, this erasure has been accomplished by the narrative of violence against women. "Women's rights as human rights" represents the apotheosis of what has been called dehistoricized and deterritorialized "mappings of Otherized communities and their worlds." As a formula, it can be simplistic or complex, but in either case, what is difficult to introduce into "women's rights as human rights" is the notion of First World domination.[9]

As a consequence, the recognition of gender persecution in Canada as institutionalized in the law does not take full account of the connections between the material practices in the law that work to ensure the subjugation of women of color and the global relations of complicity that sustain these relations. In particular, the law does not take full account of the narratives that circumscribe the claims to personhood for women of color as well as the national story of innocence that underscores the ideological impetus behind the legal redress for gender persecution.

Furthermore, Inderpal Grewal, like Razack, encourages us to examine whether legal rights offer women (who are differently located) any additional access to justice if they do not fall under the purview of human rights discourses. Importantly, Grewal asserts, "to become visible in the human rights framework is to become constituted as this international subject, a subject constructed through knowledge regimes of modernity and nation-state systems."[10] Human rights mechanisms in local contexts must be recognized for their material consequences for certain communities of women. As Mallika Dutt notes, "understanding human rights as the right to be human underscores the fact that the paradigm is not a language game but a mechanism through which we understand that we cannot take *rights* seriously without taking human *suffering* seriously."

In rendering "Third World women" subjects in law, the discourses surrounding human rights issues at the local/national level legally establish the global contours that determine citizen rights and (often) result in the exclusion of certain gendered and racialized communities from becoming lawful national/citizen/subject participants. Ultimately, as Grewal notes, "the issue then is whether the legal instruments of human rights can bring about social justice on the scale that is required at the present time."[12] Unless the historical argument is advanced to consider both the material practices of discrimination in the law and their connection to processes of gendering and racialization that underscore "human rights" legal provisions, feminist sociolegal scholars will remain caught within a Euro-Western framework that merely reinscribes the liberal contention that the law is somehow detached from the historical processes that both construct and sustain it. As Grewal has noted (referring specifically to debates in India over the rights of Muslim women), "it is the complexity of women *as subjects in history*, rather than generalized invocations of human rights discourses, that is necessary for practice" and social justice.[13]

The context of gender persecution reveals both the material and symbolic effects of antiracist incentives and highlights the ways in which the law functions as the *locus* of racialization and a primary site for policing and regulation of political, racial, sexual, and cultural membership in Canada. This examination of asylum based on gender persecution in Canada also illustrates that for women of color, legal personhood can only become recognizable within cultural/racial frames of reference. The context of gender persecution highlights the way in which legal provisions that purport to be justice seeking produce subjects, both legitimate (white) Canadian subjects and non-white subjects, and ultimately obscures the understanding of legal inscriptions through their "relationship to identity as well as to justice," as Razack asserts. Finally, codifying gender persecution in the law does not properly historicize gender persecution and, as a consequence, the connections between patriarchal violence and the legal practices in specific national contexts remain complicit in sustaining forms of such gendered, racialized violence.

In Conversation with Sherene Razack

Q: It has been ten years since you published work on gender-based asylum where you began by asking, "How is a petition for refugee status in Canada inevitably *an encounter between the white First World and the racialized Third World, and what are the consequences of these power relations for women seeking asylum from domestic violence or oppressive social mores?"*[14] *In your view, how does the move to historicize gender persecution, in the context of understanding gender-based asylum as precisely an encounter between the First World and the Third World, raise issues about complicity and national responsibility?*

One way to understand what gender persecution guidelines are about is to see them simply as policies that are intended to offer protection to women whose states have failed to protect them from sexual violence. This extremely simple framework becomes complex when we begin to consider how we would recognize a woman whose state had failed to protect her. In the first instance, we have to recognize that she has in fact encountered *unbearable* sexual violence and, in the second instance, that her state had failed to protect her from this violence. In effect, this process is about how we Canadians make sense (and it is a kind of legal sense) of her story.

When you look at the empirical data, you see that many times, decision makers recognize unbearable sexual violence only when they are able to understand the woman who is standing before them as a kind of ultra-victim. If the woman betrays too much personal strength, decision makers can assume that her story of being victimized does not ring true because she appears to be someone who can protect herself. Now who is an ultra-victim? We tend to understand harm, the harm that we see being done to her, if it comes packaged in images with which we are familiar. So if she tells us that women in her culture are passive, married off early in arranged marriages, subjected to cruel mothers-in-law, and made into a slave in her own home, we will believe her if the story is told in ways that bring to mind the scores of movies, news stories, pictures we have seen of passive, feminine, Indian women burned to death for having brought an inadequate dowry. We will understand the harm and risk she faces to the extent that it matches what we presume about people like her and what we presume about the countries she comes from. To this I would add, that believing in the peril she faces as one that originates in her barbaric culture also helps us to feel that we are kind and generous and able to save her. In essence, the whole encounter between the refugee claimant and the decision maker is underpinned by ideas about who we think "they" (her country, her fellow nationals) are as compared to who we think "we" are here. The "we" is clearly a national category, and it is shaped by national narratives.

When the facts of the case cannot be accommodated within the simple framework above, they tend to be discounted. A black woman from the Caribbean is known to us (through popular culture) as a "tough mammy." If we rely on the stereotype to understand her case, we will not find her pitiable and therefore deserving of our compassion. We will not believe her story that she could not protect herself or that her state failed to protect her.

I proposed that we find ways to think outside of the stereotype and the too familiar racial scripts (of their cultural inferiority and our superiority). We need to stand up against the seduction of seeing ourselves as generous and all-knowing decision makers. One way to do this is to see the woman in her historical, social, political and cultural context, something we cannot really accomplish until we put ourselves back into history as well. We will have to understand that her nation is beset by a number of forces, which limit the state's capacity to protect her. For example, International Monetary Fund (IMF) and World Bank policies (which we in the West insist upon) mean that Jamaica, for example, cannot have very many social services. Shelters for women are very few. She has fewer places to turn to for help not only because her culture is patriarchal (as is ours) but because social conditions have deteriorated to the point that no help is available. Does this mean we have to save every Jamaican woman who claims gender persecution? No. It simply means that in assessing her degree of risk, we are guided not by the logic that her culture is utterly barbaric but instead by an analysis of a multitude of factors that bear on her capacity to resist and her state's capacity to protect her. To go to what I consider the second step of analysis that is beyond the simple, racist frames, we will have to [consciously] give up this view of ourselves as superior. And that, I believe, is the heart of the challenge.

Q: You have argued both in your work on gender-based asylum and elsewhere[15] *that nations use human rights and the discourse of human rights to create a particular benevolent moral democratic leadership, which ultimately works to re-imagine the nation and its history by constructing new histories based upon international humanitarianism as it operates through terms that appeal to legality and justice. What is the relationship between Canada positioning itself internationally through legal humanitarianism and issues of national responsibility in a specifically national context?*

The process that an individual decision maker goes through, largely one of comparison between our superior culture/nation and theirs, is replicated on a national and international level when Canada announces itself as one of the most humanitarian countries. We prefer to stress our great capabilities to keep the peace and mediate rather than our humanitarian instincts (which some Scandinavian countries stress), but in the end we are making the same claim of superiority. As with all such claims, we need to ask for what purpose. Today, and no more so than after the events of September 11 [2001], the international sphere is dominated by the United States. As a superpower, the United States accomplishes many of its imperial activities through stories about saving the world from evil dictators. In such a world, where occupations, invasions, and a whole host of activities of political, military, and economic dominance are undertaken with the logic that the United States must teach the Third World how to live in a more civilized fashion, middle powers such as Canada can only secure a piece of the action (that is, the economic and political benefits that come with aligning oneself with the superpower) through participating in what is fundamentally a colonial mythology. We are developed; they are not. We know how to live; they do not. We know how to respect women; they do not. Canada enters this game through asserting that we know how to mediate and that we share in those universal values of democracy and human rights.

There would be nothing wrong with any of this if it did not mean that we set about making decisions such as those in asylum hearings, as though the world really was that simple a place, a world in which we are innocent and not fundamentally implicated in the "bad things" that happen to other people.

Q: Western or "First World" feminism has moved to a concern about location— a concern with global geopolitics and the interplay of both the "international" and the "national," using an official language of humanitarianism and a kind of international discourse of human rights as a platform. What are some of the dangers of this approach, and do these approaches obscure issues of national responsibility?

Feminists can enter into the fantasy of a superior West and inferior non-West, through adopting a framework of saving non-Western women. We can set out to save Afghan women from the Taliban without asking any questions about how the Taliban came to power and what it would take to remove them. What feminists then share with the imperial decision makers I described in the refugee hearing is an oversimplified understanding of what happens to women, an understanding premised on the notion that we are the saviors and they are to be saved.

Of course, the great paradox of all of this imperial saving is that there are women in peril, movements like the Taliban do exist, and something has to be done about it. The real issue, I maintain, is how we might go about ending the terrible situation in which many women find themselves. I am convinced that we don't stand much of a chance of changing anything if we proceed from the framework of our own innocence and superiority. What should we, as feminists, do with the fact that the Taliban was initially installed and kept in power largely through the auspices of the United States? How does this piece of history influence feminist strategy?

Q: You concluded your work on gender persecution with an imperative to educate in our own national complicity in the context of gender asylum rather than investigate so-called cultural practices that have led to some gender-based refugee claims. In that work you ask: "Can we attempt education initiatives around this

*[our own national stake in gender persecution] rather than around the intricacies
of Sharia law, customary rites, or FGM [Female Genital Mutilation], or would
the whole structure of policing the borders then collapse?"*[16] *What would you add
to this question today, or how would you further develop this imperative in light
of recent trends in law, like the emergence of Sharia arbitrations in Canada?*

Ah, the eternal Sharia debate! Until February 2006, when Ontario
banned all religious arbitration, there was a distinct possibility that a small
group of mainly Muslim men would secure the right under the Arbitration Act of Ontario to establish Sharia tribunals. In effect, when the Boyd
report on the Arbitration Act was released in December 2004, it carefully
framed the use of Muslim principles with respect to family law within the
context of Ontario and Canadian law. Muslims would have been able to
go before these tribunals to solve disputes over divorce and custody in ac-
cordance, presumably, with the laws of Islam. That there is no agreement
about the laws of Islam, and a thousand versions of Sharia exist, justifi-
ably raised feminist fears that Muslim women in Canada would have
been forced to live under Taliban-like conditions, subjected to the interpretations of Sharia proposed by a few, powerful men.[17]

To participate ethically in the debate over Sharia law, I would propose
the same cautions I did with respect to adjudicating gender persecution
claims for asylum. That is to say, we cannot approach issues such as the
introduction of Sharia law in Canada from the viewpoint—"The Taliban
are coming, let's save the women!" The Taliban may be coming to our
shores, and may already be here (in fact we know that fundamentalism of
the Christian, Hindu, and Muslim kind is on the rise everywhere, and
nowhere is this more evident than in the laws limiting women's reproductive rights introduced under George W. Bush). The problem—and it is an
immense political problem for women—has to be approached as a complex one requiring the kind of framework I proposed with respect to gender persecution. That is, it is imperative to examine not only what some
Muslim men do to Muslim women, but also what are the forces operating
to structure responses to women in Muslim communities and how are we
involved in this picture. The answers to these questions will help us to determine a strategy: how best to secure women's rights and respect the Muslim community as a whole. We can see, for example, that since the events
of 9/11, anti-Muslim sentiment and practices have greatly increased, push-
ing some Muslims to retreat to their communities and to build walls around
them constructed of patriarchal traditions. In such a climate, fundamen-
talists will thrive, and women will have less of a chance to exert their
rights within communities as well as outside them. How can we then
strengthen Muslim women's options? To even pose this question is to see
Muslim women not simply as victims to be saved but as social actors. It is
also to see Muslim communities as diverse, confronted with considerable
pressures post–9/11, and rife with internal contests for power, as are all

communities. From the basis of this complexity, we can begin to work out each of our roles, and the role of the law.

Notes

1. Canada Council of Refugees, "Refugee Women Fleeing Gender Persecution." Accessed on 10 April 2004, www.web.net/~ccr/gendpers.html

2. S. Razack, "Policing the Borders of Nation: The Imperial Gaze in Gender Persecution Cases," in *Looking White People in the Eye: Gender, Race, and Culture in Courtrooms and Classrooms* (Toronto 1998b), 88–129. This work was first published in 1995 as "Domestic Violence as Gender Persecution: Policing the Borders of Nation, Race and Gender," *Canadian Journal of Women and the Law* 8, no. 1: 4588.

3. S. Razack, *Looking White People in the Eye: Gender, Race, and Culture in Courtrooms and Classrooms* (Toronto 1998c), 21.

4. ibid, 12.

5. Indeed, the use of the term "Third World women" is highly contested and requires much more elaboration than is possible here. For the purpose of this paper, we borrow from Alexander and Mohanty who explain the concept of "Third World women" as one that encompasses "imagined communities of women with divergent histories and social locations, woven together by the political threads of opposition to forms of domination that are not only pervasive but also systemic." See C. Mohanty and J. Alexander, *Feminist Genealogies, Colonial Legacies and Democratic Futures* (London, 1996), 7.

6. Razack, 1998b. op. cit., 91.

7. ibid, 90.

8. ibid, 90–91.

9. ibid, 93–94.

10. I. Grewal, "Women's Rights as Human Rights," *Citizenship Studies* 3, no. 3 (1999): 351.

11. Emphasis in original. M. Dutt, "Reclaiming a Human Rights Culture: Feminism of Difference and Alliance," in *Talking Visions: Multicultural Feminism in a Transnational Age*, ed. E. Shohat (New York, 1998), 231.

12. I. Grewal, "Women's Rights as Human Rights," 339.

13. Emphasis mine. I. Grewal, "Women's Rights as Human Rights," 346.

14. S. Razack, 1998b. *Looking White People in the Eye*: 89.

15. S. Razack, *Dark Threats and White Knights: The Somalia Affair, Peacekeeping and the New Imperialism* (Toronto, 2004).

16. S. Razack, 1998b, *Looking White People in the Eye*: 129.

17. Author's note: Since 1991 Ontario's Arbitration Act permitted faith-based arbitration in family law. Jewish tribunals had thus existed resolving such matters as spousal support and the division of property. After the issue of "Sharia arbitration" generated worldwide protests and a racialized moral panic about "Sharia law" invading Canadian law, the government of Ontario enacted a package of reforms called the Family Statute Law Amendment Act on 14 February 2006. These amendments only permit arbitrations in family law using the laws of a Canadian jurisdiction.

Notes on Contributors

Adrienne Chambon is Professor at the University of Toronto's Faculty of Social Work. She has coedited essays on "Postmodernism and Social Work" with A. Irving (1994) and "Reading Foucault for Social Work" with A. Irving and L. Epstein (Columbia University Press, 1999). She has written on critical theory, narratives of self and institutions, and various forms of dialogue. Part of her work has focused on issues related to refugees and resettlement. She is interested in forms of writing and is currently involved in a funded project on the "Heuristics of Art Practices for Social Work," drawing upon premodern and contemporary art to help the social sciences expand their understanding of people and public spaces, and the changing space of social relations.

Patricia M. Daenzer, Ph.D., is Associate Professor, School of Social Work, McMaster University (www.patriciadaenzer.ca). She is a social welfare scholar who researches, teaches, and writes about the socioeconomic condition of racial minority immigrant and refugee women in the Canadian Welfare State. She is also Chair of the Board of Directors of Settlement and Integration Services Organization, Hamilton, and a social activist. Her book *Regulating Class Privilege: Immigrant Servants in Canada 1940s–1990s* sets the tone for illuminating the process of the construction of social location for racialized immigrant female workers in the Canadian labor force.

Malathi de Alwis is Senior Research Fellow at the International Center for Ethnic Studies, and member, Graduate Faculty of the University of Colombo, Sri Lanka. She is the coeditor, with Kumari Jayawardena, of *Embodied Violence: Communalising Women's Sexuality in South Asia* (Delhi: Kali for Women/London: Zed Press, 1996) and with Wenona Giles et al. of *Feminists Under Fire* (Toronto: Between the Lines, 2003). She is a founder-member of the National Women's NGO Forum and the Women's Coalition for Peace, Sri Lanka, and a regular contributor to "Cat's Eye," a feminist column on contemporary issues in the English daily, *Island*. www.mdealwis.squarespace.com

Madeleine Gagnon is a celebrated, award-winning poet, novelist, and essay writer from Québec (Montreal). She has obtained a Ph.D. in literature from the University of Aix-en-Provence (France). Since 1969, she has published some thirty books (poetry, novels, nonfiction). Her works have been translated into several languages and have appeared in many journals and anthologies in Québec, Canada, the United States, South America, Europe, and Asia. Madeleine Gagnon has received many literary awards, including the Prix Athanase David of Québec for her lifetime body of work. *Les femmes et la guerre* (2003) [translated, *Women in a World at War*, 2003] is a work for which she received the Governor General of Canada Award. It was followed by *My Name is Bosnia* (2006). Madeleine Gagnon has taught and has been invited as a writer in residence to several universities. She is also a gifted musician and a member of *l'Académie Canadienne-Française,* of the *Association des auteurs et compositeurs canadiens,* and of *l'Union des écrivaines et des écrivains québécois.*

Wenona Giles is a Professor and Chair of the School of Social Sciences, Atkinson Faculty of Liberal and Professional Studies at York University. She teaches and publishes in the areas of gender, migration, ethnicity, nationalism, work, globalization, and war. Her publications include *Maid in the Market: Women's Paid Domestic Labour* (Fernwood, 1994); *Development and Diaspora: Gender and the Refugee Experience* (Artemis, 1996); *Portuguese Women in Toronto: Gender, Immigration and Nationalism* (University of Toronto Press, 2002); *Feminists Under Fire: Exchanges Across War Zones,* Giles et al. (Between the Lines Press, 2003); and is coauthor with Jennifer Hyndman of the book *Sites of Violence: Gender and Conflict Zones* (University of California Press, 2004).

Rachel Gorman is a Visiting Research Fellow at the Education and Social Research Institute of Manchester Metropolitan University. She has recently completed a two-year postdoctoral research project on gender, disability, and nationalism at the Women and Gender Studies Institute of the University of Toronto. Rachel teaches courses on disability arts and culture, gender and disability, and violence against women. As an activist, she has at various times worked on disability-rights, antipsychiatry, trade unionism, antiwar and antiviolence campaigns. Rachel is also a choreographer and a member of the Canadian Alliance of Dance Artists.

Elżbieta M. Goździak, Ph.D., is the Director of Research at the Institute for the Study of International Migration (ISIM) at Georgetown University and is editor of *International Migration,* a peer reviewed, scholarly journal devoted to research and policy analysis of contemporary issues in international migration. She has taught at Howard University's School of Social Work in the Social Work with Displaced Populations Program. She has also managed a program area on admissions and resettlement of refugees in industrialized countries for the Refugee Policy Group. Her recent publications include the following edited volumes: *Beyond the Gateway: Immigrants in a Changing America* (with Susan F. Martin, Lanham, MD: Lexington Books, 2005), *Global Survey of Research on Human Trafficking* (with Frank Laczko, *International Migration* 43, no. 1–2, Special Issue 2005), and *Religion and Forced Migration* (with Dianna Shandy, a special issue of the *Journal of Refugee Studies* 15, no. 2, 2002). Currently, she is working on a book on children victims of trafficking.

Sepali Guruge is an Associate Professor at the School of Nursing, Ryerson University. She completed her Ph.D. in Nursing from the University of Toronto. Her thesis focused on postmigration experiences of intimate partner violence (IPV) in the Toronto Sri Lankan Tamil community. She is presently a postdoctoral fellow at the University of Western Ontario. Her teaching and research interests include women's health, mental health, IPV, and diversity and equity. Her current research focus is on the factors influencing immigrant and refugee women's experience of, and their response to, IPV. She has published articles, book chapters, and presented papers at many conferences.

Maroussia Hajdukowski-Ahmed holds a Doctorate in Comparative Literature from the University of Paris. She is a Professor of French and Women's Studies at McMaster University, and also teaches at the McMaster Institute on Globalization and the Human Condition. Her research focuses on the sociocultural determinants of the mental health of immigrant and refugee women. She was a principal investigator (1993–1999) and co-chair (1997–1999) of the McMaster Research Center for the Promotion of Women's Health. She is a coauthor and coeditor of *Women's Voices in Health Promotion* (1999), and the (co)author of working papers, reports, and essays on health promotion with immigrant and refugee women, on feminist theories and research methodologies, on Bakhtinian studies and on fiction by Francophone women authors. She was a member (2000–2006) of the Board of Directors of the Settlement and Integration Services Organization (Hamilton and Region).

Lynda Hayward is a Senior Data Analyst with the Center for Behavioral Research and Program Evaluation at the University of Waterloo. At the time this chapter was written, she was with the Community Care Research Center at McMaster University, and a member of the team researching Sudanese refugee women and their mental health. With training in sociology and social planning, her main research interest is planning for an aging population. Before completing her doctorate, she worked for a sociological consulting firm, contributing to a variety of research projects on ethnicity and women's health. www.cbrpe.uwaterloo.ca

Jennifer Hyndman is a Professor of Geography at Syracuse University. Her interests span the gamut of mobility, security, and globalization from feminist perspectives. Her research focuses on human displacement related to conflict and humanitarian responses to it, as well as refugee resettlement in North America. She is the author of *Managing Displacement: Refugees and the Politics of Humanitarianism* (University of Minnesota Press, 2000) and is coeditor with Wenona Giles of a collection, *Sites of Violence: Gender in Conflict Zones* (University of California Press).

Nazilla Khanlou, RN, Ph.D., is an Associate Professor at the Faculty of Nursing and Department of Psychiatry, University of Toronto. Her clinical background is in psychiatric nursing. Her research and teaching are situated in the interdisciplinary field of community-based mental health promotion in general, and mental health promotion among youth and women in multicultural and immigrant-receiving settings in particular. She is the Health Domain Leader of the Center of Excellence for Research on Immigration and Settlement (CERIS) in Toronto and a Visiting Scholar (2005–2006) at the Wellesley Urban Health Institute. She has published articles and reports on immigrant youth and women, mental health promotion, and participatory action research. Examples include "Post-Migratory Experiences of Newcomer Female Youth: Self esteem and Identity Development" (Khanlou and Crawford, *Journal of Immigrant and Minority Health*, 2006); "Participatory Action Research: Considerations for Ethical Review" (Khanlou and Peter, *Social Science and Medicine*, 2005); "Influences on Adolescent Self esteem in Multicultural Canadian Secondary Schools" (Khanlou, *Public Health Nursing*, 2004); and "Mental Health Promotion Education in Multicultural Settings (Khanlou, *Nurse Education Today*, 2003).

Judith Kumin holds a Ph.D. in International Relations and is currently the Regional Representative in Brussels of the UN High Commissioner for Refugees (UNHCR). She has served with the UNHCR since 1979, in Thailand, Yugoslavia, Germany, Canada, and at UNHCR Headquarters in Geneva. She has lectured and published widely on refugee issues. In 2003–2004 she was Visiting Professor at the Institute of Interdisciplinary Studies at Carleton University in Ottawa.

Maryanne Loughry currently holds the appointment Associate Director of Jesuit Refugee Australia. She was formerly the Pedro Arrupe Tutor at the Refugee Studies Center (RSC), University of Oxford. Maryanne Loughry is now a Research Associate of RSC. She teaches on the psychosocial impact of the refugee experience. As a psychologist, her research interests are in the fields of health psychology, communication and development, particularly in reference to refugee work. In recent years she has trained refugee workers in Southeast Asia, Africa, Sri Lanka, and the Middle East.

She is also doing research on a number of topics including the efficacy of psychosocial programs with refugees and the concerns of refugee children from a child's point of view.

Victor Malarek has been an investigative reporter over thirty years, for which he has received many awards, including three prestigious Governor General's Awards for meritorious public service journalism. He joined the newspaper *The Globe and Mail* in 1976. From 1990 to 2000 he was host of the Canadian Broadcasting Corporation (CBC) award-winning investigative documentary current affairs show, *The Fifth Estate*. Malarek has reported from countries around the world such as Afghanistan, Iran, Kurdistan, Ethiopia, Somalia, Ukraine, Germany, France, Italy, Austria, Thailand, Hong Kong, Australia, Mexico, Brazil, Chile, and Columbia. He is the author of four books, including *Haven's Gate: Canada's Immigration Fiasco* (1986); *Merchants of Misery* (1989); *The Natashas: Inside the New Global Sex Trade* (2004). He is the investigations editor for *The Globe and Mail*, as well as the senior reporter for the Canadian Television Network (CTV) current affairs' show *W-FIVE*.

Shahrzad Mojab is the Director of the Institute for Women's Studies and Gender Studies at the University of Toronto and Professor at the Department of Adult Education and Counseling Psychology, the Ontario Institute for Studies in Education. Shahrzad Mojab's areas of research and teaching are minority women's access to education; educational policy studies; comparative and international education; antiracism education; critical and feminist pedagogy; feminism and nationalism; gender, state, diaspora, and transnationality; women, war, militarization, and violence; women, war, and learning; feminism, colonialism, and imperialism; and cultural relativism as an ideological tool. Her publications include, among others, articles and book chapters on "Islamic Feminism," feminism and nationalism, adult education and the construction of civil society in the Middle East, women's NGOs and transnationalism, and diaspora, feminism and neoliberalism. She is the editor of *Women of a Non States Nation: The Kurds*, coeditor of, *Of Property and Propriety: The Role of Gender and Class in Imperialism and Nationalism*, and *Violence in the Name of Honour: Theoretical and Political Challenges*. She is currently conducting SSHRC-funded research on war, diaspora, and learning; women political prisoners in the Middle East; and war and transnational women's organizations (Women, War, Diaspora, and Learning: Research Resources: www.utoronto.ca/wwdl)

Helene Moussa, Ed.D., works as a policy, research, and program consultant on uprooted people with special focus on women. She is the author of *Storm and Sanctuary: The Life Journey of Ethiopian and Refugee Women* (1993);

Challenging Myths and Claiming Power Together—A Handbook to Set Up and Assess Support Groups for and with Immigrant and Refugee Women (1994). She is the coeditor with Wenona Giles and Penny van Esterik of *Development and Diaspora: The Experience of Refugee Women* (1996); cowriter and editor with Patrick Taran: *A Moment to Choose: Risking to be with Uprooted People—A Resource Book* (World Council of Churches, Geneva, Switzerland, 1996). She compiled *Stormy Seas we Brave: Creative Expressions by Uprooted People* (1998)—lyrics, reflections, drama, and visual art work by uprooted people from all regions of the world. She has published articles in numerous journals, such as *Canadian Women Studies, Refuge, Journal of Refugee Studies*. She coordinates the Board of Editors of *Refugee Update*, a national grassroots advocacy magazine and is a Member-at-Large of the Gender Core Group, Canadian Council for Refugees.

Carmela Murdocca is a doctoral candidate in the Department of Sociology and Equity Studies in Education at the Ontario Institute for Studies in Education at the University of Toronto. Her research interests include race/racism, gender, nationalism, and the law. Her doctoral work examines the relationship between race, criminal sentencing, and nationalism in Canada.

Jenny Ploeg is an Associate Professor in the School of Nursing, Faculty of Health Sciences, McMaster University, Hamilton, Canada. She was codirector of a community care research center that established research partnerships with numerous community care agencies. Her research focuses on the elderly and their caregivers living in the community. She has published work on a feminist approach to health promotion for older women and conducted research with marginalized groups of older adults. She is a recipient of the Canadian Institutes of Health Research/St. Joseph's Healthcare investigator award. Her primary reseach interests include qualitative research, evaluation of health services for older adults and their caregivers, and evidence-based practice.

Sherene Razack is a Professor of Sociology and Equity Studies in Education at the Ontario Institute for Studies in Education of the University of Toronto. Her research and teaching interests lie in the area of race and gender issues in the law. One of her recent books is *Dark Threats and White Knights: The Somalia Affair, Peacekeeping and the New Imperialism* (University of Toronto Press, 2004). Some of her previous books include an edited collection, *Race, Space and the Law: Unmapping A White Settler Society* (2002); *Looking White People in the Eye: Gender, Race, and Culture in Courtrooms* (1998); and *Classrooms and Canadian Feminism and the Law: The Women's Legal and Education Fund and the Pursuit of Equality* (1991).

Geraldine Sadoway received her L.L.B. from Osgoode Hall Law School in 1981 and was called to the Ontario Bar in 1983. She received an L.L.M. (Masters in Law) degree in the field of International Human Rights Law from Cambridge University (June 2003). From 1983 until 1997 she was a lawyer in private practice in Toronto, specializing in immigration and refugee law. From 1995 to 2000, she taught the Immigration Law Course for Queen's University Faculty of Law. Since 1997 she has been the staff lawyer and an Adjunct Professor for the immigration law group at Parkdale Community Legal Services in Toronto, representing refugees and immigrants and supervising law students in the Osgoode clinical law program. She is a member of the Refugee Lawyers Association, the Canadian Council for Refugees, and the Canadian Center for Victims of Torture. Her major area of interest is in defending the rights of the most vulnerable immigrants and refugees including women, children, survivors of torture, the elderly, and persons with serious illnesses or disabilities.

Pamela Sugiman is an Associate Professor in the Department of Sociology at Ryerson University, and currently president-elect of the Canadian Sociological Association. She has a strong interest in the study of memory and oral history, with a focus on the ways in which gender and "race" relations shape memory, as both a process and a product. She is currently writing a book on Japanese Canadian women's memories of the Second World War internment, and is working on a related project based on the oral testimony of Japanese Canadian men who were interned as Prisoners of War and/or forced to work as laborers on road and in lumber camps.

Karen Trollope-Kumar is an assistant clinical professor in the Department of Family Medicine, McMaster University, Hamilton, Ontario. She has been a practicing family physician for over twenty years, including eleven years in rural areas of Northern India. She has a special interest in the healthcare of marginalized populations. She also holds a Ph.D. in medical anthropology, with research interests in crosscultural aspects of healthcare. She teaches both in the Department of Anthropology as well as in the Department of Family Medicine at McMaster University.

Sarah V. Wayland is Research Associate at the Joint Center of Excellence for Research on Immigration and Settlement–Toronto (CERIS) and owner of Wayland Consulting, which specializes in research on various aspects of immigration and settlement in Canada. One recent report is *Unsettled: Legal and Policy Barriers for Newcomers to Canada*, commissioned by Community Foundations of Canada and the Law Commission of Canada. She obtained her Ph.D. in government and politics from the University of Maryland. Her articles have appeared in *Ethnic and Racial Studies, Canadian Ethnic Studies, Review of International Studies*, and elsewhere.

References

Aarts, P. G. H. 2001. "Psychosocial and Mental Health Care. Assistance in (Post) Disaster and Conflict Areas." *Draft Guidelines for Programs.* Utrecht: Netherlands Institute for Care and Welfare.

Abbey, R. 2000. *Charles Taylor.* Princeton: Princeton University Press.

Abdo, N. 1997. "Critical Issues in Immigrant Research: Gender Issues." In *Responding to Diversity in the Metropolis: Building an Inclusive Research Agenda,* ed. B. Abu-Laban and T. Derwing. Proceedings of the Metropolis Project First National Conference on Immigration. Edmonton: Prairie Center of Excellence, 95–99.

Abeysekera, C. and N. Gunasinghe, eds. 1987. *Facets of Ethnicity in Sri Lanka.* Colombo: Social Scientists' Association.

Abu-Laban, Y. and T. Derwings, eds. 1997. *Responding to Diversity in the Metropolis: Building an Inclusive Research Agenda.* Proceedings of the Metropolis Project First National Conference on Immigration. Edmonton: Prairie Center of Excellence.

Abu-Laban, Y. 1998. "Welcome/STAY OUT: The Contradictions of Canadian Integration and Immigration Policies at the Millennium." *Canadian Ethnic Studies* 30, no. 3: 190–211.

Ackerman, L. K. 1997. "Health Problems of Refugees." *Journal of American Board of Family Practitioner* 10: 337–348.

Adachi, K. 1991. *The Enemy That Never Was. A History of the Japanese Canadians.* Toronto: McClelland and Stewart.

Adelman, H., A. Borowski, M. Burstein, and L. Foster, eds. 1994. *Immigration and Refugee Policy: Australia and Canada Compared, Volume I.* Toronto: University of Toronto Press.

Adelman, H., A. Borowski, M. Burstein, and L. Foster, eds. 1994. *Immigration and Refugee Policy: Australia and Canada Compared, Volume II.* Toronto: University of Toronto Press.

Ager, A. 2002. "Psychosocial Needs in Complex Emergencies." *The Lancet* 360 (Suppl. 1): 43–44.

Agger, I. 1992. *The Blue Room: Trauma and Testimony Among Refugee Women: A Psycho-Social Exploration,* trans. M. Bille. London: Zed Books.

Agger, I. and S. B. Jensen. 1995. *Trauma and Healing Under State Terrorism.* London: Zed.

Agnew, V. 1993. "Canadian Feminism and Women of Color." *Women's Studies International Forum* 16, no. 3: 217–228.

Ahmed, S. 1998. "Islam and Development: Opportunities and Constraints for So-mali Women." In *Gender, Religion, and Spirituality,* ed. C. Sweetman. Oxfam Focus on Gender. Oxford: Oxfam, 69–72.

Alexander, J. C. and C. T. Mohanty. 1997. "Introduction: Genealogies, Legacies and Movements." In *Feminist Genealogies, Colonial Legacies, Democratic Futures,* ed. M. J. Alexander and C. T. Mohanty. New York and London: Routledge, xiii–xlii.

Allman, P. 1988. "Freire Gramsci and Illich: Their Contributions to Education for Socialism." In *Radical Approaches to Adult Education: A Reader,* ed. T. Lovett. New York and London: Routledge, 85–113.

Allodi, F., B. Berger, J. Beyersbergen, and N. Fantinin. 1986. "Community Consul-tation on Refugee Integration: Central American Refugees and Survivors of Torture in Ontario." *Canada's Mental Health* 34: 10–12.

Ammerman, N. T. 1997. *Congregation and Community.* Piscataway: Rutgers Univer-sity Press.

Anderson, M. B. 1994. *People-Oriented Planning at Work: Using POP to Improve UNHCR Programming.* Geneva: United Nations High Commissioner for Refugees.

Andric-Ruzicic, D. 2003. "War Rape and the Political Manipulation of Survivors." In *Feminists Under Fire: Exchanges Across War Zones,* ed. W. Giles, M. de Alwis, E. Klein, and N. Silva; with M. Korac, D. Knezevic, and Z. Papic (advisory ed-itors). Toronto: Between The Lines, 103–114.

Ankenbrand, B. 2002. "Refugee Women Under German Asylum Law." *Interna-tional Journal of Refugee Law* 14, no. 1: 45–56.

Anker, D. E. 2002. "Refugee Law, Gender, and the Human Rights Paradigm." *Har-vard Human Rights Journal* 15 (Spring): 133–155.

Anthias, F. and N. Yuval-Davis. 1993. *Racialized Boundaries.* New York and Lon-don: Routledge.

Anzaldúa, G. and A. L. Keating, eds. 2002. *This Bridge We Call Home.* New York and London: Routledge.

Arat-Koc, S. 2002. "Imperial Wars or Benevolent Interventions? Reflections on 'Global Feminism' Post September 11th." *Atlantis* 26, no. 2: 53–65.

Armour, A. and R. Northey. 2001. "Law and Community: A Conceptual Analysis to Guide Research." Research Paper prepared for the Law Commission of Canada.

Arun, K., N. 2007. " The Great Kidney Bazaar." *The New Sunday Express Magazine,* section 2, 18 February: 1.

Ayott, L. and L.Willamson. 2001. *Separated Children in the U.K: an Overview of the Current Situation.* London: The Refugee Council and Save the Children.

Baines, E. 2006. *Gender, The UN and the Global Refugee Crisis.* Burlington, VT: Ashgate.

Bakhtin, M. 1981. *The Dialogic Imagination,* ed. M. Holquist. Austin: University of Texas Press.

———. 1986. *Speechgenres and Other Late Essays,* ed. C. Emerson and M. Holquist, trans. V. McGee. Austin: University of Texas Press.

———. 1986a. "Toward a Methodology for the Human Sciences." In *Speech Genres and Other Late Essays,* eds. C. Emerson and M. Holquist, trans. V. McGee. Austin: University of Texas Press, 159–172.

———. 1993. "The Author and Hero in Aesthetic Activity." *Toward a Philosophy of the Act.* ed. V. Liupov and M. Holquist. Austin: University of Texas Press.

Bakhtine, M. 1980. *Ecrits sur le freudisme,* trans. Guy Verret. Paris: Editions de l'Age d'Homme.

———. 1984. *Esthétique de la création verbale,* trans. Alfreda Aucouturier, preface by T. Todorov. Paris: Gallimard.

Balibar, E. 2004. *We, the People of Europe? Reflections on Transnational Citizenship.* Princeton: Princeton University Press.

———. 2006. "Strangers as Enemies. Further Reflections on the Aporias of Transnational Citizenship." Paper presented at the Institute of Globalisation and the Human Condition, McMaster University, 16 March.

Balibar, E. and E. Wallerstein, 1988. *Race, nation, classe, les identités ambigües.* Paris: La Découverte.

———. 1991. *Race, Nation, Class: Ambiguous Identities.* London: Verso.

Bannerji, H. ed. 1993. *Returning the Gaze: Essays on Racism, Sexism and Feminist Politics.* Toronto: Sister Vision Press.

———1995. *Thinking Through: Essays on Feminism, Marxism, and Anti-Racism.* Toronto: Women's Press.

Barnes, D. M. 2001. "Mental Health Screening in a Refugee Population: a Program Report." *Journal of Immigrant Health* 3, no. 3: 141–149.

Basu, A. 2000. "Globalization of the Local/Localization of the Global: Mapping Transnational Women's Movements." *Meridians: Feminism, Race, Transnationalism* 1, no. 1: 68–84.

Bauer, T. 1989. *Feminist Dialogics, a Theory of Failed Community.* Albany: University of New York Press.

Begovac, I., V. Rudan, B. Begovac, V. Vidović, and G. Majić. 2004. "Self-image, War Psychotrauma and Refugee Status in Adolescents." *European Child and Adolescent Psychiatry* 13, no. 6: 381–388.

Behar, R. 1996. *The Vulnerable Observer: Anthropology that Breaks Your Heart.* Boston: Beacon Press.

bell hooks. 1984. *Feminist Theory: From Margin to Center.* Boston: South End Press.

Benhabib, S. 1992. *Situating the Self: Gender, Community and Postmodernity.* London and New York: Routledge.

———. 1994. *From Identity Politics to Social Feminism: A Plea for the Nineties. The Paradigm Wars of Feminist Theory* http://www.ed.uiuc.edu/EPS/PES Harvard University_docs/BENHABIB.HTM.

———. 2002. *The Claims of Culture: Equality and Diversity in the Global Era.* Princeton: Princeton University Press.

Bennett B. 1993. "Toward Ethno-Relativism: a Developmental Model of Ethnocultural Sensitivity." In *Education for the Intercultural Experience,* ed. R.M. Paige. Yarmouth: Intercultural Press, 21–71.

Bergin, A. E. 1980. "Psychotherapy and Religious Values." *Journal of Consulting Clinical Psychology* 48: 95–105.

Berkowitz, N. and C. Jarvis. 2000. *Immigration Appellate Authority: Asylum Gender Guidelines.* Government of United Kingdom.

Berman, H. 2001. "Children and War: Current Understandings and Future Directions." *Public Health Nursing* 18, no. 4: 243–252.

Bhabha, H. 1994. *The Location of Culture.* New York and London: Routledge.

Bhabha, J. 1996. "Embodied Rights: Gender Persecution, State Sovereignty and Refugees." *Public Culture* 9, no. 3: 32.

————. 2004. "Demography and Rights: Women, Children and Access to Asylum." *International Journal of Refugee Law* 16, no. 2: 227–243.

Bhaloo, S., A. Carias, M. Hadjukowski-Ahmed, L. Hayward, J. Ploeg, and K. Trollope-Kumar. 2005. "Refugee Women from Sudan and Their Mental Health." Report. McMaster University, Hamilton, Ontario: Community Care Research Center.

Bhatia, S. and A. Ram. 2001. "Locating the Dialogical Self in the Transnational Migrations, Border Crossings and Diasporas." *Culture and Psychology* 7, no. 3, September: 297–309.

Birman, D. 1998. "Biculturalism and Perceived Competence of Latino Immigrant Adolescents." *American Journal of Community Psychology* 26: 335–354.

Blair, R.G. 2001. "Mental Health Needs Among Cambodian Refugees in Utah." *International Social Work* 44: 179.

Blanchot, M. 1986. *La Communauté inavouable*. Paris: Les Editions de Minuit.

Boddy, J. 1989. *Wombs and Alien Spirits: Women, Men and the Zar Cult in Northern Sudan*. Madison: University of Wisconsin Press.

Boelaert, M., F. Vautier, T. Dusauchoit, W. Van Damme, and M. Van Dormel. 1999. "The Relevance of Gendered Approaches to Refugee Health: A Case Study in Hagadera, Kenya." In *Engendering Forced Migration. Theory and Practice*, ed. D. Indra. Oxford and New York: Berghahn Books, 165–176.

Bourdieu, P. 1993. *La misère du monde*. Paris: Editions du Seuil.

Bowen, S. 1999. *Resilience and Health: Salvadoran Refugee Women in Manitoba*. University of Manitoba: 1–5.

Boyd, M. 1999. "Gender, Refugee Status and Permanent Settlement." *Gender Issues*. (Winter): 5–25.

Bracken, P. 1998. "Hidden Agendas: Deconstructing Post-Traumatic Stress Disorder." In *Rethinking the Traumas of War*, ed. P. Bracken and C. Petty. London: Free Association Press, 415–417.

Bradbury, H. and P. Reason. 2003. "Action Research: an Opportunity for Revitalizing Research Purpose and Practices." *Qualitative Social Work* 2, no. 2: 155–175.

Brah, A. 1996. *Cartographies of Diaspora: Contesting Identities*. London and New York: Routledge.

Brewer, R. M. 1997. "Theorizing Race, Class and Gender." In *Materialist Feminism: A Reader in Class Difference and Women's Lives*, ed. R. Hennessy and C. Ingraham. London and New York: Routledge, 236–247.

Briggs, S. 1987. "Women and Religion." In *Analyzing Gender: A Handbook of Social Science Research*, ed. B. B. Hess and M. M. Ferree. London: Sage Publications, 408–441.

Brown, K. M. 1991. *Mama Lola: A Voodou Priestess in Brooklyn*. Berkeley: University of California Press.

Brun, C. 2003. "Finding a Place: Local Integration and Protracted Displacement in Sri Lanka." Ph.D. diss., Dept. of Geography, Trondheim: Norwegian University of Science and Technology.

Budick, S. and W. Iser. 1996. *The Translatability of Cultures. Figurations of the Space Between*. Palo Alto: Stanford University Press.

Buel, B. 2005. "The Tsunami Women" http://www.oxfam.org.uk/press/releases/tsunami_women260305.htm. Accessed 12 August 2005.

Buijs, G. 1993. *Migrant Women: Crossing Boundaries and Changing Identities. Cross-Cultural Perspectives on Women* 7. Oxford: Berghahn Publishers.

Bunch C. and N. Reilly. 1994. *Demanding Accountability: The Global Campaign and Vienna Tribunal for Women's Human Rights.* New Brunswick: Center for Women's Global Leadership, Rutgers University and New York: United Nations Development Fund for Women (UNIFEM).

Butler, J. 1990. *Gender Trouble: Feminism and the Subversion of Identity.* London and New York: Routledge.

———. 1992. "Contingent Foundations: Feminism and the Question of 'Postmodernism'." In *Feminists Theorize the Political,* ed. J. Butler and J. W. Scott. New York and London: Routledge, 3–21.

———. 1997. *Excitable Speech: A Politics of the Performative.* London and New York: Routledge.

Calloni, M. 2000. "International Women's Networks, Social Justice and Cross-Border Democracy." In *Crossing Borders and Shifting Boundaries. Vol II: Gender, Identities and Networks,* ed. I. Lentz, H. Lutz, M. Morokvasic, C. Schoning-Kalender, H. Schwenken. Project Area Migration. Hannover, Germany: International Women's University, 179–206.

Cameron, D., ed. 1999. *The Feminist Critique of Language.* 2nd ed. London and New York: Routledge.

Camus-Jacques G. 1989. "Refugee Women: The Forgotten Majority." In *Refugees and International Relations,* ed. G. Loescher and L. Monaham. Oxford: Oxford University Press, 141–147.

Canada. 1988. *The Multicultural Act of Canada.* Ottawa: Queens Printer.

Canada. 1982. "The Canadian Charter of Rights and Freedoms." In *The Canadian Constitution Act.* http://www.uni.ca/charter.html

Canada, Citizenship and Immigration. 2002a. "Canada's Program for Women at Risk." www.cic.gc.ca/english/refugees/women-1.html

———. 2002b. "Do Women at Risk Have to Meet Settlement or Admissibility Criteria." www.cic.gc.ca/english/refugees/women-3.html

———. 2002c. "Who Can Come to Canada Under the Women at Risk Program." www.cic.gc.ca/english/refugees/women-2.html

———. 2002d. "Who is Eligible for Selection?" www.cic.gc.ca/english/refugees/resettle-2.html

———. 2002. "Facts and Figures 2002: Immigrant Overview." Ottawa: Citizenship and Immigration Canada. www.cic.gc.ca/pub/facts2003/permanent/7.html. Accessed 29 March 2005.

———. 2004. "Resettling Refugees in Canada." www.cic.gc.ca/english/refugees/resettle-1.html

Canada, Department of Foreign Affairs and International Trade and the Department for International Development, U.K. 2002. *Gender and Peacekeeping Training Course* at www.genderandpeacekeeping.org/participant-e.asp

Canada, Immigration and Refugee Board. 1996a. *Backgrounder. Women Refugee Claimants Fearing Gender-related Persecution. Update. Guidelines Issued by the Chairperson Pursuant to Section 65(3) of the Immigration Act.* Web document. www.irb.gc.ca/en/media/background/back_women_e.htm

———. 1996b. *Guideline 4. Women Refugee Claimants Fearing Gender-related Persecution. Update. Guidelines Issued by the Chairperson Pursuant to Section 65(3) of the Immigration Act.* Web document. www.irb.gc.ca/en/media/background/back_women_e.htm

————. 2000. *Gender-related Persecution, Key Point Guide to Refugee Law for CRDD Member.* http://www.irb-cisr.gc.ca/en/about/tribunals/rpd/keypoints/pointso5_e.html

————. 2003. *Compendium of Decisions: Guideline 4: Women Refugee Claimants Fearing Gender-Related Persecution: Update.* Web document. www.irbcisr.gc.ca/en/about/tribunals/rpd/compendium/index_e.htm

Canada, Status of Women. 2002. *Bill C-11: Immigration and Refugee Protection Act: Gender-based Analysis Chart.* Web document. www.cic.gc.ca/english/irpac/c11-gender.html

Canada, Statutes of Canada. 2001. *Immigration and Refugee Protection Act, Bill C-11.* Web document. www.cic.gc.ca/english/irpa/c11-overview.html

Canadian Center for Victims of Torture. Faculty of Social Work, University of Toronto, and School of Social Work, York University. 2000. *Befriending Survivors of Torture: Building a Web of Community Support.* Training Manuals. Submitted to Citizenship and Immigration Canada.

Canadian Council of Churches. 1998. *Doing More to Address the Causes and Ensure the Rights of Uprooted People.* Statement to the 54th Session of the UN Commission on Human Rights, April. http://www.web.ca/~iccr/docs/Cccunchr

Canadian Council for Refugees. 2001. *State of Refugees in Canada.* Web document. www.web.net/~ccr/state.html

Canetti, E. 1984 [1975]. *La conscience des mots.* trans. R. Lewinter of *Das Gewissen der Wörte.* Paris: Albin Michel.

Carr, A. *Transforming Grace: Christian Traditions and Women's Experience.* San Francisco: Harper and Row.

Carruth, C. 1995. *Trauma Explorations in Memory.* Baltimore: The Johns Hopkins University Press.

Castel, J. R. 1992. "Rape, Sexual Assault and the Meaning of Persecution," *International Journal of Refugee Law* 4, no. 1: 39–56.

Castles, S. 1994. "Democracy and Multicultural Citizenship. Australian Debates and their Relevance for Western Europe." Paper read at the conference "From Aliens to Citizens." Vienna, November 1993. In *From Aliens to Citizens: Redefining the Status of Immigrants in Europe,* ed. R. Bauböck. Aldershot: Averbury, 3–27. Cited in D. Morley, 2000. *Home Territories: Media, Mobility and Identity.* London and New York: Routledge, 125.

Chambers, L. 1997. *Married Women and Property Law in Victorian Ontario.* Toronto: University of Toronto Press.

Chambon, A. 1995. "Life History as Dialogical Activity: 'If you Ask me the Right Questions, I Could Tell you!'" *Current Sociology* 43, no. 2: 125–135.

————. 1999. "A Foucauldian Approach: Making the Familiar Visible". In *Reading Foucault for Social Work,* ed. A.S. Chambon, A. Irving, and L. Epstein. New York: Columbia University Press, 51–81.

Chambon, A., M. Abai, T. Dremetsikas, S. McGrath, and B. Shapiro. 1998a. "Methodology in University-Community Research Partnerships: The Link-by-Link Project as Case Study." Metropolis Year II: The Development of a Comparative Research Agenda. In *Proceedings of the Second National Conference, Montréal, 23–26 November 1997,* ed. M. McAndrew and N. Lapierre Vincent. Montréal: Inter-University Research Center of Montréal on Immigration, Integration, and Urban Dynamics, 151–169.

Chambon, A., M. Abai, B. Shapiro, S. McGrath, T. Dremetsikas, and S. Dudziak. 1998b. "L'interculturel à l'aune des traumatismes communautaires: Les réfugiés survivants de la torture." In *Champs multiculturels, transactions interculturelles: des théories, des pratiques, des analyses,* ed. K. Fall and L. Turgeon. Paris: L'Harmattan, 133–155.

Chambon, A., S. McGrath, M. Abai, T. Dremetsikas, B. Shapiro, S. Dudziak, M. Kumsa, and M. Millard. 2000. "From Research to Service Training: Trustworthy Knowledge to Work with Survivors of Torture and War." Paper presented at the *National Metropolis Conference,* Toronto, 23 March.

Champassak, N. N. 1995. "Strategy for Survival." *Refugees Magazine* 100, special issue on *Refugee Women*: 16–19.

Chan, S., ed. 2003. *Not Just Victims. Conversations with Cambodian Community Leaders in the United States.* Urbana and Chicago: University of Illinois Press.

Chappel, M. and M. Morrow. 2000. "Hearing (Women's) Voices: Mental Health Care for Women." *Canadian Journal of Community Mental Health* 19: 217–219.

Charlesworth, H. and C. Chinkin. 2000. *The Boundaries of International Law: A Feminist Analysis.* Manchester: Manchester University Press.

Charron, G. 2002. "Canada Hides Behind U.S. to Attack Refugees." *World Socialist Website.* www.wsws.org.

Chartlon, J. C. 1987. "Women in Seminary. A Review of Current Social Science Research." *Review of Religious Research* 28: 315–318.

Chatterjee, P. 2001. "The Nationalist Resolution of the WomMen's Question." *Nations and Identities,* ed. V.P. Pecora. New York and Oxford: Blackwell Publishers: 325–333.

Chatty, D. and M. Colchester, eds. 2002. *Conservation and Mobile Indigenous Peoples: Displacement, Forced Settlement, and Sustainable Development.* Oxford and New York: Berghahn Books.

Chavez, M. 1997. *Ordaining Women.* Boston: Harvard University Press.

Chen, G. 2004. "A Global Campaign to End Refugee Warehousing." *US Committee for World Refugee Survey:* 21.

Childers, M. M. 2002. "'The Parrot or the Pit Bull': Trying to Explain Working-Class Life." *Signs Journal of Women in Culture and Society* 28, no. 1: 201–220.

Chindarsi, N. 1976. *The Religion of the Hmong Njua.* Bangkok: The Siam Society 65, no. 1: 390–392.

Christiano, K.J. 1991. "The Church and the New Immigrants." In *Vatican II and US Catholicism: Twenty Five Years Later,* ed. H. R. Ebaugh. Greenwich: JAI Press, 169–186.

Churchill, W. 1998. *Pacifism as Pathology: Reflections on the Role of Armed Struggle in North America.* Winnipeg: Arbeiter Ring.

Clandinin, D. J. and F. M. Connelly. 1994. "Personal Experience Method." In *Handbook of Qualitative Research,* ed. N. K. Denzin and Y. S. Lincoln. Thousand Oaks: Sage, 413–427.

Clark, M. A. 2004. *Trafficking in Persons: An Issue of Human Security.* Accessed 20 July 2004 from http://www.protectionproject.org

Clay, J. and B. Holcomb. 1985. *Politics and the Ethiopian Famine, 1984–1985.* Cambridge, U.K.: Cultural Survival, Inc.

Clayton, M. 1994. "Afflicted Women Find Hope in Canada's Refugee Rules." *Christian Science Monitor,* 9 March: 2.

Cleaver, T. and M. Wallace. 1990. *Namibia Women in War*. London and New Jersey: Zed Books.

Cockburn, C. 1998. *The Space Between Us: Negotiating Gender and National Identities in Conflict*. London and New Jersey: Zed Books.

Cockburn, C. and L. Hunter. 1999. "Transversal Politics and Translating Practices." *Soundings. A Journal of Politics and Culture* 12 (Summer), special issue on *Transversal Politics*: 88–93.

Cohen, J. 2002. "Questions of Credibility: Omissions, Discrepancies and Errors of Recall in the Testimony of Asylum Seeker." *International Journal of Refugee Law* 13, no. 3: 293–309.

Cohen, R. and F. M. Deng. 1998. *Masses in Flight: The Global Crisis of Internal Displacement*. Washington, D.C.: Brookings Institute Press.

Cohen, S. 2001. *States of Denial. Knowing About Atrocities and Suffering*. Cambridge: Polity.

Cole, E., O. Espin, and E. Rothblum. 1992. *Refugee Women and Their Mental Health: Shattered Societies, Shattered Lives*. New York: The Hawthorn Press.

Coles, R. 1992. *Self/Power/Other. Political Theory and Dialogical Ethics*. Ithaca: Cornell University Press.

Collier, J. and S. Yanagisako, eds. 1987. *Gender and Kinship: Essays Toward a Unified Analysis*. Stanford: Stanford University Press.

Collyer, M., F. Crepeau and D. Nakache, eds. 2006. *Forced Migration and Global Processes: a View from Forced Migration Studies*. Lanham MD: Rowman and Littlefield Publishers.

Colson, E. 1993. "Uprooted by 'Development.'" In *Engendering Forced Migration, Theory and Practice*, ed. Doreen Indra. *Refugee and Forced Migration Studies*, 5: 23–40.

Committee for Humanitarian Assistance to Iranian Refugees. 1996. *Fact Sheet: Gender-Based Persecution*. Document. www.hambastegi.org/reports/fact_sheet .htm

Committee for Rational Development. 1984. *Sri Lanka The Ethnic Conflict: Myths, Realities and Perspectives*. New Delhi: Navrang.

Connerton, P. 1985. *How Societies Remember*. Cambridge and New York: Cambridge University Press.

Cooper, M. 1998. "General Pinochet Still Rules: Twenty-five Years after Allende." *The Nation Magazine*, 23 March 1998. Document. http://www.thirdworldtraveler .com/History/Pinochet_StillRules.html

Crawley, H. 2001. *Refugees and Gender: Law and Process*. Bristol: Jordan Publishing.
———. 1999. "Women and Refugee Status. Beyond the Public/Private Dichotomy in U.K. Asylum Policy." In *Engendering Forced Migration: Theory and Practice*, Refugee and Forced Migration Series 5, ed. D. Indra. Oxford and New York: Berghahn Books, 308–334.

Crewe, E. and E. Harrison. 1998. *Whose Development? An Ethnography of Aid*. London: Zed Books.

Crooks, D. L. 2001. "The Importance of Symbolic Interaction in Grounded Theory Research on Women's Health." *Health Care Women International* 22: 11–27.

Cutrufelli, M. 2004. *Women of Africa: Roots of Oppression*. New Jersey: Zed Press.

Da Rocha Lima, V. 1984. "Women in Exile: Becoming Feminists." *International Journal of Oral History* 5, no. 2: 81–99.

Daenzer, P. 1997. "An Affair Between Nations: International Relations and the Movement of Household Service Workers." In *Not One of the Family: Foreign Domestic Workers in Canada,* ed. A. B. Bakan and D. Stasiulis. Toronto: University of Toronto Press, 81–118.

Daley, K. and K. Ninette. 2000. "Particular Social Group: A Human Rights Based Approach in Canadian Jurisprudence." *International Journal of Refugee Law* 12, no. 2: 148–174.

Daly, M. 1973. Beyond God the Father: *Toward a Philosophy of Women's Liberation.* Boston: Beacon Press.

Daniel, E. V. 1996. *Charred Lullabies: Chapters in An Anthropology of Violence.* Princeton: Princeton University Press.

de Alwis, M. 2004. "'The Purity' of Displacement and the Reterritorialisation of Longing: Muslim IDPs in North western Sri Lanka." In *Sites of Violence: Gender and Conflict Zones,* ed. W. Giles and J. Hyndman. Berkeley: University of California Press, 213–232.

de Alwis, M. and J. Hyndman. 2002. "Capacity-Building in Conflict Zones: A Feminist Analysis of Humanitarian Assistance in Sri Lanka." Columbo: International Center for Ethnic Studies (January).

De Beauvoir, S. 1974 [1949]. *The Second Sex,* translated and edited by H.M. Parshley. Boston: Vintage Press.

———. 1992. "Conclusion of *The Second Sex.*" In *Ethics, a Feminist Reader,* ed. E. Frazer, J. Hornsby, and S.Lovibond. Oxford: Blackwell, 194–212.

De Jong, K., M. Mulhern, N. Ford, S. Van Der Kam, and R. Kleber. 2000. "The Trauma of War in Sierra Leone." *The Lancet* 355: 2067–2068.

De Laureitis, T. 1984. *Alice Doesn't: Feminism, Semiotics, Cinema.* Bloomington: Indiana University Press.

———. 1987. *Technologies of Gender: Essays on Theory, Film, and Fiction.* Bloomington: Indiana University Press.

Deleuze, G. and C. Parnet. 1977. *Dialogues.* Paris: Flammarion.

De Mujer a Mujer, Collective. 2003. *I Was, I Am and I Will Be.* Hamilton, Ontario. Unpublished play.

Denton, M., M. Hajdukoswki-Ahmed, M. O'Connor, K. Willians, and I. U. Zeytinoglu. 1994. *A Theoretical and Methodological Framework for Research on Women, Work and Health.* Working Paper. Hamilton, Ontario: McMaster Research Center for the Promotion of Women's Health.

Denton, M., M. Hajdukowski-Ahmed, M. O'Connor, and I. U. Urla Zeytinoglu, eds. 1999. *Women's Voices in Health Promotion.* Toronto: Canadian Scholars Press.

Denton, M., M. Hajdukowski-Ahmed, M. O'Connor and I. U. Urla Zeytinoglu. 1999. "Epistemological and Methodological Considerations." In *Women's Voices in Health Promotion,* ed. M. Denton, M. Hajdukowski-Ahmed, M. O.Connor, I. U. Zeytinoglu. Toronto: Canadian Scholars Press, 30–45.

DeSantis, A. 2001. "Caught Between Two Worlds: Bakhtin's Dialogism in the Exile Experience." *Journal of Refugee Studies* 14, no. 1: 1–19.

DeVoe, P.A. 1997. "Lao." In *Case Studies in Diversity: Refugees in America in 1990s,* ed. D.W. Haines. Westport, Conn: Praeger Publishers, 107–126.

Diamond, I. and L. Quinby. 1998. *Feminism and Foucault. Reflections on Resistance.* Boston: Northeastern University Press.

Djebar, A. 1980. *Vaste est la prison,* Paris: Editions des Femmes.

————. 1995. *Femmes d'Alger dans leur appartement,* Paris: Albin Michel.

Diaz-Diocaretz, M. 1989. "Bakhtin, Discourse and Feminist Theories." In *The Bakhtin Circle Today,* ed. M. Diaz-Diocaretz. *Critical Studies,* Amsterdam: Rodopi, 121–139.

Diaz-Stevens, A. M. 1993. *Oxcart Catholicism on Fifth Avenue: The Impact of the Puerto Rican Migration upon the Archdiocese of New York.* Notre Dame Studies in American Catholicism. Chicago: University of Notre Dame Press.

Dolan, J.P. 1988. "The Immigrants and Their Gods: A New Perspective in American Religious History." *Church History* 57: 61–72.

Donelly, N. 1994. *Changing Lives of Refugee Among Women.* Seattle: University of Washington Press.

Dougherty, M. C. Southern. 1978. "Southern Lay Midwives as Ritual Specialists." In *Women in Ritual and Symbolic Roles,* ed. J. Hoch-Smith and A. Spring. New York: Plenum, 151–164.

Dufva, H., ed. 1998. "From Psycholinguistics to a Dialogical Psychology of Language: Aspects of the Inner Discourse(s)." In *Dialogues on Bakhtin: Interdisciplinary Readings,* ed. M. Lahteenmaki and H. Dufva. University of Jyvaskyla, 87–105.

Dutch Refugee Association. 1985. *International Seminar on Refugee Women—Proceedings.* Amsterdam. The Netherlands.

Dutt, M. 1998. "Reclaiming a Human Rights Culture: Feminism of Difference and Alliance." In *Talking Visions: Multicultural Feminism in a Transnational Age,* ed. E. Shohat. New York: MIT Press, 225–246.

Ebaugh, H. R. and J. S. Chafetz. 1999. "Agents for Cultural Reproduction and Structural Change: The Ironic Role of Women in Immigrant Religious Institutions." *Social Forces* 78, no. 2: 585–612.

Eisenbruch, M. 1991. "From Post-Traumatic Stress Disorder to Cultural Bereavement: Diagnosis of Southeast Asian Refugees." *Social Science and Medicine* 33, no. 6: 673–680.

Ellis, R. 1994. "Help for Single-Parent Refugee Families." *Refugees Magazine* 95 (The international year of the family): 21–24.

Epp, M. 1997. "The Memory of Violence: Soviet and East European Mennonite Refugees and Rape in the Second World War." *Journal of Women's History* 9, no. 1 (Spring): 58–87.

Epp, M. 1999. *Women Without Men: Mennonite Refugees of the Second World War.* Toronto: University of Toronto Press.

Erdman J. N. and A. J. Sanchez. 2004. "Talking about Women: The Iterative and Dialogic Process of Creating Guidelines for Gender-Based Refugee Claims." *Journal of Law and Equality* 3, no. 1: 69–83.

Erikson, E. H. 1950. *Childhood and Identity.* New York: W.W. Norton.

————. 1963. *Childhood and Society.* 2nd ed. New York: W. W. Norton.

————. 1968. *Identity: Youth and Crisis.* New York: W. W. Norton.

Ernest, A., ed. 1998. "Best Practices in Peace Building and Non-Violent Conflict Resolution—Some Documented African Women's Peace Initiatives." Interagency document prepared and edited for UNHCR, UNESCO, UNDP, UNFPA, and UNIFEM. http://www.peacewomen.org/resources/Organizing/BestPractices 1998.pdf United Nations Educational, Scientific, and Cultural Organization

Eschle, C. 2001. *Global Democracy, Social Movements, and Feminism. Feminist Theory and Politics.* ed. V. Held and A. Jaggar. Boulder: Westview Press.

Essed P., G. Frerks and J. Schrijvers, eds. 2004. *Refugees and the Transformation of Societies: Agency, Policies,Ethics, and Politics.* Studies in Forced Migration. Oxford and New York: Berghahn Books.

Evans, H. and Advokaat, E. 2001. "The Language of Community in Canada: Social Relationships." Paper prepared for the Law Commission of Canada.

Fabian Global Forum. 2002. *Global Knowledge: Refugees.* Document. www .fabianglobalforum.net/knowledge/article006.html

Fazel, M. and A. Stein. 2002. "The Mental Health of Refugee Children." *Archives of Disease in Childhood* 87: 366–370.

Felman, S. 1992. "Education and Crisis, or the Vicissitudes of Teaching." In *Testimony: Crises of Witnessing in Literature, Psychoanalysis, and History.* ed. S. Felman and D. Laub. London and New York: Routledge, 1–56.

Fiorenza, E. Schussler. 1992. (Copyrighted in 1983.) *In Memory of Her: A Feminist Theological Reconstruction of Christian Origins.* New York: Crossroads.

Fleishman, S. 1998. "Gender, the Personal, and the Voice of Scholarship: A Viewpoint." *Signs Journal of Women in Culture and Society* 23, no. 4 (Summer): 975–1016.

Forbes-Martin, S. 2004 [1991]. *Refugee Women.* 2nd ed. London: Zed Books.

———. 2001. "Global Migration Trends and Forced Migration." *The Journal of Humanitarian Assistance.* www.jha.ac/articles/u041.htm. Accessed 2 July 2004

Foss, N. 2002. "Nerves in Northern Norway: the Communication of Emotions, Illness Experiences, and Health-Seeking Behaviors." *Qualitative Health Research* 12:194–207.

Foucault, M. 1969. *L' archéologie du savoir.* Paris: Editions Gallimard.

———. 1971. *L'ordre du discours.* Paris: Editions Gallimard.

———. 1978. *The History of Sexuality Volume 1: An Introduction,* trans. R. Hurley. New York: Pantheon.

———. 1979. *Discipline and Punish: The Birth of the Prison,* trans. A. Sheridan. New York: Vintage Books.

Fraser, M. W. and P. J. Pecora. 1985–1986. "Psychological Adaptatation Among Indochinese Refugees." *Journal of Applied Social Sciences* 10: 29–30.

Fraser, N. and L. Nicholson. 1990. "Social Criticism without Philosophy: An Encounter Between Feminism and Postmodernism." In *Feminism/Postmodernism,* ed. Linda Nicholson. New York and London: Routledge, 20–38.

Freeman, M. P. 1993. *Rewriting the Self: History, Memory, and Narrative.* London and New York: Routledge.

Freire, P. 1968. *Pedagogy of the Oppressed.* New York: The Seabury Press.

Fujii, J. S., S. N. Fukushiima, and J. Yamamoto. 1994. "Psychiatric Care of Japanese Americans." In *Culture, Ethnicity and Mental Illness,* ed. A.C. Gaw. Washington, D.C.: American Psychiatric Press, 305–346.

Gagnon, M. 2000. *Les Femmes et la guerre.* Montréal: VLB.

———. 2001. *Las Mujeres dan la vida, los hombres la quitan (Mujeres en guerra),* trans. C. de Silvia Furio, Ares y mares, editorial critica, Barcelona.

———. 2003. *Women in a World at War. Seven Dispatches from the Front,* trans. P. Aronoff and H. Scott. Vancouver: Talon Books.

Galanter, M., D. Larson, and E. Rubenstone. 1991. "Christian Psychiatry: The Impact of Evangelical Beliefs on Clinical Practice." *American Journal of Psychiatry* 148: 90–95.

Geiger, S. 1990. "What's So Feminist About Women's Oral History?" *Journal of Women's History* 2, no. 1 (Spring): 169–182.

Gerard, A. 1989. *Dictionnaire de la Bible*. Paris: Laffont.

Gergen, M. M. and K. J. Gergen. 2000. "Qualitative Inquiry: Tensions and Transformations." In *Handbook of Qualitative Research*. 2nd ed., ed. N. Denzin, and Y. Lincoln. Thousand Oaks: Sage, 1025–1046.

Getu, H. and Joyce Nsubuga. 1996. "Heath Issues Affecting Sub Saharan African Women Refugees." In *Development and Diaspora, Gender and the Refugee Experience*, ed. W. Giles, H. Moussa, and P. Van Esterik. Dundas, Ontario: Artemis Entreprises, 199–208.

Gilad, L. 1996. "Cultural Collision and Human Rights." In *Development and Diaspora, Gender and the Refugee Experience*, ed. W. Giles, H. Moussa, and P. Van Esterik. Dundas, Ontario: Artemis Entreprises, 74–87.

Giles, W., H. Moussa, and P. Van Esterik, eds. *Development and Diaspora, Gender and the Refugee Experience*. Dundas, Ontario: Artemis Entreprises.

Giles, W. 1996. "Aid Recipients or Citizens? Canada's Role in Managing the Gender Relations of Forced Migration." In *Development and Diaspora: Gender and the Refugee Experience*, ed. W. Giles W., H. Moussa, and P. Van Esterik. Dundas, Ontario: Artemis Entreprises, 44–60.

———. 1997. "Re/membering the Portuguese Household: Culture, Contradictions and Resistance." *Women's Studies International Forum: Special Issue on 'Concepts of Home'* 20, no. 3: 387–396.

———. 1999. "Public and Private Constructions of Gendered Violence in Ethnic National Conflict." In *Engendering Forced Migration*, ed. D. Indra. Oxford and New York: Berghahn Books, 83–93.

Giles, W. and J. Hyndman, eds. 2004. *Sites of Violence: Gender and Conflict Zones*. Berkeley: University of California Press.

Giles, W. and J. Hyndman. 2004a. "Directions for Feminist Research and Politics." In *Sites of Violence: Gender and Conflict Zones*, ed. W. Giles and J. Hyndman, Berkeley: University of California Press, 301–317.

———. 2004b. "Introduction: Gender and Conflict in a Global Context." In *Sites of Violence: Gender and Conflict Zones*, ed. W. Giles and J. Hyndman. Berkeley: University of California Press, 3–24.

Giles, W., H. Moussa, and P. Van Esterik, eds. 1996. *Development and Diaspora, Gender and the Refugee Experience*. Dundas, Ontario: Artemis Entreprises.

Gilligan, C. 1982. *In a Different Voice: Psychological Theory and Women's Development*. Cambridge, MA: Harvard University Press.

Glaser, B. and A. Strauss. 1967. *The Discovery of Grounded Theory*. New York: Aldine de Gruyter.

Glenn, E. N. 2002. *Unequal Freedom: How Race and Gender Shaped American Citizenship and Labour*. Cambridge, MA: Harvard University Press.

Gluck, S. B. and Daphne Patai, eds. 1991. *Women's Words: The Feminist Practice of Oral History*. London and New York: Routledge.

Gomez, I. 1993. "A Space for Remembering: Home. Pedagogy and Exilic Latina Women's Identities." In *Engendering Forced Migration, Theory and Practice*, ed. D. Indra. *Refugee and Forced Migration Studies*, Vol. 5, 200–218.

Goodson, J. 2003. "The Opposite of Free Love: Dispatches from the World of Human Trafficking." *Regeneration Quarterly* 8, no. 2: 23–26.

Gorman, R. 2001. "Book Review of Grif Foley's 'Learning in Social Action: A Contribution to Understanding Informal Education' (1999)." *Studies in Continuing Education* 23, no. 1: 130–134.

———. 2002. "The Limits of 'Informal Learning': Adult Education Research and the Individualizing of Political Consciousness." *Canadian Association for Studies in Adult Education Conference Proceedings*. Ontario Institute for Studies in Education of the University of Toronto: 122–127.

Goździak, E. M. 2002. "Spiritual Emergency Room: The Role of Spirituality and Religion in the Resettlement of Kosovar Albanians." In *Religion and Forced Migration*, eds. E. M. Goździak and D. J. Shandy. Special Issue: *Journal of Refugee Studies* 15, no. 2 (June). Oxford University Press: 136–152.

Goździak, E. M. and D. J. Shandy. 2002a. "Editorial Introduction: Religion and Spirituality in Forced Migration" In *Religion and Forced Migration*, ed. E. M. Goździak and D. J. Shandy. Special issue of *Journal of Refugee Studies* 15, no. 2 (June): 130–135.

Goździak, E. M. and D. J. Shandy, eds. 2002b. *Religion and Forced Migration*. Special Issue: *Journal of Refugee Studies* 15, no. 2.

Goździak, E. M. and J. J. Tuskan, Jr. 2000. "Operation Provide Refuge: The Challenge of Integrating Behavioral Science and Indigenous Approaches to Human Suffering." In *Rethinking Refugee and Displacement*, ed. E.M. Goździak and D.J. Shandy. *Selected Papers on Refugees and Immigrants* VIII. Fairfax: American Anthropological Association, 194–222.

Goździak, E. M., M. Bump, J. Duncan, M. MacDonnell, and M.B. Loiselle. 2006. "The Trafficked Child: Trauma and Resilience." Forced Migration Review 25 (May): 14–15.

Goździak, E. M. "Refugee Women's Psychological Response to Forced Migration: Limitations of the Trauma Concept." Prepared for SAMSHA contract 280–03–2900, 2005.

Goździak, E. M. and K. Long. 2005. "Suffering and Resiliency of Refugee Women: An Annotated Bibliography," 1980–2005. Prepared for SAMSHA contract 280–03–2900, 2005.

Gramsci, A. 1971. *Selections from the Prison Notebooks*. London: Lawrence and Wishart.

Greely, K. M. 1996. "Changing the Rules: It's Time for the United States to Better Address the Gender Perspective Problem in Immigration." *New England International and Comparative Law Annual* 2: 1–18. http://www.nesl.edu/intljournal/vol2/gender.htm

Greenblatt, S. 2000. "The Touch of the Real." In *Practicing New Historicism*, ed. C. Gallagher and S. Greenblatt. Chicago: University of Chicago Press, 20–48.

Green-Powell, P. 1997. "Methodological Considerations in Field Research: Six Case Studies." In *Oral Narrative Research with Black Women*, ed. K.M. Vaz. Thousand Oaks: Sage Publications, 197–222.

Grewal, I. 1999. "Women's Rights as Human Rights." *Citizenship Studies* 3, no. 3: 337–354.

Grewal, I. and C. Kaplan. 1994. "Introduction: Transnational Feminist Practices and Questions of Postmodernity." In *Scattered Hegemonies: Postmodernity and Transnational Feminist Practices*, ed. I. Grewal and C. Kaplan. Minneapolis: University of Minnesota Press, 1–33.

Guarnaccia, P.J. and L.H. Rogler. 1999. "Research on Culture-Bound Syndromes: New Directions." *American Journal of Psychiatry* 156: 1322–1327.

Gupta S., S. Koppikar, and A.Raman. 2007. "The Lie of the Land." *Outlook*, 12 February: 32–36.

Guruge, S. and N. Khanlou. 2004. "Intersectionalities of Influence: Researching Health of Immigrant and Refugee Women." *Canadian Journal of Nursing Research* 36, no. 3: 32–47.

Guruge, S. 2004. "Gender Roles, Power Relations, and Informal Social Support Systems in the Context of Post-Migration Domestic Violence in the Sri Lankan Tamil Community of Toronto." Doctoral dissertation proposal, Faculty of Nursing, University of Toronto. Unpublished.

Hackett Nied, B. 1996. *Pray God and Keep Walking. Stories of Women Refugees.* Jefferson, NC: McFarland and Company, Inc.

Haddad, Y. and J. I. Smith. 1994. *Muslim Communities in North America.* Albany: SUNY Press.

Haines, D.W., D. A. Rutherford, and P. Thomas. 1981. "Family and Community Among Vietnamese Refugees." *International Migration Review* 15, no. 1: 310–319.

Hajdukowski-Ahmed, M. 1993. "The Framing of the Shrew: Discourses on Hysteria." In *Critical Studies,* special issue on *Bakhtin, Carnival and Other Subjects,* ed. D. Shepherd. Amsterdam: Rodopi, 177–195.

———. 1998. "Bakhtin without Borders: Dialogism in the Social Sciences." *South Atlantic Review,* special issue on *'Bakhtin'/Bakhtin. Studies in the Archive and Beyond,* ed. P. Hitchcock. Durham, NC: Duke University Press: 643–669.

———. 2003. "On the Borders of Language, Language Without Borders: Non-verbal Forms of Communication of Women Survivors of Torture." In *Exile, Language and Identity,* ed. M. Stroinska and V. Cecchetto. Frankfurt: Peter Lang, 213–229.

Hajdukowski-Ahmed, M., D. Maraj, and B. Dabrowska-Chudyk. 2000. "Wasted Skills: the Costs of Non-Accreditation; a Participatory Action Research Project with Foreign-Trained Female Physicians." Hamilton, Ontario: McMaster Research Center for the Promotion of Women's Health (MRCPOWH), Technical Report.

Hajdukowski-Ahmed, M., M. Pond, M. Farragheh, and S. Justin. 1999. "Healing from Torture: Women Survivors of Torture Living in Hamilton; A Participatory Action Health Promotion Project." Hamilton, Ontario: McMaster Research Center for the Promotion of Women's Health (MRCPOWH), Technical Report.

Hall, S. 1994. "Cultural Identity and Diaspora." In *Colonial Discourse and Post-Colonial Theory: A Reader,* ed. Patrick Williams and Laura Chrisman. London: Harvester Wheatsheath, 392–401.

Handa, A. 2002. *Of Silk Saris and Mini Skirts: South Asian Girls Walk the Tightrope of Culture.* Toronto: Women's Press.

Harding, S. 1986. *The Science Question in Feminism.* Ithaca and London: Cornell University Press.

Hargrove, B. J. 1987. "On Digging, Dialogue, and Decision-Making." *Review of Religious Research* 28: 395–401.

Hartsock, N. 1997. *The Feminist Standpoint Revisited and Other Essays.* Boulder: Westview Press.

Harvey, C. J. 2001. "Review Essay: Gender, Refugee Law and the Politics of Inter- pretation." (Review of Heaven Crawley: *Women as Asylum Seekers: A Legal Handbook*. 1997. Refugee Action, RWLG, ILPA). *International Journal of Refugee Law* 12, no. 4: 680–694.

Hashim, I. 1998. "Reconciling Islam and Feminism." In *Religion, and Spirituality. Oxfam Focus on Gender*, ed. C. Sweetman. Oxford: Oxfam, 7–14.

Hathaway, J. C. and M. Foster. 2003. "Membership in a Particular Social Group." Discussion Paper No. 4. Advanced Refugee Law Workshop, International As- sociation of Refugee Law Judges. *International Journal of Refugee Law* 15, no. 3: 444–461.

Heckman, G. P. 2003. "Securing Procedural Safeguards for Asylum Seekers in Canadian Law: An Expanding Role for International Human Rights Law?" *In- ternational Journal of Refugee Law* 15, no. 2: 212–253.

Helman, C. G. 1990. *Culture, Health and Illness*. Oxford: Butterworth.

Helms, E. 2003. "Gender Essentialisms and Women's Activism in Post–War Bosnia- Herzegovina." In *Feminists Under Fire: Exchanges Across War Zones*, ed. W. Giles, M. de Alwis, E. Klein, and N. Silva; with M. Korac, D. Knezevic and Z. Papic (advisory editors). Toronto: Between The Lines, 181–198.

Herman, J. L. 1997. *Trauma and Recovery: The Aftermath of Violence—From Domestic Abuse to Political Terror*. New York: Basic Books.

Hermans, H. 2001. "The Dialogical Self: Toward a Theory of Personal and Cultural Positioning." *Culture and Psychology*, special issue on *Culture and the Dialogical Self. Theory, Method and Practice* 7, no. 3 (September): 243–283.

———. 2003. "Construction and Reconstruction of a Dialogical Self." *Journal of Constructivist Psychology* 16, no. 2 (April–June): 89–131.

Hermans, H. and E. Hermans-Jansen. 1995. *Self-Narratives: The Construction of Meaning in Psycho Therapy*. New York: Guilford Press.

Hermans, H. and H. Kempen. 1993. *The Dialogical Self: Meaning as Movement*. San Diego: Academic Press.

Heshusius, L. 1994. "Freeing Ourselves from Objectivity: Managing Subjectivity or Turning Toward a Participatory Mode of Consciousness? " *Educational Re- searcher* 23, no. 3: 15–22.

Heyzer, N. 2005. "Celebrating our Gains, Accelerating Change." Statement by Noleen Heyzer, Executive Director, *United Nations Development Fund for Women (UNIFEM)*. New York, March 8. Document www.kwdi.re.kr/data/wotrend2/ wd2005-statement.eng.pdf. Accessed May 15, 2006.

Himmelstein, J. L. 1986. "The Social Basis of Antifeminism: Religious Networks and Culture." *Journal for the Scientific Study of Religion* 25: 1–15.

Hitchcock, P. 1993. *Dialogics of the Oppressed*. Minneapolis: University of Min- nesota Press.

Holt, M. 2007. "The Wives and Mothers of Heroes: Evolving Identities of Palestinian Refugee Women in Lebanon." *Journal of Development Studies* 43, no. 2: 245–264.

Horowitz, M., N. Wilner, and W. Alvarez. 1979. "Impact of Event Scale: A Meas- ure of Subjective Stress." *Psychosomatic Medicine* 41, no. 3: 209–218.

Human Rights Watch. 1999. "Promises Broken: An Assessment of Children's Rights on the 10th Anniversary of the Convention on the Rights of the Child. Document." www.hrw.org/campaigns/crp/promises/index.html. Accessed August 15, 2005.

Human Rights Watch. 1996. "Shattered Lives: Sexual Violence during the Rwandan Genocide and its Aftermath." Report prepared by Binaifer Nowrojee. New York. http://hrw.org/reports/1996/Rwanda.htm

Hunt, S. and C. Posa. 2001. "Women Waging Peace: Inclusive Security." *Foreign Policy*, (May–June): 1–5.

Hyndman, J. 1996. "Organizing Women: UN Approaches to Gender and Culture Among the Displaced." Paper presented at the *Women in Conflict Zones Network Meeting*. (November). York University, Toronto.

Hyndman, J. and M. De Alwis. 2000. "Capacity Building, Accountability and Humanitarianism." *Forced Migration Review* 8: 16–19.

———. 2002. "Beyond Gender: Toward A Feminist Analysis of Humanitarianism and Development in Sri Lanka." *Women's Studies Quarterly* 3–4: 212–226.

Iacovetta, F. 1999. "Postmodern Ethnography, Historical Materialism, and Decentring the (Male) Authorial Voice: A Feminist Conversation." *Histoire Sociale/Social History*, 32, no. 64 (November): 275–93.

Iacovetta, F., R. Perin, and A. Principe, eds. 2000. *Enemies Within: Italian and Other Internees in Canada and Abroad*. Toronto: University of Toronto Press.

Ice, M.L. 1987. *Clergywomen and Their Worldviews: Calling for a New Age*. Westport, CT: Praeger.

Ina, S. 1997. "Counselling Japanese Americans: From Internment to Reparations." In *Multicultural Issues in Counselling: New Approaches to Diversity*. 2nd ed., ed. C. C. Lee. Alexandria: American Counselling Association, 189–206.

Indra, D. M. 1987. "Social Science Research on Indochinese Refugees in Canada." In *Uprooting, Loss and Adaptation. The Resettlement of Indochinese Refugees in Canada*, ed. K. B. Chan and D. M. Indra. Ottawa: Canadian Public Health Association, 12–13.

———. 1996. "Some Feminist Contributions to Refugee Studies." In *Development and Diaspora, Gender and the Refugee Experience*, ed. W. Giles, H. Moussa, and P. Van Esterik. Dundas, Ontario: Artemis Entreprises, 30–44.

———. 1999a. "'Not a Room of One's Own': Engendering Forced Migration Knowledge and Practice." In *Engendering Forced Migration*, ed. D. Indra. Oxford and New York: Berghahn Books, 1–22.

———. ed. 1999b. *Engendering Forced Migration. Theory and Practice*. Oxford and New York: Berghahn Books.

International Conference on Uprooted Women. 1994. "The Sharjah Declaration, Recommendations of the International Conference on Uprooted Muslim Women." (12–15 September), Sharjah, UAE: 1. (Photocopy).

International Labour Organization. 2005. "A Global Alliance Against Forced Labour." Report. (11 May) Accessible on ILO Internet site: www.ilo.org/declaration

Irigaray, L. 1992. "This Sex Which is Not One." In *A Reader in Feminist Knowledge*, ed. S. Gunew. London and New York: Routledge, 204–211.

Irwin-Zarecka, I. 1994. *Frames of Remembrance: The Dynamics of Collective Memory*. New Brunswick, NJ: Transaction Publishers.

Jacobs, J. L. 1996. "Women, Ritual, and Secrecy: The Creation of Crypto-Jewish Culture." *Journal for the Scientific Study of Religion* 35: 97–108.

Jayawardena, K. 1985. *Ethnic and Class Conflicts in Sri Lanka*. Colombo: Sanjiva Books.

Jay, N. 1992. "Gender and Dichotomy." In *A Reader in Feminist Knowledge*, ed. S. Gunew. London and New York: Routledge, 89–109.

Jeganathan, P. and Q. Ismail, eds. 1995. *Unmaking the Nation: The Politics of Identity and History in Modern Sri Lanka*. Colombo: Social Scientists' Association.

Jhappan, R. 1996. "Postmodern Race and Gender Essentialism or a Post–Mortem of Scholarship." *Studies in Political Economy* 51 (Fall): 15–63.

Jones, L. 2002. "Adolescent Understandings of Political Violence and Psychological Well being: a Qualitative Study from Bosnia Herzegovina." *Social Science and Medicine* 55: 1351–1371.

Jones, L. and Kafetsios, K. 2002. "Assessing Adolescent Mental Health in War-Affected Societies: the Significance of Symptoms." *Child Abuse and Neglect* 26: 1059–1080.

Jopling, D. 1997. "A Self of Selves?" In *The Conceptual Self in Context*, ed. U. Neisser and D. A. Jopling. Cambridge: Cambridge University Press, 249–269.

Kaplan, C. 1992. "Resisting Autobiography. Out-Law Genres and Transnational Feminist Subjects." In *De/colonizing the Subject: The Politics of Gender in Women's Autobiography*, ed. S. Smith and J. Watson. Minneapolis: University of Minnesota Press, 115–138.

Katz, C. 2001. "On the Grounds of Globalization: A Topography for Feminist Political Engagement." *Signs: Journal of Women in Culture and Society* 26, no. 4: 1213–1234.

Kaufman, D. R.1991. *Rachel's Daughters: Newly Orthodox Jewish Women*. New Jersey: Rutgers University Press.

Kelly, N. 1989. "Working with Refugee Women: A Practical Guide." Geneva, Switzerland. (A report drawing exclusively from presentations and discussion at the *International Consultation on Refugee Women* held in Geneva, Nov. 1988). (September).

———. 2001. "The Convention Refugee Definition and Gender-Based Persecution: A Decade's Progress." *International Journal of Refugee Law* 13, no. 4: 559–568.

Kempadoo, K. 1999. *Sun, Sex, and Gold: Tourism and Sex Work in the Caribbean*. New York: Rowman and Littlefield.

Khanlou, N. 2007. "Youth and Post–Migration Cultural Identities: Linking the Local to the Global." In *Diasporic Ruptures: Globality, Migrancy and Expressions of Identity*, (Volume II), ed. A. Asgharzadeh, E. Lawson, K.U. Oka, and A. Wahab. Rotterdam: Sense Publishers, 81–94.

———. 2005. "Cultural Identity as Part of Youth's Self-Concept in Multicultural Settings." *eCOMMUNITY: International Journal of Mental Health and Addiction* 3, no. 2: 1–14.

Khanlou, N. and C. Crawford. 2006. "Post–Migratory Experiences of Newcomer Female Youth: Self esteem and Identity Development." *Journal of Immigrant and Minority Health* 8, no. 1: 45–56.

Khanlou, N., M. Siemiatycki, and P. Anisef. 2003. *Immigrant Youth and Cultural Identity in a Global Context*. Funded by Social Sciences and Humanities Research Council of Canada. (Grant period: 2003–2006).

Khanlou, N., M. Beiser, E. Cole, M. Freire, I. Hyman, and K. Kilbride. 2002. *Mental Health Promotion Among Newcomer Female Youth: Post–Migration Experiences and Self esteem/Promotion de la santé mentale des jeunes immigrantes: Expériences et estime de soi post–migratoires*. (English and French versions). Ottawa: Status of Women Canada.

Kibread, G. 1987. *Refugee and Development in Africa: the Case of Eritrea*. Trenton: The Red Sea Press.

Kim, A. R. 1996. *Women Struggling for a New Life: The Role of Religion in the Cultural Passage from Korea to America*. Albany: State University of New York Press.

Kim, J. H. 1996. "The Labour of Compassion: Voices of 'Churched' Korean Women." *Amerasia Journal* 22: 93–105.

Kirmayer, L. J. 2001. "Cultural Variations in the Clinical Presentation of Depression and Anxiety: Implications for Diagnosis and Treatment." *Journal of Clinical Psychiatry* 26: 22–30.

Kirmayer, L. J. and A.Young. 1998. "Culture and Somatization: Clinical, Epidemiological, and Ethnographic Perspectives." *Psychosomatic Medicine* 60: 420–430.

Kitagawa, M. 1985. *This Is My Own. Letters to Wes and Other Writings on Japanese Canadians 1941–1949*, ed. R. Miki. Vancouver, Brtitish Columbia: Talon Books.

Kleinman, A. 1977. "Depression, Somatization and the 'New Cross-Cultural Psychiatry.'" *Social Science and Medicine* 11: 3–10.

———. 1987. "Anthropology and Psychiatry; The Role of Culture in Cross-cultural Research on Illness." *British Journal of Psychiatry* 151: 447–454.

Kobayashi, A. 1989. "A Demographic Profile of Japanese Canadians and Social Implications for the Future." Ottawa: Department of the Secretary of State.

Kourula, P. 1997. *Broadening the Edges: Refugee Definition and International Protection Revisited*. Dordrecht: Martinus Nijhoff Publishers.

Krulfeld, R. M. 1994. "Buddhism, Maintenance, and Change: Reinterpreting Gender In A Lao Refugee Community." In *Reconstructing Lives, Recapturing Meaning: Refugee Identity, Gender, and Culture Change*, ed. L. A. Camino and R. M. Krulfeld. Basel: Gordon and Breach Publishers, 97–127.

Kvale, S. 1996. *InterViews*. London: Sage.

Lamphere, L., H. Ragoné, and P. Zavella, eds. 1997. *Situated Lives. Gender and Culture in Everyday Life*. London and New York: Routledge.

Larson, D. M., G. Milano, and F. Lu. 1998. "Religion and Mental Health: The Need for Cultural Sensitivity and Synthesis." In *Clinical Methods in Transcultural Psychiatry*, ed. S.O. Okpaku. Washington, D.C.: American Psychiatric Association, 191–210.

Lather, P. and C. Smithies. 1997. *Troubling the Angels: Women Living with HIV/AIDS*. Boulder: Westview Press.

Lederer, L. 2004. "Consequences of Commercial Sexual Exploitation." The Protection Project at the School of Advanced International Studies, Johns Hopkins University, 2000. Document. www.protectionproject.org/main2.htm. Accessed 15 July 2004.

Lehman, E. C., Jr. 1985. *Women Clergy: Breaking Through Gender Barriers*. New Brunswick: Transaction Books.

León, L. D. 1998. "Born Again in East Los Angeles: The Congregation as Border Space." In *Gatherings in Diaspora: Religious Communities and the New Immigration*, ed. S. R. Warner and J. G. Wittner. Philadelphia: Temple University Press, 163–196.

Lequin Y. and J. Metral. 1980. "A la recherche d'une mémoire collective: les métallurgistes retraités de Givors," *Annales* E.S.C., no. 1: 149–166.

Lewis, R. E., M. W. Fraser, and P. J. Pecora. 1988. "Religiosity Among Indochinese Refugees in Utah." *Journal for the Scientific Study of Religion* 27, no. 2: 272–283.

Li, H. 2000. "Defining Mental Illness and Accessing Mental Health Services: Perspectives of Asian Canadians." *Canadian Journal of Community Mental Health* 19: 143–159.

Lipson, J. G. and P. A. Omidian. 1997. "Afghan Refugee Issues in the US Social Environment. *Western Journal of Nursing Research* 19: 110–126.

Lock, M. 1993. "Cultivating the Body: Anthropology and Epistemologies of Bodily Practice and Knowledge." *Annual Review of Anthropology* 22: 133–155.

Loescher, G. 2001. "Protection and Humanitarian Action in the Post–Cold War Era." In *Global Migrants, Global Refugees: Problems and Solutions*, ed. A. Zolberg and P. Benda. Oxford and New York: Berghahn Books, 171–205.

Loescher, G. and L. Monahan, eds. 1989. *Refugees and International Relations.* Oxford: Oxford University Press.

Long, L., and E. Oxfeld, eds. 2004. *Coming Home? Refugees, Migrants, and Those who Stayed Behind.* Philadelphia: University of Pennsylvania Press.

Loo, C. M. 1993. "An Integrative-Sequential Treatment Model for Post Traumatic Stress Disorder: A Case Study of the Japanese American Internment and Redress." *Clinical Psychology Review* 13: 89–117.

Lorentzen, L. A. and J. Turpin, eds. 1998. *The Women and War Reader.* New York University Press.

Loughry, M., M. McCallin, and G. Bennett. 1993. *Women in Detention.* Hong Kong: Community Family Services International.

Low, S. 1985. "Culturally Interpreted Symptoms or Culture Bound Syndromes." *Social Science and Medicine* 21: 187–97.

Lummis, A. and A. Stokes. 1994. "Catholic Feminist Spirituality and Social Justice Actions." In *Research in the Social Scientific Study of Religion*, ed. Monty L. Lynn and David O. Moberg, vol. 6. Greenwich, CT: JAI Press, 103–138.

Lustig, S. L., M. Kia-Keating, W. G. Knight, P. Geltman, H. Ellis, J. D. Kinzie, et al. 2004. "Review of Child and Adolescent Refugee Mental Health." *Journal of American Academy of Child and Adolescent Psychiatry* 43(1), 24–36.

Mabe, A. 1994. "Taking Care of People Through Culture: Zimbabwe's Tongogara Refugee Camp." In *Selected Papers on Refugee Issues: III*, ed. J. L. Mac Donald and A. Zaharlick. Arlington, VA: American Anthropological Association, 78–97.

Macklin, A. 1995. "Refugee Women and the Imperative Categories." *Human Rights Quarterly* 17: 213–277.

———. 1996. "Opening the Door to Women Refugees: a First Crack." In *Development and Diaspora, Gender and the Refugee Experience*, ed. W. Giles, H. Moussa, and P. Van Esterik. Toronto: Artemis Entreprises, 118–143.

———. 1998. "Cross-Border Shopping for Ideas: A Critical Review of United States, Canadian and Australian Approaches to Gender-Related Asylum Claims." *Georgetown Immigration Law Journal* 13, no. 1: 25–71.

———. 2003. "Dancing Across Borders: Exotic Dancers, Trafficking and Immigration Policy." *International Migration Review* 37, no. 2: 464–500.

———. 2004. "Like Oil and Water, with a Match: Militarized Commerce, Armed Conflict and Human Security in Sudan." In *Sites of Violence: Gender and Conflict Zones*, ed. W. Giles and J. Hyndman. Berkeley: University of California Press, 75–108.

MacMullin, C. and Odeh, 1999. J. "What is Worrying Children in the Gaza Strip?" *Child Psychiatry and Human Development* 30, no. 1: 55–66.

Maguire, P. 1987. *Doing Participatory Research. A Feminist Approach.* Amherst: Center for International Education, University of Massachussetts.

———. 1993. "Challenges, Contradictions and Celebrations: Attempting Participatory Research as a Doctoral Student." In *Voices of Change: Participatory Research in the US and Canada.* ed. P. Park, M. Brydon-Miller, B. Hall, and T. Jackson. Westport: Bergin and Garvey, 157–176.

Mahler, S. 1999. "Engendering Transnational Migration: A Case Study of Salvadorans." *American Behavioral Scientist* 42, no. 4: 690–719.

Major, R. 1977. *Rêver l'Autre.* Paris: Aubier-Montaigne.

Malarek, V. 2003. *The Natashas. The New Global Sex Trade.* Toronto: Viking.

Malcuzynski, P. 1992. *Entre-Dialogues Avec Bakhtine ou Sociocritique de la [De]raison Polyphonique.* (InterActions 1). Amsterdam: Rodopi.

Malkki, L. H. 1995. "Refugees and Exile: From 'Refugee Studies' to the National Order of Things." *Annual Review of Anthropology* 24, no. 1: 495–524.

———. 1996. "Speechless Emissaries: Refugees, Humanitarianism, and Dehistorisation." *Cultural Anthropology* 11, no. 3: 377–404.

Manning, E. 2003. *Ephemeral Territories: Representing Nation, Home and Identity in Canada.* Minneapolis and London: University of Minnesota Press.

Marchand M. and J. Parpart, 1995. *Feminism/Postmodernism/Development.* New York and London: Routledge.

Marcus, G. 1992. "Past, Present and Emergent Identities." In *Modernity and Identity. Requirements for Ethnographies of Late Twentieth-Century Modernity Worldwide,* ed. S. Lash and J. Friedman. Oxford: Blackwell, 309–330.

Marfleet, P. 2006. *Refugees in a Global Era.* Basingstoke: Palgrave Macmillan.

Markus, H.R., P. R. Mullally, and S. Kitayama. 1997. "Selfways: Diversity in Modes of Cultural Participation." In *The Conceptual Self in Context,* ed. U. Neisser and D. A. Jopling. Cambridge University Press, 13–62.

Marsella, A. J. 1993. "Counselling and Psychotherapy with Japanese Americans. Cross-Cultural Considerations." *American Journal of Orthopsychiatry* 63: 200–208.

Martin, B. and C. T. Mohanty. 1986. "Feminist Politics: What's Home Got to Do with it?" In *Feminist Studies/Critical Studies. Theories in Contemporary Culture 8,* ed. T. De Laurentis. Bloomington: Indiana University Press, 191–212.

Martin, P. and E. Taylor. 2001. "Managing Migration: The Role of Economic Policies." In *Global Migrants, Global Refugees: Problems and Solutions,* ed. A. Zolberg and P. Benda. Oxford and New York: Berghahn Books, 95–120.

Martin, S. F., P. Weiss Fagen, K. Jorgensen, L. Mann-Bondat and A. Schoenholtz. 2005. *The Uprooted: Improving Humanitarian Responses to Forced Migration.* Lanham MD: Lexington Books.

Mathew, P., J. C. Hathaway, and M. Foster. 2003. "The Role of State Protection in Refugee Analysis." Discussion Paper No. 2. Advanced Refugee Law Workshop, International Association of Refugee Law Judges. *International Journal of Refugee Law* 15, no. 3: 444–460.

May, J. 1999. *Nomadic Identities. The Performance of Citizenship.* Minneapolis: University of Minnesota Press.

McAllister, K. E. 1999. "Remembering Political Violence. The Nikkei Internment Memorial Center." Ph.D. diss., Department of Sociology and Anthropology, Carleton University, Ottawa, Canada.

McCallin, M. 1992. *Living in Detention*. Geneva: International Catholic Child Bureau.

McCloud, A. 2003. *African American Islam*. Chicago: Kazi Publications.

McDonald, S. 2000. *The Right to Know: Women, Ethnicity, Violence and Learning about the Law*. Ph.D. diss., Ontario Institute for Studies in Education of the University of Toronto.

McMaster, D. 2001. *Asylum Seekers: Australia's Response to Refugees*. Melbourne: Melbourne University Press.

McSpadden, L. A. 1993. "Negociating Masculinity in the Reconstruction of Social Place: Eritrean and Ethiopian Refugees in the United States and Sweden." In *Engendering Forced Migration, Theory and Practice*, ed. D. Indra. *Refugee and Forced Migration Studies* 5, 242–261.

McSpadden, L. and H. Moussa. 1993. "I Have a Name: the Gender Dynamics in Asylum and in Resettlement of Ethiopian and Eritrean Refugees in North America." *Journal of Refugee Studies* 6, no. 3: 203–226.

———. 1996. "Returning 'Home'?" The Decision-Making Processes of Eritrean Women and Men." In *Development and Diaspora: Gender and the Refugee Experience*, ed. W. Giles, H. Moussa, and P. Van Esterik. Dundas, Ontario: Artemis Entreprises, 216–238.

Meitzen, M. O., R. J. Seime, and H. E. Ward. 1998. "Religious Knowledge and its Use in Psychiatry." *Journal of Religion and Health* 37, no.1: 5–8.

Mertus, J. 2003. "Sovereignty, Gender, and Displacement." In *Refugees and Forced Displacement: International Security, Human Vulnerability, and the State*, ed. E. Newman and J. Van Selm. Tokyo: United Nations Press, 250–277.

Michaels, A. 1996. *Fugitive Pieces*. Toronto: McClelland and Stewart.

Miernissi, F. 1991. *The Veil and the Male Elite: A Feminist Interpretation of Women's Rights in Islam*. London: Addison-Wesley.

Migrationsverket. 2001. *Gender-Based Persecution: Guidelines for Investigation and Evaluation of the Needs of Women for Protection*. Norkoping: Swedish Migration Board. www.migrationsverket.se/infomaterial/asyl/allmant/kvinno_en.pdf Accessed 30 August 2005.

Miki, A. 1991. "Preface." In *Justice In Our Time. The Japanese Canadian Redress Settlement*, ed. R. Miki and C. Kobayashi. Vancouver: Talon Books, 9–13.

Miki, R. 2005. *Redress: Inside the Japanese Canadian Call for Justice*. Vancouver: Raincoast Books.

Miki, R. and C. Kobayashi. 1991. *Justice In Our Time. The Japanese Canadian Redress Settlement*. Vancouver: Talon Books.

Miki, R. 1989. "Canadian Ethnic Studies Association Panel on Redress." Calgary, October 17, 1989. Excerpted in *Re-shaping Memory, Owning History. Through the Lens of Japanese Canadian Redress*, ed. G. E. Thomson. Burnaby, B.C.: Japanese Canadian National Museum, 6–34.

Miki, R, ed. 1985. *This Is My Own: Letters to Wes and Other Writings on Japanese Canadians* by Muriel Kitagawa. Vancouver: Talon Books.

Min, P. G. 1992. "The Structure and Social Function of Korean Immigrant Churches in the United States." *International Migration Review* 26: 1370–94.

University of Minnesota. 1954. Human Rights Library. *Convention Relating to the Status of Refugees*, 189, U.N.T.S.150; entered into force 22 April 1954. Web document. www.umm.edu/humanrts/instree/v!crs.htm

Moghissi, H. 1999. "Away from Home: Iranian Women, Displacement, Cultural Resistance and Change." *Journal of Comparative Family Studies* 30: 207–217.

Mohanty, C. 2003. *Feminism Without Borders. Decolonizing Theory, Practicing Solidarity.* Durham: Duke University Press.

Mohanty, C. and J. Alexander, 1996. *Feminist Genealogies, Colonial Legacies and Democratic Futures.* New York and London: Routledge.

Mohanty, C. 1991 [1984]. "Under Western Eyes. Feminist Scholarship and Colonial Discourses." In *Third World Women and the Politics of Feminism,* ed. C. Mohanty, A. Russo, and L. Torres. Bloomington and Indianapolis: Indiana University Press, 51–81. First published in *Boundary 2,* Vol. 12, no. 3, "On Humanism and the University I: The Discourse of Humanism" (Spring–Autumn 1984): 333–358.

Mojab, S. 1997. "Crossing Boundaries of Nationalism, Patriarchy, and Eurocentrism: The Struggle for a Kurdish Women Studies Network." *Canadian Woman Studies* 17, no. 2: 68–72.

———. 2000a. "The Feminist Project in Cyberspace and Civil Society." *Convergence* 33 (1–2): 107–119.

———. 2000b. "Vengeance and Violence: Kurdish Women Recount the War." *Canadian Woman Studies Journal* 19 (4): 89–94.

———., ed. 2001a. *Women of a Non-State Nation: The Kurds.* Costa Mesa, CA: MAZDA Publishers.

———. 2001b. "The Politics of 'Cyberfeminism' in the Middle East: The Case of Kurdish Women." *Journal of Race, Gender and Class* 8, no. 4: 42–61.

Mojab, S. and R. Gorman. 2003. "Women and Consciousness in the Learning Organization: Emancipation or Exploitation?" *Adult Education Quarterly: A Journal of Research and Theory* 53, no. 4: 228–241.

Mojab, S. and S. McDonald. Forthcoming. "Women, Violence and Informal Learning," In *Making Sense of Lived Experience in Turbulent Times: Informal Learning,* ed. C. Church, N. Bascia, and E. Shragge. Waterloo, Ontario: Wilfrid Laurier Press.

Mojab, S. 2005. "Kurdish Women" In *Encyclopedia of Women and Islamic Cultures.* Volume II, *Family, Law and Politics,* ed. S. Joseph. Leiden and Boston: Brill Academic Publishers, 358–366.

Mollica, R. F., Y. Caspi-Yavin, P. Bollini, T. Truong, S. Tor, and J. Lavelle. 1992. "The Harvard Trauma Questionnaire. Validating a Cross-Cultural Instrument for Measuring Torture, Trauma, and Post–traumatic Stress Disorder in Indochinese Refugees." *Journal of Nervous and Mental Disease* 180, no. 2: 111–116.

Monture, A. 1999. *Journeying Forward: Dreaming First Nations Independence.* Toronto: Fernwood Publishing.

Morley, D. 2000. *Home Territories: Media, Mobility and Identity.* London and New York: Routledge.

Moussa, H. 1993. *Storm and Sanctuary: The Journey of Ethiopian and Eritrean Refugee Women.* Dundas, Ontario: Artemis Enterprises.

———. 2000. "The Interconnections of Globalisation and Migration with Racism and Colonialism: Tracing Complicity." Toronto, Canada. Unpublished.

Mulvey, L. 1989. *Visual and Other Pleasures.* Bloomington: Bloomington University Press.

Mudimbe, V. Y., ed. 1997. *Nations, Identities, Cultures*. Durham: Duke University Press.

Musarrat, Akram. S. 2000. "Orientalism Revisited in Asylum and Refugee Claims." *International Journal of Refugee Law*. Oxford: Oxford University Press 12, no. 1: 7–40.

Musalo, K. 1999. "Matter of R-A-: An Analysis of the Decision and its Implications" 76. *Interpreter Releases* 1177 (9 August).

Nagata, D. K. 1999. "Long-Term Effects of Internment During Early Childhood on Third- Generation Japanese Americans." *American Journal of Orthopsychiatry* 69, no. 1: 19–29.

Nason-Clark, N. 1987. "Are Women Changing the Image of Ministry? A Comparison of British and American Realities." *Review of Religious Research* 28: 330–340.

Neisser, U. and D. Jopling, eds. 1997. *The Conceptual Self in Context. Culture, Experience, Self-Understanding*. Cambridge University Press.

Neitz, M. J. 1995. "Constructing Women's Rituals: Roman Catholic Women and Limina." In *Work, Family and Religion in Contemporary Society*, ed. N.T. Ammerman, and W. C. Roof. New York and London: Routledge, 289–305.

Newman, E. and J. Van Selm, eds. 2003. *Refugees and Forced Displacement: International Security, Human Vulnerability, and the State*. Tokyo: United Nations Press.

Newland, K., and K. Asomani, eds. 2003. *No Refuge : the Challenge of Internal Displacement*. New York and Geneva: OCHA.

Nolin C. 2006 *Transnational Ruptures: Gender and Forced Migration*. London: Ashgate.

Numrich, P. D. 1996. *Old Wisdom in the New World: Americanization in Two Immigrant Theravada Buddhist Temples*. Knoxville: University of Tennessee Press.

Nyers P. 2006. *Rethinking Refugees. Beyond States of Emergency*. New York: Routledge.

Ohye, B. Y. and D. J. Henderson, 1999. "The 'Other' Adolescent Girls: Who Are They?" In *Beyond Appearance: A New Look at Adolescent Girls*, ed. N. G. Johnson, M.C. Roberts, and J. Worell. Washington, D.C.: American Psychological Association, 115–129.

Oikawa, M. 1999. "Cartographies of Violence. Women, Memory, and the Subject(s) of the 'Internment'." Ph.D. diss. Toronto: Ontario Institute for Studies in Education, University of Toronto.

Okley, J. and H. Callaway, eds. 1992. *Anthropology and Autobiography*. New York and London: Routledge.

Ollman, B. 1971. *Alienation: Marx's Conception of Man in Capitalist Society*. London and New York: Cambridge University Press.

———. 1993. *Dialectical Investigations*. London and New York: Routledge.

Ong, A. 2003. "Budddha Is Hiding." *Refugees, Citizenship, the New America*. Berkeley: University of California Press.

Ortner, S. B. and H. Whitehead, eds. 1981. *Sexual Meaning: The Cultural Construction of Gender and Sexuality*. New York: Cambridge University Press.

OSCE (Organization for Security and Cooperation in Europe), Office for Democratic Institutions and Human Rights. 2004. *National Referral Mechanisms—Joining Efforts to Protect the Rights of Trafficked Persons: A Practical Handbook*. Warsaw: OSCE/ODIHR.

Oxfam Press Release. 2005. *Three Months On: New Figures Show Tsunami May Have Killed up to Four Times as Many Women as Men.* http://www.oxfam.org.uk/press/releases/tsunami_women260305.htm. Accessed 15 May 2006.

Paley, D. 2007. "This is What Development Looks Like. Part One: Skye Resources and Land Occupation in Guatemala." Z-Net. Latin America. http://www.dominionpaper.ca/articles/899. Accessed 1 March 2007.

Passerini, L. 1989. "Women's Personal Narratives: Myths, Experiences, and Emotions." In *Interpreting Women's Lives: Feminist Theory and Personal Narratives*, ed. Personal Narratives Group. Bloomington: Indiana University Press, 189–197.

Pearce, H. 2003. "An Examination of the International Understanding of Political Rape and the Significance of Labeling it Torture." *International Journal of Refugee Law* vol. 14. no. 4: 534–539.

Pearce, L. 1994. *Reading Dialogics.* London: Edward Arnold.

Pecora, V.P., ed. 2001. *Nations and Identities.* New York and Oxford: Blackwell Publishers.

Phan, T. 2000. "Investigating the Use of Services for Vietnamese with Mental Illness." *Journal of Community Health* 25: 411–425.

Pollock, M. 1993. "What is Left Out: Bakhtin, Feminism and the Culture of Boundaries." In *Bakhtin, Carnival and Other Subjects*, ed. D. Shepherd. Special issue of *Critical Studies*. Amsterdam: Rodopi, 229–242.

Portelli, A. 1981. "The Time of My Life: Functions of Time in Oral History," *International Journal of Oral History* 2, no. 3: 162–180.

———. 1991. *The Death of Luigi Trastulli and Other Stories. Form and Meaning in Oral History.* Albany: State University of New York Press.

———. 1991a. The Best Garbage Man in Town: Life and Times of Valtèro Peppoloni, Worker. In *The Death of Luigi Trastulli and Other Stories.Form and Meaning in Oral History* by A. Portelli. Albany, NY: State University of New York, 117–137.

———. 1997. *The Battle of Valle Guilia. Oral History and the Art of Dialogue.* Madison: University of Wisconsin Press.

———. 2003. *The Order Has Been Carried Out: History, Memory, and Meaning of a Nazi Massacre in Rome.* Palgrave: Macmillan.

Portes, A. and R. G. Rumbaut. 1996. *Immigrant America: A Portrait.* 2nd edition. Berkeley: University of California Press.

Poyatos, F., ed. 1987. *Cross-Cultural Perspectives in Non-verbal Communication.* Toronto: C. J. Hogrefe, 75–107.

Pratt, G. 2004. *Working Feminism.* Edinborough University Press and Philadelphia: Temple University Press.

Pupavac, V. 2002. "Therapeutising Refugees, Pathologising Populations: International Psycho-Social Programs in Kosovo." *New Issues in Refugee Research. Working Paper No. 59.* Geneva: UNHCR.

Qouta, S., R. L. Punamaki, and E. El Sarraj. 1995. "The Impact of the Peace Treaty on Psychological Well being: A Follow-up Study of Palestinian Children." *Child Abuse and Neglect* 19, no. 10: 1197–1208.

Radford Ruether, R. 1990 *Women and Religion in America (1900–1968). A Documentory History.* San Francisco: Harper.

Ramsay, R., S. Welch and E. Youard. 2001. "Needs of Women Patients with Mental Illness." *Advances in Psychiatric Treatment* 7: 85–92.

Razack, S. 1996. "The Perils of Storytelling for Refugee Women." In *Development and Diaspora, Gender and the Refugee Experience,* ed. W. Giles, H. Moussa, and P. Van Esterik.Toronto: Artemis Entreprises, 164–176.

———. 1998a. "From Pity to Respect." In *Looking White people in the Eye: Gender, Race and Culture in Courtrooms and Classrooms.* Toronto: University of Toronto Press, 130–155.

———. 1998b. "Policing the Borders of Nation." In *Looking White people in the Eye: Gender, Race and Culture in Courtrooms and Classrooms.* Toronto: University of Toronto Press, 88–129.

———. 1998c. *Looking White People in the Eye: Gender, Race, and Culture in Courtrooms and Classrooms.* Toronto: University of Toronto Press.

———. 2004. *Dark Threats and White Knights: The Somalia Affair, Peacekeeping and the New Imperialism.* Toronto: University of Toronto Press.

Redwood-Campbell, L., N. Fowler, J. Kaczorowski, E. Molinaro, S. Robinson, M. Howard, and M. Jafarpour. 2003. "How are New Refugees Doing in Canada?" *Canadian Journal of Public Health* 94: 381–385.

Reinharz, S. 1992. *Feminist Methods in Social Research.* New York: Oxford University Press.

Richmond, A. 1994. *Global Apartheid: Refugees, Racism and the New World Order.* London and Toronto: Oxford University Press.

Rick, K. and J. Forward, 1992. "Acculturation and Perceived Intergenerational Differences Among Hmong Youth." *Journal of Cross-Cultural Psychology* 23: 85–94.

Rieff, D. 2003. Displaced Places: Where Refugees Try to Make a Home. *New York Times Magazine* Sept. 21, Section 6: 36–41.

Roberts, G. 2000. "Narrative and Severe Mental Illness: What Place Do Stories Have in an Evidence-Based World?" *Advances in Psychiatric Treatment* 6: 432–441.

Roberts, M. K., and J. D. Davidson. 1984. "The Nature and Sources of Religious Involvement." *Review of Religious Research* 25: 334–350.

Rousseau, C., A. Drapeau and E. Corin. 1997. "The Influence of Culture and Context on the Pre- and Post–Migration Experience of School-Aged Refugees from Central America and Southeast Asia in Canada." *Social Science and Medicine* 44: 1115–1127.

Royle, M. H. 1984. "Women Pastors: What Happens After Placement?" *Review of Religious Research* 24: 116–126.

Rubin, G. 1975. "The Traffic of Women: Notes on the Political Economy of Sex." In *Toward Anthropology of Women,* ed. R. Reiter. New York: Monthly Review Press, 157–210.

Rumbaut, R. G. 1994. "The Crucible Within: Ethnic Identity, Self esteem, and Segmented Assimilation among Children of Immigrants." *International Migration Review* 28, no. 4: 748–794.

Sachithanandan, S. 1999. "Participatory Approaches to Development under Civil War Conditions. The Experience in Batticaloa, Sri Lanka, 1991–95." In *Assessing Participation: A Debate from South Asia,* ed. S. Bastian and N. Bastian, in association with D. Nivaran. New Delhi: Konark, 181–211.

Said, E. W. 1999. *Out of Place: A Memoir.* New York: Alfred A. Knopf.

Sangster, J. 1998. "Telling Our Stories: Feminist Debates and the Use of Oral History." In *The Oral History Reader,* ed. R. Perks and A. Thomson. New York and London: Routledge, 87–100.

Satzewich, V., ed. 1998. *Racism and Social Inequality in Canada. Concepts, Controversies and Strategies of Resistance.* Toronto: Thompson Educational Publishing.

Satzewich, V. and L. Wong, eds. *Transnational Identities and Practices in Canada.* Vancouver: University of British Columbia Press.

Schulte-Tenckhoff, I. 2001. *The Concept of Community in the Social Sciences and its Juridical Relevance.* Research prepared for the Law Commission of Canada.

Sells, M. A. 1995. *The Bridge Betrayed: Religion and Genocide in Bosnia.* Berkeley: University of California Press.

Sevensky, R. L. 1984. "Religion, Psychology, and Mental Health." *American Journal of Psychotherapy* 39: 75–85.

Sharing our Experiences. 1988. *The Refugee Women's Workshop.* Photocopy. Toronto, June 1988.

Signs. *Journal of Women in Culture and Society.* 2002. Special Issue on *Gender and Memory* 28, no. 1 (Autumn).

Silove, D., Z. Steel, P. McGorry, V. Miles, and J. Drobny. 2002. "The Impact of Torture on Post–Traumatic Stress Symptoms in War-Affected Tamil Refugees and Immigrants." *Comprehensive Psychiatry* 43: 49–55.

Simon, R. and C. Eppert. 1997. "Remembering Obligation: Pedagogy and the Witnessing of Testimony and Historical Trauma." *Canadian Journal of Education* 22, no. 2: 175–191.

Smith, D. 1997. "From the Margins: Women's Standpoint as a Method of Inquiry in the Social Sciences." *Gender, Technology and Development* 1, no. 1: 113–135.

Smith, L., and M. Mattar, 1998. "Creating International Consensus on Combating Trafficking in Persons: US Policy, the Role of the UN, and Global Responses and Challenges." *Fletcher Forum of World Affairs* 28, no. 1: 155–178.

Smith, M. 2004. "Warehousing Refugees: A Denial of Rights, A Waste of Humanity." *U.S. Committee for World Refugee Survey*: 38–56.

Sondergaard, H. P., S. Ekblad and T. Theorell. 2001. "Self-Reported Life Event Patterns and their Relation to Health Among Recently Resettled Iraqi and Kurdish Refugees in Sweden." *Journal of Nervous and Mental Disease* 189: 838–845.

Sontag, S. 2003. *Regarding the Pain of Others.* New York: Farrar, Straus, and Giroux.

Specter, M. 1998. "Traffickers' New Cargo: Naïve Slavic Women." *The New York Times,* 11 January 1998.

Spencer, J., ed. 1990. *Sri Lanka: History and the Roots of Conflict.* New York and London: Routledge.

Spivak, G. C. 1987. *In Other Worlds: Essays in Cultural Politics.* New York and London: Methuen.

———. 1995. "Subaltern Studies: Deconstructing Historiography." In *The Spivak Reader: Selected Works of Gayatri Spivak,* ed. D. Landry and G. MacLean. New York and London: Routledge, 203–235.

Srinivasaraju, S. 2007. "Stolen Acres," *Outlook,* 12 February: 14–16.

Stasiulis, D. 1987. "Rainbow Feminism: Perspectives on Minority Women in Canada." *Resources for Feminist Research* 16, no. 1: 5–9.

———. 1999. "Relational Positionalities of Nationalisms, Racisms, and Feminisms." In *Between Woman and Nation: Nationalisms, Transnational Feminisms, and the State,* ed. C. Kaplan, N. Alarcón, and M. Moallem. Durham: Duke University Press, 182–218.

Stein, B. 1980. "The Refugee Experience: An Overview of Refugee Research." Paper presented at *A Conference on the Refugee Experience* sponsored by the Royal Anthropological Institute and the Minority Rights Group. London (February).

Stepick, A. 1998. *Pride Against Prejudice: Haitians in the United States.* Boston: Allyn and Bacon.

Stevens, C. A. 2001. "Perspectives on the Meanings of Symptoms Among Cambodian Refugees." *Journal of Sociology* 37: 81–98.

Strauss, A. and J. Corbin. 1990. *Basics of Qualitative Research. Grounded Theory, Procedures and Techniques.* Newbury Park, CA: Sage Publications.

Sugiman, P. 2003. "Understanding Silence: Finding Meaning in the Oral Testimonies of Nisei Women in Canada." In *Changing Japanese Identities in Multicultural Canada,* ed. J. F. Kess, H. Noro, M. M. Ayukawa, and H. Lansdowne. Victoria, British Columbia: Center for Asia Pacific Initiatives, 353–363.

———. 2004a. "Passing Time, Moving Memories: Interpreting Wartime Narratives of Japanese Canadian Women." *Histoire Sociale/Social History* XXXVII, no. 73 (May): 51–80.

———. 2004 b. "Memories of Internment: Narrating Japanese Canadian Women's Life Stories." *Canadian Journal of Sociology* 29, no. 3: 359–88.

———. 2006. "Unmaking a Transnational Community: Japanese Canadian Families in Wartime Canada." In *Transnational Identities and Practices in Canada,* eds. V. Satzewich and L. Wong. Vancouver: University of British Columbia Press, 52–68.

Summerfield, D. 1999. "A Critique of Seven Assumptions Behind Psychological Trauma Programs in War Affected Areas." *Social Science and Medicine* 48: 1449–1462.

Sunahara, A. G. 1980. *The Politics of Racism. The Uprooting of Japanese Canadians During the Second World War.* Toronto: James Lorimer.

Surin, K. 1997. "On Producing the Concept of a Global Culture." In *Nations, Identities, Cultures,* ed. V. Y. Mudimbe. Durham: Duke University Press, 199–219.

Swedish Integration Board. 2002. *Swedish Integration Policy for the 21st Century.* www.naring.regeringen.se/fragor/integration/index.htm

Swidler, L. and A. Swidler, eds. 1977. *Women Priests: A Catholic Commentary on the Vatican Declaration.* Rome: Paulist Press.

Swyripa, F. 2000. "The Politics of Redress: The Contemporary Ukrainian-Canadian Campaign." In *Enemies Within. Italian and Other Internees in Canada and Abroad.* ed. F. Iacovetta, R. Perin, and A. Principe. Toronto: University of Toronto Press, 355–378.

Tapp, N. 1988. *Sovereignty and Rebellion: The White Hmong of Northern Thailand.* Singapore: Oxford University Press.

Tatham, M. 2004. "Women Refugee Claimants Fearing Gender-Related Persecution." *Education Wife Assault Newsletter* 8, no. 2. On line www.womanabuseprevention.com/html/women_refugee_claimants.html

Taylor, C. 1983. *Social Theory as Practice.* Oxford: Oxford University Press.

———. 1985. "Understanding and Ethnocentricity," *Social Philosophy and the Human Sciences, Philosophical Papers 2.* Cambridge: Cambridge University Press, 116–134. Also in C. Taylor. *Social Theory as Practice:* 1–27.

———. 1989. *Sources of the Self: The Making of the Modern Identity.* Cambridge, MA: Harvard University Press.

————. 1994. "The Politics of Recognition." In *Muticulturalism. A Critical Reader*, ed. T. Goldberg. Oxford, U.K./Cambridge, MA: Basil Blackwell, 75–107.

Temple B., and R. Moran. Eds. 2006. *Doing Research with Refugees*. Bristol: the Policy Press.

Terkel, S. 1986. *Hard Times. An Oral History of the Great Depression*. New York: The New York Press.

The Refugee Council. 2002. *Sri Lanka: Return to Uncertainty, Sri Lanka Project, London*. www.refugeecouncil.org.uk/downloads/rc_reports/srilanka_uncertainty.pdf. Accessed 22 July.

Thiruchandran, S. 2003. "The Other Victims of Terror: Households in Chaos." In *Feminists Under Fire: Exchanges Across War Zones*, ed. W. Giles, M. de Alwis, E. Klein, and N. Silva; with M. Korac, D. Knezevic, and Z. Papic (advisory editors). Toronto: Between The Lines, 131–140.

Thomas, C. 1999. "Introduction." In *Globalization, Human Security and the African Experience*, ed. C. Thomas and P. Wilkins. Boulder/London: Lynne Rienner Publishers, Inc., 3–18.

Thomas, S., S. Thomas, B. Nafees, and D. Bhugra. 2004. "'I Was Running Away from Death'—the Pre–Flight Experiences of Unaccompanied Asylum Seeking Children in the U.K." *Child: Care, Health and Development* 30, no. 2: 113–122.

Thomson, A. 1995. "Life Histories, Adult Learning and Identity." In *The Uses of Autobiography*, ed. J. Swindells. Bristol, PA: Taylor and Francis, 163–176.

————. 1995a. "Writing About Learning: Using Mass-Observation Educational Life Histories to Explore Learning Through Life." In *The Uses of Autobiography*, ed. J. Swindells. Bristol, PA: Taylor and Francis, 177–186.

Thomson, C. 1989. "Mikhail Bakhtin and Contemporary Anglo-American Feminist Theories." In *The Bakhtin Circle Today, Critical Studies*, ed. M. Diaz-Diocaretz. Amsterdam: Rodopi, 141–161.

Tobin, T. 2004. "Without a Doubt." http://www.dioceseofprovidence.org/our_diocese/news_and_media/library/?id=1531) May 19th, Providence, NJ. Accessed 15 May 2006.

Turner, S. 1999. "Vindicating Masculinity: the Fate of Promoting Gender Equality." *Forced Migration Review* 9: 8–10.

United Nations. 1996. *Platform for Action and the Beijing Declaration*. Fourth World Conference on Women. Beijing China 2–15 September 1995. New York: United Nations Department of Public Information.

United Nations Commission on Status of Women. 2005. *Report on the Forty-Ninth Session* (28 February–11 March, 2005). *Economic and Social Council. Official records, 2005 Supplement 7* (EC/2005/27-E/CN.6/2005/11). http://www.un.org/womenwatch/daw/Review/english/news.htm

United Nations Department of Public Information. 2004. *The Millennium Development Goals and the United Nations Role*. 2002. http://www.un.org/millenniumgoals. Accessed 4 June 2004.

————. 2007. "Disturbed by Escalating Violations of Ceasefire in Sri Lanka, Secretary-General Urges Parties to Return to Negotiations Without Preconditions." http://www.un.org/News/Press/docs//2007/sgsm10925.doc.htm. Accessed 28 March 2007.

United Nations Division for the Advancement of Women. 2004. Convention on the Elimination of All Forms of Discrimination Against Women. United Nations. www.un.org/womenwatch/daw/cedaw

United Nations High Commissioner for Refugees. 1980. The Situation of Refugee Women the World Over. World Conference for the Decade of Women. Copenhagen. Printed document.

———. 1985. UNHCR Executive Committee, 36th Session, *Resolution No.39, Refugee Women and International Protection.* www.refugeelawreader.org/files/pdf/61.pdf. Accessed 10 April 2007.

———. 1988. UNHCR Executive Committee, 39th session, *Refugee Women in Conclusions on the International Protection of Refugees, Adopted by the Executive Committee of the UNHCR Program.* Geneva, UNHCR 1980–1988.

———. 1990. Executive Committee of the High Commissioner's Program. *UNHCR Policy on Refugee Women. United Nations.* 9 pages. www.UNHCR.org/pub/PUBL/3d4F92712.pdf

———. 1991. *Guidelines on the Protection of Refugee Women, Geneva* (June 1991). www.icva.ch/doc00000822.html

———. 1994. *Refugee Children: Guidelines on Protection and Care.* www.asylumsupport .info/publications/unhcr/refugeechildren.pdf. Accessed 15 August 2005.

———. 1996. *Women Refugee Claimants Fearing Gender-Related Persecution.* Guidelines Issued by the Chairperson, (March 1993, updated November 1996). http://www.irb-cisr.gc.ca/en/notices/cgi_e.html

———. 2000. *United Nations Security Council. Resolution 1325.* Adopted by the Security Council at the 4213th meeting, on 31 October 2000. S/Res/1325.

———. 2000. *United Nations Protocol to Prevent, Suppress and Punish Trafficking in Persons, Especially Women and Children,* Supplement to the United Nations Convention against Transnational Organized Crime (November 15). 11 pages. www .uncjin.org/Documents/Conventions/dcatoc/final_documents_2/convention %20traft_eng.pdf

———. 2001a. *Practical Aspects of Physical and Legal Protection with Regard to Registration,* UN Doc. EC/GC/01/6, 19 February 2007.

———. 2001b. *Good Practices on Gender Equality Mainstreaming: A Practical Guide to Empowerment.* Geneva. www.unhcr.org/cgibin/texis/vtx/protect/opendoc .pdf?tbl=PROTECTION&id=3bbc24532

———. 2002a. *Guidelines on International Protection No. 1: Gender-Related Persecution within the Context of Article 1A(2) of the 1951 Convention and/or its 1967 Protocol Relating to the Status of Refugees* (HCR/GIP/02/01). Geneva (May).

———. 2002b. *Respect our Rights: Partnership for Equality. Report on the Dialogue with Refugee Women.* Geneva, 20–22 June 2001. 50 pages. www.UNCHR.org/protect/PROTECTION/3bb44d908.pdf

———. 2002c. *Statistical Yearbook. Refugees, Asylum-Seekers and Other Persons of Concern—Trends in Displacement, Protection and Solutions.* Geneva (October). www.unhcr.org/cgibin/texis/vtx/template?page=home&src=static/statistical _yearbook/2002/toc2.htm

———. 2000. *United Nations Protocol to Prevent, Suppress and Punish Trafficking in Persons, Especially Women and Children,* Supplement to the United Nations Convention against Transnational Organized Crime (15 November). www.unhcr .org/home/RSDLEGAL/3ae6b3428.html

———. 2003a. "Executive Committee of the High Commissioner's Program. Conclusion on Protection from Sexual Abuse and Exploitation," no. 98 LIV. *International Journal of Refugee Law* 16, no. 1: 157–161.

————. 2003b. "Sexual and Gender-Based Violence against Refugees, Returnees and Internally Displaced Persons—Guidelines for Prevention and Response". Geneva, 31 May 2003. 168 pages. www.UNHCR.org/cgibin/texist/vtx/protect/opendoc.pdf?tbl=PROTECTION&id=3f69bcc4-

————. 2004. "Global Refugee Trends, 2003" http://www.unhcr.org/cgibin/texis/vtx/statistics/opendoc.pdf?tbl=STATISTICS&id=40d015fb4. Geneva. Accessed 15 August 2004.

————. 2006. *Gender-related Persecution Guidelines.* www.unhcr.org/cgi-bin/texis/vtx/publ/opendoc.pdf?tbl=PUBL&id=3d58ddef4 and www.unhcr.org/cgi-bin/texis/vtx/publ/opendoc.pdf?tbl=PUBL&id=3d58de2da. Accessed 15 May 2006.

————. 2006. *Guidelines on International Protection: Relating to the Status of Refugees to Victims of Trafficking and Persons at Risk of Being Trafficked,* UNHCR 59th session (6 April) (HCR/GIP/06/07). www.unhcr.org/cgi-bin/texis/vtx/publ/opendoc.pdf?tbl=PUBL&id=443b626b2 (April).

United Nations Office on Drugs and Crime. *Protocol to Prevent, Suppress and Punish Trafficking in Persons, Especially Women and Children,* supplementing the United Nations Convention against Transnational Organized Crime. (www.unodc.org/unodc/en/crime_cicp_signatures_trafficking.html

United Nations Standing Advisory Committee on Security Questions in Central Africa. 2001. "Press Release: Central African Conference on Protecting Women, Children in Armed Conflict Held in Kinshasa, 14–16 November." United Nations. 2 pages. 7 November 2001.www.unhcr.ch/huricane/huricane.nsf/view01/0B29BE0E7FAD89D4C1256FE002D58BB?opendocument.

US Department of State. 2004. *Trafficking in Persons Report.* (June). http://www.state.gov/g/tip/rls/tiprpt/2004/. Accessed 15 July 2004.

US Committee on Refugees. 2000. *Worldwide Refugee Information: Country Report: United Kingdom.* www.refugees.org/world/countryrpt/europe/united_kingdom.htm

Valji, N. 2003. "Women and the 1951 Refugee Convention: 50 Years of Seeking Visibility." http://www.isanet.org/archive/valji.html. Accessed 15 May 2006.

Valji, N. 2000. "Seeing Refugee Women as Refugees." *Track Two* 9, no. 3 (November) www.queensu.ca/samp/sampresources/migrationdocuments/documents/2000/2.htm. Accessed 30 March 2007.

Valji, N. and L. A. De La Hunt. 1999. *Gender Guidelines for Asylum Determination. National Consortium on Refugee Affairs.* European Union Foundation for Human Rights.

Valji, N., L. A. De La Hunt, and H. Moffett. 2003. "Where Are the Women? Gender Discrimination in Refugee Policies and Practices." *Agenda* 55 http://www.queensu.ca/samp/migrationresources/gender/documents/valji.pdf. Accessed 30 March 2007.

Vio Grossi, F., V. Gianotten, and T. de Wit, eds. 1983. *Participatory Research: Theoretical Frameworks, Methods, and Techniques.* Toronto: International Council for Adult Education.

Volochinov, V. N. 1977. *Le marxisme et la philosophie du langage,* traduit du russe et présenté par Marina Yaguello. Paris: Les Editions de Minuit.

Von Sternberg, M. R. 2002. *The Grounds of Refugee Protection in the Context of International Human Rights and Humanitarian Law: Canadian and United States Case Law Compared.* The Hague: Martinus Nijhoff.

Vorst, J. et al., eds. 1991. *Race, Class, Gender. Bonds and Barriers.* Toronto: Society for Socialist Studies/Garamond.

Wachtel, N. 1986. "Introduction. Between Memory and History." *History and Anthropology* 2, no. 2: 207–24.

Walker, K. 1996. "The Importance of Being Out: Sexuality and Refugee Status." *Sydney Law Review* (18): 598.

Wallace, R.A. 1975. "Bringing Women In: Marginality in the Churches." *Sociological Analysis* 36: 291–303.

———. 1992. *They Call Her Pastor.* New York: SUNY Press.

Wallerstein, I. 1997. "The Insurmountable Contradictions of Liberalism: Human Rights and the Rights of Peoples in the Geoculture of the Modern World-System." In *Nations, Identities,Cultures,* ed. V.Y. Mudimbe. Durham: Duke University Press, 81–197.

Wane, N. N., K. Deliovsky, and E. Lawson, eds. 2002. *Back to the Drawing Board: African-Canadian Feminism.* Toronto: Sumach Press.

Ward, J. 2002. "If not now, when? Addressing Gender-Based Violence in Refugee, Internally Displaced, and Post-Conflict Settings: A Global Overview." Reproductive Health for Refugees Consortium.

Warner, R. S. and J.G. Wittner, eds. 1998. *Gatherings in Diaspora: Religious Communities and the New Immigration.* Philadelphia: Temple University Press.

Watters, C. 2001. "Emerging Paradigms in the Mental Health Care of Refugees." *Social Science and Medicine* 52: 1709–1718.

Weaver, M. J. 1986. *New Catholic Women: A Contemporary Challenge to Traditional Religious Authority.* New York: Harper and Row.

Weidman, J. L., ed. 1985. *Women Ministers: How Women are Redefining Traditional Roles.* New York: Harper and Row.

Weiler, K. 1991. "Freire and a Feminist Pedagogy of Difference." *Harvard Educational Review* 61: 449–74.

Weinberg, S. S. 1992. "The Treatment of Women in Immigration History: A Call for Change." *Journal of American Ethnic History* (Summer): 25–45.

Weine, S. M., L. Razzano, N. Brkic, A. Ramic, K. Miller, A. Smajkic, Z. Bijedic, E. Boskailo, R. Mermelstein, and I. Pavkovic. 2000. "Profiling the Trauma Related Symptoms of Bosnian Refugees Who Have not Sought Mental Health Services." *Journal of Nervous and Mental Disease* 188: 416–421.

Welaratna, U. 1993. *Beyond the Killing Fields: Voices of Nine Cambodian Survivors in America.* Stanford: Stanford University Press.

Wellman, B. 2001. "The Persistence and Transformation of Community: From Neighborhood Groups to Social Networks." *Report to the Law Commission of Canada.* Ottawa: Law Commission of Canada.

Wellmeir, N. 1994. *Rituals of Resettlement, Selected Papers on Refugee Issues.* Fairfax: American Anthropological Association.

Williams, C. 2001. "Increasing Access and Building Equity into Mental Health Services: An Examination of the Potential for Change." *Canadian Journal of Community Mental Health* 20: 37–47.

Williams, C. and J. Westermeyer. 1983. "Psychiatric Problems Among Adolescent Southeast Asian Refugees." *Journal of Nervous and Mental Disorders* 171: 79–85.

Williams, R. B. 1988. *Religions of Immigrants from India and Pakistan: New Threads in the American Tapestry.* New York: Cambridge University Press.

Willis, K. and B. Yeoh. 2000. *Gender and Migration*. Cheltenham, U.K.: Edward Elgar Publishing.

Wilsher, D. 2003. "Non-State Actors and the Definition of a Refugee in the United Kingdom: Protection, Accountability or Culpability." *International Journal of Refugee Law* 15, no. 1: 68–86.

Winland, D. N. 1994. "Christianity and Community: Conversion and Adaptation among Hmong Refugee Women." *Canadian Journal of Sociology/Cahiers Canadiens de Sociologie* 19, no. 1: 21–45.

Winnicott, D. W. 1965. *The Maturational Process and the Facilitating Environment*. New York: International Universities Press.

Women's Commission for Refugee Women and Children. 2002. *UNHCR's Policy on Refugee Women and Guidelines on their Protection: An Assessment after 10 years of Implementation* (May).

Worby P. "Refugee Return and Reintegration in Guatemala. Lessons Learned by UNHCR through its presence and intervention 1987-1999": http://www.unhcr.ch/evaluate/reports99gtm.htm

World Council of Churches. 1995a. *A Moment to Choose: Risking to be with Uprooted People. Statement on Uprooted People*. Adopted by the World Council of Churches Central Committee, Geneva, 14–22 September. http://www.wcc-coe.org/wcc/what/international/uprooted/moment1.html

———. 1995b. *Policy Statement on Uprooted People. A Moment to Choose: Risking to be with Uprooted People*. Geneva: World Council of Churches.

———. 1996. *A Moment to Choose: Risking to be with Uprooted People. A Resource Book*. Geneva: World Council of Churches.

Wuthnow, R. 1994. *Sharing the Journey*. London: Free Press.

Yaeger, P. 1988. *Honeymad Women: Emancipatory Strategies in Women's Writings*. New York: Columbia University Press.

Yaguello. 1979. *Les femmes et la langue*. Paris: Payot.

Young, I. M. 1989. "Polity and Group Difference. A Critique of the Ideal of Universal Citizenship." *Ethics* 99, no. 2: 250–274.

Young, J. E. 2000. *At Memory's Edge, After-Images of the Holocaust in Contemporary Art and Architecture*. New Haven: Yale University Press.

Yourcenar, M. 1951. *Les mémoires d'Hadrien*. Paris: Gallimard.

———. 1968. *L'oeuvre au noir*. Paris: Gallimard.

Yuval-Davis, N. 2004. "Gender, the Nationalist Imagination, War and Peace." In *Gender and Conflict Zones*, ed. W. Giles and J. Hyndman. Berkeley: University of California Press: 170–193.

Zetter, R. 1988. "Refugees, Repatriation, and Root Causes." *Journal of Refugee Studies* 1, no. 2: 99–106.

Zolberg, A., A. Suhrke, and S. Aguayo, 1989. *Escape from Violence: Conflict and the Refugee Crisis in the Developing World*. Oxford: Oxford University Press.

Index

national, 258
oral, 137
of the past, 44, 194
of refugee women, 51
research method, 98
resilience, 40, 52, 164
of strength, 40
women's, 20, 124, 127, 131n10, 135, 163
National Association of Japanese Canadians. *See* NAJC
National Geographic Magazine, The, 22n14
natural disasters, 16, 33, 69
Neitz, M., 193
Newman, E., 33
New York City, *Beijing +10* conference in, 11
Nexus of Gender and Religion in Refugee Women, 188
NGOs (Non Governmental Organizations), 2–5, 7–9, 43, 68, 77, 79, 83, 86, 90, 94–5, 172n1, 222
Nisei women, 117–20, 124–7, 129, 134n26
Non Governmental Organizations. *See* NGOs
Nordstrom, C., 188
North, South, 4, 5, 26, 33–4, 36, 55–6, 58, 60, 65, 72, 153, 184, 192, 199
Numrich, P.D., 192

O
Office of Refugee Resettlement (ORR), 181, 195n2
Ohye, B., 177
Oikawa, M., 120, 133n21
Okley, J., 137
Ollman, B., 148–9
Ong, A., 171, 191
Operation Provide Refuge (OPR), 183, 188
oppression, 6, 29, 40, 64, 135, 138, 144, 149, 189, 249
causes, 57
forms, 38, 65, 139, 245–7
practices, 34
relations, 143, 146–7

structure, 146
violence and, 42, 246–7
OPR (Operation Provide Refuge), 183, 188
organizations
community-based, 86, 93
mainstream, 197, 203, 207, 213
ORR (Office of Refugee Resettlement), 181, 186–7
Ortner, S., 187
"othering," 13, 207
of trafficked women, 26, 70
victims, 76
of women, 13, 69, 75

P
Paley, D., 33
PAR (Participatory Action Research), 50–1, 212
Parnet, C., 154
Passerini, L., 132n10, 133n16
patriarchal construct, 26
patriarchal control, 42–3
patriarchal culture, 259
patriarchal division of labor, 17
patriarchal family, 60, 140
patriarchal fundamentalism, 17
patriarchal hegemony, 43
patriarchal ideologies, 15
patriarchal labor, 17
patriarchal nationalism, 140
patriarchal power, 23n15, 38, 88
patriarchal relations, 88, 139–41, 145–6
patriarchal social order, 69
patriarchal societies, 6, 217
patriarchal subjugation, 98
patriarchal traditions, 261
patriarchal violence, 140, 255, 257
peace, 12, 22n12, 55, 64, 66n3, 85, 87, 94, 107, 159, 225–7
development, 2
human rights, 9, 178
justice, 3
and security, 10, 220, 224, 227n20
war and, 10, 33, 61, 158, 224
Pecora, V.P., 190
Pearce, H., 229–30, 241

www.ingramcontent.com/pod-product-compliance
Lightning Source LLC
Chambersburg PA
CBHW072050020426
42334CB00017B/1456